LHÙ’ÀÀN MÂN

KEYÍ DAŃ

KWÁNJE NÀÀTSAT

LHÙ'ÀÀN MÂN KEYÍ DAŃ KWÁNJE NÀÀTSAT

KLUANE LAKE COUNTRY PEOPLE SPEAK STRONG

KLUANE FIRST NATION

Figure.1
Vancouver/Toronto/Berkeley

front cover Lhù'ààn Mân (Whitefish Place Lake, Kluane Lake) in summer splendour with fireweed blooming under the midnight sun. KFN Archives. EMPC. Landscape Images #1. PHOTOGRAGHER ROBERT POSTMA

back cover top Kluane First Nation Harvest Camp, 2017. KFN Archives. EMPC. Landscape Images #40. PHOTOGRAPHER UNKNOWN

back cover bottom Burwash seen from the bay on a windy day in fall 2022. KFN Archives. EMPC. Landscape Images #21. PHOTOGRAPHER ALISTAIR MAITLAND

this spread Lhù'ààn Mân (Whitefish Place Lake, Kluane Lake) at dawn with ice forming and snow on the Ruby Range mountains to the east. KFN Archives. EMPC. Landscape Images #2. PHOTOGRAPHER ROBERT POSTMA

23 24 25 26 27 5 4 3 2 1

Cataloguing data is available from Library and Archives Canada
ISBN 978-1-77327-206-1 (hbk.)

Design by Teresa Bubela
Editing by Michael Leyne
Copy editing by Marnie Lamb
Proofreading by Renate Preuss
Indexing by Stephen Ullstrom

Maps on pages 37 and 99 are adapted from work by Richard Vladars originally created for *Kwanlin Dün: Dä Kwändur Ghày Ghàkwadîndur—Our Story in Our Words*, Vancouver, Figure 1 Publishing, 2020.

Maps on pages 345 and 349 are by Frank Anderson, KFN Lands, Resources & Heritage.

Printed and bound in Canada by Friesens

Kluane First Nation
Burwash Landing YT Canada
kfn.ca

Figure 1 Publishing Inc.
Vancouver BC Canada
figure1publishing.com

Figure 1 Publishing works in the traditional, unceded territory of the xʷməθkʷəy̓əm (Musqueam), Sḵwx̱wú7mesh (Squamish), and səlilwətaɬ (Tsleil-Waututh) peoples.

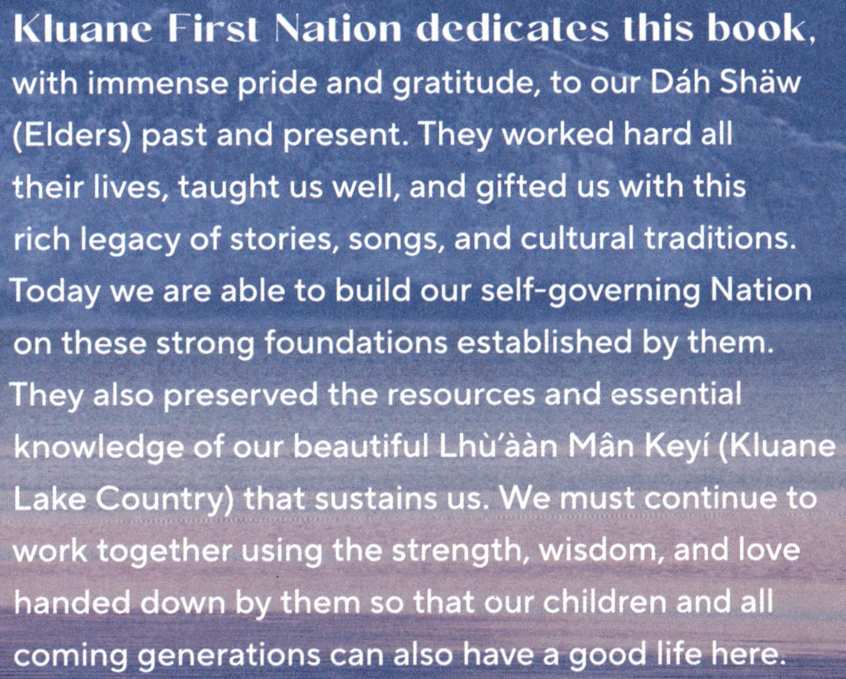

Kluane First Nation dedicates this book, with immense pride and gratitude, to our Dáh Shäw (Elders) past and present. They worked hard all their lives, taught us well, and gifted us with this rich legacy of stories, songs, and cultural traditions. Today we are able to build our self-governing Nation on these strong foundations established by them. They also preserved the resources and essential knowledge of our beautiful Lhù'ààn Mân Keyí (Kluane Lake Country) that sustains us. We must continue to work together using the strength, wisdom, and love handed down by them so that our children and all coming generations can also have a good life here.

SHÀW NÍTHAN (THANK YOU)!

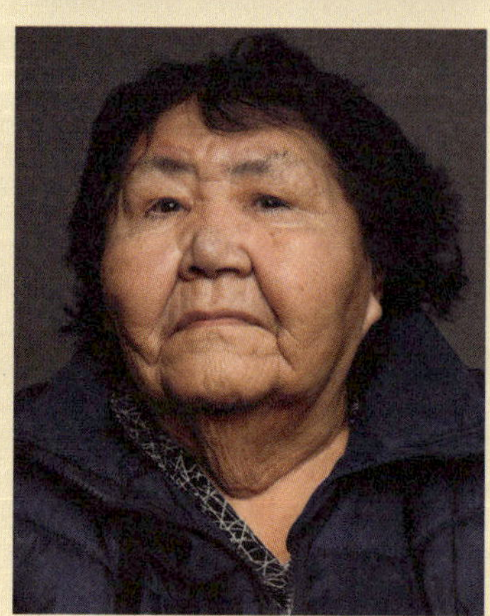

KWÄDAY DAŃ UYE KWÀNJÌ

(Our Elders Remember)

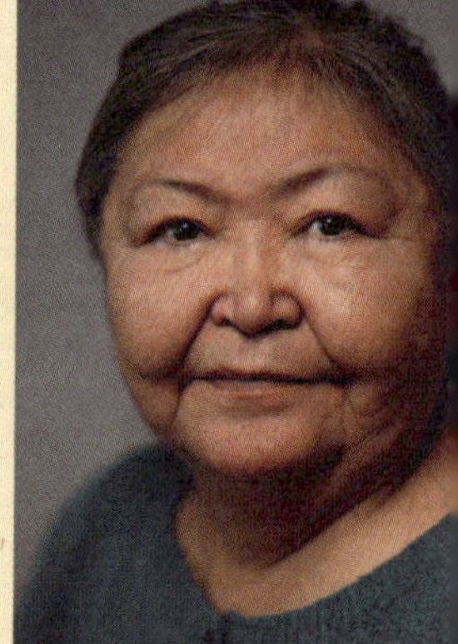

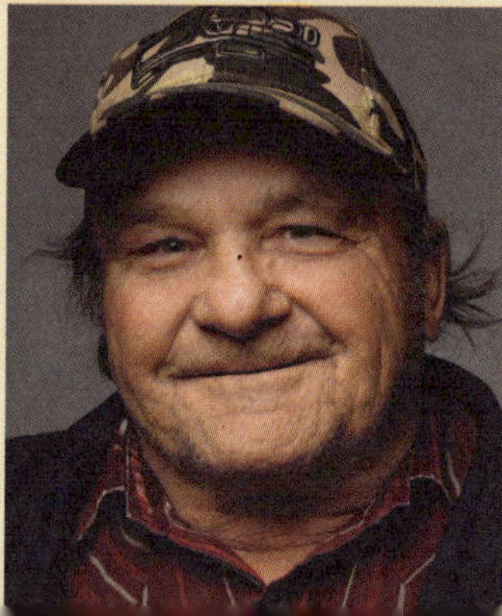

Contents

facing Kluane First Nation Elders whose stories are told in this book.

facing Cabin remains surrounded by fireweed at Silver City, circa 2011. KFN Archives. EMPC. Landscape Images #4
PHOTOGRAPHER ROBERT POSTMA

The stories shared by Elders in this book include their experiences with Indian Residential Schools, Missing and Murdered Indigenous Women and Girls, the Sixties Scoop, Indian Hospitals, and many government policies that affected Lhù'ààn Mân Ku Dań families and children. Their stories are sensitive in nature and we ask that respect be shown when reading this book.

COUNCIL MESSAGE

As Kluane First Nation's Chief and Councillors we thank our Elders of today for this very special gift they have created for all future generations. In this book they tell their individual life stories, and through them we learn about our past generations of grandparents, great-grandparents, aunties, and uncles—all those who came before us and who worked so hard to build our Nation.

Our Elders grew up before there were modern conveniences like electricity, cars, television, and the internet. Their parents and grandparents taught them traditional skills and values to live as totally self-sufficient people on the land and the water. With their extended families they travelled, hunted, fished, and gathered foods to survive year-round in this beautiful land we call Asì Keyí (Grandfather's Country). In those earlier times, and for thousands of years, our people lived peacefully and cooperatively—sharing, respecting, and caring for each other, the animals, and all living things, along with the environment surrounding them. It is because of them that we thrive today.

Their stories also reveal the many hardships that overtook our people during and after World War II. The building of the Alaska Highway brought thousands of newcomers into our land. With the highway came missionaries, government officials, and many more newcomers who had different customs and the power to enforce profound changes in our lives. Residential schools disrupted our families, removing children from their parents, homeland, culture, and language. Other government policies took our traditional hunting areas from us to create Kluane National Park and Reserve, causing serious food shortages and deep despair among our people.

Our Elders travelled, worked hard, studied, gained new skills, and gathered fresh ideas for dealing with these challenges. They joined with other Yukon First Nations to launch a comprehensive land claims movement. Our Elders were leaders in that movement—a movement built on resilience, courage, collaboration, knowledge of the land and its resources, strategic planning, and forward thinking for future generations. In 1973 *Together Today for Our Children Tomorrow*, a policy paper developed by Yukon First Nations and presented to the federal government, laid the foundations for our Kluane First Nation Final and Self-Government Agreements in 2003.

facing Kluane First Nation Council members, left to right: Chief Robert Dickson, Elder Salkaaya Bertha Doris, and Youth Coleson Ford, at Burwash, 2023. (Not shown: Joyce Albert-Johnson and Elizabeth Johnson, elected July 2023.)
KFN Archives. EMPC. Elders Portraits #1.
PHOTOGRAPHER KATIE JOHNSON

facing The dedication of the future site for a new school at Burwash was a big celebration for Council, Elders, and Youth in June 2023. *Left to right:* Geraldine Pope, Assembly of First Nations Grand Chief Mary Jane Jim, Mary Cameron (Yukon Government), KFN Chief Robert Dickson, Marissa Mills, Kona Lewis, Samantha Villegas, Mia Arca, Alexis Lopez, Liam Dubois, Yukon Government Minister of Education Jeannie McLean, First Nation School Board Executive Director Melissa Flynn, Elder Sandy Johnson, Elder Gùdia Mary Jane Johnson. *Back row below/behind sign:* Adam Hicks, Samantha Asselstine behind brother Billy Asselstine, Sierra Easterson-Moore behind Amirah Miller-Hundrup, Samara van Lieshout, Skáyda.û Jules, Minister of Highways and Public Works Nils Clarke. Government of Yukon photograph. Elders Portraits #61.

Our community has worked together to achieve many other goals through the years. This book documents the stories behind those projects, so that our children and grandchildren will understand the sacrifices and hard work involved in building the benefits we enjoy now. Our pledge to the Elders and Ancestors who began these journeys long ago is to continue their work by protecting our land, our culture, our language, and our community, raising future generations with our Ancestral Knowledge and deep respect for the world around them.

Shàw níthan (thank you in Kluane dialect), Gunalchéesh (thank you in Tlingit). Thank you to our Elders and everyone who made this beautiful book.

ELDERS COUNCIL MESSAGE

We are very happy to share our stories with our children, grandchildren, and all the ones who will come after us, just as our Ancestors passed on their knowledge to us. We created this book so that our families will know who they are and how we came to be the self-governing Kluane First Nation of today. We want to share our stories with our northern neighbours, too, and with people who come to visit our land from around the world, so they will understand what we value as a people, how we care for our environment, and how we work hard to fulfill our responsibilities in the present day and to plan for our future goals as a community.

We come from strong and hard-working people, who were completely at home in our Asì Keyí (Grandfather's Country) around Lhù'ààn Mân (Kluane Lake). They knew and respected all living beings on the land, in the waters, and up in the skies. They had wisdom and knowledge built upon thousands of years of experience and traditions. They adapted to many changes through the years, using ingenuity, well-practiced skills, and complete dedication to their families to overcome any and all challenges that came their way.

Our generation experienced an era of rapid and destructive change after the building of the Alaska Highway. We were forcibly separated from our grandparents and parents, aunties and uncles, who loved us and wanted to teach us how to live in good ways as they had been taught by their Elders. They and we endured those difficult years and still maintained our language, our culture, and our Ancestral Knowledge. With them we started the processes that led to settling our Yukon First Nations land claims peacefully. They helped guide us to establish new forms of governance to reclaim our lands, regain control over our lives, and most important re-establish our ways of raising our children with respect for our culture and language.

We look forward to the future with pride and with gratitude to all who have contributed to our Nation. We believe this book and our stories will provide important details about our past that will help our Nation continue to grow in positive and peaceful ways. That is our wish for all our children, grandchildren, and future generations. Enjoy and share this beautiful land as we have done, and keep it safe for all time!

YOUTH COUNCIL MESSAGE

Kluane First Nation has created a self-governing framework that incorporates our traditional values of inclusivity for the whole community in decision-making. The KFN Youth Council comprises all our Youth ages 13 to 25 and currently has 45 members. We hold several meetings annually and communicate in a contemporary way with members, including through social media. We have an Executive group, who meet more regularly to provide input to Council on any and all issues that concern KFN Youth and the broader community.

As KFN Youth we are very conscious of the valuable lessons and the legacy of Ancestral Knowledge passed on by our long-ago Ancestors and our present-day Elders. Their exceptional talents, strength, perseverance, and resilience are a source of great inspiration to us. They have demonstrated over and over again their ability to adapt to any circumstance. They have survived the arrival of newcomers to our land over the past century, the building of the Alaska Highway, which changed so much so fast, the terrible conditions of residential schools, and the imposition of colonial policies that undermined our culture and communities. They have reclaimed our rights through our Final and Self-Government Agreements.

Our Elders have taught us about kinship and family, values which connect us to our land and our shared experiences as Kluane First Nation people. Our women—grandmothers, mothers, aunts, and sisters—are a key source of strength and continuity for us all. Our people are exceptional hunters, guides, and resource managers. As Youth we are called to join them as leaders and keepers of our culture, language, and homelands.

Our First Nation is our organization, and our Self-Government Agreement is our tool to enact our will and destiny as a people. Our Nation is growing and maturing as a government, working towards incorporating our traditions with technologies and practices to meet our needs. We employ consensus decision-making within our government and community. Consensus building is not an easy process; we believe it is the best way forward so our citizens can live with the collective decisions that are made. We seek processes and outcomes that carefully consider our past, present, and future needs from many perspectives. As Youth we welcome and appreciate the opportunity to be part of our First Nation's governance, along with our Elders and all other citizens. We work together with other First Nations to build a strong future for our lands and our people.

Today, as in past times, we are a small population with a high calibre of talent and dedication to hard work. We know our future is in our hands and will be what we make of it. To maintain and enhance our identity as Kluane people, we must continue to work towards expressing ourselves through our language and culture. Our governance processes have to fit our contemporary setting while upholding our core values.

Our people are not and have never been stagnant. As Youth we contribute to finding ways for new technology and ideas to benefit our whole Nation. We have always had living values that evolved as circumstances required change. Our challenge today is the fast pace and enormity of change, with little time to adjust. In a few short years our people have gone from being shut out of many institutions to being sought out for our cultural background, our expertise, and our talents. As the Youth of today we have many extraordinary opportunities that were denied to our Elders and Ancestors. This sudden change is overwhelming at times. We will always need love and understanding from our Elders and our whole community. Their patience, support for education, sharing of knowledge, and trust in us are essential for us and our Nation to reach our full potential.

TURNING MEMORIES INTO A BOOK

top Katie Johnson, Gùdia Johnson, and Linda Johnson discuss archival images at Jacquot Hall in Burwash, fall 2017. KFN Archives. EMPC. Elders Portraits #2. PHOTOGRAPHER ALISTAIR MAITLAND

bottom Linda Johnson setting up a recorder for Elders recording sessions at Jacquot Hall, fall 2017. KFN Archives. EMPC. Elders Portraits #3. PHOTOGRAPHER ALISTAIR MAITLAND

In the summer of 2017 we were engaged by the Kluane First Nation (KFN) to begin documentation for the KFN Elders Memory Project. We built on the 1995 Elders booklet initiated by Chief Joe Joe Johnson, for which Katie Johnson recorded Elders in the community. For this new book the goal was to produce digital audio recordings of today's Elders, using their life histories, transcripts, and portrait photographs to create a book of memories for them, their families, and the community.

We have worked with nineteen Elders who are citizens of KFN and three more who have been long time residents and married into our families. Each Elder contributed photos from their personal family albums. We also selected images from the KFN Archives, the Yukon Archives, the Yukon Archaeology Unit, Parks Canada, and contemporary landscape photographers. The resulting life histories, images, and maps convey a unique and deeply personal history of Lhù'ààn Mân Keyí (Kluane Lake Country).

It has been our great honour to work with the Elders and KFN to complete this Elders Memory Project and publication. Many people have contributed to making the book a rich and beautiful treasure for the whole community. Our publisher, Figure 1, has been creative and dedicated in bringing forward the final published form of the project. Staff at the Yukon Archives, the Yukon Archaeology Unit, and Parks Canada, and many others have provided significant support. We thank everyone for their assistance in realizing the Elders' vision for their book.

Most of all we thank the KFN Elders for their diligent work and their steadfast trust in our team to help them bring their stories into the light. Sadly a number of Elders passed away between the time we first recorded them and the publication of this book. We extend our deepest condolences to their families and thank them for helping us complete their family members' chapters.

Shàw níthan (thank you) to all!

KATIE JOHNSON, LINDA JOHNSON, ALISTAIR MAITLAND

top Katie Johnson and Hank Jacquot recording his memories at his home in Haines, Alaska, February 2019. KFN Archives. EMPC. Elders Portraits #4. PHOTOGRAPHER ALISTAIR MAITLAND

bottom Alistair Maitland shooting landscape images at Burwash, fall 2022. KFN Archives. EMPC. Landscape Images #5. PHOTOGRAPHER LINDA JOHNSON

A NOTE ON LANGUAGE

As Lhù'ààn Mân Ku Dań (Kluane Lake People), we are constantly evolving to meet new ways and opportunities that come to us—as they always have and always will—from near and far. Our languages have been evolving too!

Dáh Shäw (our Elders) have been our teachers for millennia, and until recent decades their medium for passing on knowledge was oral, through spoken word and song. Our Ancestors came from many different directions, so our Elders often spoke one or more related First Nations languages: Southern Tutchone, Northern Tutchone, Tlingit, Upper Tanana, and others, depending on where they were born or travelled in their lifetimes. Today we acknowledge all our Elders' languages and recognize the Lhù'ààn Mân dialect of Dań Kwánje (people's word), Southern Tutchone, as our main language.

The transition from oral to written languages occurred only in the past few decades, when Elders and fluent speakers began working with linguists to develop a standardized writing system, including diacritics to indicate high and low tones plus other elements of pronunciation. This has been a complex and ongoing process, owing to the diverse origins of speakers and the subtle yet significant differences between the way our languages are spoken from one region to another and even differences between generations. It is very challenging to standardize spelling within written texts in a book like this one, which includes the life histories of Elders from various distinctive origins.

The process for selecting particular spellings in each Elder's chapter included consideration of the individual's background and identification with a particular language, as well as family preferences for the spelling of personal and place names known to them. Most, but not all, names have been standardized to Lhù'ààn Mân Kwánje, using the Easy Spelling System developed by KFN linguist Daanjì (Daniel Tlen). We consulted a number of speakers and language champions including Elders Tùlhàsèn (Lena Johnson), Gushàka (Margaret Johnson), Salkaaya (Bertha Doris), Da Kwäthala mą (Joyce Johnson-Albert), and Gùdia Mary Jane Johnson, along with younger language learners Diyet van Lieshout and others, to determine the best approach to use. Different spellings occur in various chapters and we respected family wishes for particular versions of names.

We know our languages will continue to grow and change as we reclaim and reinvigorate our cultural legacies. This book is an important step forward in that process!

overleaf Waves crash on the south shores of Lhù'ààn Mân (Whitefish Place Lake, Kluane Lake) as glacial silt from 'A'äy Chù (Lone Mountain There, Slims River) drifts across the water with Thechàl Dhàl (Rock-Scraper Mountain, Sheep Mountain) rising to the west—the rugged landscapes our Ancestors have navigated for thousands of years. KFN Archives. EMPC. Landscape Images #6. PHOTOGRAPHER ALISTAIR MAITLAND

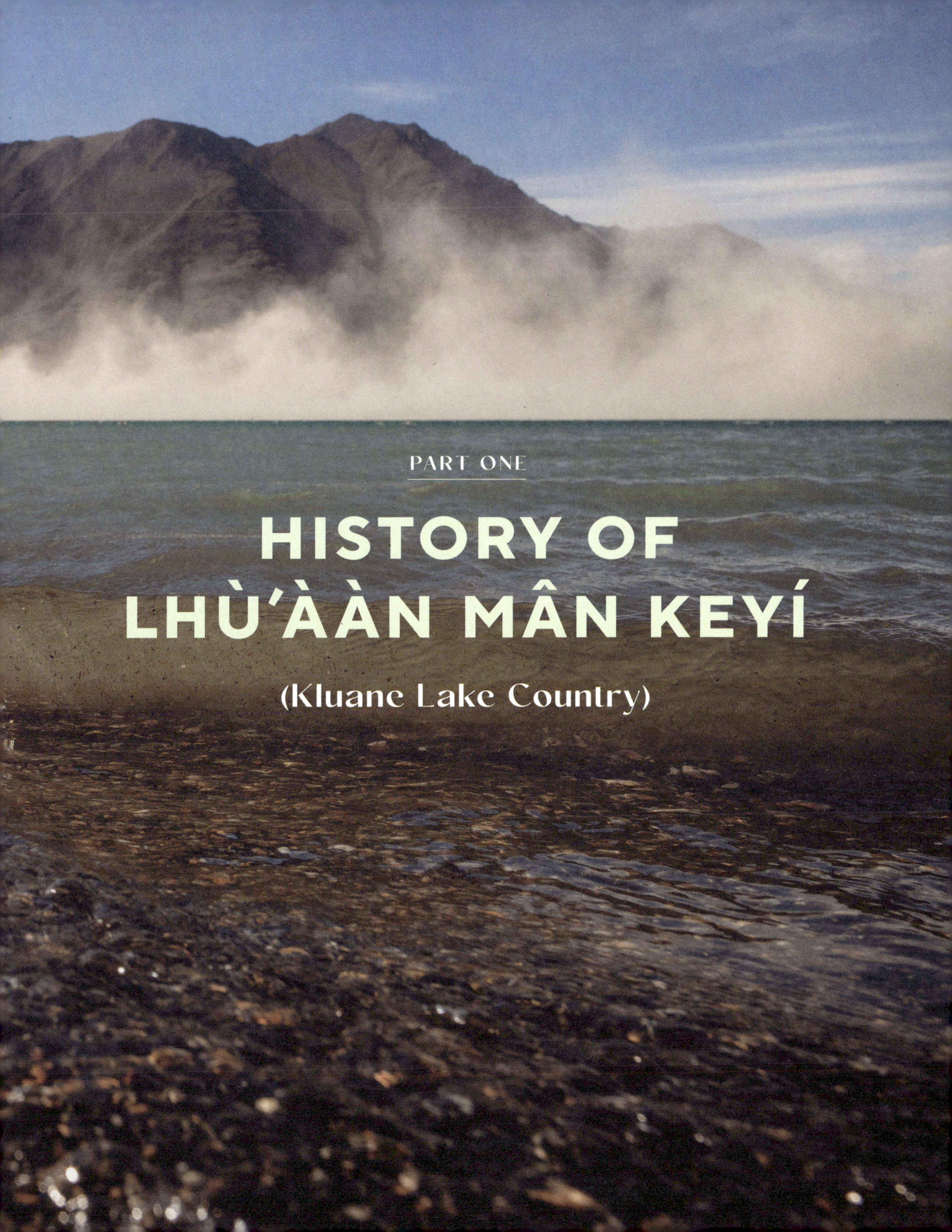

PART ONE

HISTORY OF LHÙ'ÀÀN MÂN KEYÍ

(Kluane Lake Country)

The Ways of Our Ancestors

overleaf Fall colours signal hunting season in the Kluane Range to the west of the Alaska Highway near Burwash. KFN Archives. EMPC. Landscape Images #7. PHOTOGRAPHER ALISTAIR MAITLAND.

top Horses graze on The Point across from Burwash in early fall, circa 1995. KFN Archives. EMPC. Paul Nadasdy Images #4. PHOTOGRAPHER PAUL NADASDY

bottom Moose skin Potlatch drum and wooden drumstick made by Jimmy Joe. Drum is painted with four pink areas around the black outline of a circle divided into four segments. Kluane Museum of Natural History #1974_19a_x. PHOTOGRAPHER UNKNOWN

We are the Lhù'ààn Mân Ku Dań (Kluane Lake People). Our homeland is Asì Keyí (Grandfathers' Country), the beautiful lands centred on Lhù'ààn Mân (Kluane Lake), bounded on the west by the awe-inspiring St. Elias Mountains, and extending north, south, and east through the rich lands and waters that have sustained our people for countless generations.

Ye Shäw (Elders) have taught us their ways of survival through Oral Traditions passed down from one generation to the next. Lhù'ààn Mân Da Shäw K'e (Our Elders' Way) of knowing the lands and waters we call home was developed through travel in all the seasons of the year to observe, hunt, and gather. We are blessed with abundance in so many ways, with many species of fish, small and big animals, birds, plants, minerals, clean air, and water—all contribute to the aromas, sights, and sounds that inspire us daily.

Ye Shäw have a special place in our culture. They are the keepers of life, preserving and teaching essential knowledge through our languages and today in English too. Elders are like multilingual archives. Older generations knew two or more of the inland Athapaskan languages of our region: Southern Tutchone, Northern Tutchone, and Upper Tanana. Some also spoke coastal Tlingit, plus English, and some knew French as well. We refer to our Southern Tutchone language as Dań K'è, which translates as "people speak." The Oral Histories in this book reflect the amazing wisdom, skills, and steadfast dedication of our Elders. In telling our history we honour them above all.

Elders share stories of well-travelled routes over vast areas used for hunting, fishing, gathering, and far-reaching trade networks that linked our people to other Indigenous peoples. Some of our relatives followed those routes from the Upper Tanana and Copper rivers north of the Kluane region; others came from Tlingit communities in coastal Alaska.

Together with people from the interior Yukon they became founding members of our Nation, and their descendants are all part of our community today.[1]

Our Lhù'ààn Mân Ye Shäw tell many stories and sing beautiful songs about how the world began. These stories—of how Ts'ark'i (Crow) brought light to the world; the beginnings of animal, human, and plant life; and the good ways for people to live together in harmony with the land, animals, and all beings in this world—provide a firm foundation for our community. They guided people in years past, and they are important for us today. We know people by their stories and by their songs, so our history begins with them.

The two stories shared here are reproduced with permission from Kwädāy Kwändür, compiled and translated by Margaret Workman and published by the Yukon Native Language Centre in 2010. The text was transcribed from recordings made by Daanji (Daniel Tlen) in Burwash Landing on November 9, 1984.[2]

top Looking west up the 'A'äy Chù (Lone Mountain There, Slims River) valley towards the Kaskawulsh Glacier, circa 2005. KFN Archives. EMPC. Parks Canada, Healing Broken Connections Program Images #166. PHOTOGRAPHER UNKNOWN

bottom Bright red "low bush" cranberries (lingonberries) loaded with vitamin C are harvested in early fall to provide tasty and healthy treats all winter. KFN Archives. EMPC. Landscape Images #3. PHOTOGRAPHER KATIE JOHNSON

above Renowned storyteller Tsal KàJana (Gopher Lady, Copper Lily Johnson) walking along a trail in Burwash circa 1980s with her walking stick and backpack. KFN Archives. EMPC. Dorothy Johnson Family Images #1. PHOTOGRAPHER UNKNOWN

THE CROW MADE THE WORLD

Tsal KàJana (Copper Lily, Copper Lilly)

1. Ts'ű̈rk'i äzhà kẫdìnya kwädą̄y zhän nän kay. Nän k'ẫtl'àásį ch'e kwäni.
2. Äyet äzhà gúch'än kek'àyedìnłè. Dazhän nän ķay dàshe ts'ẫn ts'ű̈rk'i äzhà nän k'ẫtl'àásį. Łàshe ch'äw chu ch'ī ăch'e, yèts'enia: äghẫn nt'ąy shų̄, äyet sha, hų zhazha. Ätl'a ghẫyenẫ'į k'e uyè nanẫt'à k'e nän kay łàshe ch'äw uyè kwälanẫt'à.
3. Äju kų̄ ts'ùdlẫw kwäni ts'ű̈rk'i. Kwädą̄y ch'äw änäwkwäkhį uthe yèts'eni shų. Däkenäkäw yèts'eni udunèna, äyet yìnlà tth'ay. Dunèn ughą äsį tth'ay.
4. Uthe chu k'ẫnàka yū, sän ughą dẫkènatl'ű̀r tth'ay. Kàch'e nayedẫtl'ű̀r k'e, chu k'ẫnàka ch'äw, sän dakènatth'et. Ätl'a ts'ű̈rk'i daghày kẫkwäch'į. Ätl'a däzhän chu nu'į̀ du. Ädaghày kàch'į. Kàch'e ch'äw chu yedẫdą kwänįą.
5. Äyet k'ètl'ą̀, äju nẫkwẫnthat ch'äw, udunèn kų̀lį. Ätl'a äyet ts'ű̈rk'i dunèna.
6. Ätl'a äyet dän k'e chu nẫ'į. K'ètl'ą̀ kẫjänadhử, tth'ay, ẫdāy. Ẫ'àn uyè nännt'ay, tth'ay, äyet chu k'e. Äyet sha ẫdāy yè yat'ay äla shų łàashe ch'äw yenẫ'į ch'e kwäni.
7. Dazhän kwändür ts'ẫndü äch'e. Äju ulan ts'ẫn kìinjì. Kwäch'e tl'àhų̀. Änaàtą̄y kwẫtl'et yè äju kìinjì kų̀lį. Tl'áhų̀ kwändür. Zhą ts'ināy änaàtą̄y kwatth'ät.
8. Ts'ű̈rk'i shų nłäts'ẫn kekwänjī k'e n-ndų̄ kwädałel k'e keni. Kẫnàni nà dän kwädą̄y.
9. Ją̀ ädè Mary Jacquot yè dághà mę̀l ta k'ẫnit'ẫr k'e kàch'į nà łų̀ ts'ű̈rk'i łẫki dákē k'ànädäl k'e nłäts'ẫn ghàkwänjē ghẫnàni. Łų̀ kẫnàni ch'äw, dákē kànät'a.

above Ravens are present year round in Yukon communities, offering continual commentary on everything they see around them. KFN Archives. EMPC. Wildlife Images #9. PHOTOGRAPHER MIKE ASHBEE

10. Kàk'e shèni Mary, "Dä̀nàni nū äyet ts'ǘrk'i. Äju kä̀nàni ch'e nà. Ye ka änū?" shèni. "Aju sòothän kwädajèl ka äni." Kàk'e, nänìzhä̀t ka, äk'äl dákų̀ ts'ä̀n nadìit'är.

11. Äyet ts'än äju kwädä̀dhät ch'äw, Ńthenada (Annie Ned) dägàlį̄ yè Burwash yū łäkea'ä̀r. Ä́ghą nä̀nya k'e shèni, "Nla ghą nàniya. Kwändür ndäw äch'į," shèni. Ä́dāy kwäts'ä̀n dèya.

12. Shekenä́'į k'e Margaret yè ä́dų̀ ä́yèdų̄ kedä̀'är. Łų̀ Margaret ä́ghą łääntal k'e, ä́k'waánjì äsay yè. Kàk'e shèni, ä́shela Jimmy Joe ä́thè hospital yū ächį hą. "Kwändǖr dìtth'ay," shèni.

13. Äyet kwändür dìtth'ay k'e łų̀ tänùusha níthän. Ä́yenjì k'ekwänìdà yák'è. Äju uk'e keni níthän. Ją äju łä̀ki nį̀įkhèla Jimmy ní'į kwäts'än, ätl'a ä́thè Whitehorse mbä̀t ka dèya k'e.

14. "Shän ní'į jèk'e kwädänùłì shį̀," kwäyèdíshį. "Ä́thè nä̀sháchè," kwäyèdíshį.

15. Kàk'e ch'äw Whitehorse ts'ä̀n dän ä́yè dä̀jel. Äyū łiíshal k'e, doctor ä́shela chē ghą̀ nä̀shèchį k'e, kàk'e sa udäníłi.

16. Kàk'e kwäts'än ch'äw dazhän dunèna kwäts'àn kwíshe. "Tl'áhų ädą, 'en kúthį däw kwàk'ù k'e."

17. Äyet kwäts'ǟn ch'äw udä̀nìłì ch'e ts'ǘrk'i iyènjì dä̀kwädanjèl yū. Äyet k'ètl'ą̀ cheshų kàkwä̀zhà nà. Ätl'a äyet Bessie ughra danjèl hą k'e shų.

18. Jessie Joe ä́tsh'ä̀n kį̀įya k'e, shèni, chįch'a äda ch'äw, ts'ǘrk'i łä̀ki umbät nä̀ninjēl k'e, kekwänje ǹtth'ay. "Ye ka kenū?" shädä́kät. Äyet dzänù ch'äw äzhà Bessie ughra motorcycle yè ujädègį. Kùka díshį, udä̀nìłi ch'e ts'ǘrk'i dän ts'ä̀n ghàkwänjē k'e.

19. Tl'áhų̀.

above 'A-dzi-zha (moon) rising over mountains on the east shore of Lhù'ààn Mân (Whitefish Place Lake, Kluane Lake) in early spring. KFN Archives. EMPC. Landscape Images #8. PHOTOGRAPHER ALANNA DICKSON

facing Ts'ark'i (raven) soaring high in the sky. KFN Archives. EMPC. Wildlife Images #1. PHOTOGRAPHER ALANNA DICKSON

ENGLISH INTERPRETATION

1. A long time ago it was the crow that came down onto this land. He made all of the world, they say.
2. Now it is the white man that really likes it. The crow that made the land, everything on this land. It was all of it, even the water, they say: those plants too, that sun, also the moon. After he stole these things, while he flew around with them, he covered everything on this land with them.
3. They say that you can't beat the crow. A long time ago a rich man had a daughter, they say too. The child of the one they call God, that's that one, they say. It made a child for her, they say.
4. His daughter, where she was dipping water, dirt fell into the container for her, they say. When she would spill it out and dip water again, dirt fell into it again. It happened according to the will of the crow. Finally, she just drank the water, they say.
5. After that, not long at all, she had a baby. That was the crow's baby.
6. It was then that person stole some water. After, he flew far away, they say, way up. He flew all around with it, they say, that water. That sun way up there in the sky too, he stole all of it, they say.
7. This is a long story. I don't know it to the end. That's it. Because I have forgotten everything, I don't remember anything. That's all the story. From here on I have forgotten it.
8. Also, when two crows talk to each other, they are passing on some bad news, they say. People a long time ago used to say that.
9. While checking on our snares down that way with Mary Jacquot, then as two crows were flying behind us, it was just like they were talking to each other. All the while talking, they were flying around us.
10. Then Mary asked me, "What are those crows saying? They never did that before. Why are they talking?" she asked me. "They talk because something not good is going to happen." Then, because we got scared, we returned to our house in a hurry.

11. Not very long from then, Annie Ned came to Burwash with her husband. When she came to me, she said, "Go to your brother-in-law. He has news for you," she told me. Then she went up there.

12. When they saw me, they came down towards me with Margaret. Really, when Margaret came to me, she hugged me while crying. Then she told me my younger brother Jimmy Joe died in the hospital down there. "I heard the news," she told me.

13. When I heard this news, I really felt like jumping in the water. Then I felt really bad. I thought what they said was not true. Not even two nights had passed from when I had seen Jimmy, when he went down to Whitehorse to get some groceries.

14. "When I see for myself, then I will believe you," I told them. "Take me down there," I told them.

15. Right away some people went to Whitehorse with me. When I arrived there, when the doctor took me to my younger brother's body, only then I believed.

16. From that day on I have talked to the young people. "Quit that drinking, give it up when it is cold."

17. From that day on I believe that crow knows that something bad is going to happen. After that it happened again. It did also when something was to happen to Bessie's son.

18. When Jessie Joe came to me, she said, that while she was sitting outside, when two crows landed in front of her, they started talking to each other, she said. "Why are they saying that?" she asked me. The very same afternoon, Bessie's son was killed with a motorcycle. That's why I say, I believe it when the crows talk to people.

19. That's all.

above KFN Elder Tàa'aana (Jessie Joe) is fondly remembered for her kind ways and storytelling. KFN Archives. EMPC. Elders Portraits #5. PHOTOGRAPHER MATH'IEYA ALATINI

THE WOLF STORY

Tàa'aana (Jessie Joe)

1. Ägay shų̄ äju unātą̄y ughā kwäts'ǟłè. Dän yàkinlį ch'ē tth'ay.
2. Äyet ch'ē tth'ay dän dämbȁt ka k'ànadàl, kanday ka. Äyet zhà, tth'ay, dän k'e dätth'ǟn k'enghȕr dā. Utth'ǟn k'èagür.
3. Äju nats'ädúche. They got tired of him. Utth'ǟn łänadȁgür. Äyet shàch'ea dän k'ànadäl yū, uzi ts'äghą. Äyet hàts'įlà dän k'e, nats'änńchį. Äthȁn mür all łų̀ äthȁn k'e ughą ämür ts'ǟsį. Ghàk'e ät'ȁts'įchį äyet dän.
4. Uzí dhȕ unathų̄ ts'įla. Äyet t'àt nats'ínchį. Hàk'e hàch'ea. What can he do? He can't get up, utth'ǟn k'èagür yè. Sür shų̄ ughą hų zhąts'ȁn pile ts'ǟsį. Tláhų̀, äju shų̄ ughą shàkwädį̀ch'e hą.
5. Äyet zhà ch'e. Äyet dän utth'ǟn k'èagür äyet shàch'e. Hahų̀, yäw uyè kwäyenńkhyȁw yū shachį. Don't know how long shachįų.
6. Äyet shànįą, kàch'e äda shachį, na. Dùuch'į k'e. He don't make fire, usǖr shų̄ ughą nàts'änlà gwȁn däw. Thų̀ shàch'ea dän shachį. Łų̀ dàkwàádhat k'e äthȁn tän keyé'įą yékhȕ. Ätl'a ughą yets'èmür yékhȕ. Äyet kį̀ kwänjì.
7. Äyet zhà ch'e, shachį ch'äw tl'áhų̀, yäw t'ay shachį ch'äw, ädįtth'ay. Dän ghàkwȁnjē, tth'ay. "Gaay, dȁkwȁch'e k'e zhą̄̈w? Jų̄ jenītrȕ k'e?" kenų. "Ätthyèn yū sür ätlą äyet ńshän ätlą yū t'àt kwȁn dàk'ą̀," kenų. Dän k'e áhų̀ yäw t'ay shachį̄.
8. Äyet ch'e, ǟ'àn dän kų̀ kwäzhät ta k'àkedȁl k'e, "Sür kajänȁya kay kwȁn kedìnk'ą," ätl'a ägay änų.
9. Äyet shànįa äyū uzí dhȕ äla. Äyet kàkinlà. Ǟdāy uzí dhȕ kàkinlà. Uzí dhȕ nashänȁtän. Äyet kàch'e uzí dhȕ kàkinlà k'e äyet dän äthų̄ ghàkwäjäntl'ȕr káthą̄. Dän k'e kuk'wänǟta k'e cheèjäl. "Nàday khį̄ äghȁn t'ay," kenų. "Dän äda." Kàkeni, "Dän äda. Dän kwänjì uzí dhȕ t'ay," kenī. Yäw ukay nìíkhyäw ch'ā äyet.
10. Nàghay, ätl'a ägay undü ch'e yèts'äni. Quite a while ägay kē kį̀ya. Kàk'e kàni nàghay demǖra ke ta, "Heey! Dàkwȁzhà kā dàáth'i?" änų.
11. "Dän äda," yèts'änu. "Dän äda ǟyī yū. Äyet uzí dhȕ t'ay dän kwänjì äda," yèts'änų. Kàk'e änįą, äyet uzí dhȕ dāy äshȁt k'e, ǟyī dän uk'änǟta k'e, łų̀ äju kwäjē, tth'ay. Äju hello ch'i änų.

12. Äyet yèni, "Dän jenìda ch'e. Ǟyī äda," kwäyènī. "Dàdáłèl k'e? Dùunje du áthā̀n k'e uts'à'ų dàátth'i," änų.

13. Kàk'e kànų, "Dùúch'e? Mäts'ä̀n kwänje," keyènų ägay.

14. Tl'ą̀ äni tth'ay nàghay, "Ǟla-a? Dìnńzhà kwä̀ch'äw?" yèni.

15. Äyet dän shàni, "Ah kwädā̧y ch'äw ä́tth'ā̀n k'äägür. Ǟt'ä̀shets'į́chį kwä̀ch'e," änų. "I can't get up," änų.

16. Ägay kutth'āt nlį̄ tth'ay tl'áhų̀ nàghay. Kàk'e kànįa, "Hähooyh! Tl'ákų̀, dákē íshal nji ä́yè k'ànudā nį, ä́ghą nási," änu. "Kwä̀n dàk'ą̀," kwäyèni. Ughày ch'äw kwä̀n kā̀nk'ą, ägay.

17. Łų thāją ts'į́mür ts'įlà. Ughą ghàts'émür. Keghä̀nnshä̀t. Kàk'e ich'ākwädä̀la. Tl'áhų̀ äyet dän utth'ā̀n k'äagür, tl'áhų̀ nīya k'e, äyet dän k'ä̀nada làch'į.

18. Äyet shànįą, "Äkų̀ dän kē ä́yè k'ànųda. Ǟyè company ųlè. Dákē k'ànūt'ä̀r shį," änų.

19. Äyet kànįą, dän ghàdinjäl tl'ą̀, tth'adā̧y nakinchį. Ketth'ā̀n ńtth'įla. Äyet shànįą, "Dįįzha kwä̀ch'äw," keyènų.

20. "Äkįízhà ä́tth'ā̀n k'äagür kwä̀ch'e," änų. "Äyet shäts'ìnlà, ät'ä̀shäts'ínchį," änų.

21. Äts'ämür tl'ą̀, dän ghàdinjäl. Kàk'e hàni näw nàghaya, "'Hùha' ákų̀! Dákē dīnshal thān shäwa. Äyįdų̀khąn," äni. "Dákē k'ànūt'ä̀r shį. Utth'ā̀n kay ä́ghą shàw náłe. Utth'ā̀n nási," änų.

22. Hùch'à ägay dùsèla nįįya. Nìįya k'e, "Ǟ'ų ntth'ā̀n jų̄ kä̀nń'į," yèts'änų̄. Dätth'ā̀n jų̄ kà'į. Nch'ā ägay däshè yè łų̀ ugà níkhäl dāy. Łų̀ ätl'ą̀, dä̀shų̄, łày hų̄, "Ntth'ā̀n nchįą," yènų. Äyet ye'į. Dätth'ā̀n zhā'į. Däshè yè ye'į. Utth'ā̀n gà yeyé'į ä́nāy.

23. Ją̀ dän neètla k'e chèètla tth'ay ä́'àn chùzhan. Ätlą̀ k'e dän kē kedä̀'är. Ńtl'ē ch'äw dän dä̀jäl. Kwänáthe ägay dä̀'är. Dän kē keat'ä̀r. Kàkech'į ch'äw dän kē k'àket'ä̀r all winter long.

24. Äju dän yèenjì yū. Kathana ch'e dhäl kay dų̀ dän shaájäl lą k'e dän kanday jenàjäl lą̄'. Äyet k'e dän kē kya'ä̀r ch'äw. Ǟ'ų kwä̀n shäw k'e kįì'a äthèn yū jà.

25. Ją̀ kwä̀n shäw dä̀k'ä̀n ghāy kay k'e kanday shį̄ ts'ä́ch'ù̀ hą'. Kanday ts'ä̀äkhį hą' k'e. Ńtl'e näts'äni dän kē ha'ä̀r. Dän kē kä̀kį'är k'e k'à chį ätą k'akädä̀'är. Ägay t'ä̀ke'är k'e, "Ǟla äk'ā k'à kò nį́'į?" äni tth'ay.

above Thechàl Dhàl (Rock-Scraper Mountain, Sheep Mountain) in winter. KFN Archives. EMPC. Landscape Images #9. PHOTOGRAPHER KATIE JOHNSON

facing Aerial view of Kluane Range in winter. KFN Archives. EMPC. Landscape Images #10. PHOTOGRAPHER ALANNA DICKSON

26. "Ē̜hę, k'à kò ätą ní'ią ǟdāy yū. Sǟl k'à kò ätą ní'į ts'än k'e ägay kegǟn ut'àdìnch'i shų̄ ní'į," äni tth'ay. Äyet zhà ägay kuyàkwįdhät.

27. "Äju, äju deyènjì kà ni. Kùkā zhà dáyàkų̀dhät," nų, ägay ts'ǟn. Ägay give up. Ätl'ą̀ k'e ńtl'e dän kwäshą dädǟl k'e dädän k'e shäkenächį̄. Atl'a hų̀ jų̄ kǟkenje dän kē kyä'ǟr. Ts'ǟtläw dän kē k'àkät'ǟr, kanday yè uzi shų̄ keghą̄.

28. Äyet ts'än kedǟjäl kàch'ią dän kàanjäl kē kyadǟl. Kanday k'e tän shajennch'ür. Kàch'e dän ukē shach'ea ǟ'ų.

29. Ägay dayān shų̄, ätl'a udaghà, ätl'a nena daghà, uyèdà dayān ätą ǟyiyū äzhän shų̄ ägay shèlà. Ushèlà, ägay shè lan yèts'äni ushèlà yèts'äni.

30. Äye nų, dän kē ńtl'e łäka'ǟr. Äthàn k'e ghàts'ǟch'ü. Ämür kanday shį̄ yè ts'ǟch'ü. Łäka'ǟr k'e, yeka kàni k'e keyedákät k'e, "Ǟla?" keyènu, "Ǟla! K'à kò äk'ā ní'ią?" keyènu.

31. "Ē̜hę, k'à kò ní'į."

32. "Dàhų̀ch'į k'à kò ńlà?" yèts'änū.

33. "Ägay dayān ätą ǟdāy äyet k'e ushèlà shų̄," äni. Ägay yàkwįthät k'e, łų̀ keyàts'adǟch'äl. Keyedǟkhį.

34. Ätl'ą̀ k'e shànią, dän dǟjäl. Tl'ą̀ k'e áhų unāy next camp. Kàk'e shànią áhų nàghaya k'e äsay, äsay. "Ála," nų k'e, "Äju shetlą -haaaaw- aju shetlą ąąą-haaaa." Ńtl'e nāy nàghaya k'e, ńtl'e nāy äsaya, äsay, "Äju shetlą-haaaaw- äju shetląąa."

35. "Gwaay! Dän uts'ämala nįyet. Tl'áhų̀! Dän shuyàni," ts'ènu. "Nda," yèts'ǟnų. "Ädǟw ughą nǟnńda k'e, uthǟn nashįįlè," yèts'ǟnų.

36. Kàkų̀ nädǟzha ǟdāy utän. Ukē nayenįkü ù yu. Äyet kǟnch'e łų̀ uthǟn ch'i nashēla. Ulà uts'ǟn ghànazhā tth'ay dā. Ńtl'e tàket'är ńtth'ay edǟką k'e.

37. Ätl'ą̀ shànī ahų ula uyè łänadāl ńtl'ē ch'äw. Äyet ts'än dǟjäl k'e tl'áhų̀ dän k'ų̄ k'ekejäl, nàghay. Tl'áhų̀ dän k'e kwǟn shäw ghàdǟk'ǟn. Łǟts'ì ätlą kų̀lį. Kàk'e kàch'e, dän udu dǟtth'i, keni. Ätl'a äkhī ät'ànkįji.

38. "Dän nànje ní'ią?" keyènų. "Ughą nǟnńzhàa?" keyènų.

39. "Ē̜hę'," änų. "I am going to see them."

40. "Łǟwa ka, "Ägay nashäkíkhì," ch'e dųnį nà. Don't tell nobody," keyènų. "Łäw ughą kųndǖr nà," keyènų.

41. Äyet shànį̨ą, "Ughą nų̀nzhàa?" keyèni tth'ay.

42. "Ę̀hę'," änī.

43. "Łä̀ki ńkhēl jè nka huts'unjē hį̀. Kàk'e dän ghą nūnzhà," yèts'änų. "Łäwa dághą kųndṻr nà, ntth'ā̈n nayītsį yū," keyènų.

44. Ätl'ą̀ k'e dän tännya k'e, änų.

45. "A'ay! Dį̀įzhà ch'äw? Ntth'ā̈n shä̀w nazhà," kèyènų.

46. Łų̀ ch'äw, "Ägay nashäkį́khì ch'e," änų. Łų̀ keyùųnjì dü ätl'a äyet, "Ägay nashäkį́khì ch'e ä́tth'ā̈n," änų.

47. Ätl'à k'e ahų̀ two night ägay tl'áhù kų̀ yana ägay nį̀į'ä̀r k'e ghàsāy yè k'e, "Gho-ow-ow-ow-ow." Ńtl'e nāy yènsay, yènsay.

48. Äyet änį̨ą, "Hähooyh!" Uyèkwį̨dhät.

49. Ägay uyenàsay nā ńtl'e. "Dáts'ä̀n łaadúzhà du." They want him to come back.

50. Äyet nį ntth'ay, "Hähooyh! Shèk'ān. Yambä̀t ye ghą nū tànń'är ä́day," änų jà. He cuss them down ägay ts'į̀. They know it's him. Ätl'a dädän änį yū keyènjì, ägay.

51. Äyet kàch'į tl'áhų̀ nadä̀zha ä́dāy kuta ts'ä̀n. Äyet keyį̀là. Ägay keyèts'àdä̀ch'äl, łų̀ usä̀la ts'ä̀n. Ät'àkįyį̀chį nū. No more. Dän ät'àkį̀chį.

52. Tl'ą̀, "Äju dän ts'ä̀n nànnìnji. No more."

53. Ägay ts'ädä́khē k'e dän ts'ädaä́khe làch'e. Ätl'a long time ago ägay shų̄ dį̀įkhį jè nà, zhän uch'ä̀t, sinew, kàkhā ts'änä̀lè. Lāyde.

54. Ätl'a kwädą̄y ts'än k'e kä̀nàch'į̄ ch'e ka díshį. Unāl ughą kwíndür zhän. Ätl'a uch'ä̀t kànį̀ch'i, yänù shų, uyāch'ä̀t shų, ätl'a first time ägay ts'ädä́khē k'e, ätl'a kä̀ts'ä'į yū, änį̨ą ä́ta. Ughą kwändṻr k'e ghày díshį shą̨hų̄. Äju ní'į. Gwä̀n ch'äw just kwändür ghày díshį.

55. Uka shädį́kät kā n-nàdíshį däzhän kwändür. Ätl'a ä́tà ä́ndāl kwändṻr k'è níshį. N-nāl kwíndür.

56. Uncle Sam [Johnson] yè Jesia [Johnson] shų dųnkä̀t ǹjè. Ätl'a ts'enke kwändṻr yèkenjì ka.

57. Tl'áhų̀ kwä̀ch'e.

ENGLISH INTERPRETATION

above Dawn over The Point south of Burwash in winter. KFN Archives. EMPC. Landscape Images #11. PHOTOGRAPHER UNKNOWN

1. Wolves too, you cannot talk about them without them being aware of it. They were people too, they say.

2. It was like this, they say that people used to travel around all over, looking for their food, for moose. That's when it happened, they say, that this one man broke his legs. His legs were broken.

3. There was no way for them to pack him back. They got tired of him. His legs were really broken. That's when, as the people were walking around, they killed some caribou. When the people had done that, they left him. Boiled meat, all (kinds), lots of meat, they made boiled for him. Then they left this man behind.

4. They put a caribou hide over him. They put him in that. And then it happened. What can he do? He can't get up with his legs broken. They made a pile of firewood close to him this high. My goodness, they were not concerned about him at all.

5. This happened too. This man with the broken legs was sleeping. And then it started to snow with him, covering him right over, where he was sleeping. I don't know how long he was sleeping.

6. So, they say, then he lay sleeping. What else could he do? He didn't make a fire even though they had put firewood there for him. So that man just kept sleeping. I don't know for how long after he was chewing on the frozen meat. And then he was chewing on what they had boiled for him. He lived on that.

7. Thus it happened, in fact while he was sleeping, while he was sleeping under the snow, he heard something. People were talking, they say. "Gee, what has happened here? Where do we sleep?" they asked. "Down there we could light a fire in that place with lots of wood and stumps," they said. The man, though, was still sleeping under the snow.

8. And then it happened, when they were moving about in the people's old camp site around there, the wolf said, "You guys make fire on the pile of wood."

9. So they say, there was a caribou skin lying there. That's the one they lifted. They lifted that caribou skin. The caribou skin was frozen. It happened that when they lifted that caribou skin, that person suddenly glared up at them. As he looked at them they jumped back. "Frozen lynx under there!" they said. "It is a person." They said, "It's a person there. A living person is under the caribou skin," they said. It happened that the snow had snowed on him.

10. Well, they say that the wolverine is the wolf's maternal uncle. After quite a while he arrived behind the wolves. Then the wolverine said, to all his nephews, "Hey! What happened that you are all sitting around?" he asked.

11. "A person is there," they told him. "There's a person down there. Under that caribou skin there is a live person," they said to him. Then they said, as he lifted up that caribou skin, as the person down there looked up at him, he did not talk at all, they said. He did not even say hello.

12. Then he said, "The person is sick. The one down there," he said to them. "What are you guys going to do? What do you guys want him to do as you all sit around in front of him?" he asked.

13. Then he said, "What about you? You talk to him," said the wolves.

14. After, the wolverine spoke, they say. "Brother-in-law! What happened to you?" he asked him.

15. That man said, "Ah, a long time ago my legs got broken. They left me behind, they did," he said. "I can't get up," he said.

16. The wolverine is in fact the boss of the wolves, they say. Then he said, "Hähooyh! Okay, fix him for me in order that he will walk places with me as I walk behind you guys," he said. "You guys make a fire," he told them. Now the wolves made a fire, following his order.

17. They made very strange boiled things. They boiled it for him. They fed him. Then they uncovered him. Finally, when that man whose legs were broken finally stood up, that man walked around.

18. Then he said, "Ok, he will walk with me behind the people. He will keep me company. We will walk behind you guys," he said.

19. Then they say, after the people had eaten, they sat him upright. They straightened his legs out. Then they said, "What happened to you?" they asked.

above 'Agay (wolf) on lake near Burwash in winter. KFN Archives. EMPC. Landscape Images #12. PHOTOGRAPHER ALANNA DICKSON

facing 'A-dzi-zha (moon) on the rise. KFN Archives. EMPC. Landscape Images #13. PHOTOGRAPHER ALANNA DICKSON

20. "It happened to me that my legs got broken," he said. "Then they did this to me, they abandoned me," he said.

21. After they cooked, the people ate. Then the wolverine said, "My goodness sakes! I walk by myself behind you guys. Heal him," he said. "We will walk behind you guys. Make good his legs for me. Heal his legs," he said.

22. After a while a little wolf got up. When he got up, "Straighten your legs toward me like this," they told him. He did his legs like this [narrator gesture]. Then the wolf patted with his tail all along, all the way up (one leg). After that, again, the other one too. "You do this with your legs," he told him. Then he did it. He did this to his legs [narrator gesture]. He did it with his tail. He did it along his legs, all the way up.

23. All of a sudden, when the man got up, he marched, they say, to outside. After that, they went behind the people. Early in the morning, the people left. Before them, the wolves had left. They followed behind the people. This is what they did, they followed behind the people all winter long.

24. He had not been with people for a long time. All of a sudden, down the mountain, it looked like people had come around and it looked like people were chasing after a moose. Then, while they were following these people, way down there a big fire was rising up, way, way, down there.

25. There, where the big fire was burning, they were roasting moose ribs. They had killed a moose. In the evening, they say, they were still following the people. When they arrived behind the people, they passed a bow laying there. When they caught up to the wolves, "Brother-in-law, did you see an arrow shaft?" he asked, they say.

26. "Yes, I saw the arrow shaft lying up there. When I saw the gopher arrow shaft lying there, I also saw a wolf's toenail attached," he said, they say. That's when the wolves got really mad.

27. "No, they do not know you people. That's why it is, that you guys are mad," he said to the wolves. The wolves gave up. After that, at night while those two were sleeping, the people moved out, but those two kept on sleeping. So when they found out, they went after the people. Always while following the people, those two killed moose and caribou too.

28. As they left from there, that's when they followed where the people were going. The moose tracks and the trail were together. It could be the people's trail this way.

29. A wolf's lower jaw too, even its chin hair, even the chin hair of an animal, the lower jawbone was lying down there, as was a wolf's tail-tip too. His tail-tip, is what they call the end of a wolf tail. His tail-tip they call it.

30. And so, they arrived at night behind the people. They cooked meat. They cooked boiled meat and moose ribs. When those two arrived, that's when they asked those two, "Brother-in-law!" they asked those two. "Did you see that arrow shaft?" they asked those two.

31. "Yes, I saw the arrow shaft."

32. "What kind of arrow shaft was it?" they asked him.

33. "A wolf's jawbone is lying up there, and this tail-tip too," he said. The wolves, getting mad, thoroughly ripped him apart. They killed him.

34. After that, they say, the people left. After that, (they went to) the next camp, over that way. That's when, they say, the little wolverine was really crying and crying. "My brother-in-law," he cried, "Äju shetlą -haaaaw- aju shetlą ąąą-haaaa." All night long the little wolverine, all night long he was crying and crying, "Äju shetlą-haaaaw- äju shetląąa."

35. "Gee wiz! You are chasing the people's sleep away. Enough! Let people sleep," they told him. "Sit," they told him. "Then go back for him and gather his body parts," they told him.

36. Then he went back way up along his trail. He followed along it exactly. When he got there, he gathered up every last bit of his body parts. He made sure even about the parts of his hand, they say. He returned at night, they say, when it was just getting light.

37. After, they say, he came back with his brother-in-law early in the morning. When those two left from there they finally passed a people's camp, the wolverine. In fact the people had several big fires burning. Lots of smoke was billowing. That's when people were waiting for him, they say. Then there was a healing through hands-sweeping-over.

38. "Do you see the people living?" they asked him. "Do you want to go back to them?" they asked him.

39. "Yes," he replied. "I am going to see them."

40. "Don't you ever tell them, 'the wolves healed me.' Don't tell anybody," they said to him. "Don't tell about it," they said to him.

41. Then they said, "Do you really want to go back to them?" they asked, they say.

42. "Yes," he said.

43. "We will call for you after two nights. Then you will go back to those people," they told him. "Don't tell them about us, that we healed your legs," they said.

44. After, when he came among the people, he talked.

45. "Hey! What happened to you? Your legs got better." they said.

46. Suddenly, "The wolves healed me," he said. So that they would know about this, "The wolves, they healed me, my legs," he said.

47. Because of this, after two nights the wolves gathered all around the camp and they started to cry. "Gho-ow-ow-ow-ow." All night long they cried and cried.

48. The man shouted, "Hähooyh!" He got mad.

49. The wolves were crying for him all night. "We want him to return to us." They wanted him to come back.

facing 'A-gay (wolf) hunting in winter. KFN Archives. EMPC. Wildlife Images #2. PHOTOGRAPHER ALANNA DICKSON

50. That man said, "Hähooyh! Go away! You go back up that way for your food," he said. He cursed the wolves. They knew it was him. Then the wolves knew that it was he himself that spoke.

51. After a while he finally went back up among them. They did this. The wolves ripped him apart into really little pieces. They threw him away. No more. They shunned the people.

52. After, "we will not help people. No more."

53. When you kill wolves, it is just like killing people. Since a long time ago, also, if you kill a wolf, you have to pull out this back leg sinew, the sinew. That's what you do.

54. Because they have done that from long ago I am telling this. For that reason I am telling about it. The sinew that stretches this way, this way too, the leg muscle too, the first thing when you kill a wolf, this is what you do, my father said. I too am telling according to the story about it. I have not seen it. But now I tell just according to the story.

55. I am telling you this story because you asked me for it. Just like my father told me the story, I am saying it. I am telling it to you.

56. You ask uncle Sam [Johnson] and Jesia [Johnson] too. They know lots of Ancestor stories very well.

57. That's all.

above Nàch'adǹch'ea (Mary Jacquot), Tsal KàJana (Copper Lily), and Tàa'aana (Jessie Joe) recording traditional Yēn (songs) outside Big Grandma Èna Johnson's house in 1968 at Burwash.
KFN Archives. CYFN Archives. Photograph Collection #b47_f28_s2_17. PHOTOGRAPHER GEORGE ADAMSON

The six songs shared here were published in *Dáh Shäw Yên, Songs of Our Elders, Lhù'àan Mân Kwanje Kluane Dialect* by the Tutchone Heritage Society and Kluane First Nation in March 2022. From 2017 to 2022 a core group—Daanjì (Daniel Tlen), Diyet van Lieshout, Tùlhàsèn (Lena Johnson), and Gushàka (Grace Margaret Johnson)—worked on translations, transcriptions, and research into the origins of twenty songs preserved in archival recordings of Burwash Elders from 1942 to the early 1980s. The booklet provides the texts accompanied by sound recordings of past and contemporary singers performing them so that KFN citizens can hear, learn, and sing them together at family and community gatherings. These six songs were selected for this book to present some of the singers and songs familiar to past generations, which are appropriate to share with all readers. The Elders and the Tutchone Heritage Society ask that people who are not KFN citizens respect Protocol and seek permission from KFN before singing or sharing these songs in public.[3]

BIAH NÀÀTSAT NÀ (THE BEER WAS STRONG)

COMPOSED BY GĂ LHÊLA (MOOSE JOHNSON)

No known recording. Passed on orally.

Lhù ù-tlą̀w, Bí-ah nàà-tsat nà.
Ma ye-nar-lhį di-nų̂, hiy hah, hay yah
Da-zhan Asì Keyí ke-nar-lhį di nų̂
'oh ho, hay yah
It's really true, the beer was strong.
I tell you I love it.
This One is my Grandfather's Land. And I love it.

Gă lhêla was widely regarded for his good nature, bush skills, and love of singing and dancing. He loved a good gathering, and his distinctive laugh was his trademark. Tùlhàsèn (Lena Johnson), his oldest daughter, described this song as an expression of his love and connection to the land.

"After some drinks with his friends, maybe they are outside; his emotions come through and he's filled with love for his country when he's looking around. It just comes over you."[4]

HUDSON BAY JÀ? (WHERE'S THE HUDSON BAY BOYS?)

COMPOSER UNKNOWN

Sung by Èna (Emma Johnson)

Hey-yah Hudson Bay jà?
Shań nĭ-zhą nà, Nį ghą.
Zù 'ă-lhį nań dį-nų 'oh-hoh 'Oh Hey
Hey-yah 'Oh hoh 'Uuuu 'Uu 'Uu Hah,
Haay-yaah
Ye kų̂ nà, nų̂-wah. Shań nĭ-zhą nà, Nį ghą. Ts'è khe zù 'í-lhį dĭ-nų
'Oh Hoh, Hey,
Heey-yaah Ya hah 'Uuuu 'Uu 'Uu Hey,
Hey-yah Ye kų̂ nà, nų̂-wah. Shań ní-zhą nà,
Nį ghą. Ts'e-khe zù 'í-lhį dí-nų 'Oh Hoh, Haay-yaah
'Oh hoh 'Uuuu 'Uu 'Uu 'Uu
Haay-yaah Ye kų̂ nà, nų̂-wah. Shań ní-zhą nà, Nį ghą. Ts'è-khe zù 'í-lhį
dí-nų-wah. Hey.
Where's the Hudson Bay Boys?
I'm getting older for you
You're the one who said about me,
"She is young and pretty!"
Why did you say that?
It's Me! I'm getting older for you!
I say to you, I am a beautiful young woman!

top Gă lhêla (Moose Johnson) hunting sheep in the mountains, circa 1950s. KFN Archives. EMPC. Elders Portraits #6. PHOTOGRAPHER UNKNOWN

bottom Èna Johnson, known by all as Big Grandma, holding eagle feather gopher snares in Burwash Lodge, with great-grandson Arnold Johnson, circa 1965. KFN Archives. EMPC. Elders Portraits #7. PHOTOGRAPHER UNKNOWN

Daanjì (Daniel Tlen) previously recorded a version of this song as he had learned it from Tàa'aana (Born in an Area That Provides Lots or Everything, a Place of Abundance, Jessie Joe). Tàa'aana said that she learned this song from Èna, who heard it at Fort Selkirk. Daniel's recording of this song, transcribed below, has become the popular version that most sing today.

Ye kų̂ nà, lhų̀
Shan ní-zhą nà,
Nį ghą
Ts'è-khe zù 'í-lhį dí-nų
Hudson Bay jà?
Shan ní-zhą nà,
Nį ghą
Ts'è-khe zù 'í-lhį dí-nų

This song is adpated into Southern Tutchone from the original Northern Tutchone version. Èna leads the song in this recording. In this song there is an Upper Tanana word for young woman: ts'è-khe zù (young woman, pretty). It is unknown who composed this song and who it was for.

During the song session Tùlhàsèn (Lena Johnson) told a story about how Èna had come to live in the Southern Tutchone lands and the Potlatch that took place when she was introduced to her new husband's family:

"Up by Fort Selkirk was a big trading post. They got school and everything there. Must be about sixteen or seventeen when she [Èna] got married to Grandpa [Sida Tà (Jimmy Johnson)]. He was from Aishihik [Àshèyi (Tlingit: Áa-shaa-yík, Dań K'è: Mân Shäw)].

When she was young they had a big potlatch in Aishihik. People worked all summer, working hides and tanning hides. That's all that [they] could give Grandma. She was the leader of the guests coming in. She had a caribou dress with long white skin gloves on. They put a big curtain up and the Aishihik people stood behind the curtain. Guests on other side. When they drop the curtain she lead the dancing with all the people behind her. After that they could all mingle together."[5]

JIMMY JOHNSON-A (JIMMY JOHNSON)

COMPOSED BY JIMMY JOE

Sung by Èna (Emma Johnson), Tsal KàJana (Copper Lily), Tàa'aana (Jessie Joe), and Nàch'adn̈ch'ea (Mary Jacquot)

Jimmy Johnson-a, Jimmy Johnson-a
Dăh dų̂ nįn-tlel-a.
Įn du 'í-shru-a
Ah hey-ah Hey-yah. Ah hey-ah Hey-yah.
Ah hey-ah Hey-yah. Haay Yah

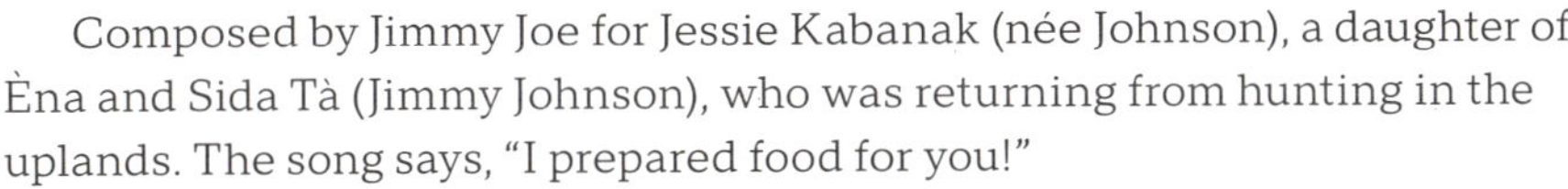

Composed by Jimmy Joe for Jessie Kabanak (née Johnson), a daughter of Èna and Sida Tà (Jimmy Johnson), who was returning from hunting in the uplands. The song says, "I prepared food for you!"

This song is well known in the Yukon and over the years has had other variations added to it.[6]

LITTLE ARM TATÄY (LITTLE ARM NARROWS)

COMPOSED BY 'ACH'ALA (CHARLIE DAVID)

Sung by Èna (Emma Johnson), Tsal KàJana (Copper Lily), Tàa'aana (Jessie Joe), and Nàch'adn̈ch'ea (Mary Jacquot)

Little Arm Ta-täy Kû-'į kwa-tth'at
Hweey 'Ă-nų̀ He-Nu-a-a-a-ay 'I-Ya Hey Yah
Hweey! Le-'i Ha-Yo-oo-o 'I-Ya Hey yah
Lhų̀ 'ù-tląa-ąąy
Little Arm Narrows
Disappearing out of Sight
From across the Water
They Say

'Ach'ala composed this song for his younger sister Èna. Charlie David is the older brother to Èna. Little Arm Narrows is on the north arm of Kluane Lake. Jimmy Johnson had a summer camp there on the north shore. When leaving the Narrows after the Shàkaat (summer/fall harvest season) by boat, Èna sang this song about how the Narrows is disappearing behind the mountains.[7]

facing Tùlhàəə̀n (Lena Johnson) tanning moosehide at her home in Burwash. KFN Archives. EMPC. Elders Portraits #8 and #9. PHOTOGRAPHER UNKNOWN

top Shäw Nàts'àli Tà (Expect Something from Hunting, Jimmy Joe) leading a horse on a trail near Burwash. KFN Archives. EMPC. Elders Portraits #10. PHOTOGRAPHER UNKNOWN

bottom Little Arm Tatäy seen from a bluff at the north end of Lhù'ààn Mân. KFN Archives. EMPC. Landscape Images #23. PHOTOGRAPHER UNKNOWN

top Red dawn sky in Kluane country. KFN Archives. EMPC. Landscape Images #14. PHOTOGRAPHER ALANNA DICKSON

bottom Daanjì (Daniel Tlen) recording with Nàch'adn̈ch'ea (Mary Jacquot) at Burwash in 1977. CYFN Archives. Photograph Collection #b47_f28_s2_5. PHOTOGRAPHER GEORGE ADAMSON

facing Ńtthe (red fox) hunting on snow near Burwash. KFN Archives. EMPC. Wildlife Images #10. PHOTOGRAPHER ALANNA DICKSON

ŃTTHE SHÈ LÀ (RED FOX TAIL TIP)

COMPOSER UNKNOWN, LEGEND SONG
Sung by Daanjì (Daniel Tlen)

Ń-tthe she-la-a-a-a-ah
Ń-tthe she-la-a-a-a-ah
Ka-ma dį̀n-jal-a!
Ń-the she-la-a-a-a-ah
Ń-the she-la-a-a-a-ah
Yaa-da-ka!
Wah! Wah!
Red fox tail tip, Red fox tail tip
Orange-red sky at dawn
Red fox tail tip, Red fox tail tip
The day is breaking soon
Wah! Wah!

Daniel learned this song from Tàa'aana (Jessie Joe). The song is from a story about creatures: Ts'àgagia (Chickadee) stole fire from Shar Shäw (Grizzly), Ńtthe (Red Fox) gave Kwàn' (fire) to Dań (humans) and created Day, and Grizzly got revenge by creating Death. The "wah! wah!" at the end is the cry of the Red Fox. The Dawn is the colour of Red Fox as it flies over the mountain to pierce the membrane skin that covered the Earth. The white tail tip of the Red Fox is the Sun. There are various versions of this story from each community, but the song remains the same. This song dates back to the time of legend.[8]

SHA KWATA ZÙA (MY OWN SWEET ONE)

COMPOSER UNKNOWN
Sung by Tsal KàJana (Copper Lily)

Sha-kwat-a Dzų̂-a
Nį-tsį̂-a nŭ-tsan
Nŭ-than-a
'Ah Yah 'Iy Yah
Hey Yah 'Iy Yah
Haa-ey!
'Įy Yah Hey Nah
My own Sweet One
I wish I could smell your Nose
That's what I'm thinking about!

Tsal KàJana says, "This is our Uncle's song. We inherited it that's why we're going to sing it again. Dăh Nuh-a Yên' Our Uncle's Song." "Smell your nose" means "Kiss you." It is unknown what uncle they are referring to.[9]

Kwäday Dań (Long-Ago People)

10,000 YEARS BEFORE PRESENT TO 1700s

overleaf Spectacular view of dhàl (mountain) and tän shi (glacier) in Kluane National Park. KFN Archives. EMPC. Landscape Images #15. PHOTOGRAPHER ROBERT POSTMA

above Nàch'adnch'ea (Mary Copper Jacquot) learned our Ancestors' stories as a young girl and faithfully carried them forward for future generations. KFN Archives. EMPC. Elders Portraits #11. PHOTOGRAPHER NORMA MCBEAN

In addition to retelling and recording long-standing Oral Traditions, Kluane First Nation collaborates with linguists, anthropologists, archaeologists, paleontologists, geologists, botanists, historians, and others who come to study our country. This information furthers our knowledge about our rich history. Our country and its people from long ago to the present offer fertile ground for everyone to learn and grow!

Oral Traditions and archaeological evidence confirm the presence of ancestral people in this region for thousands of years. Elders speak of powerful natural forces that affected people in those long-ago times. Some stories tell about the edge of the world where one side was white and very cold and on the other side it was summer. Tagish Elder Ch'óonehte' Ma/Stóow (Angela Sidney) told how animals on the winter side "poke a hole through the sky so they have summertime, too."[10] Burwash Elder Nàch'adnch'ea (meaning "A Disappointment," Mary Copper Jacquot) told stories about a great flood when water covered all the land.[11] She also spoke about a time when summer never came and the resulting two winters caused great hardships for people and animals alike.[12] During hard times it is said that some people travelled to far-distant places to find food and safety.[13]

Those descriptions echo events documented by western scientists. They speak of glaciers that covered the southern Yukon for thousands of years, receding around 10,000 years ago to leave dry land where humans could travel, hunt, and gather together. Glacial melting resulted in massive inland lakes, which gradually shrank in size. Sandy ridges high above today's southern lakes occasionally yield intriguing remains of human activities on those ancient beaches. Archaeological sites reveal more evidence of people—their tools, shelters, and hunting and travel patterns.

Two massive volcanic eruptions over 1,000 years ago occurred at Mt. Churchill near the present-day Alaska-Yukon border. White ash rained from the skies and likely blocked the sun for weeks or months, causing disruptions to food and water for all living beings. The story of two winters without a summer told by many Elders refers to a later, more distant volcanic eruption in 1815 at Mt. Tambora in Indonesia; however, it provides some idea of the disastrous effects from the earlier Mt. Churchill eruptions.[14] Linguistic studies link northern Athapaskan languages like our Dań K'è (Southern Tutchone and other interior languages) to those of people across northwestern Canada and south to the Navajo and Apache Peoples, suggesting widespread travels and migrations in the past, perhaps in response to events like volcanic eruptions.[15]

The mountainous lands, extreme variations in weather, and strong winds in our region have always been challenging, requiring specialized knowledge, skills, and endurance to survive. Our Ancestors did that successfully for thousands of years, depending totally on resources found in their immediate surroundings. They traded for some unique goods from afar with their neighbours, adding to the store of local goods that

FIRST NATIONS LANGUAGES IN THE YUKON

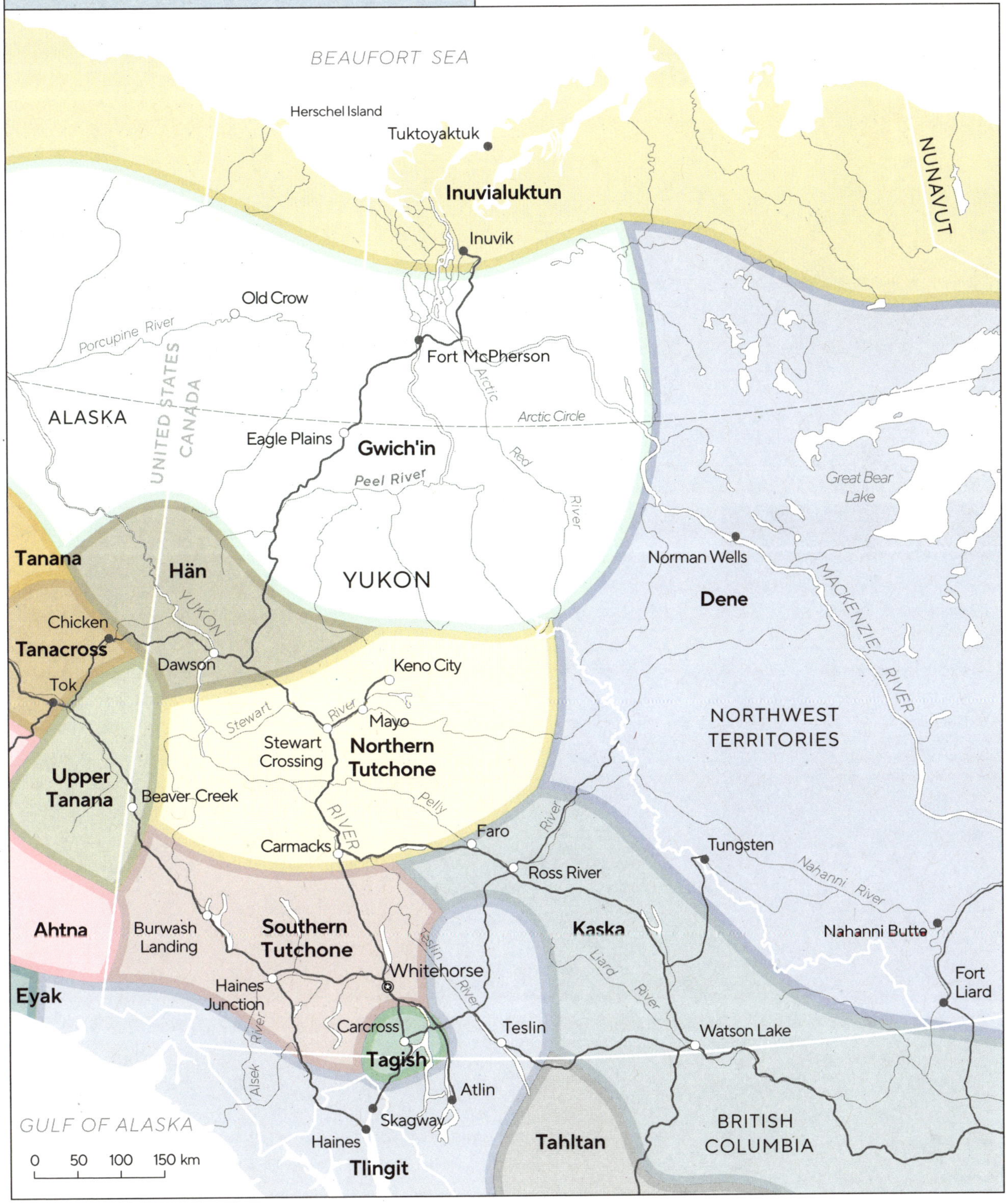

BEAUFORT SEA
Herschel Island
Tuktoyaktuk
NUNAVUT
Inuvialuktun
Inuvik
Old Crow
Porcupine River
Fort McPherson
Arctic Red River
UNITED STATES
CANADA
ALASKA
Arctic Circle
Eagle Plains
Gwich'in
Peel River
Great Bear Lake
Tanana
Hän
YUKON
Norman Wells
Dene
MACKENZIE RIVER
Chicken
Tanacross
Dawson
Keno City
Tok
Stewart River
Mayo
NORTHWEST TERRITORIES
Stewart Crossing
Northern Tutchone
Upper Tanana
Beaver Creek
Pelly River
Carmacks
Faro
Tungsten
Ross River
Nahanni River
Ahtna
Burwash Landing
Southern Tutchone
Kaska
Nahanni Butte
Whitehorse
Teslin River
Liard River
Fort Liard
Eyak
Haines Junction
Alsek River
Carcross
Teslin
Watson Lake
Tagish
Atlin
GULF OF ALASKA
Skagway
BRITISH COLUMBIA
Haines
Tahltan
Tlingit
0 50 100 150 km

Map adapted from work by Richard Vladars, courtesy of Kwanlin Dün First Nation

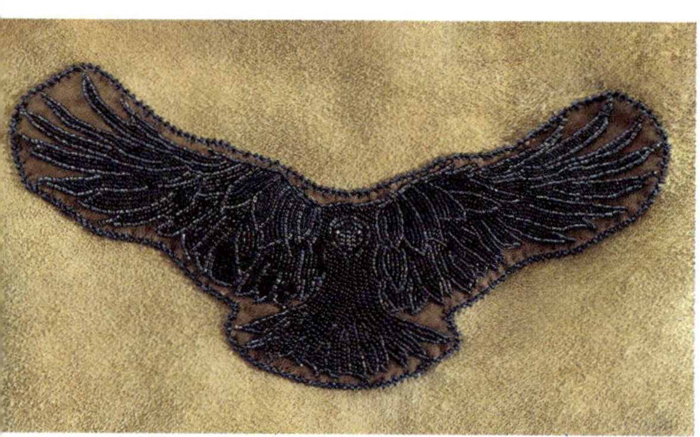

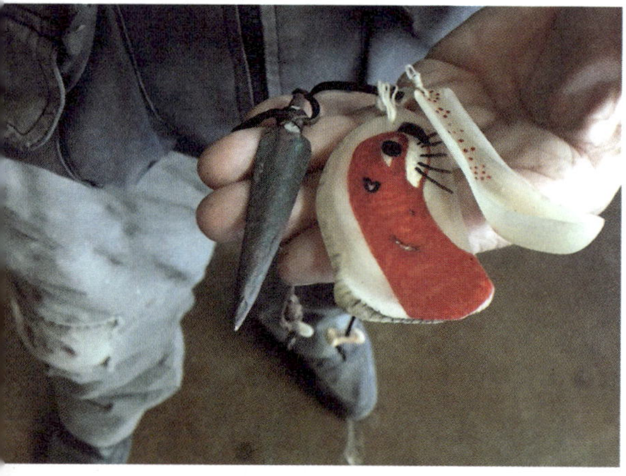

top and middle Emblems for Agunda (Wolf) and Khàjèt (Crow) beaded by Robin Bradasch for Clan regalia. KFN Archives. EMPC. Wildlife Images #15 and #16. PHOTOGRAPHER ROBIN BRADASCH

bottom Ron Chambers found this copper arrow point at a Burwash area mine site. Also shown is his artwork: a painted otter image on wood and a small sheep horn spoon with decorative design. KFN Archives. EMPC. Wildlife Images #17. PHOTOGRAPHER LINDA JOHNSON

facing Da-gäy (swan) parents on their nest in spring near Burwash. KFN Archives. EMPC. Wildlife Images #3. PHOTOGRAPHER ALANNA DICKSON

supported their lifeways. Essential and exotic goods like obsidian, copper, fish oils, and shells were brought by people from the north and south to exchange for the beautiful furs, hides, and resources of the Kluane region. Travel was constant and well defined—people went to specific places at particular times of the year when they knew various animals, birds, fish, and plants would be available. They adapted to changing weather and landforms through time and adopted new ideas and technologies as needed.

Archaeological sites yield tools and other evidence of camps at many places still very familiar to our people today. Burwash Landing was known as Lhù'ààn Mân (Kluane Lake). Jedäl̨i Tl'äw Käy (Duke Meadow), to the north of our community, dates to thousands of years before the present. Other sites at Little Arm Tatäy (Little Arm Narrows) and Chin K'ùa (Taye Lake) bear witness to our early ancestral cultures. Our people had winter gathering areas at Lhù'ààn Mân, K'amà Dzêa (Ptarmigan Heart), Àshèyi (Aishihik, at the head of Aishihik Lake), and Tatü Nà'į (Lynx City) at the Nisling confluence with the Dän Zhür Chù (Donjek River). Bone, stone, and copper tools; animal hunting blinds; and fire pits with bone remnants of animals provide clues to their hunting practices.[16]

The first archaeological expedition in our region was guided by our grandfathers and great-grandfathers in 1948. Travelling by boat and on horseback from Burwash they led a team of American archaeologists, geologists, and botanists through the mountains they knew so well to sites long used by their Ancestors. From those studies our understanding of the Yukon's earliest human occupations and changing natural environments has grown to encompass many narratives linking the Oral Traditions of our people and western scientific knowledge.[17]

For an understanding of how people lived together in earlier times, Elders today provide first hand details, brought forward from their own experiences and teachings from their grandmas and grandpas, aunties and uncles. They tell of small groups of people composed of several generations linked by kinship, travelling together throughout the year, following familiar pathways on their seasonal hunting and gathering rounds. People organized their interactions within two matrilineal moieties or Clans—Agunda (Wolf) and Khàjèt (Crow). Strict customary laws required an Agunda Clan member to marry only a Khàjèt Clan member, usually a distant member of the extended family, thereby maintaining healthy blood lines and wide ranging access to a variety of resources. In this way Clan members were closely intertwined and mutually dependent throughout their lifetimes.[18]

Some of our Ancestors came from coastal Tlingit Clans at Dyea, Klukwan, and Juneau. Northern Tutchone relatives came from the Fort Selkirk area. Other families are descended from Ahtna people around Copper Center in Alaska and the Upper Tanana at Tetlin and Tanacross. Southern Tutchone people came from Klukshu, Ta'an Män (Lake Laberge), and Àshèyi.

top Dhàl Da Tà (Copper Joe) seen here circa 1950s with ladle made from the horn of a mäy (sheep). KFN Archives. CYFN Archives. *Their Own Yukon*, #125, credit Jessie Joe. PHOTOGRAPHER UNKNOWN

bottom Kwan-zhì-a (chipmunk) is a frequent visitor to campsites, delighting people with friendly chittering. KFN Archives. EMPC. Wildlife Images #4. PHOTOGRAPHER ALANNA DICKSON

facing Mäy (sheep) moms and babies are a welcome sign on mountain slopes in spring, signalling the return of longer and warmer days. KFN Archives. EMPC. Wildlife Images #5. PHOTOGRAPHER ALANNA DICKSON

Everyone followed their mother's Clan, with traditional personal names, songs, and stories passed down through maternal relatives. Clan relationships ordered responsibilities and activities at Potlatches and gatherings to honour births, deaths, marriages, achievements like a young person's first moose kill, and other occasions. Sharing and caring for one another through reciprocal Clan relationships provided a strong and resilient social framework that has persisted through countless generations to present times.[19]

Respect was a key value taught to children from their earliest years. It was expected within all human relationships and extended to all living beings, as well as the lands, waters, and skies surrounding our people. Hunters and fishers carefully observed Protocols to demonstrate gratitude to the animals who gave their lives to sustain our people. Every part of the animal was used—meat for food, hides for clothing, bones for tools—and nothing was wasted. Women as well as men hunted and fished to feed and clothe their families, generally trapping small animals such as gophers and rabbits, and setting nets for fish close to home, while they tended fires and watched over children and Elders. Men hunted larger animals such as moose, caribou, and sheep, which required long distance treks for extended periods away from camp. Knowing the ways of animals and how they behave was essential for success. That wisdom was passed down orally from one generation to the next. For many years now our Elders, such as Mary Copper Jacquot, Jessie Joe, Jimmy Copper Joe, and Copper Lily, have also recorded stories for publication.[20]

Education was a lifelong series of lessons imparted by Elders as well as parents. Every child was taught and looked after by everyone within their extended family to provide a broad and rich continuum of expertise. Children had responsibilities that built bush skills from a young age—hauling water and wood, picking berries, and performing many other tasks. Storytelling was central to their learning about the world around them and the behaviours that would keep them and their relatives safe. Elders told about long-ago days when people and animals talked the same language, and they cautioned children not to make fun of animals, who might hear them and leave their hunting grounds. Stories about the beginning of time when Crow (Raven) and other animals travelled on long journeys to make the world safe for people reinforced those ideas.[21]

In earlier times our people had access to everything they needed on the land and in the water. We shared our riches, working together to organize our families and activities, and as Elder Lena Johnson has said, "They got a good plan."[22]

Guch'àn (Other People) Come to Our Land

1740s–1890s

overleaf Cultus Bay at the south end of Lhù'ààn Mân (Whitefish Place Lake, Kluane Lake), where some of the earliest Guch'àn (Other People) explorers, including Edward Glave and Jack Dalton, travelled in the late 1800s, meeting our Ancestors, learning about our country from them, and introducing them to horses plus the clothing and other new items from faraway places. KFN Archives. EMPC. Landscape Images #16. PHOTOGRAPHER JOHN MEIKLE

above Chù-näy (bald eagle) sits high in a treetop scouting the landscape for prey. KFN Archives. EMPC. Wildlife Images #6. PHOTOGRAPHER ALANNA DICKSON

facing Tlingit Clan leader K̲aalax̲ch (also known as Kohklux and Shotridge) with his wives Tu-eek and Kaatchxixich drew the Kohklux map for American scientist George Davidson. It is the earliest known map of the southern Yukon drawn by Indigenous people. It details landforms, place names in Tlingit and Dań K'è languages, meeting sites and routes traversed by Coastal Tlingit each summer on foot and by river craft from Klukwan, Alaska to Fort Selkirk on the Yukon River, returning overland back home along the route now followed by the Haines Highway. They visited and traded among our people, with some marrying and remaining in the Yukon as members of our Ancestral families. Map image courtesy of The Bancroft Library, Kohklux, and George Davidson. "Map of the Chilkaht: [Alaska and Yukon]." [1869]. G4370_1852_K6_CaseXD_Large YukonRectoPr

Guch'àn began travelling into northwest North America in the mid-1700s. Danish Captain Vitus Bering sailed to coastal Alaska across the waters now named for him in 1742. He named the highest peak he saw along the Alaska coast Mt. St. Elias, after a Russian saint. From that time to the mid-1800s Indigenous people in coastal Alaska had ever-increasing and more complex encounters with newcomers, including Russian, British, Spanish, and American explorers and traders. They exchanged goods they harvested from their lands and the sea for manufactured goods the newcomers brought: tea, sugar, flour, iron pots, steel knives, axes, traps, guns, cloth, beads, and many more interesting and useful things.

Those new goods were carried inland by coastal Tlingit traders, gradually replacing the traditional, ocean-based products they had brought to trade with our people in earlier generations.[23] For almost a century inland Athapaskan Peoples had no direct contact with the Guch'àn, learning about them from stories told by coastal Tlingit traders or more northerly relatives who had met newcomers in the Mackenzie region, on the Copper River, or at the mouth of the Yukon River. Sadly those stories were accompanied by deadly diseases brought from afar by the Guch'àn, diseases that spread inland, the first of many epidemics to devastate our families.[24]

By the 1840s some Guch'àn had moved inland to establish trading posts along the Yukon River. These white traders displaced Tlingit and other Indigenous middlemen, bringing their manufactured goods directly to our people. Our Ancestors first met Guch'àn at Fort Selkirk and at Fort Yukon, where the Hudson's Bay Company built trading posts in 1848. Later American traders established more posts along the rivers where our people traded. Early Indigenous maps (Kohklux 1869, Kandik 1880) document those sites and the travel routes of our people and nearby relatives during those years.[25]

Those maps show no boundaries between Alaska, the Yukon, and northern British Columbia, because our people travelled throughout those regions, working with trading partners from different groups, observing their own Clan and other local Protocols for access to lands and resources. Russian and British diplomats drew border lines on their maps in 1825, designating lands to the east of the Alaska Panhandle and along the 141st meridian from Mt. St. Elias to the Arctic Ocean as British, with everything to the west assigned to Russia. No surveyors marked those boundaries on the ground, and it would be another six decades before government officials began to prevent our Ancestors from continuing their wide ranging travels and trade.[26]

The arrival of newcomers on the Alaska coast presented both opportunities and difficulties, and encouraged more movement of Indigenous people across the southwestern Yukon. Coastal peoples told stories of armed conflicts with Russians during their early years in Alaska, and later with Americans after the United States purchased Alaska from Russia in 1867. Those upheavals caused some coastal peoples to migrate inland where they established new lives, adapting to interior lands and resources.

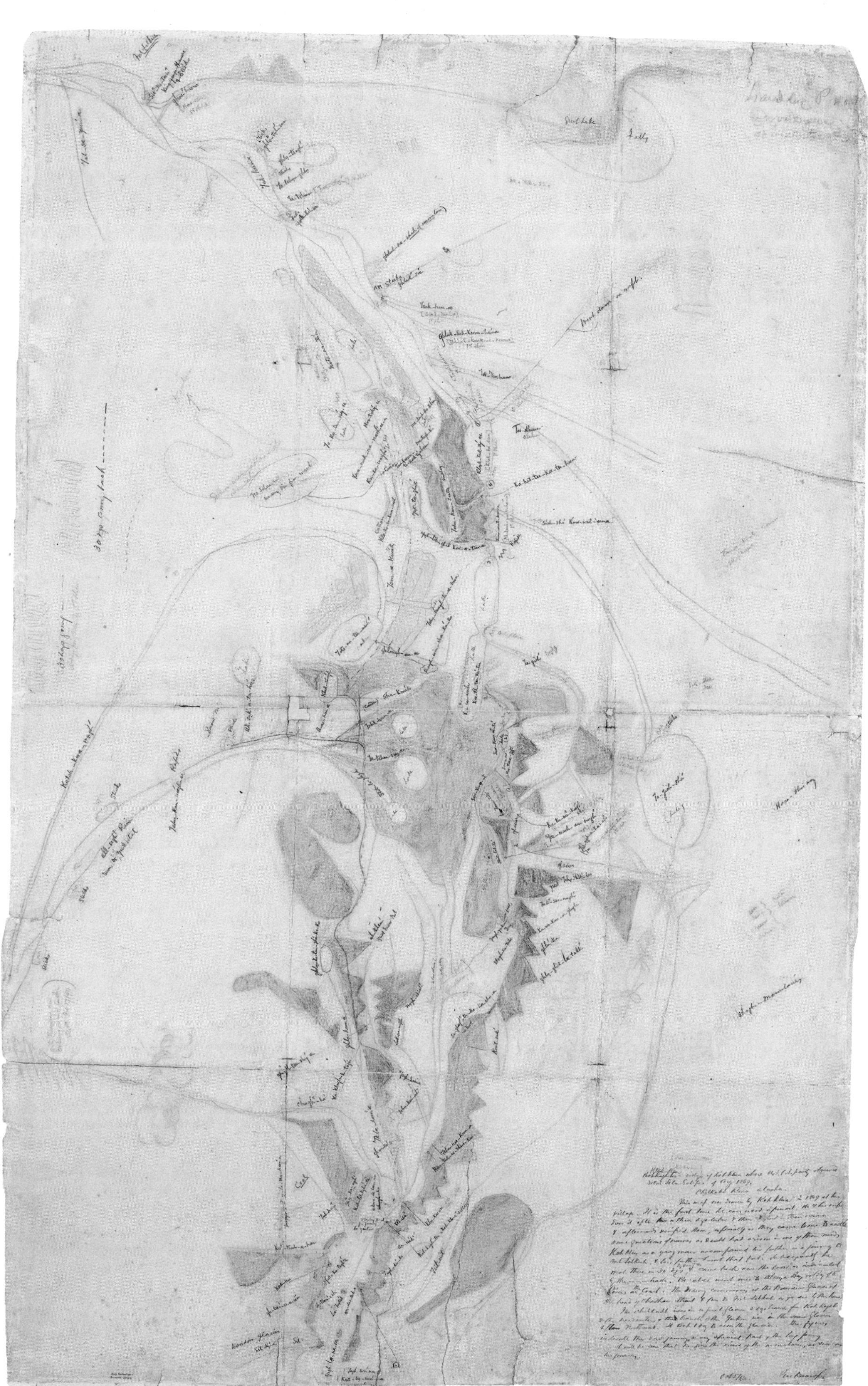

above The Kandik Map drawn by Hän river pilot Paul Kandik in 1880 with lettering by French Canadian fur trader François Mercier depicts the Yukon and Tanana river drainages in the Yukon and Alaska, along with the Upper Kuskokwim River, with place names in Tanana, Hän, French, and English. The map shows trading posts and overland trails used by our Tanana Ancestors between the Tanana and the Yukon, along with the route to the interior used by our Tlingit relatives from coastal Alaska. Map image courtesy of The Bancroft Library. Kandik, Paul, and François. Mercier. "Map of Upper Yukon, Tananah and Kuskokwim Rivers [Alaska and Yukon Territory]." 1880. G4370_1880_K3_CaseXB_Yukon1850RectoPr

Some married into Interior Athapaskan families at Àshèyi (Aishihik), Fort Selkirk, Ta'an Män (Lake Laberge), Lhu' Ghą (Dalton Post), and other areas. Expanding economic prospects, abundant food resources, and family connections encouraged migration into our region by peoples from areas to the east, as well as from the Copper and Tanana rivers to the northwest. Those circumstances brought some of our founding families to Lhù'ààn Mân Keyí (Kluane Lake Country), including the Johnson, Copper, and Allen families.[27]

Sida Tà (Jimmy Johnson) was born at Aishihik Lake, son of Nàday (Old Man Johnson) and his wife Gųya, sometime in the late 1800s.[28] He was a Southern Tutchone head man and very well known among the people at Aishihik, Hutshi, Laberge, Carmacks, and Fort Selkirk. He travelled extensively throughout the region from Aishihik to K'amà Dzêa (Ptarmigan Heart), Little Arm, Duke Meadow, and the Donjek and White rivers. He met and married Èna (Emma Jackson) at Fort Selkirk on a trading trip there. They stayed first at Aishihik Lake, then moved to Little Arm on Kluane Lake and over to Burwash Landing in the early 1900s. Sida Tà built the first cabin at the northwest end of the lake by a small creek. He took a second wife, Tsal KàJana (Gopher Lady, Copper Lily), daughter of K'akhyuama[29] and Copper George Joe, at the insistence of Èna (mispronounced in English as Emma), known as Asuà Shäw (Big Grandma).

Sida Tà held a Potlatch honouring his mother while she was still alive. The Jimmy Johnson song, as noted on page 31, is well known and still sung

above Gùdia (Mary Johnson), Tàa'aana (Jessie Joe), and an unidentified girl with Sida Tà (Jimmy Johnson) in Burwash, circa 1921. They are wearing store-bought clothing except for their homemade footwear. CYFN Archives. *Their Own Yukon*, #98, credit Jessie Joe. PHOTOGRAPHER UNKNOWN

at Potlatches to honour him. His children with Èna were Sam Johnson Sr., Mary (married name Johnson), Jessie (married name Kabanak), Jenny, Alice, and Peter. Copper Lily's children were Peter, Tommy, Freddy, Billy, Gene, Harry, Bessie, Elsie, Margaret, Rita, Bertha, and Helen. The two groups of Jimmy Johnson siblings grew up together, and several of the Elders whose stories appear in this book are descended from these two related families.[30]

Äsì Shäw, meaning "Big Grandfather" or "Big Man," was widely known as Copper Chief. He was an Ahtna man of the Khàjèt (Crow) Clan from the Copper River in Alaska who moved into the Yukon in the late 1800s. His wife Ná-Thyá-Thée-a, meaning "Thick Brush" or "Dry Brush Country," was of the Wolf Clan and came from Fort Selkirk. They established their seasonal rounds near the Generc and White rivers at Kletsan Hill, which was rich in copper nuggets. They had two daughters, who died young. Their five sons were all of the Wolf Clan after their mother; they all married Northern and Southern Tutchone women and settled down in various Yukon communities: Copper Joe at Selkirk, Copper Jack at Snag, Copper Jim and Copper Charlie at Carmacks, and Copper George Joe at Burwash Landing.[31]

Copper George Joe's traditional name was Dhàl Da Tà, also spelled as Thul-da-ta, meaning "Mountain Man." He was renowned for his copper knives, made from nuggets found at the head of the White River. After travelling through the Nisling and White river regions for many years,

top Chù-näy (eagle) keeping a sharp eye out for prey. KFN Archives. EMPC. Wildlife Images #11. PHOTOGRAPHER ALANNA DICKSON

bottom White avens flourish in Kluane country. KFN Archives. EMPC. Landscape Images #17. PHOTOGRAPHER ROBERT POSTMA

facing Chisana caribou grazing up the Natazhat Glacier near the Yukon-Alaska border. The high peak on the right is Mount Natazhat; the peak just visible on the top left is Mount Riggs. KFN Archives. EMPC. Landscape Images #12. PHOTOGRAPHER JOHN MEIKLE

he moved from Lynx City to settle in Burwash after his wife died. He had married a Ta'an Män woman from the Takhini River region near the mountain called Nalin and the settlement known as Hir-d-yil, meaning "A Place Where the Sand Always Blows" (Little River in English, on the Old Dawson Trail). They had eight children: Da Kwäthala mą, meaning "Nice Face" (Kitty, married name Jamieson); a baby boy who died young; Sul-ki ya or Tsal KàJana (Copper Lily); another boy who died young; Nàch'adǹch'ea (Mary, married name Jacquot), meaning "A Disappointment," because a boy was expected after the one who had died; Shäw Nàts'àli Tà, meaning "Expect Something from Hunting," or U Ts'àn Nëkhì Ts'ulia, meaning "Him to Go Hunting Luck Go to Him" (Jimmy); Shan che'a, meaning "Poor Little Thing" (Bertha), who died at Champagne; and Tàa'aana, meaning "Born in an Area That Provides Lots or Everything, a Place of Abundance" (Jessie Joe, who never married). Their descendants are part of our Nation and other Yukon First Nations.[32]

Old Man Allen came from the Chisana River near Northway and Tetlin in the Upper Tanana region of Alaska. After his parents died in 1900, he moved to Canada to live with the Copper family. He met Kändhäda (Monica Big Salmon from Laberge area) at Lhu' Ghą at Village Creek near Klukshu. They married and moved to Burwash Landing to build a permanent house. Their seasonal rounds extended from Beaver Creek to Champagne, with camps at Duke Meadow, Burwash Creek, Swede Johnson Creek, and on the northeastern shore of Kluane Lake. The Allen family practiced traditional shaman rituals. It is said that Monica Allen also introduced Christian elements into traditional Indigenous beliefs. Their children were Jessie Allen (married Sam Johnson Sr.), Nellie (married name Stick; married Moose Johnson after his first wife, Mary, died), Jack Allen, Johnny Allen, Lilly (married name Birckel; also spelled Lily), Paul, Billy, Ked-da-sher-Ma, Nashyea, and Shanchea. Stories of them and other founding families are told by several Elders in this book.[33]

By the 1880s and 1890s many more newcomers were travelling into our region. Prospectors were looking for gold, silver, copper, and other metals. Missionaries were seeking new people to convert to their religions. Explorers and surveyors from Canada and the United States travelled on the Yukon, Tanana, and tributaries, claiming our lands as their own and drawing physical markers on the ground to stake their territory. Canada sent William Ogilvie and other members of the Yukon Expedition to map the Upper Yukon River around the boundary in 1887–88, followed by the American Boundary Survey party of 1889–91. Jack Dalton and Edward Glave travelled from Klukwan through the southwest Yukon in 1890, and returned again in 1891 to the southern end of Kluane Lake, where they met some of our Ancestors.[34] American Army officer Frederick Schwatka gathered more information about our region on his 1891 expedition from the Yukon to the White River and across the St. Elias Mountains.[35] Many more official reports and stories in the popular press publicized accounts of rich northern prospects—leading to the momentous events at the end of the nineteenth century that changed our homelands forever.[36]

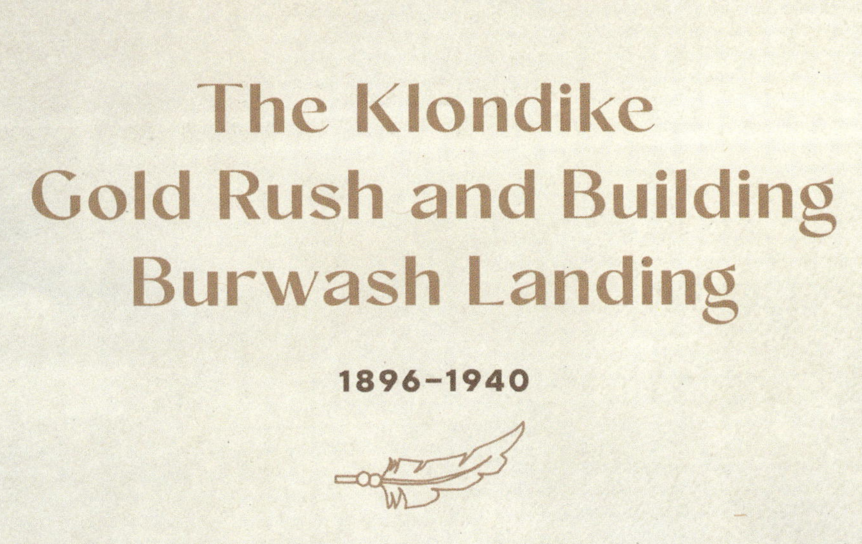

The Klondike Gold Rush and Building Burwash Landing

1896–1940

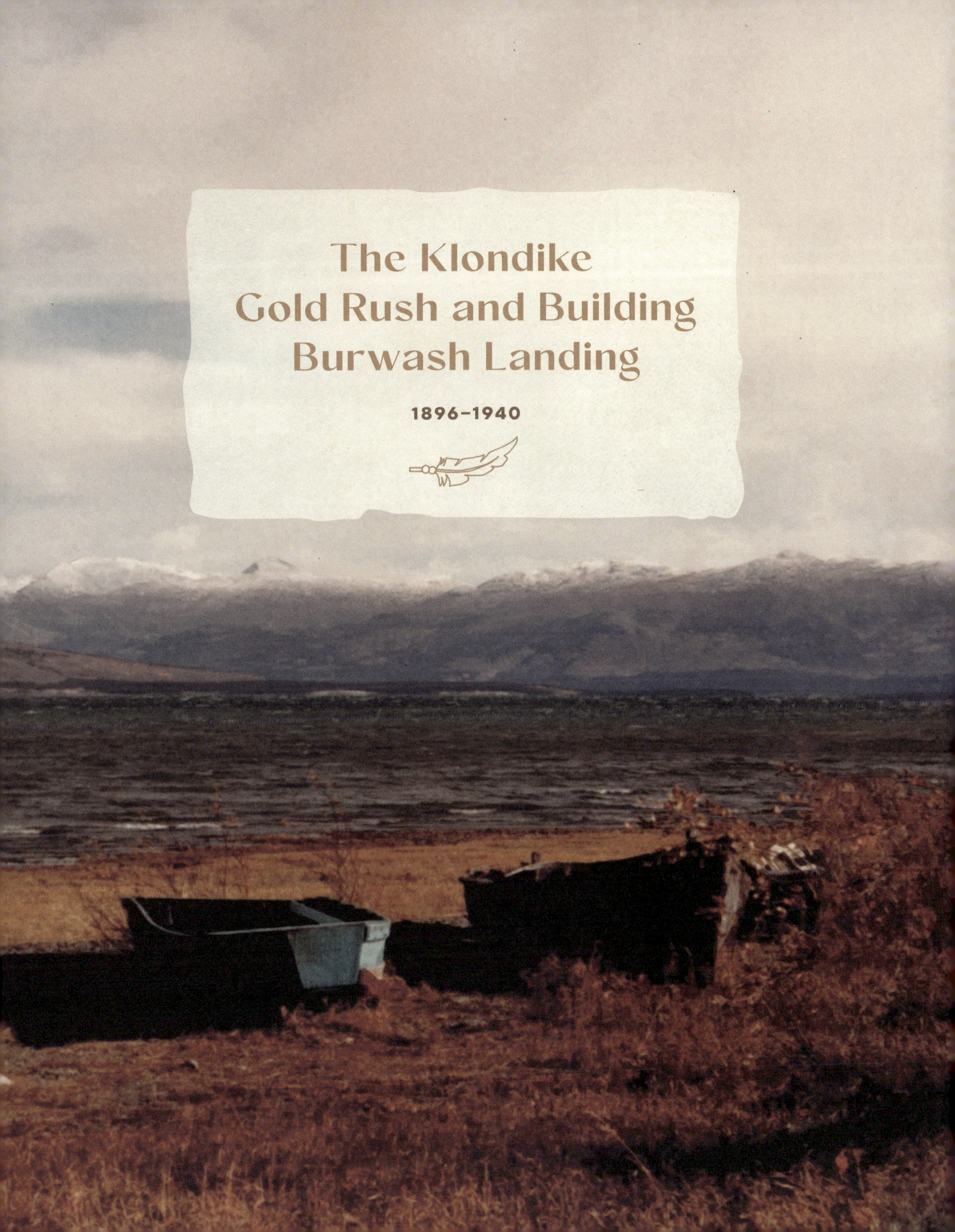

overleaf The Jacquots' *Josephine* sits on the beach at Burwash in the 1970s with other wooden boats from bygone days. KFN Archives. EMPC. Norma McBean Collection #10. PHOTOGRAPHER NORMA MCBEAN

above left Tom Dickson Sr. with son Buck and sister Lydia Dickson Dunk, and his wife Louise seated with baby Grace and daughters Ruth and Mary to her right and Susan to her left at their Kluane River homestead, circa 1914. KFN Archives. EMPC. Hank Jacquot Family Images #1. PHOTOGRAPHER UNKNOWN

above right Keish (Skookum Jim Mason) and family at his house in Carcross, circa early 1900s. *Left to right:* George Carmack, Tom Dickson, Keish's wife Daakuxda.éit (Mary Mason), Keish's daughter Saayna.aat (Daisy Mason), Keish with gold pan, and a young Koołseen (Patsy Henderson). CYFN Archives. *Their Own Yukon*, #7, image provided by Anglican Synod Archives, Toronto. PHOTOGRAPHER UNKNOWN

The Klondike Gold Rush, from 1896 to 1899, brought tens of thousands of newcomers to the Yukon for a few years of frenetic activity, though most of the original stampeders left soon after. The gold fever spread beyond the Klondike to the Kluane region in the early 1900s, with active claim staking and mining continuing to the present day. Skookum Jim and Dawson Charlie, who had been instrumental in the Klondike Gold Rush, staked claims at Fourth of July, Twelfth of July, Bullion, and Ruby creeks in the Kluane region in 1903.[37]

At the south end of Kluane Lake the settlement originally named and known today as Silver City was officially called Kluane when it had a Mining Recorders Office, an NWMP post, several stores, a post office, and miners' cabins. Burwash Creek and Burwash Landing were named for Lachlan Burwash, the Mining Recorder at Silver City. From 1907 to 1911 the Kluane Gold Rush saw dozens of miners prospecting from the Slims River to Fourth of July Creek for silver and gold. In 1908 exciting new prospects to the north in Alaska started a new stampede to the Chisana River, with more prospectors travelling through Kluane country heading to that region. Some of our people worked as packers and guides during those years.[38]

The Dickson and Jacquot families were established as founding families at Burwash Landing in the years following the Klondike Gold Rush. Thomas (Tom) Dickson was an NWMP officer working on the Chilkoot Trail during the first years of the stampede. He met and married Louise George (later Davis), a coastal Tlingit woman from Yandeist'akyé (near Haines, Alaska), with close family connections to Skookum Jim and his relatives in Carcross. They established their homestead at the mouth of the Kluane River in the early 1900s, raising a large family of thirteen children,

with many descendants today throughout the Yukon, including members of our First Nation. Their children were Molly Grace (who died at age 5), Ruth ("Pete," married to Gene Jacquot), James ("J.R." or "Buck"), Mary (married name James), Susan (married name Chambers, later Van Bibber), Grace (married name Chambers, later Duensing), Kluane (married name Leroy, later Hash, then Metz), Robert ("Bobby" adopted into the Auston family in Carcross), Dorothy (who drowned as a teen), Isabelle ("Belle," married name Desrosiers), twins Richard ("Dick") and William Olaf ("Oley"), and Edna ("Babe," married name Southwick).[39]

Louis and Eugene Jacquot—brothers from Alsace, France—first came north to the Klondike in 1898, then moved into the Kluane region in 1903. They were cooks, prospectors, miners, and above all visionary entrepreneurs who pursued every opportunity to develop their enterprises. They met Tom Dickson on their way to the Klondike, who encouraged them to come to Kluane country to pursue business and mining interests. Their families have since been closely intertwined through several generations. Following traditional Protocols for arranged marriages Louis married Copper George Joe's daughter Mary Copper Joe in 1920, and their children were Louis Jr., Rosalie, and Josephine (married name Sias), born between 1923 and the early 1930s. Eugene married Pete (Ruth Dickson), daughter of Tom and Louise Dickson, in 1921. Their children were Eugene Jr., Joe, Lou, Hank, and Larry born between 1923 and 1937.[40] Paul Birckel Sr., a nephew of the Jacquots, came from France and was married to Old Man Allen and Monica Allen's youngest daughter, Lilly Allen. They had Paul Jr., Rosalie, Lucie, and Frank.

Together with their wives and extended family members the two Jacquot brothers founded a thriving trading post and community at Burwash Landing, including a store and outfitting business. They freighted goods by boat across the lake to Silver City in summer and by dog team or horse-drawn sleds in winter over the ice. They worked with our men to build the first pioneer roads and trails from Burwash to Silver City and Whitehorse and throughout the area to support their trading, mining, and outfitting enterprises.

top left Dog teams freighting supplies on the ice near Cultus Bay, circa 1930s. KFN Archives. EMPC. Hank Jacquot Family Images #3. PHOTOGRAPHER UNKNOWN

top right Brothers Louis and Eugene Jacquot at Burwash, circa 1930s. KFN Archives. EMPC. Hank Jacquot Family Images #2. PHOTOGRAPHER UNKNOWN

bottom Jacquot brothers' barge loaded with supplies crossing Takhini River, circa 1930s. KFN Archives. EMPC. Hank Jacquot Family Images #4. PHOTOGRAPHER UNKNOWN

top left Trapping in Kluane region produced substantial income in the 1920s and 30s for successful trappers like Buck Dickson, standing with rifle on the left, together with unidentified man on the right. CYFN Archives. *Their Own Yukon*, #45, image provided by Mrs. Patsy Henderson. PHOTOGRAPHER UNKNOWN

top right Fishing and guiding were also big business in the 1920s through the 40s for the Jacquot brothers. Daddy Gene (Eugene Jacquot) and unidentified man at the first Kluane Inn, with fish, circa 1930s. KFN Archives. EMPC. Hank Jacquot Family Images #5. PHOTOGRAPHER UNKNOWN

bottom Tom Dickson and unidentified men with dog team taking supplies on the ice in front of Burwash. KFN Archives. EMPC. Dickson Outfitters Images #1. PHOTOGRAPHER UNKNOWN

facing, top left George John, unidentified man, Moose Johnson, and Sam Johnson at brush camp near Duke River. KFN Archives. EMPC. Robin Bradasch, Johnson Family Images #1. PHOTOGRAPHER UNKNOWN

facing, top right Young Jessie Joe holding baby Paul Birckel Jr. KFN Archives. EMPC. Robin Bradasch, Copper Family Images #1. PHOTOGRAPHER UNKNOWN

facing middle Sam Johnson Sr. after a successful sheep hunt. KFN Archives. EMPC. Robin Bradasch, Johnson Family Images #2. PHOTOGRAPHER UNKNOWN

facing bottom Davis Johnson at Burwash, circa 1940s. KFN Archives. EMPC. Robin Bradasch, Johnson Family Images #3. PHOTOGRAPHER UNKNOWN

The Dicksons and Jacquots were renowned big game outfitters, sometimes working together, at other times separately, attracting rich and famous clients from around the world. The first hunts started before World War I, with clients eager to travel on horseback into the high mountains in pursuit of sheep, moose, and bear to set new world trophy records among sports hunters. To support growth in this new industry the Jacquots and the Dicksons built barns, planted large gardens and hayfields, and steadily increased the number of horses they maintained for the hunts. The Jacquot brothers operated their outfitting business until after World War II. The Dickson family founded Dickson Outfitters, which continues to this day as one of the oldest businesses in the Yukon.[41]

Kluane people were key workers in the outfitters' operations, with the men working as expert guides, wranglers, packers, and cooks, contributing their knowledge of the land, animals, and trails. Our women were sewers, gardeners, cooks, and organizers who maintained family life while the men were away on hunts for extended time periods.

Jimmy Johnson and his wives and children, Copper George Joe and his family, along with Old Man Allen and his wife Monica and their children—Jessie, Nellie, Jack, Johnny, and Lilly—all stayed at Burwash at various times during their seasonal rounds. Moose Johnson's family also used Burwash as a supply and social centre in those years. He was the adopted son of Moose John and Lily (Moose's biological aunt) from Kloo Lake. Moose's wife Gùdia (Mary Johnson) was a daughter of Èna and Jimmy Johnson. Their children were Davis, Lena, Harvey, Joe, Màdhį̨ą, and Bernie. Another well-known seasonal resident family was Albert Isaac and his wife Elsie (sister to Jimmy Johnson), who visited often and later moved to Burwash from Aishihik Lake.

In the 1920s and 30s trapping was big business, interrupted briefly by the early Depression years. Prices were high, and the Kluane region was rich in furs. People made a good living on the land, and families were able to combine traditional seasonal rounds with trapping and short-term work in the big game guiding business. Burwash Landing, with its store and cabins, gradually became more of a central gathering place, drawing more families away from earlier travel and trade at the Yukon River, Aishihik Lake, and adjacent areas. People brought their furs to trade at the store for groceries and other goods. The Jacquot brothers built cabins for some families, ensuring their availability to work during the months-long big game guiding and hunting season. In the late 1920s and 30s air travel boosted the numbers of people accessing communities across the North, including flights that landed on Kluane Lake. All of these developments contributed to Burwash continuing as one of the oldest permanent villages in the territory.[42]

As more families settled for longer periods and the number of children increased, the desire for a local school emerged. In 1917 Tom Dickson asked Anglican Bishop Stringer for help in persuading the Yukon Government to establish an assisted school there, saying he would supply a building and all the food. He had five school-age children himself, and there were others in the vicinity, including those he called the "Aishihik Indians," who would attend. The Yukon Government had provided small amounts

top Many Non-Status children from the Dickson and other Burwash families stayed at St. Paul's Hostel run by the Anglican Church while attending the Dawson Public School from the 1920s through the early 1950s. Yukon Archives. Photo Collection #9673. PHOTOGRAPHER UNKNOWN

bottom Unidentified girl standing in front of Jacquot Bros. sign at Burwash, circa 1940s. KFN Archives. EMPC. Hank Jacquot Family Images #6. PHOTOGRAPHER UNKNOWN

to pay teachers at assisted schools in the Klondike in past years. However, World War I drained the territorial population and economy, and Dickson's request was not granted.

By the 1930s and early 40s his son Buck and his wife, Lillian (daughter of Patsy and Edith Henderson of Carcross), were living at the Dickson family homestead with their eleven children: Edith (Edie, married name Bohmer), Alexander, Russell, Tom, Douglas, Cecil, Dennis, Harry, Lawrence, Roy, Donald (died young), and baby Clifford. With no school close by, kids from two generations of Dicksons were sent to Dawson City to live at St. Paul's Hostel, run by the Anglican Church, and attend the Dawson Public School.[43]

Louis Jacquot took his two oldest children, Louis Jr. and Rosalie, to France in the 1920s, where they attended school for a few years before returning home. Eugene Jacquot sent petitions to the Yukon Council in 1934 and 1939 asking for help in establishing a school at Burwash, but once again the Yukon Government was short of funds and the request was refused.[44] Some of the Jacquot children from both families attended a convent school in Whitehorse or went to Catholic schools in Vancouver and Alaska. The lack of a school in Burwash in the 1920s and 30s began the sad tradition of children leaving the community every fall, not to return for many months or even years—a heartbreaking experience for them and their families, with long-lasting impacts on our community.

During the years before World War II all our families continued to follow the traditional seasonal rounds of our Ancestors and Elders. Extended family groups were on the land year-round—hunting, trapping, and gathering sustenance from the lakes, rivers, and mountains surrounding Lhù'ààn Mân. Most of the children, except for the Jacquots and the Dicksons, remained with their extended families, living and learning on the land during those years.[45]

Catastrophic world events in far-away places were about to disrupt lives in the Kluane Region. The trails and trading posts established after the Gold Rush became important waypoints for the wartime building of the Alaska Highway, bringing profound changes to our people within a few short years.

top Beginning in the 1920s and through the years until the building of the Alaska Highway, air travel was an important link to Whitehorse and beyond for big game hunters coming to Kluane country and for the Jacquots and Dicksons to expedite supplies. G-CARM was a familiar bush plane flying into many small Yukon settlements in the 1930s and 40s. Young Hank Jacquot is the child at right. KFN Archives. EMPC. Josie Sias Family Images #2. PHOTOGRAPHER UNKNOWN

middle Eugene Jacquot and unidentified man walking in front of the building used as an office for Pan American Airways. The company flew a regular route to Alaska, stopping at Burwash for fuel and sometimes for overnight stays at the first Kluane Inn. KFN Archives. EMPC. Josie Sias Family Images #3. PHOTOGRAPHER UNKNOWN

bottom The *Josephine* at Christmas Bay circa 1933–34 with (left to right) Anglican priest Alex Stringer, Tuffy (Lomer) Cyr, young Gene Jacquot, and Paul Cyr. KFN Archives. EMPC. Josie Sias Family Images #4. PHOTOGRAPHER UNKNOWN

top Scene of Burwash during the building of the Alaska Highway published in an unnamed source. Eugene Jacquot is standing in front of his home talking with unidentified man. A U.S. Army truck and radio telegraph poles in the background indicate wartime activities underway in the community. KFN Archives. EMPC. Josie Sias Family Images #5. PHOTOGRAPHER UNKNOWN

middle Unidentified woman on beach road at Burwash, circa 1940s. KFN Archives. EMPC. Josie Sias Family Images #1. PHOTOGRAPHER UNKNOWN

bottom Unidentified RCMP officer standing in front of the RCMP post established at Burwash in the 1940s in a log building near the Burwash Lodge. The building was used later by Darrell Duensing as a store. KFN Archives. EMPC. Josie Sias Family Images #6. PHOTOGRAPHER UNKNOWN

top The Jacquot camp at Mile 1016 in 1944. KFN Archives. EMPC. Josie Sias Family Images #11. PHOTOGRAPHER UNKNOWN

middle Buck Dickson leading a pack train along the highway, circa 1940s. World War II and the establishment of the Kluane Game Sanctuary interrupted the big game guiding business briefly, but the hunts resumed after the war, with both the Dicksons and the Jacquots leading large parties on long hunts into the mountains north of the preserve. KFN Archives. EMPC. Dickson Outfitters Images #3. PHOTOGRAPHER UNKNOWN

bottom Government surveyors also hired horse outfitters to guide them on mapping expeditions. Bobby Auston (born Dickson) on the right and Walter David on the left saddling a horse for an expedition with explorer and author Jim Bond in the Mayo district. KFN Archives. EMPC. Dickson Outfitters Images #2. PHOTOGRAPHER UNKNOWN

The Andover–Harvard Expedition

1948

overleaf The Andover-Harvard Expedition to the Yukon in 1948, organized by archaeologist Frederick Johnson and botanist Hugh Raup, arrived at Burwash Landing in late June 1948 to begin archaeological and botanical investigations in the Kluane region. They were outfitted with horses and gear by Gene Jacquot and led by the top First Nations guides of the region across the lake to Big Arm and over Henry Pass to Ptarmigan Heart, returning to Burwash via Little Arm. View of Burwash from the boat dock with the new Kluane Inn and other older Jacquot buildings, July 1948. Yukon Archives. Elmer Harp Jr. fonds, 2006/2, #143.

above When the Andover-Harvard Expedition arrived in June 1948, Burwash people were in deep mourning for Louis Jacquot, who had died recently in Vancouver. This image taken by Elmer J. Harp Jr. shows the expedition vehicles parked on the road leading from the Alaska Highway down to the newly built Kluane Inn. Yukon Archives. Elmer Harp Jr. fonds, 2006/2, #281.

The opening of the Alaska Highway to civilian traffic in 1948 facilitated a remarkable encounter between people from Burwash Landing and a group of American scientists who came to explore the archaeological and botanical resources of the Southwest Yukon. They hired Eugene Jacquot as outfitter for their investigations around Lhù'ààn Mân Keyí (Kluane Lake Country) and travelled to many significant places in Asì Keyí. The scientists relied on Kluane Elders and guides to lead them to important sites. Together they discussed the cultural uses of those locations and the types of artifacts they found for both ancestral peoples and those living in the region at that time.

Elmer Harp Jr. was one of the archaeologists, and he recorded those conversations in his field notes. He also carefully documented the travels and work of the expedition in his photographs. His notes and images provide a remarkable portrait of people and places that are foundational for Kluane First Nation. Many of the grandmas and grandpas of today's Elders are featured in the photographs and contributed detailed information about their lifeways, history, and culture. Harp's admiration and respect for his guides' knowledge and skills on the land is evident throughout his journal. Although he was an outsider, his notes form a unique transmission of Oral Histories from Kluane people who passed away long ago. They are a gift to all future generations from those Elders and Elmer Harp Jr. Harp's full report was published by the Yukon Government Archaeology Unit and is available online.[46] The following excerpts are verbatim.

FRI. 2 JULY *Burwash camp*

"Walked around the cove beyond the Post—Indian cabins strung along bluff there, a cemetery with the usual houses & Louie [Louis] Jacquot's old cabin the farthest down on a gravel point [...] Continued back [...] to Buck Dixon's [Dickson's] cabin at the point where the lake drains into the Kluane R. [...] Also an Indian site where Dixon's [Dickson's] cabins are—he mentioned arrowheads etc. & 'a piece of native copper with the edges beaten out' having been found there in the garden. Dixon [Dickson] appears to know the country like a book after some years of hunting, packing & trapping."[47]

FRI. 9 JULY *Henry Creek camp*

"Jimmy Joe says the last caribou migration thru this country was back around 1935, & then they were so plentiful the hillsides were tramped smooth [...] At lunch Moose told us of how the old people used to cook their food by boiling in a moose stomach, tying up one end & dropping in hot stones. Moose skins were also used over wooden (spruce) frames to make boats for crossing large rivers. During the eve Jimmy told of the trade that used to carry back and forth thru this country: people from the Yukon, where the spruce grows straight in the lowlands & splits easily (up here it is all twisted & bent) used to pass thru this trail from Aishihik, Henry Pass, or the Big Arm & take their spruce stock for arrows where they traded it for copper on the White River [...] Jimmy's father was called Copper [George] Joe & was noted hereabouts for his work with copper."[48]

SAT. 10 JULY *Henry Creek camp*

"Fred & I left with Moose for a hike up Henry Crk to look at a pole tipi lodge that Moose had noticed while tracking a moose 6 years ago. Simply amazing the way he led us thru the muskeg flat for about 1½ mi. then branched off to the left at just the right point & climbed 100' or so up steep ridge & brot us to the exact spot—after 6 years![49]

top Expedition crew and First Nations guides surveying the landscape from a mountain above Henry Pass, July 1948. Yukon Archives. Elmer Harp Jr. fonds, 2006/2, #163.

bottom Gă Ihêla (Moose Johnson) resting with horses in Henry Pass. Yukon Archives. Elmer Harp Jr. fonds, 2006/2, #166.

left Gă Ihêla (Moose Johnson) telling a story while sheep ribs roast beside the fire. The Burwash hunters supplied fresh meat for the whole crew over the month-long expedition. *Left to right:* Ts'adasha (George John), Ken Johnson, Gă Ihêla (Moose Johnson), Shäw Nàts'àli Tà (Jimmy Joe), and Shùglità (Sam Johnson Sr.). Yukon Archives. Elmer Harp Jr. fonds, 2006/2, #156

bottom Shäw Nàts'àli Tà (Jimmy Joe) resting on the trail while horses graze. Yukon Archives. Elmer Harp Jr. fonds, 2006/2, #167

SUN. 11 JULY *Ptarmigan Heart*

"I was following Moose by perhaps 50 ft. when suddenly a moose jumped up 100 ft. to our right and raced off [...] Moose got in 6 shots at him up to 500 yds but then he disappeared [...] Remounted and with Moose in the lead we followed his trail down the ridge. Don't know how he did it [...] only about every 100 yds or so could I pick up a foot print [...] Suddenly the moose leapt from the woods [...] Moose slid off his horse & took a quick kneeling shot at about 150 yds, which dropped the animal [...] Then Moose gave us an amazing demonstration [...] in 25 minutes by the watch he skinned out the moose & butchered it completely [...] Took a stroll back to the old cabin which Jimmy Johnson (Sam's father) built 23 years ago with the help of Moose Johnson [...] Sam was reared in this country: his father & he used to trap fox when the skins brought good prices but now they no longer do. Sam's father also built another cabin at the head of the Big Arm, and another at Red Tail Lake. Sam doesn't use these any more but has a couple of cabins down on the Kluane R (one near Mile 1119) where he spends the winter trapping mink & marten."[50]

TUE. 13 JULY *Ptarmigan Heart*

"Jimmy [Joe] spoke this morning of an old hunter he knew who came thru with his family during one summer on a hunt for the winter's food supply: this Indian came from Aishihik thru PH, then S to the Big Arm [...] across to the Little Arm & down to Burwash; then NW across the Donjek to Teepee Lake & on up to the White R.; then back E, to Tincup Lake across to PH & back to Aishihik. Every place this hunter picked up a moose or 2. Or a caribou, he built a high cache, & moved on [...] About 1½ mi. E of our camp we came to [...] a whole series of brush camps [...] The woods was full of small stumps, cut for the leaning poles [...] Moose said these shelters were very old, before his time, & before the old people had tents. We asked him about all the stumps & poles which had certainly been cut with metal axes (steel, we thought) & he reminded us that the old people had copper from the White R. [...] Moose then stripped down the outer bark of a spruce & we all ate some of the paper thin strips of the inner bark- mild & piquant;

something like palm tree hearts. The Indians eat this inner bark (cambium layer) every July when it is sweet & tender & before it turns into wood. They say that poplar bark is even better."[51]

SAT. 17 JULY *Camp on route to Boulder Creek*

"Got these following tribal designations from Sam, describing people hereabouts:

Dzantushen (Dzankutchin) [Zän Tuch'än, Tanana or Snag River People][52] = 'Muskrat People' (general term for people at Burwash, Aishihik, Champagne, Snag, Ptarmigan Heart—people who live in muskeg country. May be people who speak all one dialect.

Aishihik = 'a nice town' —a nice place to live

Klu-shen [Lhu Chän] = 'Fish People'—the Indians at Champagne (only) — (Klu = 'fish')

Tchugakushen = 'Yukon R. Indians' (Sam's mother one of these—different dialect but comprehensible to Muskrat People)

Tagrukutchin [Tàgür Tuch'än or Tàgù Ch'än, Tagish People] = 'Indians at Carcross'

Daltutchin [Dhäl Tuch'än] = 'Mountain People' —who live up by the glaciers, along the continental divide beyond White R. Never heard of these people, but they must be nomadic hunters with cultural affiliations inland although their dialect is incomprehensible & may be allied with coast.

.... = 'Moosehide Indians' —lived around Dawson City. Their dialect is incomprehensible to Muskrats.

Tchugakutchin [Chu gà Kwäch'an, Selkirk Indians] = 'Live by the river people' —Yukon R. people?

Dhun [Dàn, people] = A group of people who formerly lived around Ptarmigan Heart.

There seems to be dialect differences between people at Carcross, Snag & Ptarmigan Heart, although there are varieties among the Muskrat People & are of a lesser order than differences between Muskrats & Yukon People."[53]

top Looking south down the pass from K'àmà Dzêa (Ptarmigan Heart) to Boulder Creek and Big Arm. Yukon Archives. Elmer Harp Jr. fonds, 2006/2, #202.

bottom Scientists Hugh Raup and Frederick Johnson and First Nation guide Gä lhêla (Moose Johnson) looking down to Ptarmigan Heart from a spectacular viewpoint high in the mountains. Yukon Archives. Elmer Harp Jr. fonds, 2006/2, #182.

top Shùglità (Sam Johnson Sr.), Ts'adasha (George John), and Gă lhêla (Moose Johnson) sitting in an old stone cache on the east side of Boulder Creek. Yukon Archives. Elmer Harp Jr. fonds, 2006/2, #212

bottom Shùglità (Sam Johnson Sr.) taking a break on a mountaintop in Henry Pass. Yukon Archives. Elmer Harp Jr. fonds, 2006/2, #164

facing top Buck Dickson's place on the Kluane River, August 1948. Yukon Archives. Elmer Harp Jr. fonds, 2006/2, #229

facing bottom Pack train fording a stream in rugged mountain terrain en route to Bridge Creek. Yukon Archives. Elmer Harp Jr. fonds, 2006/2, #215

MON. 19 JULY *Boulder Creek camp*

"After lunch, we crossed the stream & on the other side struck a whole series of camps [. . .] saw about 3 of the teepee-type shelters [. . .] one [. . .] yielded a crude semi-lunar slate skin scraper: this was 6" long [. . .] Moose said his grandfather used to use one just like that only smaller for gopher skins. Also from this same shelter came a broken arrow shaft of good straight grain spruce (which may have been traded in from the Yukon as none grows around here). Jimmie Joe says that Yukon people used to come to White R. copper workings with whole bunches of spruce arrow shafts which they made or traded copper pts. for [. . .] Moose said that birch made the best bows in this country, birch dried for 2 yrs [. . .]"[54]

TUES. 20 JULY *Boulder Creek camp*

"Worked along the E side of the Crk. & down the lake as far as the cabins of Moose & Jimmy Johnson (Sam's father). This entire stretch is also full of camps [. . .] Moose discovered a splendid bone arrowpoint—actually made of horn (probably moose horn). Also among the collection of awls [. . .] was a blunt end bird point [. . .] On the way up the lake beach we discovered a burial which has a frame of logs around it [. . .] George mentioned the old-time burials at Weskatahin, the abandoned village on the Tatshenshini 2-3 miles below Dalton Post, which were raised log cache burials of burned bones [. . .] the way the old people did it before they began building the burial houses we see today. Jimmy Joe [said] all the black flint (obsidian), which is found down the Champagne way, all comes from one place back in the mts.—on the south side of the Kaskawulsh River [. . .] next to the teepee shelter [. . .] was an empty stone cache which all the Indians agreed was older than the shelters."[55]

THURS. 22 JULY *Leaving Boulder Creek camp*

"The Muskrat People are well acquainted with the floods of Boulder Crk & Sam told a nice little story about it (this from Fred): Once upon a time (in the old days?) when all the people were in their brush camps along Boulder Crk, the stream rose very suddenly in one of its floods & forced them out so fast that all their earthly possessions were swept away from them. One old man was able to save his bow and arrows & flint & steel & with that the people went into the mountains & hunted for caribou [. . .]"[56]

SAT. 24 JULY *Little Arm camp*

"About 12:30 PM we rounded a point in the Little Arm & could see Burwash perhaps 10 miles away. The Indians decided to put up a smoke signal to let them know we were coming [. . .] reached the little island opposite Buck Dixon's on the Kluane R. at 2:15 PM. Unsaddled & unpacked [. . .] & then the whole string of horses was swum across the river in high water."[57]

WED. 28 JULY *Burwash*

"Had another visitation from some of the Indian ladies of the village: Old Mrs. Jimmie Johnson (Sam's mother who came originally from Yukon R. country); Mary Jacquot (Louie's wife & sister of Jimmy Joe); Jessie Joe (another of Jimmie's 5 sisters, unmarried); also a few miscellaneous kids. Old Mrs. Jimmy had brot some of her old things to show

above Burwash residents visited the expedition crew after they returned from their travels, bringing examples of tools to demonstrate traditional lifeways. *Left to right:* Tàa'aana (Jessie Joe) holding an adze, Nàch'adǹch'ea (Mary Jacquot, Louis's widow) holding a birchbark basket, and Èna (Big Grandma, Emma Johnson) holding gopher snares. The three children left to right are Joseph Joe (adopted by Jessie Joe), Peter Johnson, and Hughie Johnson holding a sheep horn spoon. Yukon Archives. Elmer Harp Jr. fonds, 2006/2, #237.

us: birchbark baskets stitched with spruce roots [...] an old sheep-horn spoon of her mother's (fashioned by boiling to soften so it could be split, cleaned & shaped; sinew & a piece of tanned Moosehide; old Mrs. Jimmie had made herself a fine awl by setting a large steel needle in lead in a handle of black goat horn; also she had a handful of gopher snares, a long crochet stick for setting them; & a couple of sinew rabbit snares. She said one woman used to carry & set as many as 250 gopher snares in a day. The gopher hides are tough & are used sewn together for blankets, some parkas, winter moccasin liners, etc."[58]

THURS. 29 JULY *Burwash*

"In the evening Chief Albert Isaacs [Isaac] of Aishihik came to call [...] One of his best stories was about how the Old people used to hunt bear. (He & all the other Indians [...] have a very healthy respect for bears & never mess with them.) The brave stalked to close, very close range, then tried to put one killing arrow into him; immediately he flattened to ground under disguise of [a] gopher skin robe & played possum until the bear had quit thrashing around. A nervy procedure!"[59]

TUES. 3 AUG *Burwash*

"More talk by Jimmie Joe et al. of former warfare among Indians up here, especially with those of Tanana R. & Copper R. in Alaska [...] Potlatches are also given by these people, although apparently the only occasion is death. Instead of property money is the only thing given away to the guests—Jimmie said the potlatch he gave for his father cost him $1100. Usually given by eldest son or daughter & not until perhaps 2-3 yrs after the death so as to give them some time to accumulate some extra wealth. At the time of the potlatch, the little wooden grave house is also built (before that time the grave is covered only with canvas or a tent."[60]

THURS. 5 AUG *Burwash*

"Mary Joe Jacquot came out today to cook for us [...] Mrs. Jimmy came with her & had a nice pair of moccasins [...] In the eve. Mary came down to join us around the fire in the brush camp [...] She spoke of a moose being killed with a spear having a long copper blade: this copper beaten out with use of a stone maul & then the blade edge sharpened by grinding with stone. As she talked to us she was chewing on a bit of sage (Artemesia borealis) [...] this was to prevent her from getting a cold. There are many more colds among the Indians now since the Highway came thru & the whites come in from the cities. Artemesia is also boiled into tea & also spruce cones, for a cold curative & preventative. Before the whites came the Indians were better clothed for the winter [...] everyone, all the children had plenty of fur garments (gopher, sheep, etc.) & the severe cold didn't bother them; now they are inadequately clothed in whiteman's stuff, & they feel the cold."[61]

THURS. 19 AUG *Burwash*

"Albert Isaac is the chief of the Aishihik lake group of Indians, & every summer he comes across & sets up a hunting camp near the base of the Big Arm, on the N. shore [...] This camp is probably more exposed than the usual bush Indian camp, but it is apparently placed so that signal fires can easily be seen over at Burwash when they want the boat to come over with supplies [...] There were two huge drying racks loaded down with at least 6 mountain sheep & some fish [...] & no doubt more moose & sheep jerky cached away. Sometime in the fall Isaac moves his outfit to Aishihik with the winter's supply of food & when spring comes again he returns to Kluane. Wilson said Isaac has a gold claim staked out somewhere near the Raft or Gladstone, but he apparently isn't working it now. Old Albert rides a horse like an Arab, although he must be well in his 50s. Saw the moose scapula which he rubs against trees to attract another moose when he is hunting [...] Albert has his wife, daughter & younger son (both teen age), plus a married son & his wife & 2 small children, & at least one old crone peering out from behind the windbreak of poplars."[62]

top The expedition located many brush camps along their route, where the oldest trees were cut using stone adzes and other trees with copper tools or more recent steel axes. Yukon Archives. Elmer Harp Jr. fonds, 2006/2, #159.

bottom Among the items found during the expedition was a birchbark baby carrier leaning against a tree. Yukon Archives. Elmer Harp Jr. fonds, 2006/2, #158.

above Gene Jacquot, Ruth (Pete) Jacquot, and Shùglità (Sam Johnson Sr.) greet American hunters Jim Kennedy and John Osborne returning to Burwash with a truckload of trophies in late August 1948. Yukon Archives, Elmer Harp Jr. fonds, 2006/2, #315.

facing top Tsal KàJana (Copper Lily), Èna (Big Grandma, Emma Johnson), Tùlhàsèn (Lena Johnson), and Hughie Johnson on hill at Burwash, August 1948. Yukon Archives, Elmer Harp Jr. fonds, 2006/2, #338.

facing bottom Albert Isaac, Ts'adasha (George John), and Bill Jimmie at Burwash, 1948. Yukon Archives, Elmer Harp Jr. fonds, 2006/2, #328.

THURS. 26 AUG *Burwash*

"At 9 PM the rest of the folks came in from camp & we crowded into the beer parlor [. . .] to see Jim Kennedy's coloured movies of past big-game hunts in B.C. [. . .] Archie presented Kennedy with 2 lovely sheep horn spoons made by Albert Isaac & Albert was there [. . .] Then Jimmy Joe said he was going to do a dance for us [. . . and] wanted Sam to dance with him, but Sam who is very shy [. . .] left. Next Jimmy enticed Bill Jimm to join him [. . .] Jimmy gesturing with a broom, in lieu of a regular dancing ceremonial wand, & gave us part of Jimmy Johnson's potlatch dance [. . .] Jimmy's actions & voice were clear, positive, & authoritative (as would seem to fit his position of shaman, which Gene says he is)."[63]

FRI. 27 AUG *Burwash*

"In Burwash we bumped into Albert Isaac & [...] he launched into tales of early days about his boyhood at Aishihik (his father was chief before him & he is now), about the first white men who came into that country to boat up the Nisling R. to trade; how Jack Dalton blazed a trail thru & brought the first horses they had ever seen; the horses were so astounding that the Indians called them 'big dogs' & cached their food higher up in the trees so they couldn't eat it. Then Albert told the old tale about Skookum Jim who first discovered gold on the Klondike R. & so started the stampede of '98."[64]

SUN. 29 AUG *Burwash*

"Stopped in Burwash while Fred & I took our birchbark up to Mrs. Jimmie [...] She showed me how the bark is worked: the piece must be fairly solid with not too many knot holes; it is thinned down by peeling from the bark in toward the cambium; then for softness & malleability it is held over heat for a few moments after which it may be bent, folded & shaped most anyway desired. Later, when we went up to Burwash-3 [the third archaeology site] to check the profile again, we bumped into Mrs. Jimmy over there in company

above Tsal KàJana (Copper Lily) and Ѐna (Big Grandma, Emma Johnson) digging for spruce roots near Burwash. Yukon Archives. Elmer Harp Jr. fonds, 2006/2, #339.

with Copper Lillie, Lina [Lena] Johnson (Moose's daughter who works in the café), and young Hughie Johnson. Mrs. J had her canvas bag & 5 ft. double pointed digging stick & she & Copper Lillie were on a spruce-root-digging expedition. We snapped some good pictures of them, & Lina took one of all of us because she had a new Kodak, then Fred & I went along to help dig the roots. Mrs. J picked a clump of 2-3 spruces which stood about 30 ft. tall on the open slope of the terrace & proceeded to probe with her stick until she struck a root which could then be grasped by hand & pulled up along its length. Apparently the best roots are about pencil-size or slightly larger in diameter, & the longer they are the better [...]"[65]

WED. 1 SEPT *Burwash*

"Drove into Burwash with Fred & ordered 3 more pairs of moccasins from Mary Jacquot, then went up to Mrs. Jimmie's with Fred to watch her & get some pictures of her making baskets. She operates with an awl that tapers back from round into a rectangular x-section, & handles it the same way as in sewing moccasins: the awl is punched thru & momentarily left in the hole while she grasps the pointed end of spruce root (or sinew), between thumb & index-finger; then she grips the awl between 2nd & 3rd fingers, pulls it out, & while holding it thus, quickly inserts the spruce rt. into the hole before it has a chance to close, the bead running around the rim of the basket is a green willow shoot. When she comes to the end of a section of root she places an end to be laced under the next 3-4 loops; the new section is knotted before being placed thru its first hole [...] The best time to cut bark is in the spring when the sap is rising; it can be cut at the end of the growing season as 'winter bark' [...] Mary Jacquot says that bark can be cut in wintertime by building a brush fire encircling the base of the tree; then when the trunk has warmed up the bark can be stripped quickly before cooling sets in."[66]

above Burwash residents and expedition crew gathered for a farewell at the Kluane Inn at the end of August 1948. Yukon Archives. Elmer Harp Jr. fonds, 2006/2, #366.

FRI. 3 SEPT *Burwash*

"Gene Jacquot [... is] a wonderful story-teller [...] & a wonderful repository of Yukon tales [...] Gene's record wagon run from Christmas Crk. cabin to Wh = 10 days one way; 22 days round trip allowing couple of days to rest horses in WH [...] Copper Joe came from Copper River country in Alaska & his wife from Copper Center, was in that area. He was the son of a chief there & apparently just moved on into greener pastures in the Yukon. The cabin on Lake Crk which Jimmie Joe took Fred to in '44 & which Fred excavated as a contact site, was built by Copper Joe & his father—according to Gene [...]"[67]

SUN. 5 SEPT *Burwash*

"Cleared all our gear out of the tent & commenced repacking. Mrs. Jimmie & Copper Lillie came out with 2 baby carriers for Fred & me & they're both beautiful jobs. I have the small one now, all of which was done by Copper Lillie—the covering is Moosehide & the beaded decoration excellent. Price most reasonable too—the coverings being only 10.00 each [...] Mary also dropped out in the aft with my last moccasin orders [...] very nice indeed, with white caribou tongues [...] Jessie [Joe] also came out, bringing the gopher-skin boots I ordered from her. Later I picked up the 2 bone points which Albert Isaac made: actually these are made of moosehorn. Along about 5 PM Gene & his wife Pete came out for a mooserib supper in the brush camp: they furnished the ribs (actually a rack brot in by Moose & lifted from the cooler) & some beer. Paul [Nieman] had roasted the ribs all afternoon at an outdoor fire beside his tent, & his wife Agnes came out with the kids to supervise. The roasted ribs were really delicious."[68]

The Alaska Highway Brings Troubled Times

1942–1972

overleaf The Alaska Highway in early fall. KFN Archives. EMPC. Landscape Images #20. PHOTOGRAPHER ALANNA DICKSON

top Trees cut to clear the route for the Alaska Highway north of Fort St. John, June 1942. KFN Archives. EMPC. Peggy D'Orsay Alaska Highway Photograph Collection #5, credit Wide World. PHOTOGRAPHER UNKNOWN

bottom Bulldozer plowing through the forest to lay the roadbed for the Alaska Highway, October 1942. KFN Archives. EMPC. Peggy D'Orsay Photograph Collection #6, credit Associated Press Photo. PHOTOGRAPHER UNKNOWN

During one brief summer and winter from 1942 to 1943, the Alaska Highway was pushed across our land, opening a permanent, year-round transportation corridor from southern Canada and the United States through to the Yukon and Alaska. Everything changed so fast in those years—bulldozers, trucks, and troops crowded into camps along the route as the American Army occupied some of our treasured places. We had no say in the process and no means to defend our resources from the many new pressures resulting from the project. This was a very hard time for young families.

The Jacquot brothers were key intermediaries during the war years, negotiating with American Army officials to identify suitable camp locations for the highway builders. They also supplied local information, goods, and freighting services. First Nations men were scouts for routing the highway, guiding southern surveyors who had no knowledge of the landscape and conditions ahead of them. Although many of our people assisted the highway builders and some made significant income, the overall experience was very negative, with consequences that continue to resonate to this day.[69]

Our people experienced so many unfamiliar things in those years. There was large, noisy equipment working round the clock and heavy traffic due to hundreds of soldiers stationed at large camps along the highway. Illegal and wasteful overhunting of moose and other animals by some soldiers in our region caused food shortages. With the sudden arrival of thousands of foreign troops in our lands, "Outside" diseases once again ravaged our families, whose lifestyle on the land had isolated them from previous exposure to those diseases. Epidemics of measles, dysentery, jaundice, mumps, whooping cough, meningitis, tuberculosis (TB), and influenza swept through the army camps and inevitably reached our people,

striking hardest among the elderly and the young. The mortality rate among Yukon First Nations infants was 47 percent in 1942. Some diseases like TB persisted long after the road builders departed.[70]

The road was not open for travel immediately after it was completed except for military purposes, so impacts from highway travellers were minimal at first. The post–World War II era was a different matter, when the American and Canadian governments opened the Alaska Highway to all travellers in 1947. That brought a flood of people through our region on a continuing basis, along with government agents, who changed our lives in many disturbing ways. It seemed like the Outside world took control of our lives and our lands.[71]

Unquestionably the most destructive changes in the Kluane region came about as a response to reports of overhunting by the Alaska Highway builders during the war years. The territorial government amended the Game Ordinance to limit the sale of meat and hides. The federal government established the Kluane Game Sanctuary in 1943, removing our rights to hunt, trap, and fish in a vast area that had provided our main food resources for generations. The sudden imposition of these new restrictions caused massive problems for our people—in fact near starvation conditions for many years. Trapping incomes dropped and guiding in those areas also was forbidden, so our people experienced many economic hardships from these new policies.

Initially the changes were promoted by the governments as a means of stopping outsiders from destroying game animals in our region, but it soon became obvious that these restrictions were intended to apply permanently to us as well. Our people sent letters to protest the hardships imposed on our families, supported by our local priest and others. The penalties imposed for violations of the new laws were harsh and

top left Highway supply base at Silver City, October 1942. Caption on press release reads: "Highway supply base mingles old log cabins and modern motor convoys alongside each other at one of the supply bases for the 1,600-mile Alaska-Canada Defense Highway, under construction, and linking Edmonton, Alberta, with Fairbanks, Alaska. Termed 'America's Burma Road', the giant highway is being hacked through virgin territories in a construction job 'greater than the building of the Panama Canal,' engineers of the project boast." KFN Archives. EMPC. Peggy D'Orsay Alaska Highway Photograph Collection #3, credit Associated Press Photo. PHOTOGRAPHER UNKNOWN

top right Regiment of Black soldiers marching along the Alaska Highway, October 1942. KFN Archives. EMPC. Peggy D'Orsay Alaska Highway Photograph Collection #1, credit The Associated Press. PHOTOGRAPHER UNKNOWN

bottom Canadian and American officials, along with road-building crews and some local people, attended the official ribbon-cutting ceremony at Soldier's Summit on Kluane Lake to mark the completion of the Alaska Highway on a cold day in November 1942. Some people from Burwash travelled on the new road to witness the ceremony. KFN Archives. EMPC. Peggy D'Orsay Alaska Highway Photograph Collection #7, credit Associated Press Photo. PHOTOGRAPHER UNKNOWN

above Father Morisset stands in front of the newly completed Roman Catholic Church at Burwash, circa 1948. Yukon Archives. Roman Catholic Church, Whitehorse Diocese Collection, 92/19, #3. PHOTOGRAPHER UNKNOWN

facing Father Morisset opened a day school at the Burwash Roman Catholic Mission, which many of the Status Indian children and older teens attended until the Lower Post Residential School opened in 1949. Yukon Archives. Roman Catholic Church, Whitehorse Diocese Collection, 92/19, #2. PHOTOGRAPHER UNKNOWN

ongoing for decades. The Sanctuary was expanded and further restrictions imposed with the creation of Kluane National Park and Reserve in 1972, adding to our sense of injustice and deprivation.[72]

The highway also opened our community to year-round access by government officials, who started to enforce laws requiring all children to attend school. From the earliest days of the fur trade in the 1860s, Anglican and Roman Catholic missionaries had competed fiercely for converts to their churches. Competition in this "race for souls" intensified when the federal government began funding the churches to run mission schools for Indigenous children in the late 1800s. Anglican missionaries achieved greater success in the Yukon, while Roman Catholic missions became firmly entrenched in the Mackenzie River region. The Anglican Church established mission schools at Forty Mile, Moosehide, and Carcross before and after the Gold Rush, but our remote area was isolated from missionaries and police so few children were taken to those schools before World War II.[73]

The federal Indian Act and regulations divided our families into Status and Non-Status categories, with deep consequences for our women and children, lasting over several generations. Women who married non-First Nations men were designated as Non-Status, along with their children. Women who married First Nations Status men were designated as Status Indians, along with their children. Non-Status children were not funded by the federal government to go to church-run residential schools but could attend public schools funded by the Yukon Territorial Government. Status children were not allowed to attend Yukon public schools until the mid-1960s, when the federal government switched its student funding from the church schools to the Yukon Government.[74]

The Jacquot brothers invited Roman Catholic missionaries to settle in the community in 1944, providing land and assistance to establish a church and school. At first some children and young adults, both Status and Non-Status, attended the Roman Catholic day school at Burwash close to home and families. That was a convenient option for parents who were out on their traplines or away hunting because there were extended family members nearby to watch over their children.[75]

At the same time an assisted school was established in 1945 at the new highway maintenance camp at Destruction Bay, but it was open to only the children of highway workers. In order to attract married men and their families to live at the remote camp, the Yukon Government provided financial assistance for a teacher's salary and parents supplied books and other resources. The school building plus equipment were donated and maintained by the U.S. Northwest Services Command, and after 1946 by the Canadian Department of National Defence, when it assumed responsibility for Alaska Highway upkeep in the Yukon. The school grew in size over time to become Kluane Lake School, fully funded by the Yukon Government, but two decades passed before Burwash Status Indian children were allowed to attend these classes so close to their home.[76]

By the late 1940s the Roman Catholic Church had built a large residential school at Lower Post in northern British Columbia, where the majority of Burwash Status children were taken from the 1950s to the mid-1960s. The Anglican Choutla Indian Residential School at Carcross took Status children from many Yukon communities, but most people in Burwash identified with the Catholic Church owing to the presence of the priest and church there. The Dickson families continued to pay for their Non-Status children to live at Anglican-run hostels in Dawson and Whitehorse, so they, too, attended public schools far away from home for many years.

The Baptist Church in Whitehorse opened a residence and school in 1946, which operated for over a decade, accepting both Status and Non-Status children. Some Kluane region parents sent their children to this school so they would be closer to home with easy year-round highway transportation. Travel to Dawson City was limited to airplanes in winter and sternwheelers in summer until the Mayo Road was extended to become the Klondike Highway in 1954. By then Whitehorse had grown into the dominant economic and population centre of the territory and was designated the capital city by the federal government in 1953.[77]

With no school at Burwash both Status and Non-Status children and their parents experienced heartwrenching separations every fall as boats, planes, buses, and trucks took children away to distant schools, not to return until the following summer or in some cases for several years. At the schools, residences, and hostels they were subjected to harsh, racist, and abusive practices that scarred many of our people, with impacts that

above Children on steps of day school at Burwash Roman Catholic Mission. Child front row left is Joe Joe Johnson. KFN Archives, EMPC, Dorothy Johnson Family Images #4. PHOTOGRAPHER UNKNOWN

right Father Morisset drove the Burwash children to the Lower Post Residential School in his little green truck, circa 1949. Jessie Joe (standing next to the truck door) accompanied the group to see where they would be living away from home. KFN Archives. EMPC. Dorothy Johnson Family Images #2. PHOTOGRAPHER UNKNOWN

below Burwash children on the steps of the Lower Post Residential School, run by the Roman Catholic Church in northern B.C., circa 1949. KFN Archives. EMPC. Dorothy Johnson Family Images #3. PHOTOGRAPHER UNKNOWN

continued down through the generations to this day. Children were forbidden from speaking our Dań K'è (Southern Tutchone) language, so they were increasingly alienated from grandparents, parents, and extended family members. They missed our Elders' teachings of traditions, values, culture, and bush skills. They were often shamed and ridiculed for their lack of English proficiency and knowledge of the white world; back home it was difficult for them to fit into traditional routines expected by their families.[78]

In the mid-1960s Yukon Government policies changed to allow First Nations children to attend public schools. Some of our children came home from residential schools to live in Burwash and travel by bus to the school in Destruction Bay. Older students still had to leave home for Whitehorse to attend high school. They stayed in residences once again, at Coudert Hall for Roman Catholic students, or at Yukon Hall for those of Protestant backgrounds. In those years racist attitudes continued to harm our children in schools and residences. There was little effort to provide First Nations curriculum content or any academic supports, leading many of our young people to quit school early, with few skills for making a living in the fast-changing world around them.[79]

School was not the only cause of separation for parents and children. After the war rampant TB overwhelmed Indigenous people across the North. The federal government addressed the problem by building large residential hospitals in southern centres. TB patients of all ages from the Yukon were mostly sent to Edmonton for treatments that lasted from a few months to a decade. Babies and young children were sent away without parents or family members to support them; mothers and fathers were taken, leaving grandparents and extended family members to care for the youngest children left behind, while older siblings were taken to residential schools. These long separations disrupted family life in ways that took years to heal and were as destructive as the disease.[80]

Other destabilizing influences were felt in all Yukon communities with the building of roads and changing lifestyles. Alcohol was more readily available and legalized for consumption by Indigenous people in the late 1950s. Many Yukon Status Indians enfranchised in the postwar years, dropping their Status to obtain work, own a business, keep their children out of residential schools, or for a variety of other reasons. Giving up Status meant foregoing the meagre Indian Act benefits that had been available to people previously; it also allowed access to alcohol prior to amendments in the Yukon liquor laws in 1956. The introduction of minimal social assistance through federal programs for Status people and territorial programs for Non-Status families helped those in need, but left them in poverty and dependent on government officials. The Mother's Allowance introduced in the late 1940s required parents to send their kids to school and tied people to communities, reducing their ability to hunt and trap for a living.[81]

In the late 1940s the territorial government introduced new trapline registration requirements, further disrupting the traditional ways of

top Children playing outside the Choutla Indian Residential School at Carcross, run by the Anglican Church, circa 1920s. Yukon Archives. Anglican Church fonds 4/49, acc89-41#198. PHOTOGRAPHER UNKNOWN

middle After the original Choutla Indian Residential School burned in the 1940s, a number of years passed before the Anglican Church had raised sufficient funds to build a new larger school, seen here in the early 1950s. Yukon Archives 82/354, #20. PHOTOGRAPHER UNKNOWN

bottom Non-Status and Status children attended the Whitehorse Baptist Mission School in Whitehorse, circa 1950. Tom Dickson is the boy at the far end of the left row. Yukon Archives. Rolf and Marg Hougen fonds, 2009/81, #287. PHOTOGRAPHER ROLF HOUGEN

above After the departure of older children for residential schools, Burwash was very quiet, with just a few Elders, some parents, and small children in the community. Family members gathered here for a photograph, circa 1964. *Left to right:* Arnold Johnson, Sophie Watt, Jessie Joe, Elsie Isaac, Albert Isaac with Louise Joe and Art Joe, and Jimmy Joe with Bonnie Jean Joe. KFN Archives. EMPC. Robin Bradasch, Copper Family Images #2. PHOTOGRAPHER: CATHARINE MCCLELLAN

facing top Burwash residents gathered at the funeral for Louis Jacquot, held on Saturday, July 3, 1948, at the Roman Catholic Mission. Yukon Archives. Roman Catholic Church, Whitehorse Diocese Collection, 92/19, #1. PHOTOGRAPHER UNKNOWN

planning and sharing of lands and resources. Other significant changes came with the introduction of snowmobiles, which quickly replaced dog teams for trapping and hunting. That created a need for more cash income to buy machines, parts, and fuel, so more people worked away from home on highway projects or other jobs for longer periods. Trapping, hunting, and fishing were relegated to weekends and holiday times, rather than following a year-round cycle of seasonal activities.[82]

With easy access to communities along the highways, federal officials began to promote new regulations for governance under the Indian Act. Traditionally our people selected one or more headmen who led the planning to designate areas for trapping and hunting. Strong women were recognized as leaders for other aspects of community life. In the 1950s officials instructed each community to elect a Chief and Council in order to communicate plans and regulations for federal programs. This new electoral system added more divisive and disruptive pressures within Yukon First Nations communities. For administrative convenience the federal government also mandated the amalgamation of people from White River and Burwash to form the Kluane Indian Band. This meant some people relocated from Beaver Creek to Burwash. Over time the forced amalgamation caused tensions between families in the two communities over allocations of funding for housing and other issues.[83]

Among the families resident or visiting at Burwash in the 1950s and 1960s were several of the Johnson lineages, including children and grandchildren descended from Jimmy Johnson and his two wives, Èna (Big Grandma, Emma) and Copper Lily. As well several of Moose Johnson's children were in the community, including Lena, Bernie, and Joe. Some of Copper George Joe's descendants were there and some of the Allens. Although the children were away at school for much of the year, they were able to come home for summers. As Youth reached maturity, the number of job seekers outnumbered the jobs available in the region. Government hiring practices frequently discriminated against our people, forcing most to leave home for opportunities in Alaska, British Columbia, and farther afield.[84]

The Jacquot family experienced profound losses soon after the war, with Louis dying in 1948 and Eugene in 1950. They had launched their final massive venture in 1945, in anticipation of a coming boom in highway travel once the war was over. Burwash Lodge was a large log structure built by Bob Porsild and offering a restaurant, bar, four showers and nineteen rooms for rent, and spectacular views of Kluane Lake. Eugene and his wife, Ruth, operated the lodge, then after he died, she sold it to Leland Allinger and Darrell Duensing, who operated it for many more years.[85] Thomas Dickson died in 1952, leaving members of his large extended family in Burwash and other highway communities to carry on the family traditions of hunting, trapping, and guiding.[86]

In the midst of all these upheavals our community retained formidable strengths, thanks to our Elders, who never lost sight of their identity and purpose as leaders for future generations. The Alaska Highway had certainly opened up some new wage employment and learning opportunities. Big game outfitting flourished again in areas outside the National Park and Reserve. Tourism brought some additional new work options for men and women, with road building, museums, and visitor services. Many scientists, including archaeologists, anthropologists, glaciologists, and geologists, came to the North to study us, our lands, and wildlife. Our people of all ages had valuable skills to offer and were significant contributors to those studies.

Fresh winds of change were also blowing in the Kluane region and throughout the Yukon in the 1960s. Our young people were learning to walk in two worlds through school and work, building knowledge, strength, independence, and resilience. They had experienced the segregation, racism, discrimination, displacement, and disrespect that were rampant in schools, hospitals, the justice system, the Park, and many workplaces. They saw the power that government officials wielded over them, their families, and their communities. As adults their cultural traditions and community support provided a firm foundation along with new skills to resist those powers and build a new future together with other Yukon First Nations.[87]

above The new Kluane Inn was an impressive building on the lakeshore, offering accommodation to Alaska Highway travellers, hunters, and other visitors for many decades until it closed in 2013; it was later demolished. Yukon Archives. Elmer Harp Jr. fonds, 2006/2, #141

overleaf Each year chum salmon swim from the Pacific Ocean into Kluane Lake and spawn at the mouth of the Kluane River. They have been a delicious source of protein for thousands of years. Climate change and other factors are a concern for the future of the fish. KFN Archives. EMPC. Wildlife Images #7. PHOTOGRAPHER PAUL VECSEI

Kwäday Dań Jenntth'à

Hearing Our Elders, Reclaiming Our Lands and Our Lives

1970s–2003

top Yukon Chiefs met federal officials, including federal minister Jean Chrétien, in Whitehorse in 1968 to discuss their concerns with the government's White Paper that proposed major changes to the Indian Act. During the meeting the Chiefs adjourned and founded the Yukon Native Brotherhood, with Elijah Smith as President. Library and Archives Canada image e010775663. PHOTOGRAPHER UNKNOWN

bottom Elijah Smith was a founding member of the Yukon Native Brotherhood and long time advocate for Yukon First Nations rights and land claims. CYFN Archives. Box-48-File-22-01Ed PHOTOGRAPHER UNKNOWN

The Yukon land claims movement had gained considerable momentum by the early 1970s, inspired by the work of Alaska Native organizations, Indigenous organizations in southern Canada, American civil rights activists, and the American Indian Movement. The Yukon Native Brotherhood (YNB) was founded in 1968 during meetings in Whitehorse with federal Indian Affairs Minister Jean Chrétien. He came to promote the infamous White Paper, which proposed major changes to the Indian Act. Yukon Chiefs along with First Nations across Canada opposed the White Paper vehemently as a move to reduce their rights and supports, with no positive benefits for individuals or communities.[88]

In the late 1960s Dickie Dickson and Joe Jacquot from Burwash spent time with their Tlingit relatives on the coast and followed their discussions regarding the Tlingit and Haida land claims in Alaska. When they came home to the Yukon, they encouraged Yukon First Nations to get organized and pursue their rights in Canada. Joe Jacquot spent time with Elijah Smith and other Yukon leaders explaining the concepts and legal strategies employed by Alaska Native peoples.[89]

As YNB Chair, Elijah and a group of organizers began travelling all over the Yukon to gather ideas about how to regain control of Indigenous communities and build a better future for the children. Those consultations with Elders and people of all ages informed the groundbreaking *Together Today for Our Children Tomorrow* Yukon land claims manifesto. Twelve Chiefs, including our Chief, Jimmy Enoch, travelled to Ottawa with Elijah in 1973 to present the document to Prime Minister Pierre Trudeau, convincing the federal government to initiate formal negotiations for a comprehensive settlement of Yukon land claims.[90]

Yukon Non-Status people were left out of those initial discussions. YNB leaders insisted they would look after the interests of all people of Yukon Indian ancestry. Federal officials were accustomed to dealing only with Status Indians and were unlikely to broaden the base of discussions. In response Non-Status people founded the Yukon Association of Non-Status

above left In February 1973 the twelve Yukon First Nations Chiefs and Yukon Native Brotherhood President Elijah Smith travelled to Ottawa to present the Yukon land claims document entitled *Together Today for Our Children Tomorrow* to Prime Minister Pierre Elliott Trudeau. *Left to right:* Chief Johnnie Smith (Whitehorse Indian Band), Chief Charlie Abel (Old Crow Indian Band), Chief Danny Joe (Selkirk Indian Band), Chief Ray Jackson (Champagne & Aishihik Indian Band), Chief Jimmy Enoch (Kluane Indian Band), Chief Dan Johnson (Carcross Indian Band), Chief Percy Henry (Dawson Indian Band), Chief Clifford McLeod (Ross River Indian Band), Chief George Billy (Carmacks Indian Band), Chief Dixon Lutz (Liard First Nation), Chief Sam Johnston (Teslin Indian Band), YNB President Elijah Smith, and Chief Peter Lucas (Mayo Indian Band). CYFN Archives. Photograph Collection #b82_f19_s22_1. PHOTOGRAPHER UNKNOWN

above right Kluane Band Chief Jimmy Enoch, circa 1980s. KFN Archives. EMPC. Robin Bradasch Collection Scans #1. PHOTOGRAPHER UNKNOWN

Indians (YANSI) in 1972, with locals in every community to help people access services and lobby for standing in the land claims process. After the Chiefs returned from Ottawa in 1973, YANSI leaders protested outside a YNB meeting in Whitehorse. More discussions occurred at Burwash Landing at the Dalan (inlet) campground—an important neutral meeting place for critical decision-making.[91] YANSI and YNB leaders ultimately agreed to work together as Status and Non-Status people to form the Council for Yukon Indians (CYI) in 1973 to negotiate the land claims.[92]

From then until 1993 our leaders worked with people throughout the Yukon to establish the Umbrella Final Agreement (UFA), which set out the framework for restoring our rights and freedoms, including lands, financial compensation, and self-government powers for our people. The process was extremely complex and time consuming, requiring our leaders to be in meetings almost full time year-round. This was a significant sacrifice of time for them, with meagre monetary compensation, entailing loss of income from trapping or other work, as well as reduced time on the land to hunt and gather food.

Many of the negotiators were young people who had attended residential school together. The bonds and connections formed in those difficult years inspired them with steadfast resolve that sustained them through the long decades of tough negotiations with government officials. Elders supported and guided them throughout that process, too, sitting through endless days and weeks of meetings to develop and guide the principles for reclaiming rights and lands.

TOGETHER TODAY FOR OUR CHILDREN TOMORROW —

A Statement of Grievances and an Approach to Settlement by the Yukon Indian People is respectfully submitted by:

Elijah Smith, Chief
Yukon Native Brotherhood

Percy Henry, Chief
Dawson Band and member
Y.N.B. Executive Council

Roy H. Sam, Councillor
Whitehorse Band and 1st Deputy
Chief Y.N.B. Executive Council

Charlie Abel, Chief
Old Crow Band

Jimmy Enoch, Chief
Kluane Band

Danny Joe, Chief
Selkirk Band

Dan Johnson, Chief
Carcross Band

Willie Joe, Member
Y.N.B. Executive Council

Dixon Lutz, Chief
Liard River Band and member
Y.N.B. Executive Council

Raymond Jackson, Chief
Champagne-Aishihik Band and
member Y.N.B. Executive Council

Sam Johnston, Chief
Teslin Band

Peter Lucas, Chief
Mayo Band

Johnnie Smith, Chief
Whitehorse Band

Clifford McLeod, Chief
Ross River Band

George Billy, Chief
Carmacks Band

Judy Gingell, Member
Y.N.B. Executive Council

COUNCILLORS	DELEGATES
KLUANE	
Kenneth Johnson	Alice Johnson
	Lena Johnson
	Mary Easterson
LIARD	
Danny Lutz	Tim Dick
Robert Jules	Jerry Dickson
	Frank Magum
	Mathew Jimmy
	Raymond Donnessey
	Harry Dick
MAYO	
Mabel Hager	Richard Hager
Benny Moses	Alma Moses
	Johnny Simon
	Sam Peter

top Signature pages from *Together Today for Our Children Tomorrow*. On the left Elijah Smith and the Chiefs, including Kluane Chief Jimmy Enoch, plus YNB Executive Council members Willie Joe and Judy Gingell. On the right the Kluane signatories Councillor Kenneth Johnson and Delegates Alice (Alyce) Johnson, Lena Johnson, and Mary Easterson. CYFN Archives. Library Collection

bottom The iconic gold and black cover on the original poster and the published version of the Yukon Land Claims manifesto was designed in 1972 by Bernie Johnson from Burwash with ideas and photographs contributed by Yukon artist Jim Robb and others. CYFN Archives. Library Collection

top left CYI Chair Harry Allen and Joe Jacquot representing the Yukon Association of Non-Status Indians, along with two unidentified men, heading to meetings in Ottawa, circa 1975. CYFN Archives. Photograph Collection #b47_f22_s5_15. PHOTOGRAPHER UNKNOWN

top right CYI land claims negotiators meeting with Kluane First Nation at the community hall in Burwash, circa 1980s. At the table left to right: Victor Mitander, Harry Allen, Dave Joe, and an unidentified woman and Georgina Stone, with Wilbur Smarch behind them. Mabel Henry sits by the window with Betty Pope in front of her. CYFN Archives. Photograph Collection #64_25_3_19. PHOTOGRAPHER UNKNOWN

bottom CYI Chair Daniel Tlen and Vice-Chair Bill Webber at CYI executive meeting in Whitehorse, circa mid-1970s. CYFN Archives. Photograph Collection #b74_f30_n2. PHOTOGRAPHER UNKNOWN

Kluane leaders were key contributors to the Yukon land claims movement. Our Chief Jimmy Enoch was a signatory to the *Together Today* manifesto, along with Lena Johnson, Alyce Johnson, Kenneth Johnson, and Mary Easterson. Joe Jacquot continued to be involved in YANSI. Joe Joe Johnson, Mary Easterson, Daniel Tlen, Gùdia Johnson, and many others attended meetings at Whitehorse and in communities to carry forward our claims, hopes, and dreams for a brighter future for our children in our homelands. We reorganized and renamed our government in those years, as Kluane Tribal Brotherhood in the 1970s and then as Kluane Tribal Council in the 1990s.[93]

The negotiations were complicated by Indian Act designations for Status and Non-Status people based on whether a First Nations woman had married a Status Indian, Non-Status Indian, or white man. The Yukon Indian Women's Association was founded in 1973 to represent women's issues. All these organizations worked towards the reform of the Indian Act in 1985, with the passing of Bill C-31, which eliminated many of the discriminatory provisions for women who married Non-Status or white men.[94]

The need to settle Yukon land claims was suddenly propelled to a new level of urgency in 1977 when Justice Tom Berger's Mackenzie Valley Pipeline Inquiry recommended a ten-year moratorium on pipeline construction in the Northwest Territories. With rising prices and anticipated supply shortages Canada and the United States were looking to fast-track approvals for an Alaska Highway Gas Pipeline. That alarmed Yukon First Nations, who foresaw major problems with protecting our lands and rights if a pipeline proceeded before the settlement of our claims. The government of Canada hastily assembled a three-person Alaska Highway Pipeline Inquiry panel, headed by Judge Lysyk, with a short reporting deadline and narrow scope to hear testimony from Yukon people. Our Elders and leaders, together with many others along the highway, testified at the hearings, recalling the destructive forces that overtook our communities during the 1940s.[95]

top Elders from Burwash and other Yukon communities met at the new community centre in Burwash in the late 1970s to discuss progress and issues realted to land claims negotiations. CYFN Archives. Photograph Collection #b47_f18_s4_18. PHOTOGRAPHER UNKNOWN

bottom Elders from all Yukon First Nations were constant and engaged advisors throughout the long years of land claims discussions. Negotiators relied on them for their knowledge of the land and resources and of history and their aspirations for their children and all future generations to come. This meeting, held at Airport Lake circa 1977, included several Burwash Elders. CYFN Archives. Photograph Collection #b47_f20_s3_19. PHOTOGRAPHER UNKNOWN

Our former Chief Daniel (Johnson) Tlen, as the elected Chair of the CYI, had travelled to Washington to testify before the U.S. Congressional committee that was conducting hearings on the proposed project. In headlines that reverberated across the continent he declared there should be no pipelines before the settlement of land claims. It was a controversial stand, repeated at a 1976 meeting in Whitehorse with Prime Minister Pierre Trudeau and at the Lysyk Inquiry. In the end the pipeline proposal fizzled as other gas supplies and pricing reduced the economic viability of the project. The controversy resulted in massive federal funding for land claims negotiations, an unexpected but welcome outcome of this issue.[96]

During all those years of negotiations our community had to contend with many other serious issues. Most of our people, including Elders and children, lived in very substandard housing with minimal electrical connections and no sewer or water services, and lived under difficult social conditions. It took years of battling with federal and territorial governments to obtain help for our people. Many moved away to pursue higher education, find work, and make a better life for their children, leaving Elders alone at home.[97]

Some families remained in the community but still struggled with school issues long after residential schools closed and their children came home. Yukon public schools were open to Status and Non-Status children after the mid-1960s; however, the curriculum and teaching methodologies were often inappropriate for First Nations children. In the mid-1970s Burwash parents tried to convince the territorial government to include our Southern Tutchone language and First Nations culture and history

The Whitehorse Star, Friday, November 19, 1976, Page 7

In Berger Submission

CYI Calls For Settlement Before Pipeline

By ANDREW HUME
Staff Reperter

The Council for Yukon Indians recommended to the Berger inquiry this week that no pipeline be built until Yukon Indian land claims are settled and implemented.

The recommendation is one of nine points in a presentation to summation hearings before the inquiry in Yellowknife by Whitehorse lawyer Ron Veale, pipeline cousel for the CYI.

The Berger inquiry into a proposed natural gas pipeline from Alaska across the Yukon and down the MacKenzie Valley is scheduled to conclude this week in Yellowknife after 18 months of hearings.

The fundamental CYI principle is that land claims be settled first.

The CYI summation also recommends that no pipeline ever be constructed in the northern part of the Yukon that would affect the Porcupine River or the land traditonally used by the people of Old Crow.

The Old Crow council has asked that all drainage areas surrounding the village be declared a socially and ecologically sensitive area that should be managed by the local people there.

The CYI brief says that as part of the settlement of Old Crow land claims, this area be withdrawn from development forever.

Since Old Crow is the Only Indian village in the Yukon which would be directly affected by the two routes proposed by Canadian Arctic Gas, the CYI submission argues that the principle of self-determination for Old Crow should not be compromised by any northern development.

The CYI has asked Mr. Justice Thomas Berger to recommend that hearings similar to the Mackenzie Valley Pipeline Inquiry be held into the proposed alternative pipeline routes along the Alaska Highway.

"The CYI should be funded to undertake the research to provide the baseline data for all Indian communities affected by these routes as was done in the case of Old Crow," Veale told the inquiry.

There are 12 Indian communities in the Yukon and before the Alaska Highway route is considered, the CYI wants government funding to undertake a pipeline information program to inform these communities of the ramifications of a pipeline and to obtain their reaction.

A major section of the CYI final argument was taken up with the principles of the Old Crow land settlement, which covers all the area north of the 65th parallel in the Yukon between Alaska on the west and the Norhtwest Territories on the east.

"The fundamental objective of the people of Old Crow is to obtain control over their lives and their lands. The evidence at Old Crow demonstrates that for a t least 1,000 years the people of Old Crow have lived in harmony with the Porcupine caribou herd and have used the land of the Norhtern Yukon from the southern drainage of the Porcupine River to Herschel Island in the North," the CYI submission says.

Three principles were outlined in support of the CYI argument that to allow a pipeline across this territory would "prejudice" the land claims postion of the people of Old Crow.

"Caribou are the fundamental component of the survival of the people of Old Crow," Veale said.

The first of the three principles states that the Porcupine caribou herd must remain in existence under the stewardship and protection of the people of Old Crow in order that they can have an economic mainstay to "ensure the cultural integrity and provide an economic bridge with which the people of Old Crow can function and interact with the outside world on their own terms."

The second principle provides for "the exclusive use in perpetuity" of the drainage basin of the Old Crow River for the people of Old Crow and asks that they be withdrawn from any plans for development by any level of government or industry.

The final principle would grant the people of Old Crow the power to control their way of life and the environment within which they exist.

The brief contends that the pipeline routes, the energy corridor concept and the subsidiary developments of the Dempster Highway and the Beaufort Sea exploration all violate these principles.

The CYI sums up the position of the Yukon Indians. It was heard along with final summations from the two pipeline applicants during the final day of hearings in Yellowknife.

The two applicants are Canadian Arctic Gas, who propose a 48-inch natural gas pipeline from Purdhoe Bay, Alaska across the Yukon and down the Mackenzie Valley, and Foothills Pipe Lines, which has proposed to build a 42-inch, all-Canadian line from the Mackenzie Delta down the valley to Canadian markets. Foothills also has an interest in the alternate Alaska Highway route.

When final summations from the applicants and all interveners have been heard, Mr. Justice Berger will write a report and make recommendations to the federal government on conditions under which a pipeline could be built. It does not lie within his terms of reference, established by the cabinet, to decide whether or not a pipeline should be constructed.

The lengthy submission by the Yukon Indians examines in detail the impacts of both northern routes across the Yukon and their social-cultural impacts, man-land relationships, economic impacts and draws conclusions that in neither case should a pipeline ever be considered.

The brief concludes with the view that "the construction of a gas pipeline and subsequent corridor developments will have disastrous impact upon the people and the environment of the North and may trigger a violent reaction if native rights and title are not fully recognized.

top left *Whitehorse Star*, November 19, 1976.

top right Kluane Tribal Council arranged for the Alaska Highway Pipeline Inquiry hearing at Burwash to be held outside in the summer of 1977. With Kluane Lake in the background, Edith (Dickson) Bohmer, who was born at Burwash, Chair Kenneth Lysyk from the University of British Columbia, and Willard Phelps from Carcross heard testimonials from Elders, leaders, and citizens about Alaska Highway construction impacts in the 1940s and concerns about issues with a future pipeline. Christabelle (baby) and Walter Carlick are in the foreground. CYFN Archives. Photograph Collection #1977 b45_f25_8. PHOTOGRAPHER UNKNOWN

bottom Harry Allen and then CYI Chair Daniel Tlen presenting the CYI position on land claims and pipeline issues to the Lysyk Inquiry in 1977. CYFN Archives. Photograph Collection #b47_f13_s3_18 PHOTOGRAPHER UNKNOWN

at the elementary school in Destruction Bay. After years of refusal from officials to enrich their children's school days with our teachings, some parents staged a protest by withdrawing their children from the public school. In time the government agreed to some small cultural additions to the mainstream curriculum, but it was very little and the issue remained an outstanding concern for many parents and our leaders.[98]

The solution was a bold one: we started our own community school! Kêts'á dan' kų (meaning "Teaching People House," Burwash Community School) opened its doors in 1977 in one of our community buildings in Burwash. The Yukon Government initially refused all funding and other supports. It was a big struggle to run the school on our own with limited resources. We organized fundraising events—a walkathon, bake sales, roast gopher treats at Yukon Indian Days, and mail-outs to potential sponsors. We had dedicated teachers, including Mary Easterson and Sandy Johnson from our community and others from Outside, tremendous support from parents and Elders, and kids who were excited to learn in the new environment close to home. The school represented a major accomplishment for our people, and though it operated for only a few years, it fired up our imaginations and helped to fuel our drive towards self-determination.[99]

top Burwash, Beaver Creek, and Haines Junction residents fielded a baseball team for a tournament in Whitehorse, circa 1980. *Front row left to right:* Charlie Eikland Sr., Bruce Williams, Owen Miller, two unidentified boys, and Joe Bruneau. *Back row:* unidentified boy, Gene Kushniruk, two unidentified boys, Mark Eikland, Benson Joe, and Charlie Eikland Jr. CYFN Archives. Photograph Collection #62a_25_6.tif. PHOTOGRAPHER UNKNOWN

middle left Older students at school in Burwash. *Left to right:* Gerald Dickson and Larry Blair. CYFN Archives. Photograph Collection #b48_f15_s1_11. Kêts'á dan' kų Images #4. PHOTOGRAPHER UNKNOWN

middle right Burwash kids attend Elders Gathering at community hall in Burwash. *Left to right:* Lillian Johnson, Joyce Johnson, Gùdia Johnson with Diyet in baby carrier, Math'ieya Johnson, Robin Johnson, and Elodie Kabanak. CYFN Archives. Photograph Collection #b47_f28_s1_6. Kêts'á dan' kų Images #3. PHOTOGRAPHER UNKNOWN

bottom left Burwash kids running along the Alaska Highway during the walkathon fundraiser. *Left to right:* Otis Johnson, Juniper McLeod, and Lillian Johnson. CYFN Archives. Photograph Collection #b47_f28_s1_8. Kêts'á dan' kų Images #1. PHOTOGRAPHER UNKNOWN

bottom right Otis Johnson taking a break during the walkathon. CYFN Archives. Photograph Collection #b47_f28_s1_5. Kêts'á dan' kų Images #2. PHOTOGRAPHER UNKNOWN

top Kêts'á dan' kų school photograph 1985. *Front row left to right:* Sandy Johnson, Elena Isaac, Simon Johnson, Luke Johnson, Willie Sheldon, Dwayne Johnson, Ķatie Johnson, Gordie Isaac, and Mary Easterson. *Back row left to right:* Juniper McLeod, Otis Johnson, Lena Johnson, Robin Johnson, Jennifer Joe, Justina Michel, and Helen Joe. KFN Archives. EMPC. Lena Johnson Family Images #13. PHOTOGRAPHER UNKNOWN.

middle left Burwash kids enjoy an outing at Duke Meadow. *Left to right:* Ritchie Johnson, Teresa Johnson, Michelle Carlick, Juniper McLeod, and Justina Michel. CYFN Archives. Photograph Collection #b47_f26_s1_9. Kêts'á dan' kų Images #5. PHOTOGRAPHER UNKNOWN.

middle right Kêts'á dan' kų students at the community hall in Burwash, circa 1984. *Left to right:* Colette Bolneske, Robin Johnson, Helen Joe, Shane Johnson, Willie Sheldon, Otis Johnson standing, Luke Johnson, and Jennifer Joe in front. KFN Archives. EMPC. Bernie Johnson Family Images #1. PHOTOGRAPHER BERNIE JOHNSON.

bottom Kêts'á dan' kų graduates visit Yukon MP Erik Nielsen in his office on Parliament Hill in Ottawa, circa 1985. *Left to right:* Sandy Johnson, Robin Johnson, Juniper McLeod, Helen Joe, Erik Nielsen, and Otis Johnson. KFN Archives. EMPC. Sandy Johnson Family Images #17. PHOTOGRAPHER UNKNOWN

top Community people organizing rummage sale for the new Kluane Museum of Natural History, circa 1973. *Left to right:* Gùdia Johnson, Copper Lily, Daniel Tlen, Big Grandma Ëna Johnson, Robbie Johnson, Michael Johnson, Peter Johnson, George John, and Lena Johnson. KFN Archives. EMPC. Robin Bradasch, Johnson Family Images #9. PHOTOGRAPHER SANDY JOHNSON

bottom Moose Johnson with his wife Nelly in Burwash, circa 1980s. KFN Archives. EMPC. Robin Bradasch, Johnson Family Images #11. PHOTOGRAPHER UNKNOWN

Major problems with the Kluane Game Sanctuary added more cause for alarm and concerted community action. By 1972 more lands had been withdrawn from our use and access as the government established Kluane National Park and Reserve, incorporating most of the Game Sanctuary and new park lands in a vast preserve. For many years our people were excluded from the new employment opportunities created as part of the park management system—despite our deep knowledge of the region and its resources.

The Yukon political scene was evolving rapidly in those years as non-Native people campaigned for more autonomy from the federal government and responsible government status for the Yukon Territorial Government. Reforms implemented by the federal Conservative government of Joe Clark in 1979 gave the majority political party elected in the Yukon Legislative Assembly the power to select a government leader and form a Cabinet in accordance with British Parliamentary traditions.[100]

These fast-paced reforms brought new challenges for inexperienced elected territorial officials and departmental staff and in one case resulted in severe hardship for our people. In 1980 Elder Sam Johnson Sr. was trapping muskrats in an area of the Kluane Game Sanctuary when he was arrested by a Territorial Game Warden. The previous year Kluane Tribal Brotherhood leaders had staged a protest over the government's continued refusal to permit our members to hunt and trap in our traditional territories, a right taken away in the 1940s. Minister Swede Hanson met with our leaders and verbally agreed to an informal arrangement that would allow access to the area for our members, but he failed to communicate this agreement to his officials so they moved in and applied the law as they understood it. Sam Johnson suffered a stroke the day after his arrest and was subsequently unable to hunt and trap for the rest of his life. This incident, along with many other issues, added to our sense of urgency for change, providing momentum to push for a just and fair settlement through the long years of land claims negotiations.[101]

There were many controversies and setbacks prior to the 1993 Umbrella Final Agreement (UFA). An early Agreement in Principle (AIP) was rejected by some First Nations in 1984 because it lacked adequate protections for YFN land and resource management and provisions for self-government.

It contained an extinguishment clause that would have eliminated all other previous Aboriginal rights, and this was strongly rejected by a number of Chiefs and many Yukon First Nations people. That led to a stalemate that was finally broken in 1985 with new federal and territorial government leaders agreeing to a fresh mandate to permit negotiations on those key issues after 1986, leading to a new AIP signed by the CYI, Canada, and the Yukon in 1989.[102]

During the late 1980s significant changes took place affecting Kluane First Nation when the White River people decided to separate and form their own First Nation. They regained recognition as a separate First Nation in 1989 through a unanimous resolution passed at the CYI General Assembly. That resolution was eventually accepted by Canada, disbanding the amalgamation of the White River and Kluane Peoples imposed by federal officials in the 1950s. Subsequently the White River First Nation negotiated their land claims with the federal and territorial governments on their own behalf.

With goodwill and a focus on redefining the balance of powers between federal, territorial, and Yukon First Nations governments, a comprehensive UFA was finally reached in 1993, signed by Yukon First Nations Chiefs and passed in Parliament and the Yukon Legislature. Yukon First Nations rights and powers were confirmed in the Canadian Constitution in 1995, providing a resolution to many issues our Elders had battled for decades. Four First Nations signed Final and Self-Government Agreements at the same time as the UFA in 1993, while seven more including Kluane First Nation negotiated and signed agreements in subsequent years. White River First Nation, Kaska Dena Council of Ross River, and Liard First Nation are still negotiating their claims.

The UFA meant that Yukon First Nations rights to own selected lands, receive monetary compensation for final settlement, and share powers over the management of lands and resources had been recognized at last. Of paramount importance, our right to protect our languages, culture, and heritage was finally recognized in law, along with the right to educate our children in our way according to our ancestral traditions.[103]

top Elijah Smith and Joe Jacquot honoured as leaders of the Yukon land claims process at the signing of the 1989 Agreement in Principle, the framework for the 1993 Umbrella Final Agreement. *Left to right:* federal minister Pierre Cadieux, Elijah Smith, Joe Jacquot, CYI Chair Mike Smith. CYFN Archives. Photograph Collection #5_26 2007_02_72_9_17. PHOTOGRAPHER UNKNOWN.

bottom CYI Chair Akhwäda (Judy Gingell) holds up the 1993 Umbrella Final Agreement, with Yukon Government Leader John Ostashek to her left and federal minister Tom Siddon to her right. CYFN Archives. Photograph Collection #B6-93-158. PHOTOGRAPHER UNKNOWN

overleaf Burwash seen from the bay on a windy day in fall 2022. KFN Archives. EMPC. Landscape Images #21. PHOTOGRAPHER ALISTAIR MAITLAND

Kluane
First Nation
Self-Government
2003

top left Audience gathers in the large tent set up beside Jacquot Hall for the Signing Ceremony. KFN Archives. EMPC. Land Claims Signing Images #1. PHOTOGRAPHER UNKNOWN

top right Yukon Premier Dennis Fentie, federal DIAND minister Robert Nault, and Chief Robert Dickson hold up the KFN Final and Self-Government Agreements after they signed the documents in Burwash on October 18, 2003. KFN Archives. EMPC. Land Claims Signing Images #4. PHOTOGRAPHER UNKNOWN

middle Elders enter the tent, left to right: Agnes Johnson, Louise Bouvier, and Kluane Martin. KFN Archives. EMPC. Land Claims Signing Images #2. PHOTOGRAPHER UNKNOWN

bottom Kluane First Nation members seated in tent at the Signing Ceremony. KFN Archives. EMPC. Land Claims Signing Images #3. PHOTOGRAPHER UNKNOWN

Once the 1993 UFA was in place, Kluane First Nation used that framework to negotiate our Final and Self-Government Agreements. It took another ten years of gruelling debate, meetings that never seemed to end, and a lot of soul searching by our people.

Our leaders were under enormous pressure to make things right for our Nation now and for all our future generations to come. Everyone had to consider whether we were receiving sufficient compensation in our settlement in return for giving up the vast majority of our traditional lands. We had to trust that Canada and the Yukon would live up to the commitments they were making in the agreements. These were difficult decisions given the troubled times our people had experienced over the past century with colonial governments. In the end our citizens voted to accept the agreements, and we were ready to take the next giant step towards our future as Lhù'ààn Mân Ku Dań.

On October 18, 2003, representatives of our Nation, the Yukon, and Canada signed our agreements at a momentous ceremony in Burwash, with an effective date of February 2, 2004. We moved from our former federally controlled Indian Act band status to become a self-governing First Nation, with wide-ranging autonomy, rights, and responsibilities. This was a new era for us as Kluane First Nation, full of hopes and dreams, opportunities and challenges.

Our celebrations included all our Elders, who had worked so hard for us through many decades to achieve these agreements. We remembered those who had already passed on, and we looked to the future with our young people, who must carry their dreams forward with all the responsibilities involved in being a self-governing nation.

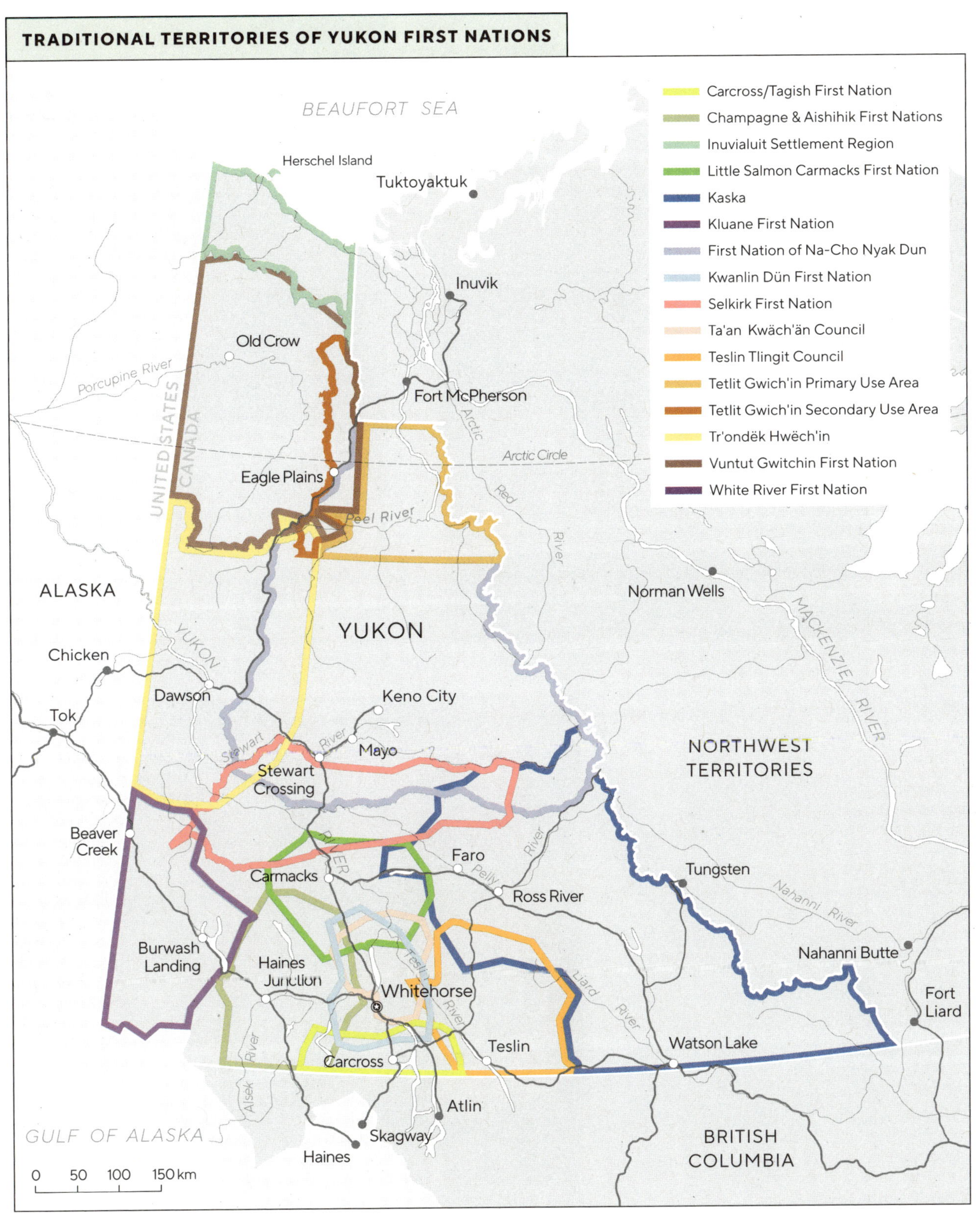

Map adapted from work by Richard Vladars, courtesy of Kwanlin Dün First Nation

top left Elder Tàa'aana (Jessie Joe), then in her late 90s, was the oldest signatory to the KFN land claims agreements, assisted by Josie Sias. KFN Archives. EMPC. Land Claims Signing Images #5. PHOTOGRAPHER UNKNOWN

top right Baby Nathan Easterson-Moore was the youngest signatory to the KFN land claims agreements, assisted by his mother, Donalda Easterson. KFN Archives. EMPC. Land Claims Signing Images #6. PHOTOGRAPHER UNKNOWN

bottom KFN land claims signatories Robin Bradasch, Bertha Doris, and Becky Miller-Hundrup with baby Nadaya Johnson. KFN Archives. EMPC. Land Claims Signing Images #7. PHOTOGRAPHER UNKNOWN

top KFN land claims signatories Monique Martin, negotiator Dave Joe, and Janice Dickson. KFN Archives. EMPC. Land Claims Signing Images #8. PHOTOGRAPHER UNKNOWN

middle KFN land claims signatories Agnes Johnson and Dick Dickson. KFN Archives. EMPC. Land Claims Signing Images #9. PHOTOGRAPHER UNKNOWN

bottom KFN land claims signatories Peter Johnson and Margaret Johnson. KFN Archives. EMPC. Land Claims Signing Images #10. PHOTOGRAPHER UNKNOWN

top KFN land claims signatories Dorothy Johnson and Lena Johnson. KFN Archives. EMPC. Land Claims Signing Images #11. PHOTOGRAPHER UNKNOWN

bottom KFN land claims signatories Josie Sias and former Chief Joe Joe Johnson. KFN Archives. EMPC. Land Claims Signing Images #12. PHOTOGRAPHER UNKNOWN

facing top KFN land claims signatories Kathleen Johnson, Gùdia Johnson, and Pauly Sias. KFN Archives. EMPC. Land Claims Signing Images #13. PHOTOGRAPHER UNKNOWN

facing bottom KFN land claims signatory George Johnson. KFN Archives. EMPC. Land Claims Signing Images #14. PHOTOGRAPHER UNKNOWN

top The Signing Ceremony event followed Potlatch traditions with gifts for people who played an important role in reaching the KFN agreements. KFN received gifts honouring the occasion from Yukon First Nations, along with the federal and Yukon governments. Ta'an Kwach'an Elder Frances Woolsey and some children admire the gifts. Kluane Member of the Legislative Assembly Gary McRobb is standing to the right in the background. KFN Archives. EMPC. Land Claims Signing Images #16. PHOTOGRAPHER UNKNOWN

middle left Specially decorated cakes are a feature at land claims ceremonies. The KFN cake featured the First Nation's logo and a pair of moccasins signifying the long journey to reach the agreements. KFN Archives. EMPC. Land Claims Signing Images #17. PHOTOGRAPHER UNKNOWN

middle right KFN Elder Sue Van Bibber reading the Signing Ceremony pamphlet with her sister Grace Chambers to her right. KFN Archives. EMPC. Land Claims Signing Images #15. PHOTOGRAPHER UNKNOWN

bottom Elders Dorothy Johnson, Lena Johnson, Darlene Northway, and Joyce Johnson-Albert sing at the celebrations after the Signing Ceremony. KFN Archives. EMPC. Land Claims Signing Images #18. PHOTOGRAPHER UNKNOWN

top left Elder Lena Johnson joyfully performs the Kerchief Dance, with Chief Robert Dickson in the background. KFN Archives. EMPC. Land Claims Signing Images #19. PHOTOGRAPHER UNKNOWN

top middle Elder Margaret Johnson dances while Luke Johnson drums for her. KFN Archives. EMPC. Land Claims Signing Images #20. PHOTOGRAPHER UNKNOWN

top right Elder Agnes Johnson dances while Samuel Johnson, Russell Dickson, and Chief Robert Dickson clap. Gùdia Johnson and Bertha Doris are on the benches in the background. KFN Archives. EMPC. Land Claims Signing Images #21. PHOTOGRAPHER UNKNOWN

bottom left Federal DIAND minister Robert Nault dances at the celebrations. KFN Archives. EMPC. Land Claims Signing Images #22. PHOTOGRAPHER UNKNOWN

bottom right Former Chief Joe Joe Johnson holds grandson Nadaya at the end of the celebrations. KFN Archives. EMPC. Land Claims Signing Images #23. PHOTOGRAPHER UNKNOWN

PART TWO

KWÄDAY DAŃ UYE KWÀNJÌ

(Our Elders Remember)

TÙLHÀSÈN (LENA JOHNSON)

(b. 1926)

The Plan Was Really Good

My name is Tùlhàsèn, meaning "strong-minded person" in Dań K'è, our people's language, and my English name is Lena Johnson. I was born in 1929 down across the lake, between U Shè Dät'äla (Redtail Lake) and K'amà Dzêa (Ptarmigan Heart). I don't know exactly what part. My mom's name was Gùdia (Mary Johnson). We got quite a few Gùdia(s) around now. I got my daughter named Gùdia. And one of my nieces is Gùdia too. There's two or three Gùdia now; we just carry the name on through the mothers' side. It's a Khàjèt (Crow) name because we are of the Khàjèt (Crow Clan). My mother's mom was Èna (Emma Johnson). Everybody called her Asuà Shäw (Big Grandma). My grandpa's name was Sida Tà (Jimmy Johnson), son of Old Man Johnson and Gųya. He was my mom's dad.

overleaf Lhù'ààn Mân (Whitefish Place Lake, Kluane Lake) at sunset in summer with brilliant fireweed. The Ruby Range Mountains line the eastern shores while Thechàl Dhàl (Rock-Scraper Mountain, Sheep Mountain) rises to the west. KFN Archives. EMPC. Landscape Images #18. PHOTOGRAPHER ROBERT POSTMA

facing Tùlhàsèn (Lena Johnson), 2018. KFN Archives EMPC Elders Portraits #12. PHOTOGRAPHER ALISTAIR MAITLAND

My dad's name was Gă lhêla (Moose Johnson). His mom was Lily and his dad was Moose John, and he was raised at K'ùà Mân (Kloo Lake). Dad's Dán Yįzhì; Indian name was Gă lhêla. I don't know how he got that name; maybe from his adopted mother, I guess. He's tall; he's got Tlingit blood in him. I don't know how much, but he said he was adopted and that's where he got that name, Moose Johnson. When you look at him, you could see his features on his face. Got a little bit Tlingit blood. I wouldn't know when I was very small, but now I do. I could see the difference. Maybe from Klukwan, probably. He didn't talk to us kids about it. He's related to Dakwàkàta (Haines Junction). Sometimes they say "Chù Ts'al Chù"; that's where he used to take us. He just lived here in Burwash since he married my mom. Then he took us to K'ùà Mân, this side of Haines Junction. There was a village there. That's where his mom and dad were living, and his sisters and the rest of the family lived there. He'd bring us there from here. I had four brothers, Davis, Harvey, Joe, and Bernie, and one sister, Màdhįą (Eva).

THE YE SHÄW (ELDERS') PLAN WAS STRONG—ALWAYS THINKING AHEAD

In those days the trappers or Ye Shäw (Elders), they got a good plan. They make plan. When I got older, my dad and me just have a little meeting with other people that trap here. In springtime when the season close, they would get together and talk about where they gonna go. One person say, "I'm gonna go to K'ùà Mân (Kloo Lake) this year. I'm gonna trap there, then I'll be back sometime in spring, probably March, before the thawing. I'll bring back the family." And another one says, "Where we gonna trap next year?" They knew where they gonna trap next year. So that's how the plan was doing really good, you know, like that.

My dad and all the men, they have meetings about where they gonna trap next year. Where they gonna spend their winter. Was their family here or K'ùà Mân or Chù Ts'al Chù (Haines Junction)? So they really know what's gonna happen for the next year.

Always thinking ahead and where they gonna camp out to trap for the winter, where they gonna be staying, where it's gonna be the main camp, where they're gonna leave their family. The dad goes out for trapping; maybe two weeks, three weeks, he'll stay. He leaves the mother and children, and he goes out to trap. I remember my mom used to tie knots on the string for a calendar. Dad give Mom the day he'd be coming back to the main cabin where the children are. He said, "If I miss a week, I'll be ok and don't worry. If I am missing ten days or more, then something could've happened and get somebody to look for me." But he always came back the right date because my mom always make supper when Dad will come home and he always made us feel real special. They must have each had a string like that.

He camped out a long ways. He couldn't have come home every day or go out. His main areas were at Big Arm, down to the end the Talbot Creek, and this way below the Tatäy (Little Arm). Sam Johnson Sr. would go trap down the Lhù'ààn Mân Jälí (Headwaters of the Kluane River). That's how traplines were before government had registration. They had their own system and planning.

The plan was strong too. When they make plans, they gotta go through with it. If they don't, they sit up and they waste a talk for nothing. If it doesn't work, they would say that. But they gotta go through with what they say they gonna do. You have to back up what you say. You just don't speak out for nothing. You have to do it. I still do today. If I say I'm gonna go to Whitehorse tomorrow and if I didn't go, it's gone. It didn't come true. I have to back up to whoever I say it to. I have to say, "I'm sorry, I didn't make it." My word is gone; it's lost to me. That's what we learned too. We learn to back up what we say and plan what to do.

EVERYBODY HAVE FUN TOGETHER!

They make a plan where they gonna meet sometimes, just for visit. They all bring their kids, wife, mother to visit. They make a feast, cook for visitors, and everybody help. Oh, everybody have fun together!

I remember the men used to play cards. Not with money, just playing for matches or .22 shells, or something like that. They play cribbage too. I remember they put a blanket out in tent and all the guys sit on the blanket and they pass the cards around. The kids are playing around, and the ladies, mothers are visiting. They laugh and they cook together. It was fun in those days. They don't have to worry about anything. Don't have to go to store and buy something.

At the Jacquots' store here they only sell dry goods. Dry potatoes, dry carrots, dry vegetables all mixed. Everything dry because the people go out and trap. They need potatoes or anything fresh, it's just gonna freeze up. So Gene Jacquot used to bring dry goods, everything, all the vegetables dry. Dry onions, I remember, in a big, large can. I remember my mom would just grab some and put it in the soup, whatever she cooked. And potatoes—you have to soak it in the morning, dry potatoes, just sliced, and they soak it. By suppertime it would be all ready, so they put it in soup. Dried fruits too. Raisins and dry apples and dry peaches. That was a big treat in the winter. Oh yes, was it ever! Make rice pudding with it—oh, just great!

We travel with dog team. My mom and dad always have six working dogs in a team then. We had more dogs too. They would have four or five plus a leader. Mom had a

facing Tùlhàsèn (Lena Johnson) relaxing at the beach, circa 1950s. KFN Archives. EMPC. Lena Johnson Family Images #1. PHOTOGRAPHER UNKNOWN

above Tùlhàsèn (Lena Johnson) remembers old time parties, when people would get together and have fun playing cards and visiting. This image was taken at Burwash in 1926 and shows Tom Dickson seated in front surrounded by family and friends. CYFN Archives *Their Own Yukon*, #189, image credit Jessie Joe. PHOTOGRAPHER UNKNOWN

facing When Tùlhàsèn (Lena Johnson) was young, girls who were entering puberty were isolated in a tent or other shelter away from the community and wore a long hood plus special garments for several days or more to prepare them for adulthood. Kluane Museum of Natural History. Puberty hood, skirt 1975_86_y. PHOTOGRAPHER UNKOWN

couple kids, and my dad had a couple kids riding in the sled. When they took us when it's a cold winter ride in 30 below zero in the big sleigh, they covered our heads, covered our face under the eiderdown bedding. We just sit there in the dark riding until we get to where we were going. Couple hours sometimes to go from our main camp to the trapping camp. You'd have to camp halfway to get back to the camp. Our main camp was way over on the other side of the lake, down at the Big Arm. We have to make a camp halfway at a place called Raft Creek by Mäy Mẹl Dhal (Sheep Net Mountain).

Got nowhere to go in those days, just Jacquot Landing (Burwash). Come back from camp close to end of March. People get packed up to move back to Jacquot Landing. Trapping season is closed. Around March is when they had the big feast. When the weather gets warm, then you can have kids on a sleigh to go where you're gonna go.

I remember we spent Christmastime down at Big Arm. Only the dad comes back to Jacquot Landing to get Christmas stuff. They can't leave the kids, three or four kids, probably the baby be there too. So only the dad or the grandpa will come into Jacquot Landing, because it's dangerous. They come back at Christmas to buy candies by the case. They buy everything by the case, dry fruit, stuff like that. They can't make too many trips when they have to trap, takes too much time.

REALLY SMART PARENTS

At our camp would be Mom and Dad, my brothers and sisters and my grandparents, Mom's parents, all together. When Dad took us to K'ùà Mân (Kloo Lake), we got Dad's parents there too. They were really smart parents. Really teaching, talking to children, parents.

Obedience was another one when we were young kids. It was really important to be obedient. If Dad sent us to get something, maybe they just do that to teach us. If they left something like axe or any valuable stuff, something important, the dad sent the kids to go and get it. If you missed it, Dad will say, "I knew that you weren't listening when I was talking to you about that." He makes some certain mark where to go. Just like you draw map. So you go there, you come back with what you go to pick up. If you don't, the dad will sit you down and say, "I know you wasn't listening. You didn't obey what I was telling you. Now you gotta go back; now you gotta really listen. Go back second time." And you just go, what he said to do, what to look for, where you mark stuff like that. You just make a beeline there when you listen, then you go.

We learned how to care for one another. The first thing when we were growing up was to look after little ones, our brothers and sisters and other kids too. Not just in the family, it's all through the village. When we get here, everybody is babysitter for one another. Not just go to your relatives—anybody. They trust each other. The trust was really strong. If the parents are gone overnight somewhere hunting, they said to Grandma, "I'm leaving the kids." Grandma agree. So to relate to one another as children, it was good too.

THE HIGHWAY CHANGED EVERYTHING

We never heard too much ahead of time about the Alaska Highway. But one day when we went by Frank Sketch's store at K'ùà Mân (Kloo Lake), we heard the army started build a road by Watson Lake. How we know that is they have Native guides, people to guide how people travel. Surveying. That's how they got this highway through from here to Beaver

Creek into Alaska, with Native people. I don't think they get too much credit for doing that. I think it was really hard work. That's how they go, by traditional trails. That's how. There's Native guys who were guiding them where the trail would go. How you get to Whitehorse from Watson Lake, and Whitehorse to Champagne, and to the head of the lake.

Here they already have that wagon road; they call that Jacquots' Wagon Road. They use wagon. I remember we went on a wagon right up to Jedälį Tl'äw Käy (Duke Meadow) from Lhù'ààn Mân (Burwash). We're all just a bunch of kids crowded on, just jump on, go for a ride.

The people knew the highway was coming through here. They know that, so they took the children and they went to Lhù'ààn Mân Jèdàlį (Down Below) or to Tatäy (Little Arm). Took their kids and they were scared. There were some older girls, and the soldiers were looking for girls. So they took all their family and camp away.

My dad tell us, "There's gonna be different looking people. We are brown people, and dark people will come." They let us know about different looking people coming from all over different countries. We were just scared of armies. I think kids were scared of them and parents probably scared too.

Us girls, we learned to sew. When highway came through, our parents teach us how to sew. We turn to be ts'agen (ladies); that's when you learnt to sew. They put you out in little tent. You have to sit there. The mother and the grandmother always come, cut out pattern for you to stitch it together. How many times that could happen. Undo it, undo it to make it perfect.

Ye Shäw (Elders) would come, tell you what to do, to sew, and to be nice to people. You don't get to keep anything; you give it away. You don't cook there; the

parents does—big pot of stew or wild meat. Whoever visit would give the girl a piece of bannock and tea, maybe soup. They put us in a ts'agen ts'at (woman's hood). Some one hundred years before me they make that. You just had to do what you're told to do, sit there; and really all these people stayed there for thirty days as young girls. But I only did two weeks. I learnt to sew. Other girls and the grandparents that I'm talking about said they stayed three to four months and longer.

When they walked, they brought you out to set the ga tth'emęl (rabbit snare) and go for traps. Whatever they're doing, you walk with them, but you have to walk underneath that hood. You don't take it off and look around outside. You just see what's in front of you, and you walk. It's the only place you can see. Now today you just

facing Tsal (Arctic ground squirrel, commonly called gopher) is a valuable and plentiful resource in the Yukon—as a source of protein for people, bears, and other predators, as well as of beautiful fur for clothing and blankets. KFN Archives. EMPC. Wildlife Images #8. PHOTOGRAPHER ALANNA DICKSON

put a nice blanket over them. The girl just sit underneath a blanket like a little hoodie.

All we know the highway gonna change the whole of Yukon, Native part. It's not gonna be the same. People always shared the trapline, like my dad say, "You're gonna trap here this year." So he traps here, couple years, maybe go back to his parents, take the kids and mother back to K'ùà Mân (Kloo Lake). Spend a winter there, probably summer too, just to be with his grandparents. And he always heard that something's gonna change, something's not gonna be the same.

Grandma Jessie Joe, her great-great grandpa, I think it was, had a dream. This was right after ice age probably. He had a dream. He said big, huge sūa (bird) landing. It landed and out of that sūa, bunch of people just came out, all over. Here he's talking about a plane. But he didn't know plane, so he calls it a sūa. He said that's going to change the whole way we live. Everything's not gonna be the same. All the people going to come out of that sūa stomach, he said.

Grandma Jessie remember when she was very young, she heard that story. He wasn't talking to her directly, but from what we know, kids are listening to hear. Even when they play around, they listen. That's how she listen to Ye Shäw (Elders) talking like that. That story went from generation to generation. Now what she said he dreamt then, that's happening now. That's why you see all these people come off the plane. They just go all over, like prospector just everywhere. And that's how his dream was, and that's how his dream came true. That's what Grandma Jessie Joe was saying.

Another thing he said, we used to have hundreds and thousands of mäzi (caribou) migrate up to Yukon, and it's not gonna happen after years passed. He said, "I dream about mäzi." And in his dream mäzi were talking to one another. And the mäzi, they were telling each other, "We gonna stop migrate, coming to this part of Yukon." They didn't say Yukon then; I don't know what they called it in those days anyway. Then they question each other, and they say, "Why are we not going there anymore?" And they said, "We were not treated good." They said, "We go there to be treated good, to look after meat. Our parts of our body got thrown all over, and nobody cared. They jumping all over our flesh and stuff like that. They not respecting us, so we gonna stop going, coming, migrate."

I remember one time we started for Jedàlį (Down Below). Here there was just big, black streak going across. It was all mäzi (caribou), going across. I was very young; I can't even remember how old I was. That was the last time Grandma Jessie Joe said mäzi came. Might be.

They tried to protect us. There were a few mäzi (caribou) left here. Nobody supposed to kill it, but sometimes people do. Village people knew they gotta save that mäzi so next generations can hunt them too. I heard some people from other place got mäzi one by one here. Now they come just across the border in Alaska—Northway, Alaska. Oh, they just all up there. We see it like that in Northway too. And it was with Dorothy Johnson, who's in hospital now; we just went to visit some friends down there. We saw mäzi go across. I wondered if somebody bulldozed across because it looked like somebody had built a road. We looked really hard, and here it was all caribou!

Well, highway change everything. You able to get a ride to Chù Ts'al Chù (Haines Junction) and down to Ät'ayat Chù (White River), where we had Zana Ka Nanáàje (Muskrat Camp). The priest here, Father Morisset, was 20 years old when he came here. He was here until about 1965. He was lots of help, with his green pickup. Moving people to Zana Ka Nanáàje in the springtime; sometime bring somebody to Kwanlin (Whitehorse) and to Chù Ts'al Chù.

After that people start cutting wood in summertime to make money, and they bought a car. I think Gene Jacquot brought a Model T Ford before the highway to the head of the lake. They had a barge to bring stuff in to The Landing, so they brought that car on the barge and it came here. My uncle Sam bought it from Gene Jacquot. He used to pile us kids up and take it to the bush. Cars were already here when I got kids, so they never really camped with a dog team like I did.

People had gas motorboat too. My great-grandpa had a big gas boat and give everybody a ride across the lake to camp. When we camp, like at spring camp, the lake melts too fast, so we just got to stay there, till the ice melt. Later Grandpa would bring the boat over and bring the kids back.

HARD TIMES

We had no warning before the Park (Kluane Game Sanctuary) was made. Park people, Game people came. We have to sign papers. Native people agree that they gonna close down that west side across the Alaska Highway. Yes, everybody sign. They talk to all the older guys, who were just young then. They said, "It's going to be tons of people going to drive through, use that land. People just gonna shoot, leave animals; they gonna kill everything off, back there. In order to save animals have to keep it closed from travellers from other side of world." Many people did shoot too many animals. That happened lots of time. People saw this.

I kind of agree they knew what they talking about then. And that's why, they said, they not shutting us out, but making Park to protect that land, to save your animals. If you don't shut it down, people from other side of world going to come through, going to shoot moose, shoot bear. Dead bear was found. Quite a few moose been found. People just cut the steak out and leave the whole thing. Setting aside the land for a park, that part was good if they did that. The older guys who sign all those paper, after they were explained what will happen, they agree and sign those papers. Village people here agree to it.

People had to fish, set nets here when the Park was made. We can't go across the road to kill anything. You get in trouble. So we just gotta push against the lake here. We just live on fish in this place. If anybody went in there and got a moose, they get charged and go to court. Yes, we change. Just had to stick to the fish and gopher and little animals like rabbits. We had to go camp other places, not stay here or we would have starved. We go down to Tatäy (Little Arm), or Ät'ayat Chù (White River), Dän Zhür Chù (Donjek); there's lots of place at the south end of the lake.

above Tùlhàsèn (Lena Johnson) with her cousin's children and her son after their confirmation ceremony at the new Roman Catholic Rectory in Burwash, circa 1968. *Left to right:* Da Kwäthala mą (Joyce Johnson), George Johnson (Lena's son), Tùlhàsèn, and Salkaaya (Bertha Johnson). KFN Archives. EMPC. Lena Johnson Family Images #2. PHOTOGRAPHER UNKNOWN

facing top Teaching her language to young people has been a long time commitment for Tùlhàsèn (Lena Johnson), which she continues in Burwash to this day. KFN Archives. EMPC. Lena Johnson Family Images #3. PHOTOGRAPHER UNKNOWN

facing bottom Granddaughter Math'ieya (née Johnson) Alatini in Burwash, early 1980s. KFN Archives. EMPC. Lena Johnson Family Images #4. PHOTOGRAPHER UNKNOWN

We camp back there in the mountains before the highway and the Park to get some sheep. When they shut it down, nobody can go in there. When anybody go in there, you feel like you're stealing. You're stealing something. So you just avoid it. We can't go in there. Sometime people do anyway, and we had to pack the moose out in the middle of night. Well, it's really hard. We have hard time for that part.

So people had to start going to court. Choppers used to just fly back and forth during season times. If government people see a moose killed, they just land right there. You get charged. And that's how my uncle Sam got trouble.

Government person said we allowed to trap muskrat down to Ät'ayat Chù (White River). And people went there camping, because they said it was ok for us to go there and trap now. Meantime other people said they were not allowed to go trap there. My uncle Sam was pretty old, about 70s or almost 80s, I guess. They camp out there, with everybody's grandchildren and his wife, like people do a good long time ago. Uncle Sam got 200, 300 muskrats on his plan. When he sells these, he's gonna buy car with it. And then the Game Officer guys from Haines Junction went down there and took all these muskrats. They went into his camp and said, "We're taking it." So they took it, and they took his gun too. Grandpa Sam got a stroke. He lost so much that he wanted to buy with that muskrat money. The ambulance had to go there because he got a heart attack. Later on they said, "Oh, it's a mistake. That part was open to trap." I don't really know what happened after that. All I know is they went to court.

ELIJAH SMITH STARTED LAND CLAIMS

I went with my brother Joe Joe Johnson to quite a few land claims meetings. Elijah Smith got him involved. Joe Jacquot and he started off all the land claims. Elijah used to work here when he was a young man. He helped to build the old lodge down here. I remember when he was working, he used to come to my mom and dad's camp to eat moose meat and stuff like that. He'd go there and visit; that's how well known a person Elijah Smith was.

He was smart as a young person. That's how, when he came back from Europe and the war, he and Joe Jacquot started all this land claims. Elijah saw what's happening in other countries. He wanted training. Training for young people here to look after their land. He said everything's gonna change. Young people have to grow up in that and learn to look after their land, their way of life for Native people. Yes, he already got everybody going to train them, to learn, and he did lots of work in his lifetime.

We don't go to all the land claims meetings that they have. They have it in Whitehorse with Elijah Smith speaking. To us I think it's not going to be the same. It's going to change. Young people will change. Ye Shäw (Elders) be gone and young people have to learn to survive. How do you survive without the store long time ago? You don't have k'wäns (potatoes), you don't have vegetables, but what you do, you pick out some thaw (bear roots) and stuff like that, and nän zhùr (berries). You pack food, and you don't eat a whole bunch at one time, just maybe once a day: nàń-dhäy (blueberries), ń-tl'àt (low bush cranberries), nän zhùr' (ground berry), just everything.

IT'S LIKE A DIAMOND TO HAVE GREAT-GRANDCHILDREN

My mom passed away just after I turned 16. Who do I have to look after then? My brothers, Harvey, Bernie, and Joe. My brother Joe Joe called me Mom for a long time. He must have been about 4 then. Bernie was the baby. Oh, not by myself, the whole community, all the people and all the grandmas helped me.

I went to the Catholic school here for a few years. I did my grade 5 here at the Burwash Indian Day School with Father Morisset. I got married and had three kids, but after my husband left, I raised my children on my own. That's how, when my partner left me with three kids, and the youngest one was just maybe 8 months old, I said, "I'm young enough and I'm strong enough to bring these kids up," and I did. They all finished school, and their children went to university. That's a part of me. My brother Joe Joe too. We had really intelligent grandparents on both sides, mother's side and dad's side.

After all my kids grew up, I went to Whitehorse to the Vocational School and did up to grade 8, and got my GED. I lived in Whitehorse probably three winters around '72. My first granddaughter was born in 1972. When I finished there, I went to study at Yukon Native Language Centre with John Ritter in Whitehorse Elementary School basement. Then I went to Yukon College for two years to study Native Language and to the University of Alaska in Fairbanks.

Any Ye Shäw (Elder) Grandma is a grandma to your children. Not just one. Got four or five of them Elder Grandma,

top Great-grandmother Tùlhàsèn (Lena Johnson) with grandkids left to right: Becky Miller-Hundrup, Math'ieya Alatini, and Geordan Clark with great-granddaughter Lenita Alatini in front. KFN Archives. EMPC. Lena Johnson Family Images #5. PHOTOGRAPHER UNKNOWN

bottom Tùlhàsèn (Lena Johnson) is renowned for her beautifully crafted slippers and other beadwork. KFN Archives. EMPC. Lena Johnson Family Images #6. PHOTOGRAPHER UNKNOWN

probably more; they are all the kids' grandma. That's my grandma too. That's how we used to be. So everybody was babysitter for one another. And everybody looking after these grandchildren like their own grandchildren. All the grandchildren here in the village just call me Grandma. Even to all the teachers I'm still Grandma Lena! Even the big guys, no matter how old they are, it's Grandma all the time.

That's where I'm really thankful today. Sometime I see kids not knowing their grandparents, and I feel sorry for them. Education really came to me from my grandparents, half and half. To listen. Listen to the stories. Listen to how you can treat people. Just to think back now, the kindest grandparents I had and that's why I am what I am today. I raise my own children, help out with my grandchildren, and now my great-grandchildren. I am going to babysit them today. It's like a diamond to have great-grandchildren. They pretty smart kids too. I mean, not coming from me, coming from way back, from grandparents who passed it on.

Today kids just watch cartoons or play computer games. They don't know what's going on. Even little baby, toddlers, they just watch that. I see some parents put cartoon on, let their baby just watch, and next thing you know, iPad. Little kids even learn to compete about something: "I got this; you don't got that." Our kids in my day learn to share. They share anything. The grandparents and parents just share everything too.

USE YOUR BRAIN TO SURVIVE AND KNOW WHAT TO DO

Now it's changed, not the same anymore. Not too many things could happen in the old, old days. Everything was just to do what they know to do. My teachers were my mother and Asuà Shäw (Big Grandma). And other Elders, ladies in town, whoever lived in that village.

To teach, Ye Shäw (Elders) sometime cut out slippers, and they'll bring it to you. Some grandmas will stitch your pattern together where it starts. Mbàt ür (gloves), ke (moccasins)—you really gotta go by direction, by the pattern. And if it's not done right, then, "I'm sorry, you have to undo it, do it again. Make it look nicer." It does, maybe second time around, come a little bit better. They don't do it too much though, because the young girl sitting there get tired too. Undo it, redo it, redo it like that. I think maybe twice, they could do it. After that they just leave it, but they use it. They know it's going to get better, as you go older.

Today bigger boys need to know how to shoot kanäy (moose) and learn how to prepare it, skin it, and bring it home. And how to take care of all parts of kanäy: than (moose meat and moose body), the kanäy dhù (skin) and kanäy thì (head),

and everything. Not too much of those older guys left now. Older women are gone, too, with their skills, and it's not the same today. Not many of them know how to skin or prepare skin. The bigger children have to want to learn. You have to tell them, "Come, learn this with me." Today's young people are just busy with their own life now, working, making money. They gotta be taught how to make money too.

I want them to learn to survive because other thing we're hearing, we're going to run out of everything in the world like processed food. They got that food now that's already cooked, and some kids don't even know how to cook. Just open up a package, heat it up. I want my great-grandchildren not to get completely out of that, but to still go down to learn how to survive, how to raise your kids. I want some of that learning to go to them.

Well, you can't prepare for that big wind on the lake. If you get down across the lake, then sometimes people get stranded a couple days across there. If you know how to catch squirrel, rabbits, gophers, then you'd be all right. Then you don't starve. Or eat nän zhùr (berries), something like that. Just cook them; säl (gophers), ga (rabbits), roast it. If you got no pot, you had to roast it. You put it on a stick, hang it by the fire, keep turning it. When you get stranded, you do that. You don't have to have pots or a pan to cook in. Always got to use your brain to survive and know what to do.

Tl'áhų kwach'e' (that's all).

above Passing on her knowledge is important for Tùlhàsèn (Lena Johnson) so that young people will know how to survive. Here she is teaching Shàwkwälita (Nathan Easterson-Moore) how to tan a moosehide. KFN Archives. EMPC. Lena Johnson Family Images #7. PHOTOGRAPHER UNKNOWN

Come, learn this with me!

TÙLHÀSÈN (LENA JOHNSON)

GUSHÀKA (GRACE MARGARET JOHNSON)

(b. 1929)

Living the Old Ways

My mom was Copper Lily and my dad was Jimmy Johnson (Sida Tà) from Selkirk. My dad was a Chief, and had two wives, Emma, and my mom. My mom's traditional name is Tsal KàJana (Gopher Lady, Copper Lily) and now my granddaughter Juanita Johnson is named after her. My traditional name is Gushàka and this name was given to me by my grandpa, Copper Joe. I was born in Burwash Landing on November 10, 1929, in a tent. I was given my English name Margaret by my family when I was born. When I went to school the Catholic Church gave me the name Grace. Today I am called Margaret by all my family and friends.

facing Gushàka (Grace Margaret Johnson), 2017. She was given the name Grace when baptized in the Roman Catholic Church; however, people know her today as Margaret. EMPC Elders Portraits #13. PHOTOGRAPHER ALISTAIR MAITLAND

PEOPLE WORKED HARD

We were taught as young children to be hard workers. In those days there were no running water or machine to split wood. We packed our own water, chopped our own wood, and used a big whip saw to cut our wood. We hauled our wood with toboggan and sled dogs. Lots of wood then, not like now. We would go anywhere and get wood on this land.

We all had to be handy. My aunt Jessie Joe would chop the ice, and we would get water. There could have been six tents, so we made sure everyone got water and wood. The kids had to be trained, so each one would help with wood and water. It stays like that for a long time. Now they got running water, so we do not see that anymore. When kids were asked to help, we did it right away, never say no, because they are training us. People worked hard a long time ago. Right now everything is easy.

My dad would make a boat out of wood, and I remember it was a long one too. They got motor behind, took us way down there to Big Arm. You need a boat like this in summertime. Take all the dogs inside the boat, come back, take us down there. I been all over there. We would hunt squirrels and rabbits. We would eat rabbits. I remember Dad catching them down the Big Arm. There were no Parks people back then to stop us from hunting when we needed food. Sometimes we get two or three moose. I remember we got six caribous around Big Arm. In the wintertime we would cut the legs off and hang them in the cache. In the summer months we would make dry meat sometime.

Long time ago people travel with toboggan and sled dogs. This is how people travel around. I travel everywhere on this land, mainly to hunting and trapping grounds. Where my mom and dad went, I would go. I was the middle child in our family and travelled a lot with my older sisters Bessie and Helen. In the wintertime my sister and dad got one toboggan each. Mom, she got five dogs; my sister got three. My dad maybe got six. My dad make toboggan with wood, and this way they haul the wood to make fire. My mom would cut down poplar trees and bring them down and tie onto the toboggan. My dad would make the whole toboggan, and sometimes he would make us a sleigh out of moosehide and babiche. We would use it to play around with, like sliding down the hill.

A lot of people made their own snowshoes. This was made from birch trees, and it had to be good ones. Snowshoes were steamed with water so that they can shape them and then laced from outside to middle with babiche. Snowshoes were used to track and chase moose or caribou. Sometime snow too deep, you stay on top of snow with snowshoes. With boots you fall in.

PEOPLE HAVE FUN

A lot of things have changed now, and how do we try to straighten it out, I really do not know. It makes me sad. Our old ways are gone, and it is hard to teach over.

above Tsal KàJana (Copper Lily) and Tàa'aana (Jessie Joe) at Burwash, circa 1970s. KFN Archives. EMPC. Dorothy Johnson Family Images #5. PHOTOGRAPHER UNKNOWN

facing top Older Elders remember the fun everyone had at Christmastime in the 1920s and 30s when people came in from their traplines and gathered together to visit and share food, stories, and laughter. CYFN Archives. *Their Own Yukon*, #188, image credit Jessie Joe. PHOTOGRAPHER UNKNOWN

facing bottom Gushàka (Margaret Johnson) cutting and hanging fish to dry in the traditional way. KFN Archives. EMPC. Sharon Kabanak Family Images #15. PHOTOGRAPHER SHARON KABANAK

Everything white man way now. Everything too easy today, cars, Ski-Doo, four-wheeler. Long time ago when we want to go somewhere, we just hook up the dogs to the sleigh, and we just go. The dogs always know we are going some place, and they were not lazy. They go through training as puppies to be leader, and this one goes up front to lead the other dogs. They know when we are going to leave for somewhere; they all bark and want to go. The dogs were taught commands to turn right, left, and stop. Little doghouses were made for the dogs when the weather is cold. You can see some homemade doghouses along the beach here. They would put grass as beds for the dogs.

We fished in the lake right across there. Who is going to set net now? My mom, aunt Jessie Joe, and sometime my sisters, we all go across the lake and set net under the ice in wintertime. Weather sometimes cold, 20 to 30 below, we still had to take the fish out of the net. They got a cache, near house over there across the lake. Sometimes 300–400 fish in one day. They used a lot of fish for dog food; dogs got to eat too. Mom and sister Bertha would go across and set fishnet too. Now it is hard to get fish over there; lake do not freeze right away.

There was no Ski-Doo that time. When the cars come this way, no more dog team. I tell you lots of story yet. Sometimes we will go down to Onion Creek. My dad had cabin there. From there they all go down Fort Selkirk for Christmas. No alcohol at that time. When everything was done at Selkirk, we come back and stay here. My dad, sisters, and Alice [Johnson], they would go to Kloo Lake for New Year's. They travelled by dog team. New Year's would be a happy, laughing, and joyous time for everyone. Men would go out and get a moose, and my mom would have campfire where they cut the meat. Men would play card games for matches and shells all day long, lots of laughter. Everything is changed now. Long time ago people have fun.

My daddy used to snare wolves, lynx, and coyotes. He also used spring traps, and they were set by putting your feet here on one side and then you open it up. There was trading post down in Burwash, and Daddy would trade furs to buy food. Once in a while we go to store, and people would give us candy.

above Gushàka (Margaret) with her son Nuzhia (Billy) and daughter Salkaaya (Bertha). KFN Archives. EMPC. Margaret Johnson Family Images #1. PHOTOGRAPHER UNKNOWN

DADDY TELLS STORIES

My daddy tells us stories about respecting animals. Yes, there are certain animals you need to respect, like otter. Stories say that he has medicine, so there are ways you take him out of the snare or traps. Bears, too, you really need to respect this animal. He is a powerful animal. Long time ago only selected people would skin this animal out, and I think it is practiced here. I know that Gracie Southwick, Luke Johnson, and Pauly Sias can do this. No woman who is pregnant could step over it when it is dead or could they work on it. The story says that the woman bearing a child could lose that child by stepping over it. It is powerful animal.

My half-sister Jenny was born at K'amà Dzêa (Ptarmigan Heart). It is shaped like a moose heart. I been there not too long ago with Gùdia Johnson, and I took a picture. The middle is shaped like a heart. Lots of cranberries there, and my mom and dad had a trapping cabin there. We spent summertime over there, hunting and picking berries. Some time Emma Johnson would come with us. Not many visitors that time. Jack Allen and Uncle Jimmy Joe once in a while would come to see us.

When I was very young, I was taught to sew beadwork and later learn to make all kinds of things, like mukluks, mitts, everything. I teach my daughter, Bertha, how to sew when she was 9 years old. I started training her then. I would cut out patterns for her, and now she does this all on her own. I always tell her try this pattern or do this one here. She always did.

WORKING FOR MY FAMILY

I started working at Joe Chouinard's at airport, used to be a restaurant and motel there. I was only 16 then. I would help with making beds and sometimes work in the restaurant. I would set squirrel snares down below at Buck Dickson's place. I wanted to work and make money so I could buy nice things, like high heel shoes, fancy shoes, and hairbands. As young girls we wanted to go to Whitehorse, but my mom said no.

First trip to Whitehorse, I was 20 years old. I moved my family—it was only Bertha then—to Whitehorse. She was just small then when they took her away to Lower Post from Burwash to go to school.

My sister Helen was already living at Jakes Corner and trapping. My husband, Gilbert Nicholson, worked for Canada Bridge, and we got to do lots of travel to B.C. and throughout the Yukon. Once he finished with Canada Bridge, he bought trapline at Jakes Corner. He built a house there, and we live there for a long time. I would go and trap for lynx, squirrels, martin, mink, and fox. I did this by myself; sometimes I carry baby on my back, but I go. I did well with trapping and money help to buy my kids clothes and food. I did this for many years until all my children had to go to school. We move to Whitehorse.

At that time Gilbert started to get sick. He taught me how to drive a car when I was 38 years old, never drive before in my life. I got my driver's licence when I was 38. Gilbert passed away in 1982, and I started working as soon as I got my driver's licence. I worked in Whitehorse in many hotels: the Westmark Whitehorse, the Shannon, and the Yukon Inn. I enjoyed working, and I still had four kids at home to feed. No more husband to help me. I retired from work at the age of 72.

above Gushàka (Margaret Johnson) is an active participant in language workshops, always generously sharing her cultural knowledge with Youth and with anyone who wants to learn. Here she is preparing porcupine feet at the 2018 Kluane First Nation Big Horn Culture Camp. KFN Archives. EMPC. Elders Portraits #14. PHOTOGRAPHER ALISTAIR MAITLAND

overleaf Gushàka (Margaret Johnson) enjoying a summer walk in the mountains during the Kluane First Nation Big Horn Culture Camp in 2018. KFN Archives. EMPC. Elders Portraits #15. PHOTOGRAPHER ALISTAIR MAITLAND

LANGUAGE COMES FROM MY HEART

We had to learn the language as young babies and children. My aunt Mary, Jessie Joe, and Grandpa would tell stories to me and to my sisters. I hear my mom telling stories to my niece Joyce in the language. We not like that anymore; it's different now. Our parents taught us about the land, the plants, birds, and animals. We would always be asking questions when we go out. "What is this? How you say it?" That is how we learn, no English those days only in the language. The land teaches the language.

In the late 70s, early 1980s, I went back to school with Daniel Tlen at Yukon College. There was Lena and a couple of older people from here. We graduated from the program to work as a language teacher. I have taught at the daycare for almost nine years. Children are cute when they speak the language. I continue to teach and mentor to whoever wants to learn. I do a lot of translation work for Kluane First Nation and do mentorship to two young people: Luke Campbell from Champagne/Aishihik First Nations and Sachi Umą (Sleeping Mother, Sharda Ayotte-O'Connor) from Burwash. I still drive, but RCMP told me not to drive to Kluane Daycare anymore, only in Haines Junction—no more highway driving for me. I passed my road test at 92 years old.

Lena and I sit on the Tutchone Heritage Society Board of Directors, and we both try to help the young people to learn the language. We are old now, and we need leaders to take our place. Who are we going to ask to do this?

Language comes from my heart, and I want to teach everyone, even children and young people who come to visit me. My aunts Jessie Joe and Mary Jacquot and my mom tell me not to hold it back and do not lose it and to share it, so that's what I do today.

Thank you for talking to me today. I am happy.

A lot of things have changed now, and how do we try to straighten it out, I really do not know.
GUSHÀKA (GRACE MARGARET JOHNSON)

KÄNDHÄDA (DOROTHY JOHNSON)

(1934–2020)

Learn from Your Parents

Kändhäda (Dorothy Johnson) of the Crow Clan was born on Christmas Day, 1934, in her parents' winter cabin at Thè K'u (Salmon Patch) along the Kluane River. Her mother was Shada Zhan Mą (Humming As She Works, Jessie Allen), daughter of Old Man and Monica Allen. Her father was Shùglità (Good Hunter, Sam Johnson Sr.), son of Èna (Emma) and Jimmy Johnson. She was the oldest of ten children, including four sisters, Agnes, Mary, Gloria, and Alyce, and five brothers, Kirk, Edward, Michael, Sam, and Gordon.

facing Kändhäda (Dorothy Johnson), 2018. KFN Archives. EMPC. Elders Portraits #16. PHOTOGRAPHER ALISTAIR MAITLAND

Dorothy resided at Thomson Centre in Whitehorse in her last years and was unable to record her stories. Her sister Agnes and other family members compiled her chapter.

CAMP LIFE AT THÈ K'U

The only way into the winter camp in those days was by dog team. Dorothy's parents continued to live there for many years, supporting their children and teaching them to live on the land. There she learned sewing and beadwork from her mother and grandmother. Dorothy followed that traditional lifestyle all her life, speaking Southern Tutchone as her first language and sharing stories about her youth. Her favourite memory was about her parents rewarding the cleanest, tidiest kid in their camp. She said she always won because she put her spruce boughs in their tent very tightly and always very neatly.

MOVING TO BURWASH

The Johnson family moved to Burwash Landing in the 1940s. Dorothy attended the Catholic mission day school taught by Father Morisset. When she was 16, she was sent to the Roman Catholic Indian residential school at Lower Post. She stayed there just one year and then came home to Burwash.

After Dorothy returned from Lower Post, she met Arnold Allinger of Chico, California, who had come to visit his brother Leland, who owned the Burwash Lodge. Dorothy worked there as a chambermaid and dishwasher. Dorothy and Arnold lived together in a house above the gas station for several years. After ten years Arnold went back to California.

Dorothy moved to the village to raise her children, Arnold, Liz, Richie, and Hughie, in the "old house," which overlooked the lake. She stayed there until the early 1990s.

Dorothy was born at a time when Dań K'è (Southern Tutchone) was spoken as her first language. She learned English when her family moved to Burwash. Being a fluent speaker she was happy to be close to the traditional Elders there, who were always speaking the language and sharing songs, laughter, and stories.

HARD-WORKING SINGLE MOM

Life was very difficult in those days. There was no running water in Burwash homes then, and Dorothy and the kids carried water in buckets up from the lake. The house was heated with wood that had to be cut, split, and packed into the house as well. Dorothy worked very hard to raise her

top Sam and Jessie Johnson at Roman Catholic Church in Burwash circa 1952 with children Kirk, Mary, and baby Gloria in Sam's arms. Unidentified priest is behind them. KFN Archives. EMPC. Dorothy Johnson Family Images #6. PHOTOGRAPHER UNKNOWN

bottom Father Morisset with children at Roman Catholic Day School in Burwash, circa 1948. KFN Archives. EMPC. Dorothy Johnson Family Images #7. PHOTOGRAPHER UNKNOWN

children alongside her sister Agnes and her family. Over time things became a little easier for people in Burwash with better housing, electricity, and running water in homes. It was a tight-knit community where everyone looked out for one another.

Dorothy was always busy. She was an incredibly hard worker, always gardening, sewing, or cleaning. She was very particular about how she kept her home, and everything had its place. She loved to walk, and every day she walked all over Burwash to visit people.

Dorothy was a very spiritual person. She attended Mass in Burwash at the famous Our Lady of the Holy Rosary Catholic Church with her children for years every Sunday. In the 1970s Dorothy, Lena, Margaret, and others from Haines Junction joined the Yukon Bible Fellowship Church and were very actively involved in it for many years. They attended prayer meetings all over the Yukon and Alaska, where they sang, praised the Lord, and studied the bible.

TRADITIONAL SEAMSTRESS AND HERITAGE WORKER

Dorothy was also very interested in heritage and cultural work. She was an avid collector of traditional songs and stories. She brought a tape recorder when she attended Potlatches in Northway, to record the music, songs, and stories to share with her family in Burwash.

In the early 1970s Dorothy's former home became the first Burwash Museum, and she worked there for several years. In 1973 a new, larger building was constructed under the leadership of Father Huijbers, and the museum was renamed the Kluane Museum of Natural History. It was located closer to the highway and attracted many visitors through the summer season. Dorothy worked seasonally for over twenty years at the new museum from its opening until her retirement in 1995. She was a founding member of the Yukon Historical & Museums Association in 1977, attending meetings and participating in heritage training workshops for many years to learn more about the care of museum artifacts.

Dorothy was also renowned for her sewing, beadwork, and jewellery, especially her beaded necklaces and hairpins, along with beaded bone and hide belts, which were very popular art pieces sold at the museum. She had a special eagle motif that she used in her beadwork, along with other distinctive Burwash designs.

top Dorothy with a visitor at the new Kluane Museum of Natural History shortly after it opened in 1973. She worked at the museum for decades and was a member of the Yukon heritage community, attending museum workshops and conferences in Whitehorse. KFN Archives. EMPC. Dorothy Johnson Family Images #8. PHOTOGRAPHER UNKNOWN

bottom Dorothy was known for her beautiful sewing, especially her beaded necklaces, which she made for family and also sold at the Kluane Museum of Natural History. KFN Archives. EMPC. Dorothy Johnson Family Images #9. PHOTOGRAPHER UNKNOWN

top Dorothy's father, Shùglità (Sam Johnson Sr.), circa 1980s. KFN Archives. EMPC. Elders Portraits #17. PHOTOGRAPHER UNKNOWN

middle Dorothy and her mom, who was known in her community as Jessia or Jessie. Her Dań K'è name was Shada Zhan Mą, which means "Humming As She Works." KFN Archives. EMPC. Elders Portraits #18. PHOTOGRAPHER UNKNOWN

bottom Dorothy Johnson, circa 1990s. KFN Archives. EMPC. Elders Portraits #19 PHOTOGRAPHER UNKNOWN

facing Dorothy loved to gather resources from the land, including picking rhubarb at this bountiful patch at Copper Joe Subdivision near Burwash. KFN Archives. EMPC. Sharon Kabanak Family Images #16. PHOTOGRAPHER SHARON KABANAK

DUKE MEADOW MEMORIES

In the early 1990s Dorothy's son Arnold wanted to renovate her house, so she moved to her late aunt Nellie's house, next to her mother, Jessie. There she stayed and never moved back to the "old house." Dorothy was a homebody who was always happiest in Burwash being close to her cherished family and familiar places.

As a very active KFN citizen and community member, Dorothy loved attending general assemblies, cultural gatherings, and events. She always generously contributed her knowledge and continued speaking her language.

Dorothy's favourite place was her parents' camp at Duke Meadow, where she spent a lot of time during the summers, trapping gophers, picking berries, and visiting and helping her parents. Whenever her dad shot a moose, she would go and help her mom cut up the meat. Even after her parents passed, she still loved going to Duke Meadow to share her memories and experiences with her children and grandchildren. They had many family trips out on the land in the summers to pick berries and go to Longs Creek to get fish.

LEARN FROM YOUR PARENTS!

In 2016 a serious fall meant Dorothy had to leave her beloved community of Burwash to live at the Thomson Centre in Whitehorse. She missed her home every day but kept her cheerful demeanour and enjoyed the many visits she received from family and community people. Although she always wanted to go home, she made many good friends during her time at the Thomson Centre with her smiles and laughter.

Dorothy left the world on her own terms and on the same day that she arrived, Christmas Day, in 2020. Her loving and caring legacy lives on in her children, grandchildren, and large extended family. She left them her many recordings of songs and language, her beautiful sewing and beadwork, and her traditional hide work and lovely patterns. She loved the Burwash Museum, where she had shared her stories, which she could do with grace because she had listened really carefully to the Elders in her early years in order to pass their words on to future generations.

Dorothy always told young people, "Learn from your parents. If they tell you what to do, you do it and then you will learn."

Learn from your parents... then you will learn.

KÄNDHÄDA (DOROTHY JOHNSON)

UNDERWATER
CONSTRUCTION, INC.
Anchorage, Alaska
Marine & Oilfield Services

KOOŁSEEN (HANK JACQUOT)

(1934–2021)

I'll Tell You a Story

I was born in Whitehorse on February 7th, 1934, at the old hospital there. My mother was Ruth Mary Dickson. Her nickname was Pete. She was born in Carcross around 1902. My dad's name was Eugene Jacquot. He was from Alsace in France. He and his brother Louie [Louis] were the founders of Burwash. After my parents married, they lived in Burwash. They had five sons: Eugene Jr., Joe, Lou, Hank, and Larry.

facing Koołseen (Hank Jacquot), 2019. KFN Archives. EMPC. Elders Portraits #20. PHOTOGRAPHER ALISTAIR MAITLAND

My mother was descended from coastal Tlingit and Tagish people. Her mother, my grandma Louise George, was born at Yandeist'akyé, a Tlingit village at the mouth of the Chilkat River near Haines, Alaska. Grandma Louise's mother was Skookum Jim's sister, and her cousin was Patsy Henderson, who was with Skookum Jim and the others who found the gold that started the Klondike Gold Rush. When Patsy Henderson passed, his wife, Mrs. Patsy [Edith] Henderson, who was at Klukshu, gave me his Tlingit name, Koołseen. This was a very proud moment for me. Grandma Louise's dad was George Kla-Naut, who was second Chief of the Chilkat Tlingits. Grandma was raised at the Haines Mission School after her parents died, and around 1900 she went to Carcross, where she later married my grandfather Tom Dickson.

LEGENDARY DICKSON FAMILY

Grandpa Tom came to the Yukon during the Klondike Gold Rush as a member of the Northwest Mounted Police. He was from a large family of Scottish descent, born and raised in Ontario. He left his job in Ontario with his brothers Adam and George to join the Northwest Mounted Police. Later his younger brother Andrew followed in their footsteps. Tom carried the title of being the best marksman in the NWMP for ten years.

In those days NWMP were not allowed to marry, so Tom left the police force to marry Grandma and they established a homestead at Kluane Lake. Grandpa and Grandma grew vegetables, cared for their horses, had a trapline, a mink farm, and a big game outfitting business. Mom was the oldest child of their thirteen children. The others were Molly, Ruth, Mary, Buck, Sue, Grace, Kluane, Bobby, Dorothy, Belle, Dick, Ollie, and Babe.

The Dickson girls were known for their trapping and hunting skills and their strength. The Dickson boys were also skilled at trapping and hunting. My mom would take her dog team into Whitehorse to pick up mail and supplies when she was 14 years old. She would stop and visit everyone along the way, picking up mail that they wanted delivered. Some of the Dickson kids had their own outfitting and guiding businesses in later years: Sue Van Bibber from Champagne, Buck Dickson from Burwash, Belle Desrosiers at Lake Laberge, and Bobby Auston from Carcross. When the grandchildren started coming, they also were trained and skilled at living off the land and helped with the guiding business.

Grandpa had a good friend, Bobby Auston, who had been in the Northwest Mounted Police with him. He and his wife couldn't have kids, so Grandpa said they could pick one of his boys and raise him as their own. Auston picked Bobby, and he went to live in Carcross. Bobby never forgot his family and stayed in contact with his brothers and sisters. When Auston died, he inherited the store and hotel in Carcross, so he did all right.

The old people were always doing something. Grandpa would get some sheep on the ice when they couldn't move. Always had fresh meat. Grandpa made sure, if he gave his kids five shells, they better come back with five animals. Bear, caribou, moose—they'd dry the meat and everything like that. They did a lot of sharing of their food too.

top Hank's grandfather Tom Dickson was a former Northwest Mounted Police Officer, known as a crack shot and famous hunter. He was blinded in his right eye by a twig, when he was out hunting. KFN Archives. EMPC. Hank Jacquot Family Images #7. PHOTOGRAPHER UNKNOWN

bottom Mary Copper Jacquot and husband, Louis, with daughter Rosalie at their home in Burwash, circa 1910. KFN Archives. EMPC. Hank Jacquot Family Images #8. PHOTOGRAPHER UNKNOWN

above left Eugene Jacquot and his little son Gene Jr., circa 1920s. KFN Archives. EMPC. Hank Jacquot Family Images #9. PHOTOGRAPHER UNKNOWN

above right Three Jacquot children (left to right) Larry, Hank, and Josephine at Burwash, circa 1920s. KFN Archives. EMPC. Hank Jacquot Family Images #10. PHOTOGRAPHER UNKNOWN

Grandma left Tom Dickson later on and married another outfitter named Alex Davis. He was a friend of my grandpa, and they remained good friends. Grandma and Alex had a mink ranch at Kathleen Lake, south of Mile 1016, which is Haines Junction today. Grandma took care of the fur. They had to walk in to their ranch. There was a big, beautiful lake by their place, and they would get six or seven different kinds of fish. She also cooked for the mining outfit.

One year Grandpa was out on a hunt and breaking trail when a twig poked his eye and he went blind in that eye and then the other eye, all in one day. Harnessing his lead dog in the middle of the night, he went to Dad's house. Everybody's dog team had different bells so that you knew who was coming from a distance. My dad said, "Tom is coming in." Grandpa went in the house and said, "Jesus, Jesus, I am blind now. I can't see!" Dad took him to Fairbanks, but there was nothing the doctors could do for him. It really bothered him that he was blind. It was a hardship, but he rose above it and did the best that he could. My dad took really good care of him. Back in those days that's what everyone did.

Grandpa lived in a small cabin by Sophie Watt's place on the top of the hill at Burwash. My brother Joe drove truck and would go into Whitehorse to get supplies. When Joe came back, Grandpa would hear Joe's truck coming before anybody else did. He'd say, "Here comes Joe." And Joe always had something special for him. One time a grizzly bear was trying to break into Grandpa's cabin. He took his gun and shot right through the cabin and killed it. Even though he was blind, he still used his gun. There are so many stories floating around about my grandpa; it is too bad somebody didn't record him. He lived to the ripe age of 94.

ENTERPRISING JACQUOT FAMILY

My dad and my uncle were Eugene and Louie Jacquot. They were born in Alsace, France, which was on the border of Germany. Germany invaded Alsace and took it over in the 1870s. My uncle Louie was lucky to get out of there and headed for America. He was very frugal with his money and saved enough to go back and sneak his brother Gene out of the country too. I am forever grateful to my uncle Louie!

above left Dog team on lake ice in winter at Burwash. Dogs were large and essential for transportation in the early days of the Jacquot enterprises. KFN Archives. EMPC. Hank Jacquot Family Images #11. PHOTOGRAPHER UNKNOWN

above right Outfitters camp with Tom Dickson, Louis Jacquot, hunters, and guides relaxing at campfire, circa 1930s. KFN Archives. EMPC. Dickson Outfitters Images #4. PHOTOGRAPHER UNKNOWN

The brothers worked as cooks in New York and different places in the U.S.A. until they saved enough money to go to the Yukon. As they were getting ready to head up to the Klondike Gold Rush, they met Tom Dickson. They never did make their fortune in the Klondike. Thank goodness they met Tom, because he gave them a job guiding for him in Kluane country.

In 1904 my dad and uncle established the Burwash Trading Post. They bought their guiding business from Morley Bones, who had a cabin at Wolverine Creek. Daddy Gene (my father's nickname) and Young Daddy (Louie) used to take out hunting parties around the Donjek. Dad was the businessman, and Uncle Louie was a miner, blacksmith, and really good at working with his hands. They were both good with horses and raised horses for sale. Through the years they were big game outfitters and guides, miners, road and bridge builders, freight haulers, blacksmiths, boat and cabin builders, gardeners, chefs and bakers, and entrepreneurs who sold supplies to miners. Between the two of them they had so much talent; they were both jack of all trades. They had all kinds of books about building cabins, bridges, medical and veterinary care. My dad had rheumatism real bad, and he was always doing research looking for a cure.

The brothers built a two-story hotel, restaurant, general store, and beer parlour at Burwash Landing. My dad and uncle slowly built up their business, being frugal and with a lot of hard work. Supplies and goods were hauled by horse and wagon to Silver City from Whitehorse in those days, then stored in the Jacquot warehouses there until they were needed and brought over to Burwash by boat or on the ice.

First Nations people were given credit once a month in the store; they were able to get a sack of sugar, salt, tobacco chew, tea, and coffee. I believe it was around $10 credit. When they made their purchases, they would call it "jawbone credit" for their purchases. They sold furs to Daddy Gene, and he traded them staples. In establishing Burwash Landing the Jacquot brothers provided the Indians a permanent place to stay and also gave them jobs in their guiding and other businesses.

The brothers also had a mining claim at Burwash Creek, with a partner named Ernest Lawrence Petrel, who was another Frenchman, and they were good friends. He went on vacation to Louisiana, where he died while visiting family. Dad brought his two nephews, François "Frank" and Paul Birckel, out from France and gave them jobs at the mine. They were in the French Foreign Legion, and it was hard to get out. Somehow Dad was able to bring them to

above Tom Dickson leading a heavily loaded pack train across a glacier during a hunt in the mountains, circa 1930s. KFN Archives. EMPC. Dickson Outfitters Images #5 PHOTOGRAPHER UNKNOWN

Canada, and I think that probably saved their lives. Paul (Sr.) and I have always been close. I would go to visit him and his wife, Lilly, would say, "Your son is here!" My dad really thought a lot of Paul too.

Uncle Louie married Mary Copper Joe in 1920 and raised three children: Rosalie, Louis, and Josephine. Mary learned to cook and shoot, and she loved horses. She decided she wanted her son to be a shaman, so she bound Louis's head. When Uncle Louie found out about it, he was really angry, but by that time the baby's head was a different shape. Later Louie took his kids to France to go to school there. When they finally came back, they had to learn how to speak English again.

Dad would often cook donuts or whatever people had a hankering for. If he shot a bear, he would render the fat down and make lots of donuts for everybody. Those donuts were big, and I have never tasted a donut that good ever since. Everyone went away with as many donuts as they wanted or could carry! If Dad shot a moose, he would cook up a big feed. He took care of everyone. He taught all of my aunts how to cook, and I used to watch them produce food that was similar to how Dad would cook. When my cousin Kluane makes pastries, she reminds me of Dad's cooking. Daddy Gene was well known for the good food that he would cook out on hunts too.

We had several dug-out root cellars that we called ice houses to store vegetables and anything else that we needed to keep cold. Dad had a sawmill, and so we had plenty of sawdust to insulate the ice to keep it from melting. The ice would be cut out from the lake, and we had big ice tongs to move it. The horses would drag the ice to the dugouts, and it would last through the summer. Life back in those days was a lot of hard work.

The Canyon Creek Bridge was in bad shape one year. The family needed that bridge to be strong, as horses and wagons with supplies were hauled over it. So my uncle Louie and Dad rebuilt the Canyon Creek Bridge. The brothers privately owned and maintained the old Kluane wagon road.

The Jacquot brothers' hunting clientele included many rich and famous people. One client was Nelson Rockefeller, the Governor of New York, and the story goes that he sat around the campfire, eating gopher with the Indians. Dad had the Mellon family, too, wealthy people from the States who used to come up every year for a long time. Another one was Sargent Shriver, who was married to one of the Kennedys, and for years we would get dates from him every Christmas. My uncle Alex Van Bibber, who was married to my aunt Sue, had Bobby Kennedy out on a hunt.

BIG GAME HUNTS

We used to hunt in the upper White River country, around St. Clare Creek. That was our hunting grounds before the government took it over for Kluane Park and Game Preserve. Some of those hunts were ninety-day hunts in the early days, which is quite a long time to be out there. They had over one hundred head of horses at one time. My dad would pick up his hunters on the Alaska side. One time up on the White River they built a raft to bring the trophies down, and it froze in. They had to go back up in the winter to chop that thing out. It's written down in *Trophies Won and Lost*. Last time I went up there, I was about six. They'd get me on a horse too.

I didn't care for all that horse wrangling, like Jim Watt and them. I just worked with Paul Birckel Sr. I stayed in camp and put up jerky and stuff like that. We used to have to keep up on the uplands area. We'd have a horse wrangler up all night, because those horses wanted to come back home. They knew where home was.

Our best hunters were Buck Dickson, Paul Birckel Sr., and my dad. Uncle Buck was a great trapper, great with horses, and could call any animal. He worked for Daddy Gene as a guide and then eventually had his own outfitter and guiding business. Buck would go out on hunts with my dad. He took care of all the game that was shot. When my uncle Buck had cancer, Kluane Martin had him stay at her house and took care of him day and night. I will be forever grateful to her. She has a good heart. When Buck became sick, he set about putting his affairs in order. He told his brother Dick he would give him the guiding outfit on condition that he care for his boys, feed and clothe them, and make sure they had schooling. Dick agreed. No money was ever exchanged, and the older ones in the family can back me up on this.

The last time that they could hunt in that area before the government made the Park was with Paul Birckel Sr. My brother Joe took a hunting party over to White River area around 1948 after that. Then the big game hunting business got too commercial, with people cutting rates and taking shorter ten-day hunts.

I went hunting with Jimmy Joe and them, hunted with them a lot when I was a little kid. They had snowshoes from Teslin. There's a pattern that the Chief made for those snowshoes there, and nobody else is supposed to use that same pattern. They're hunting snowshoes, made out of that soft babiche. My brother Joe bought them, and that's thirty to forty years ago. They were $600 then; I don't know what they'd be now. One of my cousins that I also hunted with for years is Dickie Dickson. One time the two of us headed up to White River, and I shot a caribou. The horns were over 44 inches, and I have it hanging up on my wall.

NOBODY FOUGHT WITH PETE!

Pan American Airways used to have their own overnight stop at Burwash in the 1930s. They had a hotel there, the Pan American Hotel. We lived there for a while. They'd land those big planes on the ice in wintertime. In summer they'd land just this side of where the airport is now. Their ad said: "Exclusive with Pan-American. Super-strato Clippers. Largest, most powerful airliners serving Alaska and the Yukon Territory. Pressurized and air-conditioned, two abreast seating, wide aisles, big, comfortable foam rubber seats, delicious meals served piping hot." That's from the *Whitehorse Star*, December 10, 1937.

A lot of famous people used to stop there, including some who went into the airline business. Shell Simmons ended up with Alaska Coastal, Bob Reeve with Aleutian Airlines. He went through the ice at Burwash one time. He stayed there five or six months, and the old man didn't take a cent from him. He fixed up the prop so he could go on into Fairbanks. Later he went to Alaska and became a bush pilot. Red Redell was one of the pilots for Pan Am, and when he came, I would follow him everywhere. When World War II started, he enlisted as a pilot. He died fighting at the Battle of the Bulge. Red was a good man, and I would like to honour his memory by mentioning him here.

They called Mom Pete because she worked like a man. At the Pan American Hotel we had a bar downstairs. Old Bert Cluett was an Englishman who worked for my dad as a miner at Burwash Creek, then became the bartender at the hotel. He'd come in and say, "There's a fight in here. I can't do nothing with 'em." So she'd go in, "You guys wanna fight?" Bang their heads together and throw 'em out of the bar. So that's why they called her Pete: nobody wanted to fight with her. It wasn't uncommon for the family to do the sword dance in the beer parlour. Instead of swords the kids would lay down belts. Uncle Buck and my aunts and us kids loved to sword dance.

Mom was strong. She could take a hindquarter of a moose and put it on her shoulder or barrel of fuel on her knees and throw it onto a wagon. When she was a young girl, she would do tricks on a horse for tourists in Whitehorse. She would jump on a horse, and when it was moving, she would stand up, ride backwards, and other things. In her later years her joints were stoved up, and she moved pretty slow from all the abuse on her body when she was younger. Even in her later years she was pretty daring. She loved to drive fast. My dad and her were always competing with each other on whose dog team was the fastest.

CHILDHOOD DAYS

When I was a little guy, my mom used to hook me onto the clothesline with a long rope so she would know where I was. My family always told me about Santa Claus being across the lake. I had my own sled that Young Daddy (Uncle Louie) had made for me. It was probably about 8 foot long. One day I hitched up two or three dogs to my sled and took off across the lake looking for Santa. My old man asked everyone if they had seen me. Someone told him, "Oh, I saw him going across the lake with his dogs." So they had to go and get me. One of my early memories of my dad is when we had to go and take naps in the afternoon and he would always read us stories.

facing Hank's brother Joe Jacquot backpacking in the mountains, circa 1950s. KFN Archives. EMPC. Hank Jacquot Family Images #12. PHOTOGRAPHER UNKNOWN

above Hank's parents at Burwash, circa 1940s: Ruth Mary (born Dickson), nicknamed Pete, and her husband, Eugene, shortened to Gene, Jacquot. Her Tlingit name was Łáde'. KFN Archives. EMPC. Hank Jacquot Family Images #13. PHOTOGRAPHER UNKNOWN

Mom made me go berry picking with her and the ladies one day up at Duke Meadow. She told me to just stay in the wagon. Well, I got bored pretty fast, so I started messing around with the reins and I said, "Giddyup," and the horses took off galloping. I thought it was great fun; besides I didn't know how to stop them. The horses took me all the way back to the house, and Dad said, "Where is everyone?" I told him, and all the guys had a good laugh. I am sure that they could have gone back to pick up the ladies, but I think they just wanted to watch the fireworks. Dad told me that I'd better watch out when the ladies came back. Mom was so mad that she had to walk all the way back to Burwash. When she entered the house, she yelled, "Where is Hank?" I quickly hid underneath the big kitchen table, and because she was a big woman, she couldn't get at me right away. She finally was able to grab me by the leg, and then she took me out to the water barrel and dunked me.

I used to go across the lake and stay with Grandma Louise. I would make bannock for her, and she would laugh and then she would make me some. When she laughed, her whole belly would shake. We would play crib and go fishing together, because she loved to fish. There was a lot of rabbits in those days, so she always had lots to eat. I always enjoyed my time with Grandma. Uncle Buck would go over and check on his mom and cook for her too. He loved to tease her. The two of them got along really well.

OUR OLD PEOPLE'S STORIES

As a child I heard many stories about the old days. Solomon Albert was a French trapper a long time ago who froze his feet and had to slice his toes clean off. He was hungry and in the bush in the winter. He had a hard time; without your toes you can't walk very good. Somehow he made it back to Dawson City to the hospital. The doctor amputated his feet and he was given false feet, but he never took to them. So come springtime he shot a bear, skinned out the hind feet, and used them for his own feet. When the Chisana stampede started up, the prospectors had to go through the Donjek area. Part of the band was up there watching them travelling through. The Indians came upon two bear prints, walking alongside a horse. Then a little later the bear prints disappeared, and all they saw was horse prints. It scared them because they thought it was a man bear, and they moved camp. I know this story because Solomon Albert came to Burwash for supplies, and he told my dad about it.

I knew the really old people, like Copper (George) Joe too. Copper Joe was from Copper Center, and his dad was a Chief. All the people were killed off with the exception of Mr. and Mrs. Allen (Old Man and Monica Allen), who at the time had been slaves. Copper Joe's wife was killed at Nisling River. She was climbing up a cache ladder when some moose horns came loose and killed her. Copper Joe, he moved his whole family to Burwash. The kids were Kitty John, Copper Lily, Mary Copper, Jimmy Joe, and Jessie Joe. Jessie Joe was just a young child, so my grandma took her in and raised her like her own daughter. Jessie thought of Grandma as her mom. That's why we called her Aunt Jessie. Aunt Jessie always looked out for me. Her sister Mary married my uncle Louie and also became my aunt.

Mom would go over to visit Copper Joe and talk about different things. "Copper Joe, tell me: If you get stuck in the bush, what do you eat?" Many people don't know that on the wagon road there's roots, and they get pretty big, too, and boy, they're good. You just peel them and live off them.

Copper Joe was Dad's best friend. Gas used to come in wooden boxes. A dollar would get you maybe 30 or 40 pounds of nails, but he used to have Old Copper Joe save the nails out of those boxes. Just for

above American Army camp at Mile 1016 (now Haines Junction) with tents, trucks, and the pioneer road winding north to Alaska. KFN Archives. EMPC. Josie Sias Family Images #7. PHOTOGRAPHER UNKNOWN

something to do. Not only that, he got a bottle. The old man made his own wine, 50 gallons a whack, so he'd go home with a bottle of wine in his coat. They were the best of friends. Copper Joe—we were lucky to have him. He used to have us dance. I could speak pretty good Indian in those days and understand it too. I have the only known picture of old Copper Joe on Duke Mountain. He had a .22. He's sitting there, mad at himself because he missed a gopher, so he took the gun and hit it over a rock.

Copper Joe would put sinew in his ears because he said it would help him know what kind of weather was coming. I don't know if it really worked or not. One day I think it was Red Redell, the pilot from Pan Am Airlines, who was talking about what the weather was going to be like the next day. Copper Joe takes out his sinew and puts it in his ears, and says, "No, I don't think so." Red was teasing Copper Joe about the weather and about shooting his bow and arrows. The next day Copper Joe came down to the weather station, which was a big pole painted red with a sock to indicate which way the wind was blowing. Gene comes out of the building, and Joe said, "I am going to show you something." He pulls back with his bow and lets go. Zing, the arrow went into the windsock, and then zing the next one, and zing the next one, and the windsock went limp. Then he went home.

Jimmy Joe was Copper Joe's son. We used to hunt together, and we built a cabin across the lake from Burwash for my mom. She wanted a place to stay when she went over there to fish. When the whitefish spawned, she would go over for two or three nights and put up enough fish for her dog team. Mom had dog teams, and she was going all the time. Going to Duke Meadow and getting gopher, setting fishnets. She let her sister Grace have the cabin later. When Gùdia Johnson and John didn't have a place to stay, Aunt Grace let her stay in that cabin for the winter.

Billy Blackmore was originally from Burwash; his mother was Bessie, who died of TB. His people are descended from Copper Lily. Billy went to Hollywood, trying to get into the movies. He never made it big but did get small bit parts. He was a spare in *The Lone Ranger*. One time Billy attended a powwow down in Arizona and recorded the Navajos singing. When he came back to Burwash, he played the recording for Mom, and she knew what they were talking about because it was so similar to the Athapaskan language.

TREES FALLING EVERYWHERE IN 1943

We were pretty young in 1943, when the 'dozers were coming through to build the Alaska Highway. Copper Joe used to take us for walks. Trees were falling

down everywhere. I was so inquisitive and really enjoyed watching the army, wishing at the same time that I was older. Copper Joe would say, "Come on, you kids, get out of the way. The white man are going to run you over with the Cat."

During World War II there was lots of money coming in. The Jacquot businesses really took off when the American Army had a camp near Burwash. The old man was a chef, and that's the first person he'd see at a camp, would be the cooks. They'd give him anything he wanted. You couldn't get sugar in those days or coffee, but those cooks, they took care of each other.

The old man was always doing business: writing letters to hunters, getting hunters to come in, and all kinds of things. They were always doing something all the time. After the war anthropologists used to come to see how the Indians lived. Around Burwash they found places where they had steam baths in little skin huts. They would rent horses and everything else they needed. Jimmy Joe and George Donald used to take parties up Little Arm. They found a lot of stuff up there, like atlatls and other tools.

SCHOOL DAYS

In those days people were mostly self-taught. Elijah Smith was living in Burwash in the 40s, and he had taught himself to read and write from labels on canned goods, sugar, and tea bags. My dad decided that Elijah would teach all the kids their ABCs and to learn how to count. That didn't last long, because the first time a bunch of horses went by, we were all out the door chasing the horses and he lost all his pupils, just like that. So in later years we went to different boarding schools.

Everybody went down to Dawson to school in the early days. Those old Dicksons, like Sue and Grace, and all Grandpa's kids went there. Buck and Mom had to stay home and run the trapline. Somebody had to bring money in, so they didn't go to school. I used to hear horror stories about that place because they didn't feed 'em very good. So I was smarter than that. I got some dry meat and hid out in a big hay barn. When the Pan Am plane left without me, I came out of hiding. I still wasn't able to stay home. Dad sent me to school in Whitehorse. I stayed with his friend Fred Grey, who owned the light plant. Fred treated me really well, and it was a fun year. All my cousins were in town too. We played hockey together, and we had our own team. I didn't care for Whitehorse, but I could go home in the summers.

One summer I decided I wasn't going to go back to school, so the old man said, "Well, good, don't go to school." He said, "I need 1,000 cords of wood. There's a tent there; there's a swede saw over there." George John felt sorry for me and decided to help me out cutting wood. Dang, it was so cold outside. I became tired pretty quick of sawing wood and sleeping in a tent. I don't think I even made it two weeks. I went back to my dad and told him that I had changed my mind and wanted to go back to school, and that was the end of that. I am sure that was my dad's plan all along.

I was maybe 14, 15 years old, and one day I wasn't feeling good and then I became really sick. They had to drive me into Whitehorse because of a burst appendix. In those days it took a long time to drive to town. When I arrived, I was put into a small room where they fit as many Indians as they could. Many of us were sleeping on the floor.

The doctor did not believe Indians could have a burst appendix. When my dad arrived in Whitehorse, he had me transferred to a room and fired the doctor. My stomach would swell up like a balloon, and they would cut me in the same place every day and my stomach would deflate. I wanted to die. Dad hired a French doctor by the name of Major Blais, who was in the army. He put me on antibiotics and gave me a blood transfusion. When they first hooked me up, they gave me the wrong blood and I started to shiver and shake, and the nurse immediately pulled the IV out and saved my life. I ended up missing a lot of school that year. When I was on the mend, my dad bought the doctor's wife a fur coat.

I had other accidents, too, through the years. I slipped and fell off a tower but ended up in water, so that wasn't too bad. When I was out in Vancouver, I was riding my bike and a Standard Oil truck hit me. It broke my collarbone, and I still have a dent in my right leg to this day. They did buy me a new bike.

I went to school in Haines, Alaska, in 1947 or '48. After missing so much school because of past injuries, I was way behind, so I only made it to 8th grade when I should have been in 11th grade.

We went out to school in Vancouver after that. My brother Eugene had to stay in Vancouver because the weather was easier on his health. One of his nurses was a widow named Grace, and she was very fond of him. Dad talked her into taking care of Gene. Her husband had left her well off so she didn't need the job, but she liked to be busy. Dad bought a house, and she took care of my brother and then eventually all the rest of the Jacquot kids. We all had jobs to do at the house. I had to take care of the chickens and then chop off their heads when that needed to be done, and hauled sawdust or coal into the house every day.

We were so far from home that we started calling Grace Aunt Grace, and she became like a mother to us. Aunt Grace had one son, and he would come to visit on the weekends. When my dad would call to get a report on how we were all doing, I could hear him say, "What has Hank done now?" We weren't able to come home every summer, but Dad always made a point to travel to Vancouver to see us. As we got older, I would take all kinds of odd jobs to make enough money to go home.

Dad and Uncle Louie had a 90 foot well at Burwash. Louie was down in that well when a rock slipped off the edge at the top and hit him, splitting his skull. Dad took him to New Westminster, B.C., but the

facing left First truck and unidentified driver who travelled from Dawson Creek to Whitehorse on the pioneer Alaska Highway, fall 1942. KFN Archives. EMPC. Josie Sias Family Images #8. PHOTOGRAPHER UNKNOWN

facing right American Army soldiers drill in the forest at an Alaska Highway construction camp in the Kluane region during the summer of 1942. Technically, because the construction project was considered top secret during the war years, local people were not supposed to take photographs of the soldiers or their highway-building activities. KFN Archives. EMPC. Josie Sias Family Images #9. PHOTOGRAPHER UNKNOWN

doctors couldn't do anything for him. He didn't know what was going on around him after that. Dad talked to him in French. They were really close, and it was very hard on him. Louie lived at the Vancouver house with Grace, and his daughter Josie helped take care of him until he died about one and a half years after the accident.

I went to school at High Prairie, Alberta, for a while and then moved back to Steveston. Then I went to Vancouver College. First day I got there, I had some problems. There was a little Franciscan preacher. This little guy put boxing gloves on backwards and knocked the heck out of me. So I respected them. They're fair but they're firm. You listen to them, you know. I didn't argue with them.

My dad donated some property to the Roman Catholic Church in Burwash in the 1940s because he's a Catholic. I knew Father Morisset, who built the church and school there. A lot of people from Burwash went to that school. Dad died a few years after the war on February 19, 1950, in Whitehorse at the age of 72. In my dad's will my mom ended up with one-third of Burwash, and us boys ended up with the rest. She said she gave the First Nations people the land for ninety-nine years on a lease, but she had no right to give away our inheritance without us signing off on it. Some day KFN should say, "We got it from the Jacquots." Not just Mom.

MOVING TO ALASKA

I met Edith Berry, and we were married in Our Lady of the Rosary Church in Burwash, with Father Morisset officiating, on July 1, 1951. Our children are Mary Jane and Henry. We lived in Haines.

I worked all over for thirty years commercial fishing in Alaska. I fished at Bristol Bay. Blink your eyes once when I first went there, and see a million jumpers. Just can't imagine how many you could see—fish coming out of the water. We never got very much money in those days, only about 25 cents a fish; that's all. The Nine Alive Cannery was one of the biggest. Bristol Bay is the biggest spawning area for sockeyes in the world. That was something else, by golly—you just can't imagine. The limit was 5,000 fish a day, and you could

facing Hank hunting in the mountains, early 2000s. KFN Archives. EMPC. Hank Jacquot Family Images #14. PHOTOGRAPHER UNKNOWN

left Hank and his wife, Edith, and children Henry Jacquot and Mary Jane Valentine in Haines, Alaska, circa 2015. KFN Archives. EMPC. Hank Jacquot Family Images #15. PHOTOGRAPHER UNKNOWN

stay out there and when the flag went back up, you could go out fishing again. Get another 5,000.

Freddy Chambers and I drove tankers in Haines too. There was a lot of construction work, so he moved down here from Burwash. Freddy was a real good provider and nice guy. We have so much history together and have been super close all our life. We went to school together and played together, and we never said one cross word to each other. When we lived in Burwash, we drove the Jacquot brothers' truck back and forth to 1016 to get a drum of gas. In those days that was how gas came.

I ended up building bridges. I worked on the Wells Bridge near Haines and on the docks. That's the good life, you know. We had lots of fun. That's the main thing in life. Go to work. None of the guys ever argue with you. But that's why I ended up down here. There was lots of work and fishing. With the Tlingits the tide goes out, and the table's set. They never were hungry. Athapaskans, they had to go miles and miles, but Tlingits got their strength by living together. You know, the Chief in the Yukon would say, "Go up; go get me a caribou. Go up; get me a sheep." But that fish was right here on the coast.

ONE BIG FAMILY

We have a big family, and when one of us goes, it is so hard! When my aunts Dorothy and Belle were young, they were across the lake in a little inlet. Dorothy told Belle she was going to swim across, and Belle told her she shouldn't. She went anyway and soon became unconscious. Belle put her in the boat and took her back across the lake. That was the first time I saw my grandpa Tom running. Everyone was frantic trying to get the water out of her lungs to revive her. They tried everything, but nothing worked. Imagine my grandma had to watch all of this. Grandma and Grandpa had a hard time for a long while after.

The *Whitehorse Star* had an article in December 1964 about my aunt Belle going to New York to appear on the television show *To Tell the Truth*. A panel of experts asked questions to four different people posing as a big game guide, and the panel had to figure out who was the real big

facing Kooɬseen (Hank Jacquot) recording stories at his home in Haines, Alaska, February 2019. KFN Archives. EMPC. Elders Portraits #21. PHOTOGRAPHER ALISTAIR MAITLAND

game guide. She felt she gave herself away when she knew the answer to "What is a deadfall?" After that show aired, a lot of people certainly knew where the Yukon was. She was a beautiful woman, and I think many people were surprised that she was a successful big game guide. Belle couldn't have kids, so she kept busy taking care of the dog teams and helping Daddy Gene cook.

Aunt Grace and Aunt Sue married brothers Carl and George Chambers, settled at Champagne, and had big families there. The settlement became a centre for big game outfitting. My aunt Babe was another amazing woman. One time she was going into Whitehorse and picked up a hitchhiker. He tried to choke her, but it was a good thing that she was a strong woman because she said it took all she had to throw him out of the car. Sadly she died while racing her dogs at the Sourdough Rendezvous in 1965; a memorial trophy honouring her memory is handed out at the dog races to this day. One of my many memories of her is all of us sitting around a fire. We cooked a moose nose, ate it, and told a lot of stories. That's what I love about my big family: we had so many good times and genuinely liked each other.

I am a member of Klukwan Inc. in Ałaska. All the Dicksons could've got on that because our grandma Louise was born in Alaska. That's all you had to prove. I had dual citizenship, and I was allowed to apply for Native allotment of 160 acres in Haines. I've been living in Haines for forty years off and on. My two kids, Henry and Mary Jane, are here. I have twelve grandkids and great-grandkids.

My oldest brother was Gene. He passed away in 1945 at Burwash. Joe passed away around 1989, and Lou died about twenty years ago. Mom was admitted to the hospital in Whitehorse in 1982. While she was in the hospital, she developed gangrene, and they were going to amputate her foot. My wife (Edith) and I drove up and arrived after 9:00 p.m. She was sleeping, and they wouldn't let us wake her. She passed away early the next morning before we could see her. She was only 79 years old.

The people who live in Burwash decided to tear down my parents' lodge. That building was a historical building because it was a magnet for all things to come. Without a trading post the Indians would never have lived there. My dad and Uncle Louie built up a community and welcomed all to live on their land. Nobody ever went hungry, and if anyone needed a job, they would give you one. I look back to our big happy family and the lodge and all their businesses—they all thrived, and my parents, aunts, and uncles all made that happen. I figure that without the lodge there would never have been a village there now.

That's what I love about my big family: we had so many good times and genuinely liked each other.

KOOŁSEEN (HANK JACQUOT)

SHAKWÀǸCHE (KLUANE MARTIN)

(b. 1935)

It Was Challenging Sometimes

My name is Kluane Martin, and my Indian name is Shakwàňche (Poor Thing). I am of the Wolf Clan. I was one of two family members born at Shá Dhäl (Champagne), Yukon, in the 1930s. I spent my first few years at Champagne, where my dad lived, and then my mother took me and my sister, Louise, back to her home at Burwash. My grandparents were Louise George, who was of coastal Tlingit ancestry, and Tom Dickson, who was an NWMP officer during the Gold Rush.

facing Shakwàňche (Poor Thing, Kluane Martin), 2019. KFN Archives, EMPC Elders Portraits #22. PHOTOGRAPHER ALISTAIR MAITLAND

My mother was Grace Dickson Chambers. She grew up at the Dickson homestead at the mouth of the Kluane River. My grandparents made their living there. They didn't run to the store in those days. They hunted, gardened, fished, and trapped off the land. So when people talk about going out and making gardens and all that today, that was done here long ago. So it's not new. It was hard work and all done by hand. Hauling the water for the garden by hand. I did that too. And tilling the land with a horse and plow. Mom and her sisters did that. They had big gardens and they had a big family, too, so they had lots of kids to do the work.

We moved back to Burwash before World War II and before the Alaska Highway was built. I can remember going up to Burwash along the lakeshore. The old road went out along part of the lakeshore. I remember that there used to be a whole bunch of us when we went up there from Champagne, and us kids would all be riding in the back of the truck under canvas and some of the adults too. We'd all go up to Burwash to see our relatives, Daddy Gene Jacquot's family.

My grandfather Dickson was also living at his residence on the river at that time. Even though he was totally blind, he stayed there for quite a while on his own. I remember going down to visit him, and he had a rope that he used to hang onto and walk around different areas of the house. He used to go down in the basement there and get us kids some black current jam, which we really thought was something! He would have made the jam himself. He did all his own cooking and everything. Later on he reached the point where his daughter my aunt Sue Van Bibber had to bring him to Champagne, and he lived there until he passed away. Even there he had a rope so that he could feel his way to the different areas of her house.

My grandmother Louise had left him some years before that and moved to Champagne with Mr. Davis. They ran a mink farm there. When I was five or six, she wanted my mother to send my little sister, Toots (Louise), to stay with her, but Mom sent me instead. I remember walking with Grandma all the way from the mink ranch to Champagne to buy groceries.

BURWASH COUSINS

My mother and the Jacquot boys' mother were sisters. They were both Dicksons, Grace and Ruth. Ruth married into the Jacquots, so all those kids were our cousins. In my age group at Burwash there was Larry Jacquot; Kirk, Peter, Edward, and Joe Joe Johnson; and myself. Also Lucky Johns, Alex Johns, was there when he was young. There were a few others too. Fred Jamieson, who got killed when a truck rolled over on him. He was from Champagne, but he was in Burwash with his dad some of the time.

We were all the same age, and we always did everything together. We were always getting into trouble! We'd go out and get the horses and run them around, and of course the adults didn't know! We used to sneak into where Daddy Gene had his storage area for his store. We found a way to get in there, and we would take candy—until we got caught. Oh, it was good!

Then we got into the hay barn, where they had all the hay for the horses, and they had a couple of cows then too. We used to play in the hay, but Daddy Gene didn't like it. We'd all hide in the hay when he would come around and say, "I know you kids are there!" We'd all be quiet.

We built rafts and went out on the lake, and then the adults would be mad because we shouldn't be on the water alone. So that was another thing we did. Well, we had to make our own fun. What else was there? No TV, no Ski-Doos, no four-wheelers, no video games. The only games were the games we made up.

We had our chores to do when we came home from school during the summer. We were in residential school during the winter months at Dawson City in St. Paul's Hostel. Nine years of hell! We were fortunate in our family that we were able to come home and spend the summer in Burwash. Then they'd send us back in the fall, in September. There were eighty children in that residence and only four adults. We had cousins there. The Dickson boys from Burwash and my aunt Sue's bunch from Champagne were in there too; that's my uncle George Chambers's family. So we were all there.

We always travelled in a vehicle, even when I was small. My uncle George Chambers was quite a mechanic and a very industrious man. He lived at the Champagne trading post, and he had a vehicle. Harry Joe also had a car at Champagne when we were small. We always travelled with my uncle George and aunt Sue Chambers, and there would always be a load of us. There were kids all over the place!

At Christmas there was always a dance at Champagne. Before we moved to Burwash, I remember seeing the ladies from Chu'ena Kéyí (Hutchi) there. Some of them had the old-style traditional tattoos on their faces, and they would all be sitting on chairs around the edge of the room. Elijah's brother Roddy Smith played the fiddle, and everybody had a great time.

My aunt Sue and uncle George also had a house in Whitehorse, the Chambers house. It's still preserved in Whitehorse on the waterfront now. It used to be on the street where the Whitehorse Elementary School is. There was a hill then, and the Frommes lived on one side of the hill. My aunt Annie—Meyers was her married name—lived across the street. We went down the hill and over to the Chambers's residence, and everybody camped at aunt Sue's place. We had beds all over the place when we came to town. That's when I was small.

WORLD WAR II—ARMY TRUCKS EVERYWHERE

Daddy Gene was Gene Jacquot who owned Burwash. We all called him Daddy Gene. Everybody called him that. He negotiated with the American Army when they arrived in the 40s, and he located space for their camps and facilities because he had been running the Burwash Trading Post for decades by then. So the older people at Burwash knew what was going on, that there was a possibility of a war, and they had land marked out for the airport there. They made that airport and marked it for emergency landings.

When the war came in '42, that was the year my sister and I went to Dawson, so I don't remember the war being declared and all that. We were just 6 and 7 years old then.

facing Some of Kluane's big family visiting together at Burwash in the 1930s. Children in front left to right: Kluane's cousins Frank Chambers, Harold Chambers, and Hazel Chambers. Adults in back left to right: Daddy Gene Jacquot; Sue Chambers (born Dickson and later married to Alex Van Bibber); friend of Gene's (name unknown); Kluane's mother, Grace (born Dickson) Chambers; and George Chambers (married to Sue at this time). KFN Archives. EMPC. Kluane Martin Family Images #1. PHOTOGRAPHER UNKNOWN

Somewhere in my memory I can remember going to the army camps when we came home in the summer. There was a big army camp at the head of the lake. I remember going there because we used to go and see my uncle Howard, who was a cook in the army. We used to go to the kitchen, and of course he'd feed us kids. That's why I remember it: because they'd have cakes and steaks and all that stuff. So we'd eat real good! Then we'd go on up to Burwash. My dad's sister Ida was married to Howard Cook. They went on to Fairbanks after he left the armed forces. They both are long gone now.

After 1942, when we were home in the summers, there were army trucks and jeeps everywhere at Burwash. The American Army also had a big camp at Duke Meadow. In fact if you go up there, you can still see some cement foundations. You can see the remains of some of the camp there. We used to go up there to the army dump because they'd throw cases of food away. Just full cases. Never even opened them. A lot of the packages had chocolates—those little care packages for the soldiers. Well, us kids used to find just the chocolates and eat them. They used to have cases of food there, and we used to take stuff home. Everybody did. It was good food, and if you found a chocolate bar, you hid it! No, no, we didn't share. I didn't share!

LEAVING HOME

I was in Dawson City for nine years, and that took me to grade 9. I took grade 10 in Haines, Alaska, because I had relatives there, my cousin Hank Jacquot's wife. I took grade 11 in Chilliwack, B.C., and then I came back to Whitehorse and took grade 12 at Whitehorse Elementary and High School. There were only four of us in grade 12 in 1954. Ellen Davignon (née Porsild) was one of the other students.

I didn't graduate there. I went to work at the lodge in D-Bay for a while. Then I left and went to school in Vancouver when I was 18. I stayed with an aunt and uncle down there. I just had $35 in my pocket when I left, money for my flight and $35 in my pocket.

After that I went to work in a café for about two or three months, and then a job came up at the Coqualeetza TB Hospital in Sardis, B.C. TB was very prevalent in the 50s. I was hired to work cleaning hallways, and that's how I got my beginning in my career. I used to clean at the superintendent's home, too, and when a job came up in the lab, he said, "Give her a chance." And so I went to work as a lab technician. The technician in charge of the lab trained me. That was in 1956. When I finished my training later on, I think I was one of the first First Nations people to become a registered lab technician in Canada.

While I was working there, we did experimental work with new drugs. There were several new TB drugs that we made up in dilutions. We would get tissue samples from the TB patients, and then I would plant the TB on the dilutions and see at what stage it killed the TB. Not only did it

kill the TB, sometimes it killed the people because it ruined their kidneys and their livers because the drugs were so strong in the experimental stage. I worked in Sardis for two and a half years.

BACK TO THE YUKON—OPPORTUNITIES AND CHALLENGES

I came back to Whitehorse in 1959 and got a job working at the NC, the Northern Commercial store, for about three or four months. They really desperately needed a lab tech at the hospital here. My aunt Belle said to our MP, Erik Nielsen, "You know, Kluane's had all that training." It's funny how things go! Erik mentioned it to Jim Gentleman, who was the Director at the hospital. He interviewed me, and I told him what I had done at Sardis. He said, "Come to work." I never looked back.

The Canadian Army was still in Whitehorse in the 60s. I was working with the army lab tech at the hospital, and he had not been able to get any time off, because there was nobody to replace him. So when I came there, well, right now he wanted time off. So I was there for a week or two on my own not knowing anything about this hospital, but I managed. Bill Siemens was his name. I don't know where he is now, but he was the tech in charge of the lab at that time. Bill and I worked together for a couple of years, until the army left the Yukon in 1966.

The federal government had the Northern Careers Program then, so someone put my name forward for lab training. They asked me if I wanted to go. I said, "Sure, why not?" So I took the six-month program, wrote the test, and passed it. I got my certification in the American association of lab technicians, but I wasn't certified in Canada. So I went all these many years with the U.S. certificate. There was myself and a guy that worked in the X-ray department who was First Nations from B.C. I can't remember his name. There was just the two of us First Nations people at the Whitehorse hospital in those days.

I had to do the exams and training at Vancouver General Hospital. I was very fortunate at that time because I knew the woman who was in charge of the hematology department there. At first they weren't going to take me, because the program was not proving to be successful. Only one other person had passed that exam, and so they didn't want to take me. She stood up and said, "I will guide her through," and so she did. I was only the second person that did that program in six months, but I had worked here for many years prior to that. I knew a lot already because I was doing it every day in my work.

I found it most interesting. You have to pull yourself away from the personal connections. All these years that I worked here that's what I had to do. I had to go to work and think that way and not "This is my friend." In Whitehorse I was the only lab tech there for some time. We had a hundred-bed hospital, and there were only

facing Since the mid-1940s the Alaska Highway has been the route taking Kluane people away from home and back again. The last vista of Lhù'ààn Mân (Whitefish Place Lake, Kluane Lake) is seen here at the 'A'äy Chù (Slims River) causeway when driving south, and Thechàl Dhàl (Rock-Scraper Mountain, Sheep Mountain) signals the return to home when driving north. KFN Archives. EMPC. Landscape Images, #22. PHOTOGRAPHER ALANNA DICKSON

left Kluane's Aunt Belle (born Dickson) Desrosiers, seen here circa 1960s, ran an outfitting and guiding business with her husband, Curly Desrosiers, for many years and continued on her own after he passed away. KFN Archives. EMPC. Ernie Martin Family Images #8. PHOTOGRAPHER UNKNOWN

two of us working there. Later we had three people working, and now they have twenty people doing the same work that we did. We had to make up our own reagents, all those glucose tests and other things. We had to do tests on them to make sure they were good. So we did three times the work that they're doing now, with only two people.

It was challenging sometimes when you'd have patients say, "I don't want an Indian taking my blood." More than once that happened. Sometimes when I'd have to do a cardio test, they'd say, "I'm not exposing my body to an Indian." Oh, I just laughed because there was no one else to do it! The doctors had to call me to the OR to set up intravenous too. I knew I was going to have to do it eventually because the nurses couldn't do it. They didn't do blood work then. I just laughed. I said, "Ok, fine. We'll see you later." And pretty soon they'd be lying there, and they'd say, "Here take my blood then."

I did very well. I knew I had my expertise. I got letters commending my work twice from the doctors' council. Dr. Helm, the Chair of the Medical Association, gave me a letter commending my work. At a later date I got a second letter thanking me for my dedication.

Many times tests would be needed for the First Nations patients and I knew it, so I'd just go ahead and do it. I'd look at the work and know the patient's needs, but the doctor was somewhere else and unavailable. I had doctors tell me off a couple of times, but later they would come and say thank you anyhow.

I worked from 1956 to 1998 at the Whitehorse General Hospital lab. I can remember when there was new technology for DNA analysis being introduced in our field in the late 50s and early 60s. The tech that was in charge of our lab said to me, "This is going to open up a lot of fields." I never talked about those things outside work in those days, because it was hard for people to understand.

I was raising my son and my daughter on my own in those days. I can remember putting Ernie into a little wagon or a sleigh and dragging him down the street to the babysitter's at 7:30 in the morning. I'd have him bundled right up because I didn't own a car, and then I'd catch a ride downtown. I had to walk back down to the bank to catch my ride, and then the guy would drop me off at the bank and I'd go up to the babysitter's, get Ernie, and go home. That's when he was about 2, 3 years old... And there was no babysitting services. I don't know what I paid her a month, probably $20 or something. Twenty dollars was a lot of money in the 60s. No daycares then. You had to arrange your own babysitting services.

Rendezvous Festival was really a lot of fun then. They had dances all over, and they used to bus people to the different dances. It was all free, and they don't do that anymore. My mother raced sled dogs. My aunt Babe raced, Babe Southwick.

Aunt Belle was a big game guide. She owned her own business. They were the real pioneers, and that was because of my grandfather. They had to be strong because what else could they do? They had to fish in the summer, and in the winter, hunt. My mother said that my grandfather told them, "I'm giving you six shells, and you'd better have six sheep or six caribou." And God help them if they didn't have it. They got them! Oh, they all enjoyed life. I mean, we had good times then; it's not like now. When we got together—well, of course we were young, but when they got together, they always laughed and there was always something to eat and they'd all be telling stories and then they'd go and do stuff. I mean, there was no sitting around, and they were always busy.

NEW HORIZONS AND MAKING CHANGE

I was on the Non-Insured Health Committee, and we went and did a lot of travelling across Canada. There were fifteen of us from across Canada, First Nations people. We were setting up that Non-Insured Health Benefit Program, and we went all across Canada. I'd get to Vancouver, and they'd say, "Kluane, you have to cancel your ticket home and go to Quebec!" I'd be sitting at the airport with my suitcases, and I'd have to cancel and get a hotel room in Vancouver and fly off to somewhere else the next day. I enjoyed it because I had many years of working, and I knew the system.

So when the federal government said, "Oh, we'll give you guys a red book" for non-insured issues, and "We'll give you the lab, and you people can do your own testing and everything," I said, "What?" Can you imagine the government telling you that all these First Nations could have their own labs and do their own testing? I said, "Are you kidding me?" I said, "Who's going to train all these people? And where are you going to get the money for all that equipment?" I said, "That's very expensive equipment. And who's going to look after that equipment?" Boy, that red book was gone just like that. That was the end of that red book. Didn't hear any more about it!

I did the first water quality study on the Kluane Lake area. I cultured the water in different areas and wrote up a report about where the bacteria and contamination was coming from on the lake. That was one of my little studies that Joe Joe Johnson said, "Take it over and do it."

I remember when they were beginning to organize the land claims movement. Unofficially it was starting, and it took Elijah Smith to bring it out. I kept a fairly low profile because of my job. I was a government employee, and I was not allowed to be vocal. So I could not become politically involved in anything. My mother was one of the signatories. I didn't think they'd make it.

facing Kluane Martin (middle right) with Donna Rear (middle left) and two other people speaking about professional opportunities in the health field during a career fair at Yukon College in the 1970s. CYFN Archives. Photograph Collection #b72_f3_s7_2. PHOTOGRAPHER UNKNOWN

above Kluane's mother and aunts, the legendary Dickson sisters, are seen here at the Sourdough Rendezvous in Whitehorse circa 1960s, all wearing beautiful home-sewn mukluks. *Left to right:* Sue Van Bibber, Grace Chambers, Belle Desrosiers, and Babe Southwick. Tragically Babe died suddenly after finishing as one of the top five mushers on the first day of the Rendezvous dog races in 1965. KFN Archives. EMPC. Kluane Martin Family Images #2. PHOTOGRAPHER UNKNOWN

I was part of land claims but not too much. Elijah Smith came to me way back in the 70s telling me that they're setting this up, and he said, "I'd like for you to join our group." I said, "I don't know, Elijah." And he said, "Well, think about it." I thought about it, but I'd already had ten years at the hospital at that point, so I thought in politics you're never secure. I couldn't go, because I had a family and if I lost my job with the association, where would I be? Whereas with the hospital I knew my job, I was secure in my knowledge, and I thought, "No, I couldn't join them," but I sure wanted to. I had to make up my mind, and I stayed with the hospital. I went to meetings just as a citizen. I wasn't one of the forerunners. Dorothy Wabisca, Joe Jacquot, and Joe Joe Johnson and all those guys were at meetings lots of times until midnight. So I stayed with the hospital, and I'm glad I did. I was at Burwash for the Kluane First Nation land claims signing.

When I left Burwash, we seemed to be like a family. Everybody was getting along, and we were growing up, Peter Johnson, and Kirk, and Joe Joe and them. They were going on and doing other things, too, but when I came back in the 1960s, I noticed quite a difference. It didn't seem like a tight-knit group. People were bickering at each other, and it just seemed to get worse and worse. I think because people became more independent, and they didn't have to depend on, say, Daddy Gene, so to speak, for all their jobs and everything. They were getting independent, so they had the privilege of saying what they thought. And people thought, "If I didn't want to do something, I won't do it." And so the independence was growing.

The highway contributed to that, I think, because it built up resentment, and people were beginning to feel that we were being discriminated against. They didn't know that until of course the great white society came in. Then those people were really openly saying, "Give this goddamn country back to those goddamn Indians. It's so frigging cold here." I can remember a guy saying that, not to me, but when I was standing there and that kind of stuff. So our people were saying, "Yeah, give it back to us," whereas before I left they would have just walked away.

I think we're regressing now. I think we're going back, and I think that we're going to have Yukon Territorial Government running CYFN, and we will be back to where we were in the 50s if these leaders here right now today don't start standing up. And we worked so hard to get what we got, the non-insured benefits, all those healthcare programs—all those programs that we got, we worked hard to get those. We said, "We want them; we need them; we want to be independent." Well, we're going right back. We've got government employees running our band—well, indirectly running our band. And I think we're going right back. There was a guy in Ottawa, one of the politicians, and he said, "The First Nations people are losing control." I thought, "What the heck is he talking about?," and now I'm beginning to agree with him. Like a lot of our people are working for YG now too. As soon as we get a good tech or a good person to work, they give them such good wages and they put them in a good job, how can they refuse? And then they work for YTG, and we've lost a good person.

Those were quite the years, the hospital years. I went through all that when they were talking about taking babies, you know, across Canada—the 60s Scoop. I remember them taking some of these babies up here and the mother would be crying and you know, I'd have to go and take her blood and I'd say, "Well, what's wrong?" "They're taking my baby." "Well, why?" "I don't know." Well, who was I going to talk to?

REMEMBER WHO YOU ARE!

Always remember who you are. You're as good as the guy next to you and better than some. And I had to keep that in my head, because I tell ya, I would never have gotten anywhere if I didn't. When some patients would stop and say, "I don't want that Indian taking my blood," then I said, "That's ok. We'll see you later. Bye." And after everybody else had tried and their arms would be all black and blue, they'd just put their arm out to me. I never said a word, took their blood in two seconds, and I was gone. They never said a word. Oh yeah, I had that quite often.

I say, "Remember who you are, and you're just as good as most and better than others." That's the only way you can move ahead. Take a chance if it's a good thing. That's the only way I got ahead, and boy, I'll tell you, it was pretty hard doing it with some of those people. And the prejudice—you could just see it. You know, as soon as you walked in a room, and they'd take one look at you and you could just see the expression on their face, and I thought, "No."

Well, you want to be treated equally, and you want to treat other people the way you want to be treated.

facing Kluane Martin participating in a land claims meeting, circa 1990s. CYFN Archives. Photograph Collection #b45_f9_1. PHOTOGRAPHER UNKNOWN

above Kluane with her cousins Hank Jacquot and Harry Dickson butchering meat after a successful moose hunt, late 1990s. KFN Archives. EMPC. Kluane Martin Family Images #3. PHOTOGRAPHER UNKNOWN

Remember who you are, and you're just as good as most and better than others.

SHAKWÀNCHE (KLUANE MARTIN)

LOUISE BOUVIER

(b. 1937)

Coming Home to Kluane

I was born in Whitehorse at the old hospital on October 12th, 1937, to Carl and Grace Chambers. My mother's maiden name was Dickson. She was born at Silver City and raised on the Dickson homestead at the head of the Kluane River, which is a beautiful place. Her dad, my grandfather, was Thomas Dickson, who was a Northwest Mounted Police officer during the Gold Rush. His wife, my maternal grandmother, was Louise George, and she came from Dyea, Alaska. They moved here in the early 1900s and had a very big family.

facing Louise Bouvier, 2018. KFN Archives. EMPC. Elders Portraits #23. PHOTOGRAPHER ALISTAIR MAITLAND

I'm named for my father's mother, Grandma Chambers, whose name was Anne Kershaw. She died just two weeks after I was born. We're related to old Johnny Fraser through the Chambers. My second name is for Grandma Louise, my mom's mother. I have never used the name Anne. When I went to school in Dawson, there were other girls named Annie, Anna, and Ann, so the school called me by my second name, Louise. My name Toots comes from a cousin. She called me by that name, so that's who I am today!

A REALLY GOOD CHILDHOOD AT BURWASH

I grew up here on Kluane Lake at the homestead. I spent part of my summers at Champagne. My dad's father, Harlan Chambers, started the trading post there. It was nice there, and I still like Champagne, but Burwash has always been home. We had a lot of good times and lots of fun as kids here in Burwash. We were always learning new things. There weren't as many houses as there is now. The hotel was built in the 40s. There was a blacksmith shop and a hay barn. There were cows, horses, big gardens, and hayfields.

My grandfather Thomas Dickson was blind for all of my childhood, but he knew me! I loved him very much. He taught us to make biscuits, and if they weren't right, he would throw them across the room.

I only have one sister and one brother; I'm the middle child. My sister, Kluane, lives in Whitehorse, and my brother, Ron Chambers, lives in Haines Junction. Ronnie knows a lot about history. I know all of our background and the way we were raised because of my grandmother. The standards that Grandma and Grandpa gave to Mom and her siblings became the strength of the Dickson-Chambers women. We're strong. Their work ethic was very strong, and they passed that down to us and it continues in our children and grandchildren. My aunt Babe, uncle Buck, and my mom were the ones that stayed here the longest of the Dickson family. My mom helped a lot of people around here and never said no. If somebody needed something, she was there to help them. She taught that to us kids as well.

I have three children. My boys were raised in Burwash every summer. This is their home. Ronald, the youngest, is a KFN member. My older boy, Darrell, decided to go with Champagne and Aishihik First Nations because of my dad's side. My daughter, Edna, is KFN. She has two kids, Amber and Dustin. Darrell has two kids, Alaura and Alexander. Ronald has a daughter, Alexis, who was raised in Vancouver and came to visit here in the summer.

As kids we used to walk from the Dickson homestead to Burwash by the lake or by the highway. We'd pick berries and trap gophers at the Duke. We swam in the lake and played around there. We had a good childhood. There were lots of kids. There was Paul Birckel Jr., Peter Johnson, Kirk Johnson, Larry Jacquot, Russell and Tom Dickson. Edward Johnson was a bit younger, but he tagged along with us. Most of them are gone now.

When we came home, we had chores to do, so we were always busy. We didn't have time to get into mischief. We used to run and jump off the dock here. Nobody ever threw bottles in the lake or broken glass. When my niece was 7 years old, she jumped off the wharf and cut the tendon on her foot. That's when we said, "No more." Ours was a different time. There were lots of Elders around, who taught us to be polite to everyone. We were taught to respect everyone and everything: the forests, animals, plants, and fish. We learned what the blacksmith did. We saw Uncle Dick milk the cows. We all learned how to ride horses. We used to cut hay. We had work to do before we could play. It was a good life.

Everybody was our auntie or uncle, grandma or grandpa. That's the respect that you show to your Elders to call them by those names. Margaret is my aunt. I love her; she is so much like her mother, Grandma Copper Lily, my mom's good friend. When my kids were small, Lena was Aunt Lena to them, even though she's not directly related. All the Elders were their aunts and uncles. My kids used to think they were really fortunate because they had so many aunts and uncles and grandmas and grandpas. They said, "How come?," and I said, "Because we're family, we're all family."

We had a really good childhood. It was a tough childhood. It was tough on Mom, because she raised us three by herself. Burwash was home, the old Dickson homestead by the river was home, and I knew that Little Arm was a Dickson place. The Dickson family used to go up there to their trapline. Mom, Aunt Fran, and I used to trap in Little Arm. (Aunt Fran wasn't related but they all called her that.)

Now the respect for the traditions that we used to have towards the land, water, hunting, everything—our way of life is being eroded, some of it slowly; some of it is moving at a pretty fast pace. It's disturbing to see it happen. In the past things were tough, but things were good. Mom always had her fishnets in, and she shared the fish.

This subsistence that we insist is our right is not the way I remember it. We have abused it so badly that I don't like the word subsistence. I never agreed to it, because you don't have the respect for the animals like they used to have. People killing moose in the spring, little babies. If you kill one cow, that's three moose because most of them have twins. My husband used to maintain the garbage dump here, and he also did the scrap metal dump. Every spring he'd come home just furious. There'd be fall meat thrown over the bank and new meat brought in April and May. We were taught, "You take what you need; you don't take what you want." Our family, my mom and my sister and brother, we got one moose a year. We got our fish, we got sheep, but we never had to have two moose.

My mom was 11 when she shot her first moose. My grandpa Tom gave her three shells and said, "You better come back with two shells," so she did. And that's the way we were raised. We all shared.

facing Site of the old Tom and Louise Dickson homestead at the mouth of the Kluane River, circa 1970s. KFN Archives. EMPC. Louise Bouvier Family Images #1. PHOTOGRAPHER UNKNOWN

above The *Josephine* built by the legendary Jacquot brothers to transport freight on Kluane Lake sits on shore circa 2020 in silent testimony to busy days gone by. KFN Archives. EMPC. Landscape Images #19. PHOTOGRAPHER ALANNA DICKSON

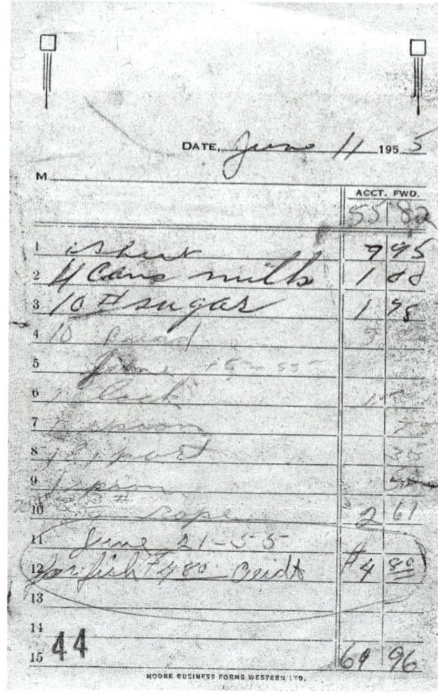

DATE June 11 1955

		ACCT. FWD. 55 82
1	shirt	7 95
2	4 Cans milk	1 00
3	10# sugar	1 95
10		2 61
11	June 21-55	
12	for fish 4.80 credit	4 80
15	44	69 96

MOORE BUSINESS FORMS WESTERN LTD.

DATE June 30 195

		ACCT. FWD. 69 96
1	Credit for fish	17 70
3	July 4-55	
4	Credit for fish	13 20
7	July 8-55	
9	Credit for fish	12 80
15	45	25.26

MOORE BUSINESS FORMS WESTERN LTD.

She went sheep hunting, too, across the lake and they probably hunted on this west side, too, but it was mostly across the lake and up the Little Arm.

We all had to help Mom with fishing. She had a little inboard motor, and she fished by boat. She sold her fish to the lodge here and to all of the lodges on the North Highway. She said it wasn't the best living in the world, because of the wind. Sometimes she didn't get out for a week, but she fished, she hunted, she trapped, she cooked on the hunts, and she cooked for the restaurants here. She did live trapping, too, for the Al Oeming Wildlife Farm in Alberta. My sister and I cooked on the hunts as well.

Mom sewed too. She learned to sew when she was young, so we had to learn too. I do beading now, but my beads keep popping up because I sew them too tight. I think Margaret, my teacher, is just about ready to throw the towel in, but she still has hope. We learned to sew and how to bead because it was something that we needed to know. Most of the younger generation here are all very talented with beads. I don't think I ever saw factory-tanned hide until the 80s. As kids we wore moccasins here, but we had boots when we were in Dawson. I know we had runners.

HORRORS AT RESIDENTIAL SCHOOLS

I was just about 6 when I went to Dawson City to St. Paul's Hostel. Mom sent us there because the Catholic convent school in Whitehorse wouldn't take us, because we were Protestants. We went to Dawson because that was the one place she could send us to a boarding residence, and we could go to the public school. When the Baptist Mission School opened in Whitehorse, we went there for one year. Then we went back to Dawson, when I was 13. My last year was in the Baptist Mission School again. I went to St. Agnes, too, a small Anglican boarding school in Whitehorse. From age 6 to 12 I was in

Dawson, then Whitehorse for a year, and then from 13 to 14 back in Dawson, and then from age 14 in Whitehorse. Kluane and I went to school in Dawson, but Ron never did go there, because he was younger and could go to school in Whitehorse.

I don't have memories about the building of the Alaska Highway, because I left here in September 1942 to go to school, and when I came back in the spring of '43, the highway was already through. We used to go over the top of Sheep Mountain and stand and look straight down and see part of the road over the hill there. We accepted the highway. I never thought of it as changing anything, because we were always able to travel even before it was built.

St. Paul's Hostel was horrible. We didn't have any sexual abuse, but the guy that ran it was an alcoholic and his wife was a sadist. We had a cook that did not know how to cook. Nothing. We used to get gruel in the morning, and right after breakfast we'd wash the pot. Then she'd put the pot back on the stove. She had two double boilers and she'd put water in, then the porridge, and it cooked for twenty-four hours on the back of the stove. One year she decided she was going to make bread. It's too bad Lepages wasn't looking for glue, because that was the best glue in the world. We kids had to mix 5 pounds of margarine, add the colouring, then add peanut butter and mix it all together. I don't remember ever getting jam. We had apples once a year. We ate Dawson City salmon. We ate a lot of bear meat, because Old Man Darim drank all the food money up. Mom used to send us her Family Allowance, and we were lucky if we got $2 a month. He took the rest of it. He had a dog that he treated better than us. The staff ate on Royal Albert china, with crystal glasses and silverware that we had to polish. Life in Dawson was tough.

I met Mrs. Darim in a store in Haines Junction a few years later. I asked her why she did the things she and her husband did, terrible things to me as a child in Dawson. Someone put a chalk mark on the door frame. It wasn't me, but her husband strapped me three times so hard that I couldn't hold a pencil at school the next day. I was sent back to the hostel, where Mrs. Darim put me on bread and water for a week, kept me in a room, and I was not allowed out even to go to the bathroom until she said I could.

Dawson was the capital of the Yukon then, until later they changed it to Whitehorse. When we went to Dawson, we hostel kids were allowed to go to the public school on weekdays. On Sunday went to church. We could leave the hostel on Sunday after church, but we had to go out of town. We couldn't stay in town. The only other time we got out of the hostel was on Friday and Saturday nights when we went to the movies, and on Saturday afternoon we were allowed to go shopping downtown for an hour.

The first year we went to Dawson by plane. Every year after that we went down by the steamboats. Mom drove us to Whitehorse. Mom would take us into Whitehorse by truck in the fall and drive us back in the spring. We went on the boats by ourselves, which was a great trip. It took five days to go down to Dawson and a whole week to come back upstream to Whitehorse. We knew all the deckhands on every boat, because we travelled on every one of them. Frank Slim was the pilot on the boats. We were not allowed up in the pilot house unless the captain said it was ok. Kluane and I were the ones that went the most. Mom used to pay room and board for us.

Harold Lee was the principal at the Whitehorse Baptist Mission School the first year that I went. We went back to Dawson the next year, and Hilda Hellaby was looking after the hostel then. It was a whole new ball game. We were treated like humans.

facing left Grace Chambers with a huge fish caught in the lake, circa 1971. KFN Archives. EMPC. Louise Bouvier Family Images #2. PHOTOGRAPHER WAYNE TOWRISS

facing middle and right For decades Grace Chambers made a living by setting nets in the lake and selling her catch to the Kluane Inn and other lodges along the highway or for credit on goods purchased at the store in Burwash. KFN Archives. EMPC. Ernie Martin Family Images Store Receipt scans #60 and 61

In the past all our mail was read. Everything we wrote was read by Old Man Darim. You couldn't talk to anybody about it, because nobody would believe the stories that you had to tell about him.

In Whitehorse we got out of the mission school on Saturdays. There were no sports for girls, but we had a gym that was part of our school. Our PE teacher came up on some weekends, and he would teach those of us that were interested in gymnastics. He was very good. The boys used to play hockey. We played baseball in the spring, but we came back to Burwash for most of the summer. I would go to Champagne for two weeks during the summer, then come back home and then go back to school in the fall.

When I was in high school, there were some problems at St. Agnes Mission, where we boarded. I had to come home to Burwash, and I did correspondence school for a while. I really didn't want to leave school in Whitehorse. It wasn't my favourite place, but I was learning different languages. My French teacher really took an interest in me, and she said when she got finished with me, I would be a translator for lots of languages. When I left, she was really, really upset, but there wasn't any place I could stay in Whitehorse.

BECOMING A MOM

I stayed in Burwash and worked in the restaurant at the lodge while I did my correspondence courses for a year or so. The restaurant was built long before the hotel was built. The Jacquot brothers built it. Then Leland Allinger and Darrell Duensing bought the whole thing. Later Leland bought Darrell out. I married at a young age and headed off to Whitehorse briefly. I went back to Burwash for another summer after I was divorced from my first husband.

I returned to Whitehorse to work at the Regina Hotel, and that's where I met my second husband, Maurice Bouvier, who came from Manitoba. We had two boys together. I wanted to come to Destruction Bay with my kids when they were small because I wanted them to go to school here. My husband had a trucking business, so we stayed in Whitehorse. I came out and worked for Leland and Betty at the lodge for two to three weeks in the summertime each year. Mom would take my kids when I was working.

We had a big lot in Porter Creek, but the laws were starting to change in Whitehorse by the 1990s. People were saying, "You can't have heavy equipment

in the backyard." The city told us that we had to move our equipment to Kulan subdivision. We weren't going to pay $125,000 for a piece of land and put a building on it.

In the end it worked out perfect. We got a house in D-Bay. As soon as we got it, we started moving and here I am. Back home and I have no intentions of leaving. We moved here in 1994, and this became Maurice's home too. He never wanted to leave it. He worked for Yukon Government for ten years and always had a truck and a loader in the yard. If somebody needed something done, he had to go to work! My kids love it here too. They come out as often as they can.

D-Bay is very different now from the 1960s. There were 250 people then plus transients. It was really, really busy. The Northwest Highway System was operating then. In 1959 a huge wind blew the roof off of the Royal Canadian Electrical & Mechanical Engineers (RCEME) building, where Yukon Electric now sits. This place has had the name Destruction Bay going way back to the Chisana stampede in the early 1900s! People drowned in that bay back then.

I lived in Whitehorse when the land claims process was starting. I was involved as much as I wanted to be until my kids got older, then I became more active in the process. I think the recognition that we got was really good. It was good for the Yukon. It was great that we were the first place to amalgamate all our people together. We were one people then. It changed the way of life for a lot of us. Some of it was really good; some of it was not. But like everything else it's still in its growing stages, and it can only get better.

I worked for YANSI, the Yukon Association for Non-Status Indians, in Whitehorse. We got housing grants to improve living conditions for people who were Non-Status. In those days people had to give up their Status to own a business or go to work for the government. There was a lot of prejudice against Native people, and it still is going on.

facing Portrait of Louise taken in Whitehorse, late 1950s. KFN Archives. EMPC. Louise Bouvier Family Images #3. PHOTOGRAPHER UNKNOWN

above left Ernie Martin, Ron Bouvier, Maurice Bouvier, and Grandma Grace visiting her cabin at Little Arm, circa 1982. KFN Archives. EMPC. Louise Bouvier Family Images #4. PHOTOGRAPHER LOUISE BOUVIER

above right Louise and fiancé Maurice Bouvier at a friend's wedding in Whitehorse, circa 1960s. KFN Archives. EMPC. Louise Bouvier Family Images #5. PHOTOGRAPHER UNKNOWN

RESPECT FOR OUR PAST WAYS

I would like my children, grandchildren, and my great-grandchildren to have respect for what was done in the past and the way it was done. The respect that my mother and aunts and uncles instilled in us. I would really, really like to see this place remain unique, but I don't think that's going to happen.

We've already done a lot of damage to our animals with subsistence hunting. It was being managed not too bad before subsistence. Everybody was hunting, but nobody was hunting excessively. We have friends in Wasilla, Alaska. It's nice to go up and visit with them, and in the spring, in their backyard, there'd be a calf and two cows. That's where they stayed for the first month. We would see people chasing moose out of their gardens because they were eating all the flowers. We don't get that here. I've seen one moose in two and a half years, and I go to Whitehorse on average at least twice a month. Now I haven't seen a moose this year at all. I haven't seen a bear. Saw a rabbit and that's it. Don't see deer. I haven't seen an elk in over a year. I don't know if it's because they've moved or what's going on. It was nice; at one time you could drive here and there, and you could see game. You don't see that anymore.

At Swede Johnson Creek there's no more fish, because the beavers have built so many dams that there's no more grayling coming up there. Same at Edith Creek. They will all be gone soon. Christmas Creek is another one. I like beaver; I think they're industrious, but they do a lot of damage, because they only stay in an area for so long and then they go to another place and do that all again. No one wants to trap them now.

We learned respect very young. And respect brings everything. So what I learned when I was young was a way of life. My grandmother Louise was a very, very, very strong person. She lived in Champagne later in her life. She was very

facing left Maurice and Louise Bouvier celebrating his 70th birthday, circa 2010. KFN Archives. EMPC. Louise Bouvier Family Images #6. PHOTOGRAPHER UNKNOWN

facing right Louise's son Ronald; husband, Maurice; and brother, Ron Chambers, after a fishing trip, circa 2010. KFN Archives. EMPC. Louise Bouvier Family Images #7. PHOTOGRAPHER LOUISE BOUVIER

left Alaura Bouvier celebrates her high school graduation with grandparents Louise and Maurice in Whitehorse, circa 2010. KFN Archives. EMPC. Louise Bouvier Family Images #8. PHOTOGRAPHER UNKNOWN

strict but also gentle. She would sew and do beadwork. I never heard her speak Tlingit. My mom was, well, amazing.

I never thought of doing anything any different with my life. If you told me I couldn't do something, you only said it once. That was the way we were taught. We were taught not only to respect everybody else but mainly to respect ourselves. If you don't have that respect, that is when you stray. You've got to have that respect that was given to us, not forced upon us—it was just there.

I would like to see some changes around here. They may come. I hope they do. I would like to see the drugs and the alcohol gone. It's doing so much damage. It's damaging the young people so they don't want to come back here. They don't want to raise a family here, which is unfortunate because it's the best place in the world! I went to Russia and I loved Russia. It's just not the Yukon.

Big Grandma (Emma Johnson) and Grandma Copper Lily were my favourite Elders here. I loved them both dearly, and that's why Margaret is really precious to me too. She is like them—yes, she is. Grandma Emma, she just had a way about her—so very good. Yes, they were all good people that lived here.

Yes, they were all good people that lived there.

LOUISE BOUVIER

DÄN JU DÄJEL
(PETER JOHNSON)

(b. 1937)

Mountain Hunting Man

Dän Ju Däjel (Where People Went, Peter Johnson, nicknamed Támày) was born at K'amà Dzêa (Ptarmigan Heart) on December 11, 1937. He is of the Crow Clan from his mother, who was Copper Lily Joe, daughter of Copper George Joe from Nįįlį Chù (Nisling River) in Alaska. His father was Jimmy Johnson from Lhù'ààn Mân (Kluane Lake), the son of Gųya and Old Man Johnson. Peter resides at Thomson Centre in Whitehorse, and family members visited him there in 2018 to photograph him and ask about his life. Although not able to record stories at that time, he was able to confirm details of his life, and family members shared more memories of him for this chapter.

facing Dän Ju Däjel (Peter Johnson), 2018. KFN Archives. EMPC. Elders Portraits #24. PHOTOGRAPHER ALISTAIR MAITLAND

Peter and his eleven brothers and sisters were raised in Lhù'ààn Mân Keyí (Kluane Lake Country), mostly in Burwash Landing, in their early years and on the land with their parents and spent their time hunting, trapping, and fishing. He travelled to many places in the Kluane region on the family seasonal rounds, including Chegär Män (Tincup Lake), U Shè Dät'äla (Redtail Lake), Onion Lake, and K'amà Dzêa (Ptarmigan Heart). Peter became an expert trapper with his father and older brother Tommy. When Peter was 15 years old, he shot his first moose with his brother.

The first school Peter attended was the Catholic Mission School at Burwash for several years. Later he was taken to Lower Post Residential School in northern B.C., where he finished grade 8.

When Peter returned home to Kluane, there were many highway and bridge construction projects happening in the region. He went to work cutting survey lines at Dän Zhür Chù (Donjek River) and Nambür Chu (Wolverine Creek). Peter helped to build the pump station for the pipeline at Mile 1124 on the Alaska Highway. He worked as a maintenance man for Betty and Leland Allinger at the Burwash Lodge for fifteen years.

Peter's outstanding knowledge of the land and his bush skills, developed from his earliest years, led him to a new career in the big game guiding industry in 1965. He started working for outfitters as a guide and wrangler, taking clients out on hunting trips in the Kluane region. He worked for Phil Temple for three years. In 1971 he

above Elders Gushàka (Margaret), Tùlhàsèn (Lena), Dän Ju Däjel (Peter), and Mats'an Nats' ats'ulia (Joe Joe) Johnson travelled by helicopter to K'amà Dzêa (Ptarmigan Heart) circa 2016 to visit the lands where they had travelled with their parents as children. KFN Archives, EMPC, Lena Johnson Family Images #8. PHOTOGRAPHER UNKNOWN

started working as a wrangler and guide for Len Berard at Bear Creek and K'ùà Mân (Kloo Lake). In 1987 he went to work for outfitters John Ostashek and Dick Dickson and continued with them for many years.

After he retired, Peter lived at Burwash, continuing to do a little trapping, hunting, and travelling. He was always a busy person around the community, visiting people and kindly helping anyone who needed a hand. He spent a lot of time with Joe Joe Johnson on Joe's Big Arm trapline and at Tayāna (Cultus Bay), trapping, hunting, working with horses, and building a log cabin.

Peter loves to laugh and to make other people laugh and smile. He is renowned for his tall tales and practical jokes. When his nieces and nephews were young, he had them convinced that he played on an NHL team. They would watch a game on CBC and see a player with his name—he told them the game had been played the day before and he had just got back!

Peter is always willing to share his knowledge and has taught many young people outdoor skills. He always participated in heritage outings and helped to preserve Ancestral Knowledge. He was very excited when he was able to return on those outings to places he had not been for a very long time. His love for Asì Keyí (Grandfather's Country) is very strong, and he still shares his knowledge with incredible detail with those that seek his advice on the best way to navigate and harvest from the land.

above Sheep hunting party with trophies. *Left to right:* guides Thomas Joe, Peter Johnson, Joe Joe Johnson, Bruce Temple (son of big game outfitter Phil Temple), and Frank Joe after a successful sheep hunting trip. KFN Archives, EMPC, Sandy Johnson Family Images #14. PHOTOGRAPHER UNKNOWN

above left Peter Johnson, circa 1990s. KFN Archives. EMPC. Sandy Johnson Family Images #15. PHOTOGRAPHER UNKNOWN

above right Peter celebrating his birthday with a snowman cake at Burwash, circa 2010. KFN Archives. EMPC. Dorothy Johnson Family Images #10. PHOTOGRAPHER ELIZABETH JOHNSON

Peter developed some medical issues over the last ten years and eventually had to move into Whitehorse to the Thomson Centre for continuing care. There he lived close by his niece Dorothy Johnson, who was also a resident there. They kept each other company and always enjoyed visits from Burwash family and friends. For some years Peter was able to come home during summers and was always out walking with his walker in the community, waving hello and visiting with people along the way.

Peter's big heart, warm smile, and infectious laugh continue to brighten the days of all who meet him. His many nieces and nephews and entire extended family and community treasure him and his life of hard work and generous gifts to his Lhù'ààn Mân people.

Peter's advice to people is based on long experience: "Always carry your rifle with you when going back to your moose carcass."

above Peter Johnson recording stories with Pauly Sias at Elders Story Camp in Kluane National Park, circa 2006. KFN Archives. EMPC. Susan Howlett Images #1. PHOTOGRAPHER SUSAN HOWLETT

Always carry your rifle with you when going back to your moose carcass.

DÄN JU DÄJEL (PETER JOHNSON)

JÈDÀLĮMĄ (AGNES JOHNSON)

(1943–2021)

Life Has Changed So Much

facing Jèdàlįmą (Agnes Johnson), 2018. KFN Archives. EMPC. Elders Portraits #25. PHOTOGRAPHER ALISTAIR MAITLAND

My name is Agnes Johnson, and my Indian name is Jèdàlįmą, meaning "Down below Mother." My parents were Jessie Allen and Sam Johnson Sr. My grandparents were Old Man and Monica Allen on my mom's side. On my dad's side my grandparents were Jimmy and Emma Johnson.

My grandpa, Old Man Allen, came from Alaska, yeah. They walked to Dawson, then from Dawson. That's where he met my grandma Monica. At Carmacks. It's a long story. I think, according to those stories, we're American people because our family came from the other side in Alaska, but they weren't able to cross back that way after they put the border in. That's why they were all born in Canada. There's Jack Allen and Johnny Allen, and Lilly, and my mom, three girls and three boys. So we became Canadian. Their relatives live at Tetlin. We go there for Potlatch. I been going up there taking my mom and dad to visit my mom's side of the family since I was 17 or 18. So I got to know a lot of people that way, and they got to know me too.

left Sam Sr. and Jessia Johnson at their cabin in Burwash with unidentified man, circa 1995. KFN Archives. EMPC. Agnes Johnson Family Images #1. PHOTOGRAPHER UNKNOWN

I was born in my family's winter cabin at Thè K'u (Salmon Patch) in 1943. That's where Mom was, with my dad all the time. Dorothy was born in 1934. I was the fifth child born there along with my older siblings, Dorothy, Kirk, and Edward. My younger brothers—Michael, Gordon, Sam Jr.—and my sisters—Mary, Gloria, and Alyce—were born at other places. We travelled around to different places where we had camps: Duke Meadow, Tincup Lake, Mile 1120 (Agnes Johnson's camp), and Edith Creek. My mom told me she had one baby who died at birth across the lake.

You go to Mile 1118, and my dad had a cabin there. My grandparents on my dad's side had a cabin nearby, on the other side of the Kluane River. So it was quite a ways away from Burwash. When we were growing up, we couldn't just get up and start playing around, because we have chores to do, and we know that. We have to do it; otherwise we don't go out, simple as that.

So much changes over the years: the highway, land claims. I remember a long time ago when my dad had a Model T car. It was one week to get to Whitehorse, one week. And it was small, holy, that time, small like that. Mary, me, Dorothy, too, I think, would go with my parents. One week. The first day we go as far as Silver Creek, then my dad said, "Oh, wait. We've gotta stop. Car's getting hot. It want water." You know, take water? For the radiator but we didn't know. So he put some more water in, and then he camp there. That's why it took us seven days to get to Whitehorse. It was a wagon road. Big change. Right now it only takes about three hours to get to Whitehorse. No more camping out, no more pulling out tents, no more setting up bed. We used to sleep on branches. Boughs, spruce boughs.

THE GOVERNMENT WAS POWERFUL

They didn't give us warning, nothing, when they made the Park. Then my dad had a cabin on the Park side, and they moved that. He had to get somebody to move it for him to Burwash Creek. It was a trapline cabin. And they got him to move it out of sight. And we even had to sneak across the highway to get our meat, pack it home to feed our kids. It was because they got the Park on one side, then you have the lake other side, so where do you get your moose? So where do you hunt? That's the big question that everybody had. We didn't know where to go, or what to do, because at that time we were just stuck between the Park and Kluane Lake.

Yeah, government was powerful in those days. Because we didn't understand them, you know, that's the power they had over us. With their language because we didn't understand what they were saying. My mom and dad didn't know, because they were raised in the bush, and so they had to do it.

above Sam and Jessia Johnson's large family gathered together in Burwash at their mother's Potlatch in 1998. *Front row left to right:* Alyce, Dorothy, Agnes, Mary, and Gloria. *Back row left to right:* Kirk, Michael, Edward, and Sam Jr. KFN Archives. EMPC. Agnes Johnson Family Images #2. PHOTOGRAPHER UNKNOWN

HUNGRY AND LONELY AT LOWER POST RESIDENTIAL SCHOOL

It was like us when we went to school in Lower Post. We had to go to Lower Post because they told my mom and dad that they were going to be put in jail if we didn't go. Well, it was either that, or they got thrown in jail. That's what Father tell 'em. Father Morisset. I mean, there was cops involved. So we went. And all I heard on the school bus, kids screaming, crying, "I wanna go home. I wanna go home. I wanna go home." That's all I heard for all my life. Till maybe grade 9 or 10.

We came home from school once a year. Not for very long, just for about a month. We went on the bus. Big, big bus. Alaska Highway bus. And the sound, I heard all the way down there, for one week later, kids crying, "Where's my mom? Where's my dad? Where's my auntie?" Yeah, that's all I heard for about one month. But they won't say it out loud, just at night. The nuns will hear them. Yeah, during the night, because they would get so lonesome for their parents.

I was about 7 or 8. My sister Mary went out a year later after I did. At night she would crawl into my bed and cry. And I would just rock her to sleep. Rock her. She's a year younger than me. Then I would rock her to sleep because if the nuns heard her crying, they would come in and strap both of us. They would do stuff like that to us, and so I would just make sure she don't cry, so that they don't hear her, and they don't punish us. So after I put her to sleep, then I pack her to her bed and I'd go to sleep. I'm just a year older than her, but I had to do all that.

There was Kirk and Gordie there too. We can't talk to each other. The boys were on one side and the girls on the other side. They separated us. Dorothy was there for one year, and then she wouldn't go back at the time she turned 16. And so that's my

experience with Lower Post, just a little, short bit of it, but I have lots of other stories. It was a long period of time.

We never get enough to eat, so we have to go to the pantry. But not me because if we got caught—man, you just get it from the nun. More strapping. We never had enough to eat. We only got one egg a year. That's at Easter time, one egg. All the rest it was bread, toast, and mush. Yeah, lots of it. Three meals a day. Mush in the morning and maybe some toast in the morning if we were lucky. Lunch time—soup. I can't remember supper. No fresh fruit or anything—no traditional food. No. So when I went home, I had to relearn quite a bit of stuff because I had to learn about all of my culture.

RELEARNING OUR CULTURE

Language was always here in me. And it still is. But what happened is that I have it all in my head because we were punished so bad if we spoke our language. They wouldn't let us speak our language. They just made sure we kept quiet about it. So a lot of times my brothers would want to talk to us, and they would make language with their fingers. Writing in the air, but I didn't know what they were saying. They would do stuff like that. They have stories, too, about what happened to them. It was different for the boys than for the girls. Totally strict.

Family is important. But, like I said, residential school separated everyone. You cannot talk to your brother or your sister or your relations. You can't. Otherwise you get hit or strapped. So it was hard for us. The only time we could talk to our brothers was when we were on the way home. On the bus.

I had to learn my culture all over again with Mom and Dad when I left school after eight years. Their trapline went all the way down from Jedälį Tl'äw Käy (Duke Meadow) to Thè K'u. Salmon Patch is quite a ways. We used to go down there with dog team. Two dog teams, six dogs each. That's a lot of dogs to feed. In the fall time in late September there's always so much thè kü (dog salmon) down that way. So they would get them, dry them, feed them to their dogs. It is a big chore. They were our main transportation.

In spring we went with our mom hunting for säl (gophers). We'd make their burrow bigger. It would be about 2 inches when they first come out. They would squeeze out. Then when we set trap, we would chop the hole bare, all the ice around. Make it bigger. Then we would set snare there. We used to go from Burwash to Duke Meadow, and then they would go on the trail in the back, towards Salmon Patch. We'd camp there for one week. Get gophers. On the other side of the river down at 1118 (John Trout's Place), they had a place. There's horse trails right down there. They go that way and get the gophers. Then skin 'em out. They would dry the gophers to preserve it. And in wintertime we'll take it out and boil it. Emergency food for winter.

SISTERS HELPING EACH OTHER

Dorothy and I worked together as sisters during the late 1950s and 1960s.

We helped each other quite a bit when we lived at Burwash. You know, we had kids, and we each have water holes at the lake. We also got wood to make fire, keep our kids warm. Joe Joe Johnson helped us too. He did. We did all kinds of heavy work like that, just to keep our family going.

We used to go out in the bush and cut wood with swede saw. At that time there was no power saw. We had to use swede saw. We cut enough wood for Dorothy one night, two nights, and then she'll do the same for me, go out and get wood for my family, my kids, because they were all little. We used to go about 5 miles with a dog team to get wood, put it in a sleigh, and then come back home with it. We kept our fires going all night for our kids to stay warm. They don't understand the hardship that we had and the work we had to do to keep them alive. In wintertime we had to take chisel, axe, and chop the hole in the ice on the lake to get our water, pack it home. We just had buckets. We didn't stay that far away from the lake; our house was close to the lake.

Dorothy and I went hunting up to Duke Meadow. All over the place, for rabbits, gophers. We had to feed our kids. So we hustled quite a bit. Had to set net in the lake for whitefish. That's how we fed our kids. When the lodge opened up, then they're selling hamburgers and stuff like that. If we didn't have any meat, we'd go down there and buy a can of meat, a can of Klik meat. And that's how we fed our kids. And hamburgers—one easy meal!

In summer we used a boat. We didn't go out too far. We just went to where Sharon [Kabanak] lives right now. We went out to the lake, put our net out, and then get fish. And we'd do stuff together like that just to keep alive. Maybe get ten, fifteen whitefish. Maybe one trout. If we got one trout, we were happy. Just medium size.

Life has changed so much from the state that we grew up in to electricity, heat, and all that now. Big difference. Water delivery. I delivered the water for Dorothy. I mean, that's our life. If we didn't do it, who's gonna do it? Our kids were too small. I had seven kids. They're just little ones. At first I had two, Kathleen, Bobby. Dorothy had three boys and one girl. Dorothy had kids later than I had kids. So we had to do it. They all pass away. Arnold pass away

facing top Agnes teaching school kids about snaring, cleaning, and roasting a rabbit, circa 2000. *Left to right:* Jeffrey Mills, Jeri Groves, G.P. Dickson, Marissa Mills, and Agnes. KFN Archives. EMPC. Agnes Johnson Family Images #3. PHOTOGRAPHER UNKNOWN

facing bottom Agnes's granddaughter Alanna Dickson took this photo of la-khel (crocus), carrying on her grandmother's tradition of being out on the land and hunting—in a new way, with her camera. La-khel were Agnes's favourite flowers, the first to bloom in the Yukon in early May. KFN Archives. EMPC. Landscape Images #24. PHOTOGRAPHER ALANNA DICKSON

above Agnes teaching school kids how to set a gopher snare, circa 2000. *Left to right:* Erika Bob, Dennis Itsi-Chitzeh, Monica Johnson, Pascale Dubois, and Agnes. KFN Archives. EMPC. Agnes Johnson Family Images #6. PHOTOGRAPHER UNKNOWN

above In summer Agnes loved to snare gophers to roast over a fire outdoors. KFN Archives. EMPC Agnes Johnson Family Images #4. PHOTOGRAPHER UNKNOWN

and her grandchild. She lost two of her grandchildren. [Including] Darren. Just in the last four years. It is sad, and then she ended up in the hospital. Right now she's in the Thomson Centre, and I go over visit her all the time. I just hope that she'll start moving her legs because she doesn't do anything, just sit there.

She really had a tough life too. You know, we all did in Burwash. We all did. Just to raise our children. Now they have children. It's much easier for them nowadays. Because they have electricity and they have heat. They have oil; they get SA (Social Assistance) from the band for that. So it's a different world. Different world.

WORKING FOR OUR PEOPLE

My first work was at the lodge as a chambermaid, when it was run by Betty and Leland Allinger. In the early 1970s I decided to get more education. I went to the Vocational School in Whitehorse for two years to study life skills and human development. Then I came back to Burwash and worked for Kluane Tribal Council from 1972 to 1998, dealing with health, education, social assistance, and as a NNADAP (National Native Alcohol and Drug Addication Program) worker. While our school was running in Burwash, I taught cultural programs to our children there. We had many programs to try and help people live healthy lives.

In 1977 Bob Dickson, Richie Johnson, Benson Joe, and Hughie Johnson moved a cabin to Down Below for me, and we called it the Louis L'Amour Cabin because it reminded us of the cabins in his books. I moved a bigger house down there later on. In 1982 Joe Bruneau and I got together, and we travelled around a lot. We set nets on Kluane Lake and at Longs Creek. We spent time at 1120, where my parents used to hunt and camp.

I would like to talk about my experience in running KFN with Joe Joe Johnson, when he was Chief. Me and Joe Joe tried to help people. Then when people get SA, we don't give them a cheque or anything. We say, "Did you split wood for George, Little Grace? Yeah, we'll help you." But they have to do it. Work for SA. It worked pretty good for a while. There was a lot of stuff we did like that, Joe Joe and I. We worked long hours. No overtime. No benefit package, no. And now everybody's getting benefits. Even how much work we did, we still get nothing. It wasn't only me. There was those people I named. They were all involved in there. Sure, we fight like everything else, but somebody always win. We had a common vision that we worked towards. It wasn't just to gain for yourself; it was to gain for the community. I was the Chief from 1989 to 1991 and served on Council for three terms (1981–1983, 1985–1989, 1993–1996).

In the 1990s I represented Kluane First Nation on several committees and attended many meetings. I was involved with land claims through the Council for Yukon Indians. I was a First Nations representative on the Yukon Government Advisory Council on Indian Child Welfare. Thinking about benefits from land claims, that's a hard one. Really hard one. We have access to the Park now.

MONEY ISN'T EVERYTHING!

There needs to be more role models to get the younger generation to start helping each other. Nowadays you have to pay young people to help the Elders, to clean their snow off, things like that. But it's just all gone. We need to set an example and get the younger generation to start helping the older people. I'm getting old, but I don't have anybody coming out to my house and helping me with snow shovelling, things like that. I gotta pay them, and that's a different message going out to the younger people. They won't do nothing for you unless you pay them. So I want those young people to start learning to help people, older people.

Long time ago when there was Potlatches in Burwash, lots of people from Aishihik would come over. Oh, from Haines Junction, all over the place. When they had meeting long time ago, it's not like today, just a few people show up to pass a resolution. Long time ago was just packed. Packed, packed with people. It was in the round building. The community hall it used to be. Not like nowawdays, only get about ten, not even fifteen, people in there. They used to have Potlatch in there, supper in there, everything, in that building.

We went down to Salmon Patch two summers ago in 2018. We went with a boat down there. We went down to look at a cabin because people want to use that as a hunting place.

I would like to see a gathering for all the people that went to residential school. Have another big reunion before they all pass away. That's what I would like to see. In Whitehorse. All the survivors, because we're all getting old, and we're all passing on to another world. Be nice to see who's living. I never come to see it when they tear down the old residences. Too many bad memories. Just be nice to get together for a visit. And a feast. Yeah, see who's still going and who's still living.

When you look back at my age now, I think of all the hardship I had with raising my kids, and Dorothy, too, with raising her kids. If it wasn't for us helping each other, I don't think we could've made it. It's not something you think about all the time. Sometimes when I think about it, I think to myself, "Holy, I'm lucky to be 75!" I worked hard all my life.

Money isn't everything. Teaching your children is very valuable so that they can pass it on and the knowledge won't be lost forever.

above Agnes with her children and grandchildren, circa 2000. *Front row left to right:* Gerald Patrick (G.P.) Dickson, Jeffrey Mills, Derek Johnson, Jasmine Walker, Janice Dickson with Austin Dickson, Agnes Johnson with Alanna Dickson, Marissa Mills, Willie Sheldon with Daisy Walker, and Russell Dickson. *Back row left to right:* Lillian Underwood, Gerald Dickson, Bob Dickson, and Kathleen Johnson with Jenna Mills. KFN Archives. EMPC. Agnes Johnson Family Images #5. PHOTOGRAPHER UNKNOWN

Teaching your children is very valuable so that they can pass it on and the knowledge won't be lost forever.

JÈDÀLI̜MĄ (AGNES JOHNSON)

DENNIS DICKSON

(b. 1943)

I Went All Over to Work in My Life

My name is Dennis Dickson. I wasn't born in Burwash, but I was raised here. I was born in Whitehorse at the old General Hospital in 1943. We had a homestead down at the end of the lake. We had gardens down there and lots of rhubarb. Keish (Buck Dickson) was my dad, and my mom was Lilly. My dad owned a big game hunting outfit here.

Mom was from Carcross, the daughter of Patsy Henderson. He was the nephew of Skookum Jim and with him at the Klondike when they discovered gold. Mom had cancer when we were young. Violet Lebarge came from Whitehorse to look after us kids.

facing Dennis Dickson, 2018. KFN Archives. EMPC. Elders Portraits #26. PHOTOGRAPHER ALISTAIR MAITLAND

Thomas Dickson was my grandfather, and he started the homestead here right at the mouth of the river, about 5 miles from here by the trail. There's no widened roads going down there. My grandmother Louise George was Tlingit from Dyea, and my grandfather was from Ontario of Scottish heritage [and he was someone] who came in the Gold Rush days. Dad probably was born here because he was older than his sister Sue. She was born in the bush. There was no highway then, just the wagon road. Grandma had thirteen kids.

My grandfather never talked much about the Gold Rush. He talked about Skookum Jim a little bit. He said that one time Skookum Jim was down in Seattle, and he had a few dollars. Well, in them days, you know, $10,000 was a lot of money. They were down in Seattle, and they were throwing silver dollars out of the hotel room window. He was about to get thrown into jail. People were just diving at it, you know, out on the street. Well, that was a lot of money—a silver dollar. You could buy lots! A little more than what you can buy now with a dollar! He said the policeman was about to ship him back to the Yukon.

Skookum Jim more or less settled at Carcross. He donated some of his money to that foundation the Skookum Jim Foundation. It's still going. I remember Skookies dances. We used to go dance there. That's in my dancing days with Bob Charlie and Malcolm Dawson, Bob Joe. The D-mans, they called their band. They held a few dances, you know, at Haines Junction. The Outfitter's Ball would hire them, and they did pretty good. Everybody had fun. See, them days of drinking everybody would go out and be socializing. D-Bay had a curling club, and there were lots of people here. Then the TV came through, and that pretty much shut everything down. Everybody would stay home and watch TV. Now it's video games and texting; it's even worse.

above Buck and Lilly Dickson with their children, late 1940s. *Front row left to right:* Dennis, Harry, Buck with Cecil, and Lillian with Lawrence. *Back row:* Douglas, Tom, Richard (Dickie), Russell, and Edith. KFN Archives. EMPC. Dennis Dickson Family Images #1. PHOTOGRAPHER UNKNOWN

MISSION SCHOOL DAYS

The highway was built already when I was born. Yeah, there was lots of army personnel and air force in Whitehorse by then. And here, too, everything was run by the army engineers. Then later the highway maintenance was run by the government, DPW (Department of Public Works). First it was army people in control, but they hired local workers. You didn't have to be in the army to work. They had a ninety-man camp at Destruction Bay, and they had running water. They had their own power units with the old circulating pump system. And labour was cheap, so they had eight-hour shifts for pump operators. They kept it going; at 50, 60 below they kept the water going.

In wintertime we kids had to leave here to go to the Baptist Mission boarding school in Whitehorse. The concentration camp—that's what they called it. I was only about 5 years old when I went because my mother had passed away. We'd go there in September, and we never come back until June. Our parents drove us in to Whitehorse. My dad had a truck. I think it was two days to go to town. The highway wasn't like it is now. He died young, when he was only 52, in 1961. I was old enough to look after myself by then.

above As a very young child Dennis attended the Whitehorse Indian Mission School in Whitehorse, run by Baptist missionaries. Whitehorse Aboriginal Women's Circle Image in *Finding Our Faces*, p.1

The Baptist Mission School principal was Reverend Harold Lee. He had two kids, a boy and a girl, Wade and Betty. They were our age and went to school with us. Harold was killed in a highway accident. Then Earl Lee took over, his brother. Well, Earl had to be strict. I mean, you got 250 kids. You've got to have a little discipline. Them days, discipline helps but you can't do that now. Most of the students are gone now, 90 percent. There's only a few left older than me. Some of them, like Gerald Isaac, were there in the later years, also Dave Joe; Bobby, his older brother; Howard Joe, the one that just passed away. Doug Joe, I don't even think he went to school. A lot of them, they stayed home.

It was like the army, with the bunks, and they run it by the same discipline. You were supposed to make your bed in the morning, bounce a quarter on it. Well, you'd never use a quarter because a quarter was worth money! Then, you know, you got certain chores. The breakfast crew, and the crew going around making fires in the classroom, and the wood crew. On weekends we had to go cut wood with a buzz saw and stuff like that. It was run by the kids. They were the workers. They had supervisors.

Food was pretty basic, oatmeal mush. And bread, homemade bread. It wasn't too bad. Dinner's the same thing, soup and sandwiches or whatever. It wasn't that bad. I know they used to bring potatoes from Alberta, a truck load—a whole truck, a 3-ton truck, and then we had to sort the potatoes. You know, how they get bruises on them? They had a cellar. And they'd get beef too.

Some days we'd go to school and it was cold, you know, 50 below, and they had barrel heaters. Then the fires in the wood stoves wouldn't start. It'd be cold in there. You know, it wouldn't take off, and it wouldn't draw. It was kind of a rough life. We had to use ink pens them days with ink bottles. They'd be frozen. Then there was lots of religion too. They pushed that Christian religion, and we'd go to Sunday school. We had Sunday school in the

morning, and I think we had Sunday school in the afternoon, too, sometimes and then church. We'd all fall asleep in church. We'd get whacks in the back of the heads to wake up. I was there for ten years, then I left and went to work.

SUMMERTIME FUN

Well, we had lots of fun as kids back here in the summer. We used to come up to Burwash from the homestead, play all night, and then walk home. There was more kids here then, and they had the barn down here. We never got in trouble, but we always got chased out. We had a swing rope in the hay barn. So in the summertime we would be running back and forth. Yeah, we'd go fishing with our aunt Grace, and we'd go hunting. We'd go across the lake, camp up the Little Arm. She had a cabin up there. Then we'd go up the Big Arm, too, over to Talbot Arm, and we'd get a moose.

Dad had a boat, a Cedar, that come from the coast. He got it through Skagway. They were good boats; they'd last. I think it was around 18 feet, with just a 10-horse motor—the old gravity-fed tank on top and the pull rope. But it would pack! He had a lifeboat, too, one of those lifeboats that come off the steamboats. They were good boats, pointed at both ends, but they cut off one end for the motor. They were good in the wind. They would ride the waves pretty good. Then he had an inboard too; quite a few people had inboard motors with a motor inside and the drive shaft. They'd buy those through Skagway, then the railroad would haul it into Whitehorse and they'd bring it here in trucks. The highway was through by then, and he had a 2-ton truck.

During my school years in summer I'd either go to Burwash or to Carcross with my grandparents. There was lots of activities at Carcross because they had the steamboat and the train. We used to pose for tourists to give us a quarter for taking our pictures. They had lots of kids there too. Carcross people—the Jims, the James—they're related to us through their mother, who was our dad's sister Mary. She married over there and raised her family. She stayed for the rest of her life; she left here and went over there. My grandparents Patsy and Edith Henderson were there too. He had kind of a workshop going for the tourists. He'd sing, and then he had things to show them, like little fish traps he made and gopher traps. Tourists liked that. He had a little lecture, and he'd donate the candy. He'd make a few dollars. In them days $10 was lots of money.

They had Potlatches there, but most of the time they never let no kids in. No, they never let us kids in there. Like here, now they're getting the kids into the tradition, so they'll dance and they learn.

My grandmother Edith was very strict, and she was busy all the time. Edith, Edie Bohmer, was our oldest sister. She was raised there with the grandparents. She left and got married when she was 16. She did good; she raised three boys and one girl. Two boys are still alive, and one got killed in a car accident. You know, when Edie passed away, she had lots of money, and the kids didn't even know that. When she and Don got married, he was working for the CN and he had life insurance. Then he got killed in a car accident, accidental death.

She had a house in Florida, two houses in Whitehorse, one in Tagish, and a condominium in Vancouver, but she was driving an old pickup! Lawrence told her, "Go and buy yourself a new one." She said, "It costs money."

OLD-TIME FAMILIES

After the highway was built, that's when the people started coming here to stay around Burwash. See, the people from Burwash, they used to live down on the Nisling River. That old Chisana stampede used to go through there from Coffee Creek and the Yukon River, over the top of the mountain to Donjek City. Then they'd go across the Donjek and the White River and up Dry Creek into Alaska, hit Beaver Creek. During the stampede they would branch out to the Fourth of July Creek too. They worked hard, them guys. In the winter they'd haul the boilers up with a horse and sleigh. They had a big town that the steamboats used to come up to, Donjek City; the small boats from Dawson would bring supplies. There were quite a few miners out of this whole stampede. Well, others were just prospectors looking for gold.

Some of our old Burwash people used to live at Donjek City. The salmon used to spawn there, and they'd get dog food. And they've got a couple little hills there, and they'd go up there for a look out and look across the flat for moose. Sometimes they'd see a moose way across. It was hard walking, but they had dogs and they'd go across and then they'd run into a moose before they got to that one and they'd put up meat and everything. They stayed there, and then they'd go from there.

Some of the people came down from Copper Center: Sam Johnson's wife and her family, the Jack Allens, all the Allens, Old Allen. They all come from Copper Center in Alaska, and they stayed right around here, trapping, and they had little cabins here.

They had cabins down on the Nisling River too. They trapped all through there.

There was nothing at Burwash then. The Jacquot brothers had started a trading post here long before the highway. They used to have a wagon trail from Whitehorse to the south end of the lake. See, at the end of the lake that was Silver City, and that was the only town. The RCMP and people who lived in there, gold miners, they grew their own gardens and dried their own meat. There was no power then.

In Burwash, too, there was no power here before the war. We had lamps at Christmastime that they'd light up. Kerosene mostly. In Burwash in the 1940s there was our Dickson family and the Johnsons—Peter and Margaret's family—they were Sam Johnson Sr., old Sam's family. And Moose Johnson, Joe Joe Johnson, and all them were here. Jimmy Joe and his kids, they were a little younger. And the Jacquot brothers, Louis and Gene. They started a business here. You know, they did lots of work. I mean, it was a good, good community then with everything.

I WORKED ALL OVER

I was 15 when I took off from mission school. I took off at Easter time. I wanted to work. Went to White Pass. The railroad.

facing Horses up in the mountains around the Donjek Valley northwest of Burwash, circa 2000. KFN Archives. EMPC. Dennis Dickson Family Images #3. PHOTOGRAPHER TED DUNROB.

above Dennis got his first truck in his early 20s and has been driving big trucks non-stop ever since! KFN Archives. EMPC. Dennis Dickson Family Images #2. PHOTOGRAPHER UNKNOWN

above In his teen years Dennis Dickson joined his father, Buck Dickson, on a month-long hunt in the mountains. He is the first person on the left in this image of the crew and clients after they returned to Burwash, circa 1959. *Front row left to right:* Dennis Dickson, Douglas Dickson, Johnny Desrosiers, John Bunbury, Joe Johnson. *Middle row:* Russell Dickson, Carl Chambers, two hunters, Tom Dickson. *Back row:* hunter, Joe Tom Tom, hunter, Buck Dickson, hunter. KFN Archives. EMPC. Louise Bouvier Family Images #9. PHOTOGRAPHER UNKNOWN

Tough job, but of course you're young. Then I got a job as a dispatch in Whitehorse; that's the trucking. They were hauling and getting fuel to different places, so I got in there. I started riding around with Jimmy Profeit, and I learned to drive the truck. It was just a 3-ton. I got in the truck business, and yeah, illegal, no licence, but see, them days it was easy to get your licence, you know. You just answered twenty questions and drive around the block, and you'd get your licence. Not like now, you know, it takes a year or so.

First I was a labourer on the railroad, working on track maintenance. We went to Robinson, just out of Carcross, just between Carcross and Whitehorse. They had a camp, bunkhouses. There were older guys working there, John Burns and Jimmy. Those guys were old railroad hands. They knew how to get us to work and then get us to do the heavy lifting. Of course we were young then. Johnny Tom Tom. He's gone. Joe Jack, a couple of other guys, Lawrence Koch, who was about my age, but we didn't last long. We worked there for about two months, and then we got rich and then I took off. We called it rich in them days.

After that I went to one of the hunting parties here for Joe, Hank's brother. He had a hunting outfit. Then my dad passed away, and I worked for Dick for a couple of summers. Then I went to the highways maintenance. I worked for them twelve years. That's where I learned to operate heavy equipment. Now I own my own. In those days actually there wasn't much work around here.

I lived at Beaver Creek for about twelve years. I got married up there and had one daughter. She lives in Haines Junction now. I have grandkids; they're grown up now. We've got four great-grandsons now. Beaver Creek was a grader station. They had a grader station and Customs and the big tourist lodges—that Yukon-Alaska border lodge. They had the RCMP too. There really wasn't that much there. There was a sawmill.

John and Freda Livesey had a store just out of town. John was a radio technician in the Second World War. That's how he met her, in England, and he brought her over after the war. I guess he was working at Snag airport in air control. See, they had radios then; they didn't have no radar. He brought her up, and then he started a little store there. They had a little store at Snag, the little village there. He worked there for a while, and that gave him the idea. I think it's Jack Dalton that owned that store long time ago because the steamboats used to come up just below Snag, and he used to go to the boat and bring the supplies. It used to land there, at Donjek City, just small boats. He'd order supplies, flour, and sugar.

They still used radios at the airports, and there was one at Snag, the one at Aishihik, then Whitehorse, and then all the way down. Mostly military. They never took no passengers or nothing, but they hauled freight. I used to go out there, not very often; it was a pretty crooked road, 17 miles in there. It closed in the early 60s.

I worked on highway maintenance out of Beaver Creek. We'd come south on the highway just on the other side of Donjek Bridge. There was one lodge at 1137, just a small one, little café and hand pumps there.

And then 1156, there was a maintenance camp, but they shut that down. Just on this side of Pickhandle Lake. The pipeline had a pump station up here, about 20 miles up, called Donjek Pump Station. They had one at Beaver Creek and one at D-Bay. About half a dozen or so people living there. They had housing for 'em. Hardwood floors, everything. They built houses in those days that would last fifty years, not five years like they do nowadays. They shut down, I think, around the early 70s.

Well, it's different nowadays, with the pipelines. Governments don't just allow it unless there's a war, but nowadays you got the environmentalists, which is good. Think about the land too. You can't just allow anything. Gold mines come in there and they tear up the land and they take off, say they went broke. What are you gonna do? Look at Faro! Well, they're still spending millions of dollars. They're just playing around. They're not doing any work. Technology, they come in there, testing for radon and stuff like that, scientific stuff.

After Beaver Creek I went all over. I ran a crane, and I built a few bridges. I built the Takhini River Bridge, the Aishihik River Bridge, Morley River Bridge. On the job training then. It was nothing to operate, just a matter of getting on. They send you to school now, and they put you on new equipment.

Up here nobody owns new equipment. Are you gonna spend half a million dollars on a loader? You got half a million dollars, you put it in the bank and live off the interest! Only the bigger companies, they got new stuff.

PEOPLE HELPED EACH OTHER

Years ago people socialized, and it was much better working conditions. Everybody got on, and we'd go out for a beer and socialize. Never get drunk. A lot of people come from down south, from Saskatchewan. They liked it up here; they stayed right here, and then their families would come up.

We never had TV then, but we had Halloween dances and curling bonspiels. Everybody from Whitehorse would come out. You didn't care if you won anything; you'd just have a few drinks. And you'd help each other; just anytime you needed a little bit of work or you wanted to put up your boat, people would help.

above Dennis Dickson with grandson Taylor Sembsmoen. KFN Archives. EMPC. Dennis Dickson Family Images #4. PHOTOGRAPHER UNKNOWN

Anytime you needed a little bit of work or you wanted to put up your boat, people would help.

DENNIS DICKSON

GÛDIA SHÄW, A NÀCH'ADǸCH'EA (MARY EASTERSON)

(1945–2021)

Good Teaching from Our Elders and Community

facing Gûdia Shäw (Mary Easterson), 2018. KFN Archives, EMPC, Elders Portraits #27. PHOTOGRAPHER ALISTAIR MAITLAND

My Northway Upper Tanana name is A Nàch'adǹch'ea, which is the same as Mary Jacquot (her Tlingit name was Łáde'). My Southern Tutchone name is Gûdia Shäw. I belong to Khàjèt, the Crow Clan. I was born in Burwash Landing according to my birth certificate, but my mother told me I was born in Shär Ch'ù Nji Chù (Edith Creek), which is a traditional area where our family used to live a long time ago. My mother, Jessie Allen, was born in Alaska, so I'm connected to the people in Northway, Tetlin, and that whole area—the Upper Tanana people. My father, Sam Johnson Sr., came from Northern Tutchone people on his mom's side. She was from Fort Selkirk, so he's connected through Carmacks and Pelly Crossing people today.

LEARNING OUR TRADITIONAL RULES—YOU HAVE TO REALLY LISTEN

I like to make sure that we abide by our traditional rules. I wrote a book, *Potlatch: The Southern Tutchone Way*, that explains our roles and responsibilities as Southern Tutchone. I try and pass that on to the children so they understand why we hold the Potlatch ceremony and what it entails. I also wrote four children's books: *Mouse Story*, *Picking Berries with Grandma*, *Bear Story*, and *Christmas Story*.

My grandmother, Monica Allen, from the Northway side was very religious—not religious in the Catholic Church sense, but she carried on our spiritual ceremonies and taught us what to do. My parents did as well. We also learned something through books and going to university, where I took courses. It's all a combination of good teaching from this community. When we were growing up, we had all the Copper family and all the Johnsons as Elders. Copper Lily and her family, my dad's family, and all my aunties: Nellie, Rita, and Margaret. So we had all those teachings. They didn't write it down in a book, but it was all passed down orally so you had to learn the information from them and really listen!

POTLATCHES, SPIRITUALITY, AND THE OLD WAYS

We grew up in the traditional areas where we still have cabins: in Duke Meadow, where we had our summer camp. In the springtime we were at Edith Creek because of the fishing. And in the winter we went to Salmon Patch. These places were traditional gathering places.

Duke Meadow was a place where we used to have Potlatches and ceremonies. At one point when there was a Potlatch happening there, I know there were Indian doctors. My two grandmothers were doctors, on my mother's side and my father's. Then there was another one from Aishihik. They came to the Potlatches that used to be held at Duke Meadow. I don't remember the early, early Potlatches, but I do remember there were a lot of people there that I wasn't really familiar with. At one point somebody fed me goat meat, and then I started choking. One of the Indian doctors came over and they did something, and then the meat came up. Then they said, "You can't be eating that, because that's your spirit helper, you see?" Everybody has a spirit helper. They just have to know what animal it is. I never heard of birds as a helper, but I know about animal helpers. And so mine was goat. You're not supposed to eat it.

above Mary picking berries, circa 1967. KFN Archives. EMPC. Mary Easterson Family Images #1. PHOTOGRAPHER UNKNOWN

Nobody really talks about it anymore; being an Indian doctor is not practiced openly anymore. I'm sure there are younger people in our generation, or the younger generation, that could follow that. I haven't seen anyone practice that, not since my grandmother passed away. That's really critical, I think, because it really shows you the different way. It's a religion, like Catholicism. They used to have their practices.

I really hope to see some time in the future when our spirituality is practiced again, because it's really an important part of our culture. It's not totally lost, I don't think, because people still pray and do a lot of things, but they are not having the ceremonies. The old people had sacred things that they kept, which they only used when they were having their ceremony. Today someone who wanted to learn would have to go somewhere where that's being openly practiced still. I think a lot of that went underground with the residential schools. People don't talk about it openly today. There are still Indian doctors in Canada that I know of. I know there's some in Alberta.

I think that's important to revive more of those practices. It's still there. There's still people that have knowledge of it. That's really important, I think, to our culture because we've lost some of the ceremonies. One particular ceremony we've lost, I guess because of the new technology, is that before when a young person became a woman, they used to put you out in the bush. You used to have to survive there for three or four days by yourself. One of these things we tried to do is to document that in our lifetime so that people know and understand that part of our ceremony, which was lost. I think this year KFN is going to do a women's camp, and hopefully that's a beginning of reviving that kind of ceremony.

We had the marriage ceremony, which we no longer have, where you exchange the moccasins. Those are ceremonies that we've lost over time, because of having residential school. This area became Catholic. Our belief system has to be recorded and transmitted to future generations so they will know what they don't know now.

I remember my grandmother, she lived in a tent and would never live in a house. They absolutely refused to live in a house, even in the wintertime. It's just the way they were in their day. I don't really know why. I just know that's what their practice was. And yet when we went to Salmon Patch, my dad built cabins over there. He built cabins all over the country, and he built two cabins over at Salmon Patch. We started to go back there last year. First time my whole family went back there. So we're gonna go again this spring and in the summer. My parents stayed in the cabin over there, not here. There were no cabins at Duke Meadow at the time. It was all tents. Wall tents.

above Mary's parents Sam and Jessia Johnson, circa 1990s. KFN Archives. EMPC. Mary Easterson Family Images #12. PHOTOGRAPHER UNKNOWN

OPENING THE DOORS TO EDUCATION

I believe I was 6 when I went to residential school, then Christ the King High School, and then I went to university at SFU and UBC. I believe there's only one other person from here that went to university when I did. I saw an opportunity in that. When I got back, I thought, "Let's open these doors for the other people who had not had a chance to go to university." Let's do something about it. So what I did in fact was make the government offer all these programs. There's still some existing now. I wasn't totally involved in the Remedial Tutor issue in the 1970s, but I pushed for the Native Teacher Education Program.

above Spring Break Carnival for the Burwash kids at Kêts'á dan' kų in 1979. Kids and adults participated in a swede saw contest near the community school. *Left to right:* Michael Belinsky, Donalda Easterson, John Clark, unidentified child, Mary Easterson, Daniel Tlen, unidentified children, teacher Peter Stewart, Joyce Johnson, and Joe Joe Johnson. KFN Archives. EMPC. Mary Easterson Family Images #3. PHOTOGRAPHER UNKNOWN

I pushed for the Native language teachers in the school system, all those kind of things so that we would see our young people as graduates. I started the Native Graduation Ceremony. The first year, in 1975, there were only six Native grads in the whole Yukon! Today we see over a hundred and close to 200.

I think what inspired me was being rooted in Burwash Landing. I was rooted here because my parents and my aunties, and all my family, really thought education was important. They did. I went to university, and then when I came back in the 70s, there were all the Black Power and Red Power people. Back then there was racism in the government—that really inspired me to try and crush that. It was so evident—right in your face. It was a struggle just to get them to change and to introduce new programs. They just refused. They wouldn't even fund our school in Burwash Landing. In the first year we had to apply to all sorts of places, all around the world. The UNESCO people in Geneva gave us money just to pay our salary.

I was on my way to the United Nations in New York one time, and I happened to stop at Ottawa. So I went to the House of Commons and was talking to some political leaders there. I asked them to bring up the school here in Burwash Landing, and they did. And you know what? Within months they sent a letter to the Government of Yukon saying if you don't fund this school in Burwash Landing, the Canadian government will fund them directly and that's going to set a precedent in the Yukon. So they had to turn around and fund us. They had to pay our wages as teachers, myself and Sandy Johnson, who was a teacher there too.

I think one of the reasons my parents supported education is because they didn't want us to struggle and have a difficult time like they did. Sometimes they couldn't get jobs. We had major barriers in this community. We had Parks Canada, we had the Game Sanctuary, we had all that history, which was their history, and they saw it. I guess they must've seen it as barriers. We had barriers to education that would stand in your way unless you knew how to overcome it. So they really pushed us to get a good education, and that was critical for them.

It was not only our family. The whole community was like that. You know, every aunt, every uncle, everybody was interested in your education, interested in kinda pushing you little bit, nudging you, like that. We had the highest graduate rates in Canada per capita. Think about that! We had all these graduates from university. We had seventeen students, and out of the seventeen I'm sure fourteen of them went to university. The other three went to trade school or did some post-secondary. They didn't drop out like today. People drop out today because they don't have the support. It's a transition they have to make to Whitehorse now.

HARDSHIPS LED TO CHANGE

My father, Sam Johnson Sr., was involved in a very famous court case. He was trapping at Pickhandle Lake in 1975. We had made an agreement with the Government of Yukon, Renewable Resources, that they would not bother us there. For a long time we were always being harassed by them, but they had finally agreed, "Ok, you can go in there and get the muskrat. You can do that, and we won't arrest anybody." We were doing this in April, going out there again, and they arrested my father. They took away all his traps, all the muskrat, and he had a heart attack. It was the Game Branch people from Haines Junction. Apparently the officials that we met with in Whitehorse didn't relay the information to their staff in the field. They just went over there and took all his stuff.

We had a meeting after my dad suffered that heart attack, and they agreed to changes. Eventually we got the Game Sanctuary back to some degree through our land claims, and we were allowed to hunt without being arrested. The reason is that we lived on this land right here, and we have the old stories where all the old people say, "We can't live on fish alone." That's a very famous Burwash Landing saying of that day because we had no access to the Park, no access to the Game Sanctuary at all. So where you gonna get moose? Way over there, I guess, somewhere on the other side and bring it back across the lake.

I was involved with another legal case about hunting access with my brother Edward Johnson and Henry Michel, who at the time was my partner. We went in to the Game Sanctuary in the summer of '78. We tried to go in there and get arrested, so our people could get access to the Game Sanctuary back and Parks Canada lands. Negotiations were going on but going nowhere. We got a sheep up there at Quill Creek one night. We went back the next day to get the sheep, but there were Game Wardens from all over hiding in the bush. They hid their vehicle. I didn't see it when we went up there. We were halfway up the mountain, and just as soon as we were going to get that sheep, they jumped us.

Our generation wasn't the only active one. My father and Grandpa Moose Johnson and all those old people sent a letter to the government in 1952 saying they were starving in Burwash Landing because they could no longer go into the Park and the Game Sanctuary to hunt. They wanted the government to allow them to go into the Game Sanctuary to get one moose. It was a long winter that year, and people went hungry.

In those days we used to hunt across the road in the Park anyway. Since we didn't

above Combatting racism and systemic injustices in government and in the education system required huge amounts of courage and energy in the 1970s. Mary was an early First Nations political activist in the Yukon, building on the work of previous generations to advocate for change to overcome barriers that prevented First Nations children from succeeding in school. Mary Easterson and Daniel Tlen presented a briefing on education issues in Whitehorse in the mid-1970s. KFN Archives. EMPC. Mary Easterson Family Images #4. PHOTOGRAPHER UNKNOWN

above Mary loved to learn; she studied her own culture passionately and also pursued Western education, graduating with a Bachelor of Education and then a master's degree from the University of British Columbia. *Top:* Mary in cap and gown with her bachelor's degree, 1984. *Bottom:* Mary with her children at her graduation from UBC, left to right: Donalda Easterson, Justina Michel, and Juniper McLeod. KFN Archives. EMPC. Mary Easterson Family Images #5 and #6. PHOTOGRAPHER UNKNOWN

have legal access to that area, if you got a moose in the day you'd have to get it out at night and sneak across. People would listen for a car and say, "Go!" and then you run across the road. It was because of all those things that changes really had to be made in the Yukon, especially in our area. There was so much racism in government policies and how they were acting in those days. Our traditional territory was removed from us by somebody in Ottawa. So that created a lot of problems for our people of that generation. I think now people are more vocal in standing up for more. It was their hunting grounds. I think it's the hardship that people go through that makes them strive for more and to change things. It's really the hardship, I think.

KEEPING OUR CONNECTIONS TO THE LAND

When I went to university, my parents supported me. Somebody in the church might have helped me, too, but I just applied like everybody else. I was 20-something. I went to Simon Fraser first, and then I transferred to UBC. All my kids went there after me. I got my Bachelor of Education from UBC, and then I got my master's degree from UBC too. It was something that had to be done, so I didn't see it as an adventure. I just saw it as something I wanted to do and at the same time try and maintain my cultural knowledge that was passed on to me.

I think you have to have a balance, and that's a balance the younger people need to know. Now they're all focused on playing their digital games, but really they have to have more of a balance. They have to learn more of the land because they're going to be the caretakers of the land in the future. They're going to be assuming that responsibility. They better learn quickly, and that's why I think they need to focus.

Now young people are expanding their focus; they're doing more science and things like that. I'm just hoping there'll be more jobs for them because there's more and more coming back every year. We need to keep that connection. If we can't record and preserve what we have, we won't be a society anymore. We'll just be like anybody else. That's why I think it's really important that the knowledge we have today is passed down to the next generation. They have to preserve it, record it, film it, everything like that. You know, there's songs that Kitty McClellan took down to the University of Wisconsin a long time ago, and we have them today. It's the old songs and the old stories that are being slowly lost, because everyone's going digital.

When I came back after university, the Education Director position within CYI was open, so I applied. It was a field that I wanted to go into because that's where you can make the most changes. You could change a lot of things there. We changed a lot of programs in the schools, so that kids would be more successful. Because they weren't graduating. I don't know why. Maybe they didn't have the support or something. I don't know. All I know is that the year I started the first Native Grad, we only had six grads. To me that's a sad statistic.

BUILDING OUR OWN SCHOOL IN BURWASH

In the 1970s we asked the government to do something about setting up a school in Burwash Landing, and they wouldn't. They just refused. Largely it was organized by myself, and Daniel Tlen helped me. Then the government refused to fund it, so I had to lobby around the world. Then we refused to send our kids to school at D-Bay. Everybody did. The whole community—it was a community then. We did everything, and everybody supported what we did. So we just started the school without funding, without getting paid. We had two buildings that were already here as housing. We just moved whoever was in there out. We had kindergarten to grade 3, I think, in one area, and then the next building was grade 4 and up. My kids went to school there.

The whole community supported us is all I can say, because without that we would never have gone as far as we did. The first class was seventeen children. They just went right on to school after that in Whitehorse, and then from there the majority of them went to university. That's the way it should be. But today some kids are not finishing school.

We had the regular school programming. We had math and all that, but we also had Elders in the classroom. Some of the Elders would sit in the back and sew, cut dry meat sometimes, just doing traditional education. We went to Muskrat Camp and things like that. Muskrat Camp's been going on for years. It didn't just start ten years ago; it's been on since we've been around.

Sandy and I were the only two teachers. We were busy all the time as young parents too. We were just busy. We had meetings with parents on a regular basis, and they volunteered too. The Elders would be in the classroom. It was a community school. I think that's the part that's missing here now is that they don't have that. After I retired, no one really picked it up, because times change.

Land claims became such a big push for so long. It took so long to finish it, and so many people had to devote themselves to that to get it done. It seems like we just spent decades working so hard on that. So the school lasted for about three years. Ultimately there were some people within Yukon Government who came out here to see it but only when they wanted to inspect it. They never said, "We like your programming." They did send some equipment when they shut down a school somewhere else.

above As a mother Mary always encouraged her children to pursue higher education, just as her parents had supported her to go to university. Graduation day in 1985 for daughter Donalda Easterson at F.H. Collins High School in Whitehorse. *Left to right:* Justina Michel, Donalda Easterson, Mary Easterson, and Juniper McLeod. KFN Archives. EMPC. Mary Easterson Family Images #7. PHOTOGRAPHER UNKNOWN

That was really, I think, a major wrong move on the part of the government. The government of the day didn't really care, because if they did, they would've helped us establish the school here. They just thought, "It's just Burwash Landing." It's still like that today, as far as I'm concerned. They don't have a school here; they don't have a swimming pool. People still have to move for their kids to go to school. At this time you'd think there'd be a high school to keep it as a community, but instead it's a scattered community. Kids still have to leave. After you're finished grade 8, you're done here. You're in Whitehorse, and then you're on a new path. After that your path opens up more, and you're like my granddaughter Jade over in England, going to university there. So that's so far away from Burwash Landing, you know. It's great for her, but they're never going to live here, I don't think.

The Yukon Government was racist, and they wouldn't fund it. Danny Lang, Hilda Watson—they all just stood against the school. I did a tour across Canada on the land claims and the school. They followed me all across Canada to Ottawa. Flo Whyard was right behind me talking to people. After I was on the radio or on TV in Calgary, next thing she's on TV in Calgary right behind me. I'll be somewhere else, and they send someone else. What a waste of government money!

above Three generations gathered together in 2013. *Left to right:* Jeremiah Groves, Sierra Easterson-Moore, Jacob Groves, Jade Groves, Nathan Easterson-Moore, Chishana Michel, and Mary Easterson. KFN Archives. EMPC. Mary Easterson Family Images #8. PHOTOGRAPHER UNKNOWN

facing top Potlatch traditions are an important aspect of culture in Kluane First Nation. In 1992 Mary worked with Elders to record stories and publish a book so that the information would be available for future generations. Here she is in her regalia at a Potlatch with her daughter Justina Michel in front; her mother, Jessia Johnson, in the middle; and her sister Alyce Johnson on the right. KFN Archives. EMPC. Mary Easterson Family Images #9 and #10. PHOTOGRAPHER UNKNOWN

facing bottom Another Potlatch image of Mary in her regalia.

The young kids went through kindergarten, grade 1, grade 2, grade 3. So it might've been open four years. Possibly five. I just remember it was sad when it did close, because it had been such a big effort. I mean, we had bake sales and fundraising. We had a walkathon—we walked all the way to Whitehorse. I remember we had all the CYI politicians come out to support us. They only walked 1 mile, really. They didn't even make it to Destruction Bay! Well, we walked and we drove, took it in segments. There was myself, Daniel Tlen, Rosie Blair-Smith, and all the younger people, all the younger kids. The whole school, really. I don't remember lots of adults doing the whole thing. That day when we got there, we went to a hotel. I guess everybody was so tired.

After our school closed, the Department of Education sent me to Mayo to teach. I think Sandy went to Haines Junction. I didn't stay in Mayo very long. I was offered different opportunities. I sat on the Education Reform Commission, and then I did the whole political thing nationally. I was on the Assembly of First Nations National Inquiry on Indian Education. My kids were growing up then, and we had to move back to UBC. My kids went to University Hill High School and then university.

WORKING TOGETHER IN BOTH WORLDS

I think that there's things that I would really like to see kept intact in our culture: the ceremonies, the language, the storytelling. Those kinds of things are really critical to pass on to the next generation, and doing all the traditional activities. We're so gifted; we had Gerald Dickson, who did the recording of cultural activities, and we have all sorts of other people who are gifted in other things. We just need to all work together to try to preserve this and make sure it's passed on. Otherwise if you don't write it, you don't record it, you don't film it, in forty or fifty years from now our great-great-great-grandchildren, will say, if they're still living here, that they need to know what people valued in our day. Otherwise you could just live somewhere where they don't have any knowledge of anything. I think that's really critical, really, really critical. Kids learn that way today; they know all these games. It's got to be recorded in books and everything you have. Otherwise we might as well just be like everybody else.

I was involved with the land claims negotiations with Harry Allen and Dave Joe from the beginning until the 1984 Agreement in Principle was rejected because it didn't permit self-government. That AIP didn't go far enough for us, so I'm glad it was rejected. I believe KFN voted against it. They would never agree on something like that.

I was gone when the UFA was negotiated. I was involved at the university with First Nation student issues. Going in

marches, doing things like that, and then getting my kids to school. There's still some things I don't like about land claims, like the taxation issues. I still really strongly believe they should never have taken that away from us, whatever little rights we had. That was one of the major rights. We voted against the taxation and lost. It's just one of those things. It's done with. We can't argue or talk about it now. Who cares? It's done. You pay taxes and you die, I guess.

I think there's things that we need to hang onto, that we can't just forget about it. It's sad that people aren't fighting for a school here, but I can understand that things have changed. People are more mobile, for one thing, and kids are really into being digital and everything like that. The school committee interviewed me and borrowed my Potlatch book so they can get background. They were trying to piece what they needed for the school here. I said it's important to have a traditional area attached to your school, like a smokehouse, because that part is as important as the inside of the school. You can do things with the kids, traditional things, and you have science in it, you have math in it, so you could learn and do projects. We do projects over at Duke Meadow. We have cabins and a classroom there. So I would like to see the younger kids have that knowledge and work in both worlds.

You have to work in both worlds today. You have to have that knowledge and survive over there, too, in the white man's world, because you can't have just a one-sided education anymore. You have to have both. I think it is important to the other kids too. That's why we have the Muskrat Camp, where they're outside learning and it's still like learning in a school.

Climate change is really important. I say to people today, "It's fine for you to be doing these things that you say you're doing, but what needs to happen is you need to tag on to the younger kids. Tag on the Youth, kids in university, so that they learn about Ancestral Knowledge while they're here in the summertime. They should know about fishing in Kluane Lake and what's happening there. They should learn about all the sciences in the area. In order to do that you need to look at your funding base and make sure it happens." Today we have students in all fields except for engineering, which I'm trying to push my grandson to go into. I think that's an area we haven't conquered yet.

I notice lots of things, but when I'm talking about preserving and transmitting culture, that is really critical. It's something our leadership need to stand up and remember. Otherwise in twenty years kids will be coming back here, and they'll say, "What is that?" It's like in a city now where they're having all high-rises, so in fifty, sixty years they'll say, "What's a house?" See? Like that kids will come back here and say, "What's a Potlatch? Why are we doing this? Why are we putting the ashes on the kids, or why are we doing that?" They wouldn't know unless someone told them why that happens. The Potlatch itself has a lot more meaning than just coming here when somebody passes away. It has responsibilities laid out.

left Lena Johnson and Mary Easterson enjoy a visit together at culture camp, circa 2010. KFN Archives. EMPC. Sharon Kabanak Family Images #17. PHOTOGRAPHER SHARON KABANAK

facing Mary at home in Burwash in 2017, cutting and drying moose meat with granddaughter Sierra Easterson-Moore. KFN Archives. EMPC. Elders Portraits #28. PHOTOGRAPHER ALISTAIR MAITLAND

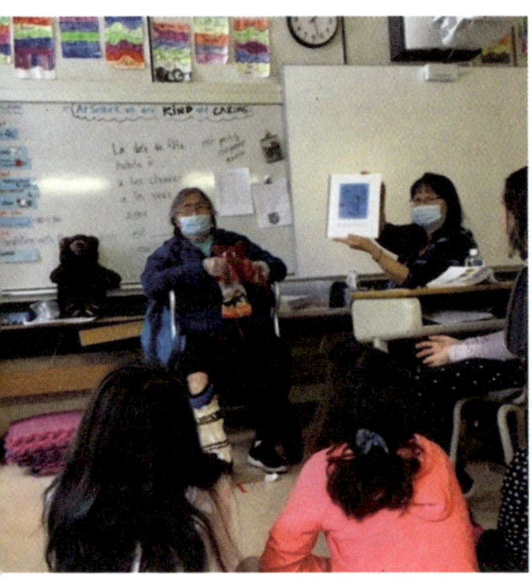

above Even in COVID times Mary continued to teach and share her culture, here in her granddaughter's classroom beside her daughter Donalda Easterson. Left to right with backs to the camera are Sierra Easterson-Moore and another student. KFN Archives. EMPC. Mary Easterson Family Images #11. PHOTOGRAPHER UNKNOWN

Crow has to do this; Wolf has to do that. So that's how you develop your belief system; you pass it on.

So I think our history has to be recorded for all the people here. We're not going to be here forever, so we need to pass it down. I think it's important to continue being vocal about things, trying to help the Council in some way or be vocal on the Elders Council. I think we need to speak up. I think it's really critical. It has to be expanded. You have to go around with film. A book alone is not good enough. Who wants to read a book in fifty years? Probably nobody, they're all digital. Might be something different; I don't know what. But it's gotta be video. That's the future. And that's how kids learn to preserve culture. That's how we've learned in the past. We've always been visual. We're just carrying on tradition.

Through the years I participated on many committees including the Yukon Teacher's Certification Board, UBC House of Learning Board of Governors, as Chair of the Yukon Land Claims Training and Implementation Committee, Yukon College Board of Governors, Yukon Indian Curriculum Advisory Board Commissioner, Education Act Commission, Standing Committee on First Nations Education in the Yukon, and the Royal Commission on Aboriginal Peoples. I had an opportunity when I was at UBC to teach, so I taught there for a couple of years, which was really an amazing opportunity.

I have had enough of school. Now I just want to cut more dry meat. I got here Monday. I cut meat all day Monday, Tuesday, and Wednesday!

I have had enough of school. Now I just want to cut more dry meat. GÛDIA SHÄW (MARY EASTERSON)

DOUG SIAS

(1952–2019)

Just Really Good People

I was born in Whitehorse, on January 17th, 1952. My mom was Josephine, called Josie by most people who knew her. My dad's name was Frank Sias. Mom's mother was Mary Jacquot, daughter of people from the Nalin area of the Takhini River and Dhàl Da Tà (Mountain Man, Copper George Joe), who settled at Burwash in their later years. Grandma's siblings were Da Kwäthala mą (Nice Face, Kitty); Tsal KàJana (Gopher Lady, Copper Lily); Shäw Nàts'àli Tà or U Ts'àn Nëkhì Ts'ulia (Expect Something from Hunting, Him to Go Hunting Luck Go to Him, Jimmy); Shan che'a (Poor Little Thing, Bertha); and Tàa'aana (Lots of Everything, Place of Abundance, Jessie). Mom was of the Wolf Clan, like her mother and all her siblings and their mother, and now me and my sister, Linda.

facing Doug Sias, 2018. KFN Archives. EMPC. Elders Portraits #29. PHOTOGRAPHER ALISTAIR MAITLAND

ALASKA HIGHWAY FAMILY

Mom spent most of her life in Burwash. My dad was from B.C. They met in the late 1940s in Vancouver. Mom had been going to school out there for a while. Then she got a job at one of the fish canneries in Steveston. My dad was working on the tugboats as a young fella. I guess the fishing industry brings people together. They met out there and got married in 1948. They drove up the original Alaska Highway in an old Model A Ford that year. That would be a real adventure. Gotta be pretty brave, you know. It would have been quite an experience, that's for sure. They came to Burwash and worked in this area for a few years.

The lodges all along the highway were getting started. People could see the writing on the wall, I guess. It would be a good business to be in. I don't know how many were actually in operation. My mom and dad ended up working at some of those lodges, from Morley River right up to Beaver Creek and in between over the years. So it provided jobs and opportunity.

They worked at the Morley River Lodge. Clyde Wann owned that. And they worked at his lodge in Beaver Creek. Mom also worked for the people at Bear Creek Lodge, and they helped out quite a bit with Betty and Leland at the Burwash Lodge.

My sister, Linda, was born in 1950. We moved around a fair bit in our younger years, that's for sure. There used to be a pipeline pump station up the road from Burwash at Mile 1124. We spent about five years at that pump station. We home-schooled there in the winter. My dad was working there. Mom would come down to Burwash to work for Betty and Leland at the lodge in the summertime. We would spend our whole summer here at Burwash. It was great. My grandma just lived down the road at her old place. She used to be down on The Point, and that's where we stayed—at Grandma Mary Jacquot's home.

Grandma was great, and there were lots of other Elders of that generation around that I can remember. They were all just down to earth, great people. Just really good people. Strong people with a real sense of a community. Everybody did things together, and everybody was happy. They had a hard way of life; most of their houses were one-room log cabins. Nobody was bellyaching. And they had this beautiful lake.

One of the cool things, I think, is that it wasn't just the men that were the hunters and the fishermen. A lot of the women did just as well, if not better. I can remember going out with my grandma, and she'd set a net down in front of her place. Maybe Jessie Joe would be down there too. They all just did it.

We went out on the rowboat. They were little rowboats, very little. No motors. Just oars. My sister and I still talk about being in Grandma's old rowboat out there on the lake. She'd let us get out of the boat and hang onto the back of the stern, and she'd keep rowing. She wouldn't go too far but plenty far out there to drown. And we never had no lifejackets, but we had a good time. Surfing behind the boat! If there had been a problem, I'm sure she would have got the job done.

It was a different way of life. Childhood was different, and I was probably one of the fortunate ones. I had a good childhood in this area wherever we were. I have a lot of good memories. My parents were welcomed at just about any place, whether it was in this area or Beaver Creek, Haines Junction, Morley River. I think they ended up of being the managers at Morley River Lodge. They were intelligent people and hard workers. Everybody was a hard worker back in those days. Those lodges were twenty-four-hour, seven-day-a-week operations. No days off or phoning in sick—nothing like that. They just went to work. People would need gas, tires changed, vehicles towed; lots of variety in their work, that's for sure.

CHALLENGES FOR SCHOOLING

I know a bit about my mom's early life here. I always wanted to sit down with her and get that history, but then she got sick and passed away in 2012. So I didn't get it all. But from what she told me she had a good childhood and pretty much all in this area. Back in those days there was no school here, so they had to leave home for schooling. My grandfather Louis was from France. He decided that his two oldest kids, Louis Jr. and Rosalie, should go to France for their schooling. I'm not sure if my mom spent one year in France. The two oldest ones did.

Mom went to school in Dawson for a little while, and then the rest of her schooling was in Vancouver, with Louis Jr. and Rosalie. Grandpa Louis had a bit of money, and he hired a nanny or a housekeeper to look after them in Vancouver while they went to a Catholic school there. I think she was out there for ten years. So it was hard for her and her brother and sister. It was also hard on my grandma and of course grandpa too. But he was looking to the future for the better. I think to my grandma it was, "You've taken my babies away, and now I don't get to see them." I think when they first went to France, they were there five or seven years before they ever got back. Too far to come back. Whereas my mom, I don't know whether she got to come back every summer from Vancouver, but she did come sometimes. She was closer, probably because she was the youngest and the most spoiled.

Then the next younger generation of Burwash kids all had to go to Lower Post or Whitehorse. It wasn't easy on any of the kids around here, for sure. I was lucky to have a little bit of homeschooling and then elementary school down the Haines Road at 48 Mile and my high school in Whitehorse. So I was pretty fortunate I didn't have to go away with the other kids. I think my mom probably had something to do with that, too, because of her experience.

Our homeschooling materials came out of B.C. We were at the pump station with her teaching us for the first part of our schooling—five years, probably. I think before that we started out in Haines Junction because she was working at Bear Creek Lodge then. And then from up here we went down the Haines Road to another pump station about 110 miles south of the Junction, just 6 miles north of Canada Customs. That was one of the reasons they wanted us to go down there: because we were two extra kids and they were trying

facing top Elders Jessie Joe, Copper Lily Johnson, and Mary Jacquot out for a walk in Burwash in the 1970s. KFN Archives. EMPC. Doug and Linda Sias Family Images #1. PHOTOGRAPHER UNKNOWN

facing bottom Doug and sister, Linda Sias, playing on an old wagon at Burwash, with Geannie Atkinson standing on the side, late 1950s. KFN Archives. EMPC. Doug and Linda Sias Family Images #2. PHOTOGRAPHER UNKNOWN

to get their own school going there. I think the first year they had school there was the year we moved there, in 1961. So then we had an elementary school up to grade 8, probably about twenty-eight kids total. After that we had to go somewhere else.

There were twelve families right in camp, and then a few more people had their own little thing going on nearby. It was a good place to grow up. We had a lot of fun down there. Lots of kids, lots of freedom, lots of snow, skiing. There again on the weekends everybody got together and went skiing, had wiener roasts, and just nothing but play. It was a good time. Pretty lucky.

When Mom was homeschooling us, we studied pretty much Monday to Friday. It was all done in the school year, like it is today, so she wasn't working at any of the lodges then. She was just a mom at home and a housekeeper, and she would teach us school. She wouldn't teach us in our house. For some reason she wanted to go to another building across the road that they weren't using. That was our school. So we actually left the house and did all our studies over there, and then came back home at night. It wasn't a free-for-all; we were going to school. From her upbringing, and maybe she got some of that from her dad, she knew education was going to be a big part of everybody's life. I think she had better luck with my sister. I think I fooled around quite a bit. Managed to get through life anyway.

JACQUOT FAMILY ROOTS

I didn't get to know too much about the Jacquot brothers, other than the name and what my mom or my grandma told me. I think Grandpa died in 1948. I wasn't born till 1952, so I didn't get to meet him. And the other Jacquot brother, Eugene, died in 1950. So I just heard the stories about them as some of the early pioneers of this area. Both were hard workers apparently. And it was a big journey for them when they came from France, I guess. They were both young men, and both were chefs. They got to the East Coast and worked their way across Canada, cooking. How they actually ended up in the Kluane area I don't know, but that's just how things happened. I know my grandfather got into the gold mining. Eugene might have been part of it too. But from what my mom says, Eugene was the business head behind everything. My grandpa was the worker guy. So they had it all figured out between themselves.

They built their pioneer road, which became part of the foundation of the Alaska Highway, and they were freighting out to Kluane region from their early days. I guess it was just a horse trail and they upgraded it to the wagon road, and it just kept going. As a kid I can remember very vividly, down in front of Burwash, there were just the two roads: one went straight to the lodge; the other one went up towards the church. When you get right at the hill and you drop down where the lodge is, they had all the old freight wagons and old trucks once they upgraded to that. I can just remember those old vehicles, and it's too bad a lot of that wasn't preserved. A lot of history went down the tubes there. They had big sleighs on runners for the winter. There were a few of them I remember, but mostly wagons on wheels. There were a couple, three of them, down at Silver City and at Christmas Bay.

They had their store here, too, and their outfitting business. They were very successful. Nowadays ten days, two weeks is a long hunt. Back in those days it was probably three months. And probably longer than that if you count the time getting here and getting back from here. They were taking out guys like the Mellons and the Rockefellers and people with money. My mom mentioned some of those names. The Jacquot brothers were known throughout the world.

The brothers both married Kluane First Nation women. Mom always told me that Grandpa was really good to Grandma and just treated her like a queen. When you look at some of the older pictures, it's understandable—the women were just beautiful, just beautiful. It was probably a good way of life and probably a hard way of life. You had to work at it, but I think the Jacquot brothers were pretty smart boys. As for the schooling and then getting into the outfitting, I think they could foresee what was needed. All of a sudden the Alaska Highway was coming in, so there would need to be more changes, but by then they were pretty much both out of time. They died shortly after the highway came through.

Mom might've been here in the summer for a little bit during the war years, but she was down in the Vancouver area in 1948, because that's when her and Dad got married down there. She was born in 1927, I believe, so she was a teenager when the war was on and the highway was built through here. Then of course there was a big change. She talked about that, but I didn't pay much attention. All I can remember is that side of the road, ever since I can remember, was the Game Sanctuary, and we were not supposed to be going in there. It was difficult because a lot of those hunts with the Jacquot brothers and Dicksons and those guys, a lot of the hunting, was done on that side of the road until they got into Alaska. Then they had to shut it down. No doubt it affected them terribly.

facing Jacquot outfitters' horses ready for a hunting trip, late 1940s. KFN Archives. EMPC. Doug and Linda Sias Family Images #3. PHOTOGRAPHER UNKNOWN

above Frank Sias collecting wild lambs in the mountains in Kluane country for export to research centres and zoos. *Left to right:* unidentified man, Frank Sias, Danny Nolan, and unidentified man. KFN Archives. EMPC. Doug and Linda Sias Family Images #4. PHOTOGRAPHER UNKNOWN

LEAVING HOME

We left the Haines Road area because the pump station closed down in '72, I believe. We were down there roughly ten years. For the last two years I went to Whitehorse for high school. I took one year, grade 8, in the school down there, but we had to take it by correspondence. I was fooling around, so that's when I went to town. At first they tried to put me in Coudert Hall, which was a Catholic residence. I didn't spend one night there—I didn't like it. So I ended up staying with private people. Three different ones over my high school years, mainly friends of our family. I went to Christ the King High School for two years and then three years over at F.H. Collins. I didn't quite make it to the graduation part. I just quit and went to work.

The first job I ever had the summer I got out of school was at the Yukon Game Farm. Danny Nolan was the owner at that time. He was a good friend and a good guy to learn how to work, that's for sure. At the time my mom and dad were working in the lodge business. Danny ended up owning White River Lodge, so I worked for Danny just for the one summer. After that I went to work for the Yukon Government. Sweeping floors and washing vehicles, that was my first job in their maintenance shop in Whitehorse. It was in Marwell, pretty much the same place as now. I drive by there and still see the building.

I got to know a few more people in businesses around town, so I can remember I was making $1.67 an hour when I went to work for the government and stayed there probably two years. Then I went over to Northern Metallic. Bob DuPont was the owner. He went up the stairs to his office, and we were on the bottom floor. Les Couch was there, Bob Darling and Dougie Phillips. Lots of gold mining and other mines going then, which we supplied. I can't remember what I was making, but I only worked there probably for one year.

Those were busy times. There was lots of stuff happening in Whitehorse. Boom times. At Northern Metallic I was on the counter at the end, but I started in Shipping and Receiving. Me and one other guy were busy making big cable slings and filling orders for nuts and bolts, supplying all the big mines: Faro, Cassiar, Clinton Creek, Keno Hill. Couldn't keep up. It was a busy time. Busy, busy time.

Then a friend of mine over in White Pass offered me a job at $4.10 an hour. They were union, and man, that was just like dying and going to heaven! Went over there in what they called the TBA Department: tires, batteries, and accessories. We were looking after the highway lodges. We brought in a lot of parts and tires, especially for White Pass Highway Division that was hauling primarily out of Faro at that time. So it was a smoking busy job too. I must've stayed there till 1973. I probably put in two or three years there. I finished off with the White Pass. I quit in '74.

At that time I'd taken on one of the road salesman jobs. I was running the North Highway from Whitehorse, and I was going south too. Checking with the lodges, making sure they had whatever they needed. We had a van all loaded up with supplies. White Pass would consign the tires to the lodges and probably some batteries too. That was part of my job to take inventory, see what they sold, so then you gotta charge them for it and replenish the stock. Kept me going. Was a good deal for the lodges and a good moneymaker for White Pass too. They were looking ahead too. That's one way of getting rid of all the tires. They had the market on the tire business.

I was not involved with the union, the Teamsters. I can't remember ever having a meeting with them. All's I know is they paid good. The department I was in wouldn't have been up to today's standards, but the work environment was plenty safe for me anyway. But there was no wearing steel-toed boots and no hard hats and all that jazz. The one thing I can remember is we sold a lot of batteries, and you're dealing with acid. There could've been something done in that department. Nobody, to my recollection, got any of that in their eyes, but it was dangerous stuff to be working around.

There was asbestos in the shed where they unloaded the Clinton Creek and Cassiar mine trucks. Dangerous conditions for sure. The thing I really remember is that I liked curling back in those days, and I still like curling today. I was a pretty avid curler, and Cassiar Asbestos down in B.C., they'd have a bonspiel and invite the corporate teams. White Pass would send a team and General Enterprises. Anyway four of us from White Pass went down there for four-five days. They gave us a tour of the mine, and in the main mill it was just like it was snowing in there. I can remember the one guy in there had a big upright sewing machine. I remember the bag would come down the assembly line, and he'd have to guide the seam through the sewing machine, sew it up, and it would keep going. There was asbestos dust just all over the place, and nobody had a mask on, including us. So I'm sure a lot of those people suffered in the end. That's bad stuff. I don't think I was there long enough.

I was over in the White Pass shed, too, but maybe I was just in a different section. I don't recall any asbestos happening over there. We'd sometimes go over there and get tires, because they'd come through there. I can remember the ore they were shipping out of Faro would be transferred there. They had the big gantry where they would drive over the trucks and pick up the container and put it on the train.

White Pass had it all: road, rail, ship—integrated system. Down in that Petroleum Division where I worked, Phil Delaney was the push there. Down on the Rail Division was Bill Jones. He was the Comptroller, whatever that meant. Don Jones was involved with Highway Division. Norm Jarvis was there. Bill Dickson was a little bit up the ladder from them guys.

BACK TO KLUANE

I decided to come back out on the highway, and I ended up meeting my wife Cecile there in '74. We moved to the south end of the lake in '75, and I've been there ever since. We just sold [our place in] Silver City last year, in 2016. My mom and dad started living there in 1972. We just kind of invaded them [by moving to Silver City] in '75. Then we did whatever we could, them included, to find jobs and make things work. They got into running youth camps for Kluane National Park and were involved in the trappers training program,

facing Doug Sias and his wild falcon, late 1960s. KFN Archives. EMPC. Doug and Linda Sias Family Images #5. PHOTOGRAPHER UNKNOWN

overleaf top Doug was a skilled and avid outdoorsman who loved to go camping out on the land. KFN Archives. EMPC. Doug and Linda Sias Family Images #6. PHOTOGRAPHER UNKNOWN

overleaf middle Doug taking Grandma Mary Jacquot for a snowmobile ride on Kluane Lake, circa 1970s. KFN Archives. EMPC. Doug and Linda Sias Family Images #7. PHOTOGRAPHER UNKNOWN

overleaf bottom Grandma Mary Jacquot, baby Jimmy Sias, and Dad, Doug Sias, at Silver City, circa 1976. KFN Archives. EMPC. Doug and Linda Sias Family Images #8. PHOTOGRAPHER UNKNOWN

hunter safety programs. We did a lot of things, especially my mom and dad. I got a job with the Highway Department up here in Destruction Bay.

My wife would pick up jobs at the Health Centre, and then when the kids got older and outgrew their school at D-Bay, she took the kids and went to Haines Junction. She worked in the store down there. So we just did whatever we could to make ends meet. Raised our two kids at Silver City until they went to Haines Junction to finish high school. After that they went to tech school out in Calgary.

Cecile Henri, my wife, was from Saskatchewan. She'd been in Whitehorse for a couple of years and was married to a different guy there. I was married to a different girl. We met through baseball, everybody separated, and we ended up together. Then Cecile and I came home to Silver City. I spent a lot of time around my parents, living in very close quarters. So it was hard when my dad died last year. We're a pretty close-knit little family.

My mom and dad had the idea for developing Silver City when they left 48 Mile. They had a vision that they wanted to work with kids, or younger people, and give them an opportunity to experience the bush. It was probably initiated by my mother. Mom always thought of the ideas, and Dad, he did the work. They made a good team.

So they were running the Youth Corps for four or five years, sponsored by Kluane National Park. They'd take sixteen kids, and they'd have 'em for seven weeks. Two weeks at our place at Silver City, and then the rest, four or five weeks, out in the bush, building cabins or whatever. So it was a great experience, a great chance for kids that would probably have never gotten an opportunity to experience that. The kids came from all over. They tried to take them from all over the Yukon. There was one or two from Winnipeg too. So it was mostly

Yukon kids, and a lot of them kids, they kept in touch. They really got something out of it. I worked on the first two camps for my dad, and here comes a busload of smart-aleck kids and lipping me off or whatever. After the seven weeks, when they flew out of the bush in the helicopter, everybody was crying; nobody wanted to leave.

I ended up working with one of the guys in Destruction Bay, Jerry Desjardins. I think he was still the boss there in 2012, and he ended up being my boss. He was from Haines Junction. Anyway he said it was the best year of his life. Kevin McLaughlin is down in Haines Junction to this day. He was one of the kids on the first camp. After my two years Kevin took my place and was one of Dad's supervisors. Tom Elliot, he's another Parks Canada guy in Whitehorse.

It was the kind of program where the kids learned a lot about this type of life. Everybody works together, and you eat together. Teamwork. Dad ran all the camps for five years, I think. Started in '74 till '79. Then they said the funding disappeared. A big shame—that program should still be going on today. They had those kids out in the bush. There's no phones; there's no texting; there's no nothing. It's all hands-on, and you pay attention while you're in the bush or you don't do very well.

We also had academics staying out there at the Kluane Research Station. We got the overflow people who needed a place to stay. The Arctic Institute was based at Silver City just across the creek from our place. That's where everybody who was studying glaciers and everything to do with education stayed. But if they had family or friends visiting, they would come over and stay at our place. We were involved there but not to a big degree. When the institute started, that's when we started the bed and breakfast down at our place. I think my mom started that in 1990, so they did that until 1999 and then we bought the place. We closed it down last year.

Walter Woods was one of the founding guys there and his wife, Renee. They stayed at our place, right in my mom and dad's house. They were good friends. Julie Cruickshank and her husband, Gary Clark, the glaciologist. Julie got my mom a position on the Polar Commission Board. So my mom was busy doing that and it might have been a little out of her element, but she wanted to learn and she was with Julie and was very good at it. Julie was a good lady.

My wife Cecile and I ran the B & B from about 2000 to 2016. We sold last year, in 2017, and the new owners took over and paid us on October 31st. I don't think they're going to run it as a bed and breakfast. The owners of Yukon Honda in Whitehorse bought it, Satman and Gureeta Ray. Of course we didn't know what their plans were, and they didn't know. We had some good customers, some Japanese groups that were coming and one group out of Germany and a couple local groups,

top Frank and Josie Sias enjoyed camping in the bush, when time permitted them to be away from their business. KFN Archives. EMPC. Doug and Linda Sias Family Images #9. PHOTOGRAPHER UNKNOWN

bottom Doug's mother, Josie Sias, meets Governor General Adrienne Clarkson while serving on the Canadian Polar Commission. KFN Archives. EMPC. Doug and Linda Sias Family Images #10. PHOTOGRAPHER UNKNOWN

and they agreed that they might not open the door to the travelling public, but they would take those groups because we recommended them. Seemed funny that the Japanese were there in early February. They had one group then and another in March. So my wife and I just drove down there to say hi to them, because they were all our old customers. Seemed kinda different to walk in there, and you don't own nothing anymore.

I don't miss the generators. I haven't missed them for a second! So the maintenance, it was getting to me. It was ok while my dad was still functional and Pauly Sias and her then husband Kelly Wroot were there. They'd give a hand, but the last few years it ended up just myself. The last year with my heart giving me a little bit of trouble, it was just sell and get the heck out of there while we could. Luckily I never even advertised the place. The people just came in, and everything worked out.

A VERY SPECIAL PLACE

Too bad my dad had to die so soon because I thought maybe we'd bring him along to Copper Joe subdivision with us, but it just didn't work out. We've got a lovely KFN house down here now, and I'm not as busy. Was lucky that way. Only had to move 40 miles, from one end of the lake to the other. I'm liking it, but it was hard to leave down there after forty-three years.

I'm not a world traveller. The boss there, Cecile, she'd jump on an airplane and go wherever. She's gonna have to do some of that on her own. But we already made up our mind last year, when we sold Silver City, that the first year we're just gonna take the little motorhome and tour the Yukon because we haven't been anywhere for forty-three years. We couldn't ever leave the place together. You could maybe get away for a day. So it's gonna be enjoyable.

We brought so much stuff from Silver City because it all happened so quick. We've got Rubbermaid containers that we gotta go through, and some of it has to be gotten rid of. We weren't just packing up our stuff. I had to empty my mom and dad's house too. My sister came down from Faro, but we didn't have time to go through it all. My mother kept everything. So I've got two Sea Cans down at our Copper Joe house full of containers. It's just stuff that's gotta be looked at. So we'll be busy doing that. Stuff I wish I could've done when Josie was alive, but I didn't take the time. I didn't have the time. It didn't happen, but I can still do it this way. Cecile and Pauly [Sias] are way better on the history end of the whole deal: land claims and the family trees and all that sort of stuff. They know way more than I do.

I was not involved in land claims. I'd hear through people or friends the general idea of what was going on. People like Katie's dad (Joe Joe) and a lot of people in

facing Josie and Frank Sias, hosts of Kluane Bed and Breakfast at Silver City. KFN Archives. EMPC. Doug and Linda Sias Family Images #11. PHOTOGRAPHER UNKNOWN

left Doug Sias hunting with his daughter, Pauly, and son, Jimmy, circa 2008. KFN Archives. EMPC. Doug and Linda Sias Family Images #12. PHOTOGRAPHER UNKNOWN

this community—they were the ones that did it all. I think pretty much everybody was relieved that it got signed. My mom was present for the signing.

We didn't have much time for meetings, just because the life we chose down there was a busy life, just keeping things running, making ends meet and all of that. I know the one thing that was important to my mom, and I don't know whether it came up to meet her expectations: she wanted to make sure that the Elders were looked after, people of her mother's age, like Lena and Annie Ned, Copper Lily, and Mrs. Jimmy [Emma Johnson]. Home care was important to her, for sure. She was wanting to see more set up out on the highways, whether it had to be in Haines Junction or Burwash, but a good facility so people didn't have to leave the area to spend their last years. So they could be closer to home, and it's a good idea. I'm for that, that's for sure. But we'll see where that all goes. I can't recall her talking about access to the Park and Game Preserve for hunting, but it probably was important to her because her dad and their family, that's where they used to make a living. When that was taken away, it was a big change in lifestyle, that's for sure.

I can see what KFN have been doing and what's happening, and I think they're doing good. I think they're doing really good. In the last few years I've really noticed parents are taking a lot of time to show their kids what living off the land is all about. The trapping and the hunting, the fishing, and that way of life. And they're also making sure that their kids are getting the education. Some of them have moved to Haines Junction, some to Whitehorse, so that they're getting the best, and they're seeing two different things. It's great that you don't always see the kids with the texting thing going on all the time.

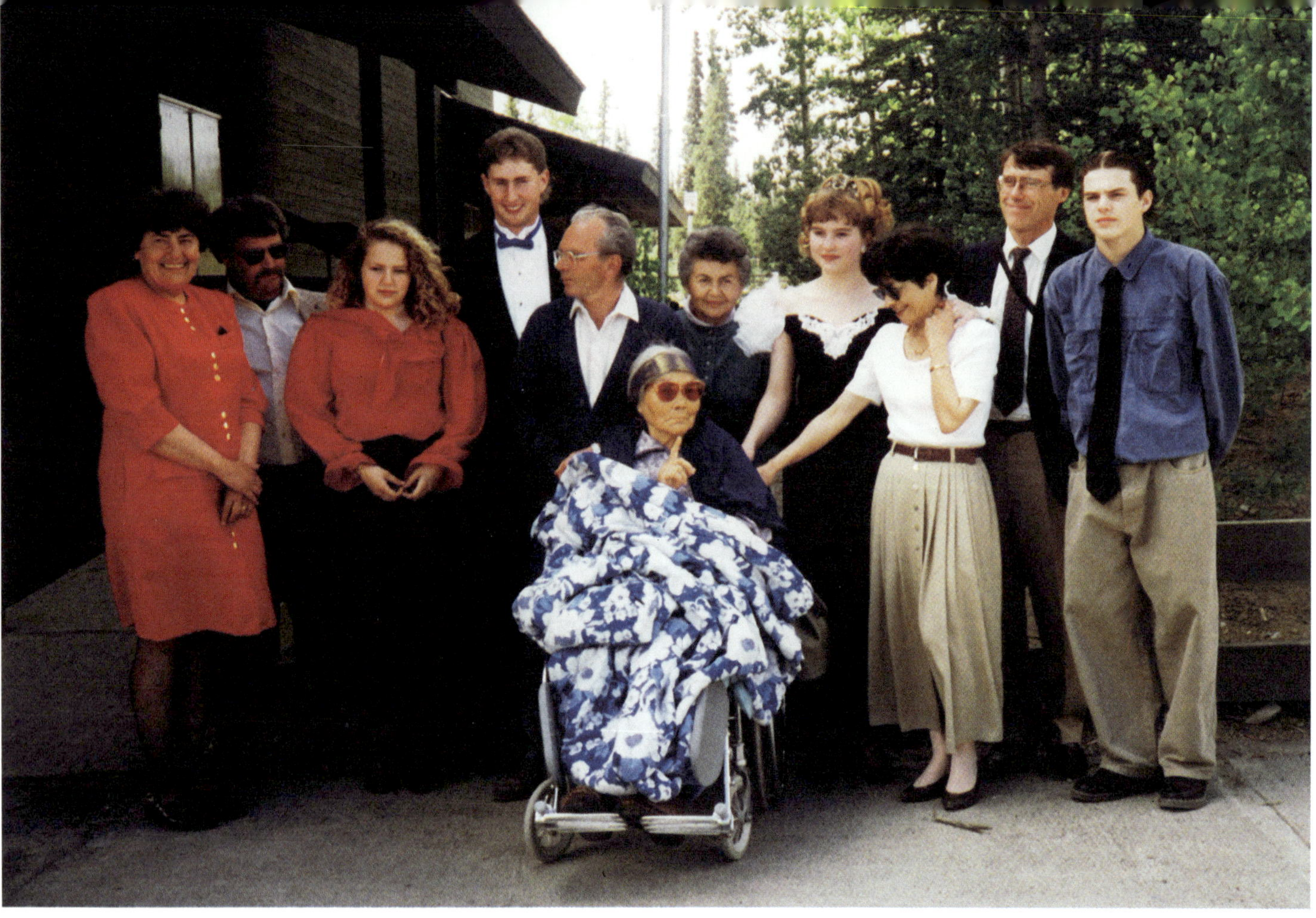

above Sias family gathering, circa 2000. *Left to right:* Cecile, Doug, Pauly, Jimmy, Frank, and Josie Sias with Grandma Mary Jacquot in front, Jennifer, Linda, Ron, and Ben Wondga. KFN Archives. EMPC. Doug and Linda Sias Family Images #13. PHOTOGRAPHER UNKNOWN

facing Doug recording stories in 2018. KFN Archives. EMPC. Elders Portraits #30. PHOTOGRAPHER ALISTAIR MAITLAND

They're out there, and some of them are pretty small; they know how to catch a muskrat, skin it. I think all that is very important, not to lose that, that's for sure. I think KFN's doing a wonderful job. They have lots of those kind of activities going on all the time it seems.

This was a good place to spend our summers when I was at that age. You'd walk down from the lodge or to my grandma's house, and you were more than welcome to walk in anywhere. I mean, knock on the door, but stop at Jessie Joe's or stop in at Sam Johnson Sr. and them. It was just a tight community. It's probably very similar to that today. I've been away from it for so long I'm kinda new to the game now. I think Kluane First Nation have done all right, and they will do all right. Just make sure the First Nation and the parents take the time to teach these kids so that they don't lose that. Because if you lose that, then you've lost a lot.

It's a special place, that's for sure. And you know, that's one thing: when you look out there to the lake, it's the same as when I first came here. Yeah, same. Lots of good memories. And then a guy like myself, I'm feeling pretty lucky, very lucky. Spend my whole life within 150 miles of here. Can't hardly do that anymore!

It's a special place, that's for sure.
DOUG SIAS

SULKAJUNAGHRAW (MAUREEN GLORIA JOHNSON)

(b. 1952)

Following Grandma—Tsal KàJana (Gopher Lady, Copper Lily)

facing Sulkajunaghraw (Maureen Gloria Johnson), 2017. KFN Archives. EMPC. Elders Portraits #31. PHOTOGRAPHER ALISTAIR MAITLAND

My name is Maureen Gloria Johnson. A missionary, Father Morisset, here named me after his sister, Maureen, and he gave me the name Gloria too. In the Southern Tutchone way I'm Crow Clan, and I was named Sulkajunaghraw (Little Gopher Lady) after Copper Lily. She was our medicine doctor for this village. I was given Copper Lily's name at birth when Copper Lily, Jessie Joe, and my aunty Jenny Johnson were present. Aunt Jenny did not have a daughter, so my mom shared me with her and she was like a mother to me. I was to follow Copper Lily's footsteps and work with people in medicine. The grandmas—Jenny Johnson, Jessie Joe, Mary Jacquot, Copper Lily, Nellie Johnson, and most Elders in the village and my mom—called me by my nickname, Ku'k, which means "paper," and I was also supposed to work with paper. I would like to give my name back to Alaska when I pass away.

FAMILY ROOTS

I was born in Burwash in the house that my dad built. It had a big front room and a big back room. I was born in 1952, and I've lived a good part of my life in this community. I've gone Outside for education purposes, but I always come back to Burwash. It's home!

My parents were Sam and Jessie Johnson. Mom was Jessie Allen from Chisana, Alaska. Her Indian name is Shada Zhan Mą and means "Humming As She Works." Mom spoke five languages: Upper Tanana, Southern Tutchone, Northern Tutchone, and some Tlingit plus English. She was from a line of Chiefs in Alaska.

My dad is Shùglità, and his name means "Good Hunter." Dad's mom came from Fort Selkirk. Her name was Emma Jackson, then Johnson after she married my grandfather Jimmy Johnson. Grandma Emma was from a line of Chiefs at Fort Selkirk. When my grandma Emma became ill, my grandpa took on another wife, and that was Copper Lily. A Chief can do that a long time ago. So he had two families, and they're related through marriage.

When I was four years old, Elders conducted a marriage ceremony for me and Arthur Joe from the Chief Albert Isaac family of Aishihik because we were meant to be married as children of Chief lineages. A Chief's daughter is always supposed to marry a Chief's son. We had to stand all day long and look each other in the eyes. We both went off to residential school, and everything changed.

We travelled on the land a lot when I was young, so I didn't really know my grandmothers. There's five boys and five girls in our family: Dorothy, born in 1934; Kirk was born in 1936, and he passed away; Edward, in 1938; Gordon in 1941, who has passed away; then came Agnes, born in 1943, who has passed away; next is Mary Easterson in 1945; Michael, in 1949; myself, in 1952; Alyce in 1955, who teaches at Destruction Bay school; and my youngest brother is Sam Jr., born in 1957.

above Shada Zhan Mą (Humming As She Works, Jessia [born Allen] Johnson) drying fish in the fall, circa 1990s. KFN Archives. EMPC. Maureen Johnson Family Images #1. PHOTOGRAPHER UNKNOWN

facing top Sam and Jessia Johnson had a tent frame and well-established camp set up at Jedälį Tl'äw Käy (Duke Meadow), just north of Burwash, seen here in the mid-1970s. They spent time there every summer with their children as part of their seasonal rounds, snaring gophers, picking berries, and enjoying visits with many relatives and friends from near and far. CYFN Archives. Photograph Collection #b47_f26_s1_1. PHOTOGRAPHER UNKNOWN

facing middle Maureen Johnson as a baby in a willow frame baby carrier. KFN Archives. EMPC. Maureen Johnson Family Images #2. PHOTOGRAPHER UNKNOWN

facing bottom Maureen Johnson in her teen years. KFN Archives. EMPC. Maureen Johnson Family Images #3. PHOTOGRAPHER UNKNOWN

LOWER POST WAS LIKE MILITARY SCHOOL FOR KIDS

We all went to Lower Post Residential School, so we were never all together, because the older ones went to school when the younger ones were still home and then they left home before us younger ones got back from Lower Post. I recollect when I went there, it was really, really frightening, but what happens in those situations is the older students took care of you and taught you the ropes.

Boys and girls were separated; you cannot interact. It was very strict, very regimental—like a military school but for kids. We'd get up in the morning early, and it's clean-up time—shower, wash, fix your bed, get ready to go down to the common room—and we'd do our prayers, usually on our knees. Then we'd go to the dining room, have our breakfast, do our chores, and then

it's off to class. You have to do your reading, writing, math, and it was a very, very strict learning situation. You had to be still, you had to listen, you had to do the work, and I think that's what helped me later on in life, too, is that regimental type of learning, because I always felt that I had to succeed. So it's drills, drills, drills, constantly. Then you're always in line marching just like a military school.

I had nine years of Roman Catholic religious training, really strict. We used to pray sometimes seven or eight times a day. We always had Mass said in Latin—High Mass and Low Mass, always in Latin. We had to speak Latin, but I don't remember any of it now.

I've seen children beaten up because they can't speak English; they could only speak their Native language. Then there were other terrible beatings too. I spoke English, and I think it's because my parents were traditional people but they always told us when we were small, "You have to learn English. You're going to go to school. You're going to learn how to work. You need to have that because things are not going to stay the same." So they knew that, and they pushed and taught us kids that way. I also was lucky I had Michael and Robbie Johnson and Daniel Johnson, because they would come back from Lower Post and bring me books they stole from school. Then they would teach me. So I started learning when I hadn't even gone to Lower Post yet. I went there for nine years, and then in 1965 we were allowed back into the community to attend Kluane Lake public school.

OUR PARENTS WERE OUR TEACHERS

We were out on the land in summers with my parents, so they were my main teachers. There's just us younger ones—myself, Alyce, and Sam—at that time. People like Copper Lily and the old ones—Mary Jacquot, Jessie Joe, Sophie Watt—the real old people would talk to you, tell you stories, and guide you. I was close to my aunt Jenny when I was small, my dad's sister. So there was a lot of movement, I remember that, and a lot of

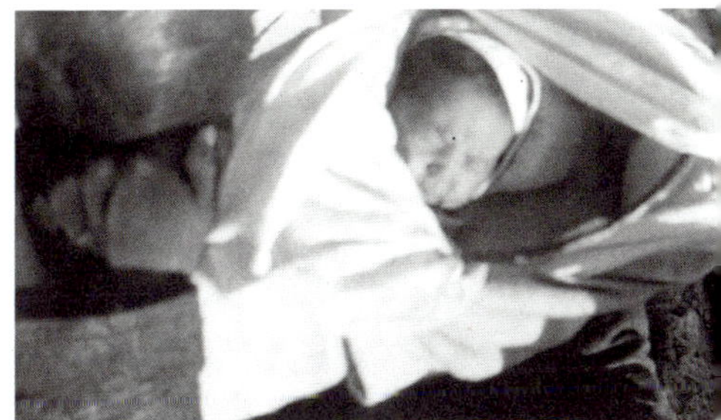

above Maureen grew up hearing stories from the many Elders living in Burwash at the time. This photograph of Lilly (Allen) Birckel, Copper Lily, Jessie Joe, and Nelly Johnson was taken at a Potlatch in Haines, Alaska, mid-1970s. KFN Archives. EMPC. Robin Bradasch Collection Scans #2. PHOTOGRAPHER UNKNOWN

facing top Otis Johnson school picture at around age 10. KFN Archives. EMPC. Maureen Johnson Family Images #4. PHOTOGRAPHER UNKNOWN

facing middle Tcha-ya Johnson as a young man always worked hard outdoors as a labourer. KFN Archives. EMPC. Maureen Johnson Family Images #5. PHOTOGRAPHER UNKNOWN

facing bottom Maureen's daughter, Shannon Johnson, as a young girl about 12 years old. KFN Archives. EMPC. Maureen Johnson Family Images #6. PHOTOGRAPHER UNKNOWN

camps, traditional camps, different places across the lake, and at Duke Meadow, Burwash Creek, Snag, and by Silver City area. We went to Haines Junction because my aunt Lilly Birckel lived there. She had a garden, her and Paul Birckel Sr. We spent two weeks there every summer, and she would teach us about vegetables and canning and all that. I remember my mom used to walk across the ice on the lake to set net and then walk back. She was a hunter and fisher and very much an outdoors person. Fish was an important diet source for us.

We had to go to Whitehorse for high school and back into the Roman Catholic residence at Coudert Hall. I didn't make it two years there, because I had a really hard time with staff. I was young at the time, but I knew I had some rights too. I used to go meet the big officials from DIA, Indian Affairs, and I would complain about the staff and what they were doing.

So I came home for a while, then I went to Eric Hamber High School in Vancouver. Well, I was young. I remember that day. We were all swimming up at the pond. I got home and I packed my bags, and my dad says, "Where you're going?" I said, "Well, I'm going down to Vancouver." "What do you mean you're going to Vancouver?" I said, "Yeah, I am." "How are you going to get there?" "I'm going to go out and hitchhike." Fifteen—so I just got on the road and got a ride. I was an adventurous person! I made it in about three days. I met some good people; they bought me meals. I only had about $10 in my pocket, and I still had it when I landed in Vancouver. My sister Mary was at UBC taking a teaching course. All I had was her phone number. It was culture shock. Spent two years there, then I went to Camosun College until I finished grade 12, about two years.

BACK HOME TO WORK

In 1974 I came home to Burwash and worked in the band office for Kluane Tribal Brotherhood. I had two boys, Otis and Tcha-yah, and a daughter, Shannon (who have passed away). The boys went to the Kêts'á dan' kų community school here for a few years. They liked it and it was right near home, right in the community, so it was great.

My mom was an avid sportsperson. She was still out hunting, fishing, and really active until she was very old. She was always doing something. She would walk across the lake, set her net, and walk all the way back, in winter temperatures too. Whitefish, trout—we had a good diet of fish, lots of fish.

In 1968 Elijah Smith, with Chuck Hume as a driver, George John, and my parents, got involved with the pipeline that was being planned in Alaska. They were talking about land claims and getting things done for the younger generation. When Elijah got off the plane, he would come out here and everyone would sit around here and discuss plans for the future. I listened a lot to what was going on. The federal and territorial governments were after me to work for them. I would ask my mom and my dad if I could go, but he would say, "No, there is lots of work to be done out here. We have to get a store going and a school. We need you here." That was the reason I didn't go to work for the governments.

LEGAL TROUBLES

When I was young, I remember my dad and uncle Moose liked to go to the Park over across the road or up to Burwash Creek or Duke Meadow area to hunt. The time of Dad's famous legal case he was hunting in his regular territory—in the Park. He was old at the time, around 77. Back then the relationships weren't good between Parks Canada and the Game Sanctuary and Elders, like my dad, that hunted. They were taking guns, traps, and trucks away. They'd fine them too. That time my dad had a stroke because he got so excited about the officers taking his property away. Ron Veale defended him in court, but he lost on a technicality.

Another time I was charged with endangering a species. I was actually saving a Harlan's hawk that had a broken foot. It was at Burwash Creek. My dad came down and said there was a hawk stuck in a tent; his foot was caught. So I got a cage and I got the hawk out and was taking it to a veterinarian in Whitehorse. The Yukon Government Conservation Officers arrested me, and the RCMP put me in jail in the Junction. I had to leave my truck at the café when they brought me to the jail. I made a phone call to my sister Mary Easterson, and she called Ron Veale. I was released late that day. I went to court, represented by Ron Veale, and we won the case. I don't know what happened to the poor hawk. I was in jail, and the officers took the bird away.

Then my brother Edward, Mary and her husband (Henry Michel), and I were at Quill Creek to hunt sheep. My young son Otis was with me that day too. My brother and Henry were in the lead. Mary, my son, and I were behind. My brother hollered, "Turn around! Look!" We were quite a ways up by then from where the trucks were parked. Five Conservation Officers were running up the hill behind us, so we knew they were going to take the vehicles, the guns, and lay charges. So I threw the key to my son and said, "Run as fast as you can, get to the truck, and lock the door." He was running down, almost made it to the truck, and the Conservation Officer got him. They told us to walk back—20 miles. We argued with them, "You know, we can't walk back; we need our trucks. We've got a child with us." So finally after arguing with them they gave our trucks back but kept our guns and laid charges. Ron Veale again came to the rescue, and we won the right to hunt in the Game Sanctuary.

I was part of AIM when I was younger, American Indian Movement, so I had a little bit of exposure to protests there. Back then, I think, it was a big challenge. It was like, "You win or you lose" type of thing. Mostly it was antagonizing, patronizing, a lot of critical stuff, and they just didn't want you to have the power. And so it was a face-to-face moment all the time. Yeah, there were worries, but you know, it's also a challenge so you have to do it.

FUTURE DREAMS

So I've spent a lot of time here and worked a lot of office jobs, not much outdoors. I like going outdoors, cutting wood, and doing this and that. I went to school in Vancouver and did university courses at UBC, Vancouver City College, and over at the Institute of Indigenous Government run by B.C. Indigenous First Nations groups. I always believed in education. I love reading, and computers now, so I always have great respect for education. Since I turned 65, I've been involved in a lot of advocacy work for people in the community or Vancouver. I'm also around kids a lot, babysitting great-nephews.

I wish we had more population here in Burwash. We have all this land here. What can we do with it? I have one idea:

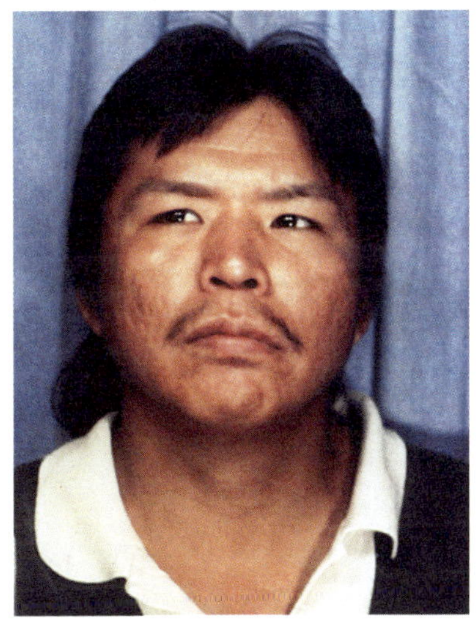

above Luminous wild phlox and Arctic avens grow in profusion in Asì Keyí. KFN Archives. EMPC. Landscape Images #25. PHOTOGRAPHER ROBERT POSTMA

facing Maureen Johnson recording stories for Elders Memory Project at Burwash, November 2017. KFN Archives. EMPC. Elders Portraits #32. PHOTOGRAPHER ALISTAIR MAITLAND

There's lots of refugees and people from different countries looking for a new home. Why don't we take some of this land here and lease it out to them? They can stay here and become involved in our community, get jobs, or look for jobs, or create jobs. We've got to start thinking about how we can make some economic opportunities. We need the population, we need children, and we need a school.

I'd like to be involved with language preservation. I think that it's really important to do preservation, the active talking and listening. I recently went to visit cultural centres in Haines Junction, Whitehorse, Teslin, Pelly, and Carmacks. Those were really great places. I used to work for some big architectural businesses when I lived in Vancouver. I saw many of the heritage buildings in the city, with interesting artifacts and archival records. The City of Vancouver wanted me to work there, but I said no, I have to go home. There is work to do there, and it's home too. We have the museum here, and we need to develop it, adding more cultural activities for our people, especially our young people.

I need to get my first aid again, and I told the school that I could volunteer to help out. We're getting our own school here finally. Well, let's just hope I stick around a little bit longer. That's all I can say.

I'd like to be involved with language preservation. I think that it's really important to do preservation, the active talking and listening.

SULKAJUNAGHRAW (MAUREEN JOHNSON)

GÙDÍA (SHARON KABANAK)

(b. 1953)

Lhù'ààn Mân Yu Nìínje (Where I Come From)

My given name is Sharon Rose (Johnson) Kabanak, and my Dań K'è (Southern Tutchone) name is Gùdía, given to me by my maternal grandma and my aunt Mary, my Southern Tutchone namesake. I am of the Khàjèt (Crow) Clan. I was born in the old army hospital in Whitehorse in 1953 before my parents were married.

facing Gùdía (Sharon Kabanak), 2022. KFN Archives. EMPC Elders Portraits #33 PHOTOGRAPHER ALISTAIR MAITLAND

My mother's name was À Thay Mą, meaning "Golden Eagle Mother," a Southern Tutchone/Northern Tutchone name given to her by her mother, who was Emma Jackson, a Northern Tutchone woman from Fort Selkirk. Mom's English name was Jessie Johnson Kabanak. It is the custom of the Kluane Southern Tutchone people that our namesake comes from our mother's Clan. The inherited names are handed down from one generation to the next. For example Jessie's name was given to my sixth grandchild by Mom's two stepsisters, Rita and Margaret Johnson, with an extra "a" on the end, signifying "little." So her name is À Thay Mą ra (Little Golden Eagle Mother). My mother was a fluent Dań K'è speaker, storyteller, and culture keeper for our local Ancestral Knowledge and ancestry.

COMMUNITY-MINDED PRIEST

Father Morisset, the Roman Catholic priest at Burwash in the 1940s and 50s, gave me my English name, when I was baptized in the church at Burwash Landing. My name is from the Rose of Sharon, a white rose that grows in Provence, France. He came from France. When I came back from overseas in December 1973, I went to visit him at the Whitehorse Roman Catholic Cathedral. Later I took my daughter as a child to visit, and we had tea with him there.

In my early childhood he was the only person with a car at Burwash besides my dad, so many people liked him and waited for a ride with him! Later on the Greyhound bus service was the only other means of transportation for those that began travelling the Alaska Highway. Mom said that everybody else had a wood truck or a Caterpillar tractor for building roads, but Father Morisset had a car—a free taxi! He would take Burwash people out to check their gopher snares or traps or whatever they needed, such as good drinking water. People were known to visit him at the rectory in Burwash to have a visit, planning to catch a ride with him up to the Duke Meadow camping area.

Father Morisset was really community minded and fit right into our community. French people are very connected to their land, and he taught a lot of people about gardening here. He helped people by planting a community garden. I remember the summer holidays when we were kids; we volunteered to help clean up his garden, and we were given food to take back to Grandma's house. He said to go pick the food when it's the right time. He grew all kinds of veggies like potatoes, carrots, turnips. He had a greenhouse too.

above Father Morisset working in his garden at the Roman Catholic Mission in Burwash, circa 1950. KFN Archives. EMPC. Dorothy Johnson Family Images #12. PHOTOGRAPHER UNKNOWN

facing top À Thay Mą (Golden Eagle Mother, Jessie Johnson Kabanak) and baby Gùdia (Sharon Kabanak) with husband Edward Kabanak and son Mädasa (Terance Kabanak) at Christmas time in their log home near Burwash, 1953. KFN Archives. EMPC. Sharon Kabanak Family Images #1. PHOTOGRAPHER MARTHA IRVINE

BEDTIME STORIES WITH MOM

Late at night my mom always told me stories about my grandpa (Asi) Jimmy Johnson. He was a Southern Tutchone man from Aishihik Lake. He was very skilled in building watercraft. He travelled to Fort Selkirk from Aishihik by waterways, and there he met Emma Jackson. He married her in the traditional way and took her back to Kluane Country. Mary was their oldest child; next came Sam, my mom (Jessie), then Jenny. Grandpa built a caribou corral out of wind driftwood and dry tree falls. Big animals like caribou and moose could not go past the barrier. He burned the grass to improve the feed for moose. One year he caught five moose there but took only enough to feed his family.

Mom told us how the old people made bows and arrows from spruce trees for hunting. The first time they got rifles was at Redtail Lake. That's where they used to go fishing for red tail trout, whitefish, and grayling. They moved around following the trails that the animals made, harvesting different foods at each place according to the seasons. Surviving on the land requires tremendous knowledge and skills; the seasons and resources available are part of the Ancestral Knowledge taught by Mom's storytelling about her life. Her life and her stories are now embedded in my language, culture, and history. Our language is the Kluane Dań K'è of the Kluane Lake people who live in this big lake area, surrounded by mountains and often experiencing high winds and cold weather. The moon and the place names of the mountains guide us, telling us what foods are available in which places, helping our people to remember where to go and when to travel.

Mom told me other stories at bedtime too. "Your grandpa built a little cabin at Tatäy (Little Arm) at the mouth of Kluane River. He had a lookout there for scouting caribou and moose. He was a very skilled hunter. He used that site for many years. That's where they made the song 'Little Arm Tatäy,' meaning 'It's tight water to get through,' because when you're crossing the river there, the sandbars are very narrow at the arm. The Jacquots used to come over there to trade flour and sugar for furs with our people there." As stormy winter days came, Mom taught me to stack up wood in case of a big storm and snowfall. I appreciated her stories, so I made sure the chores got done.

My grandparents also had a cabin on the west side of the lake at Jèdàlį Tl'äw käy, which means "The Grass on Top the Ground" (where Duke Meadow meets Kluane River). They would hunt for ducks and dry their fish in summertime, then go back over to Tatäy (Little Arm) cabin to hunt sheep and moose. Later my grandparents came over to live on the Burwash side of the lake year-round. Grandpa built a cabin at Thè K'u (Salmon Patch). Mom's older brother, my uncle Sam Johnson, lived there while growing up and began his own family between there and Mile 1124 of Alaska Highway. This place is where Grandma Emma made a homestead for her family to move back and forth into new territory and new cultural upbringing. At Mile 1124 they used to tell time by the way the sun shone through the mountain peaks there. This place is sacred land in some places because there is always a gift from the Creator to feed our families in Grandma's country.

My grandma Emma was a very skilled resource person who was quiet spoken and traditionally knowledgeable about the ways of living on the land. She taught my mom and her sisters how to harvest roots to make tools, and how to catch grayling with a little net made of braided roots. They dug the roots out of the ground and braided them together as a little net or scoop while it was wet. Then they put it into the water in a creek or river and caught grayling with that scoop. I have a small basket made with this same technique by using willows and spruce roots.

My mother didn't go to residential school. She mostly had a traditional

above Small willow and spruce root basket made by Sharon Kabanak and similar to those made long ago by her grandmother and mother to catch grayling in creeks. KFN Archives EMPC Sharon Kabanak Family Images #2. PHOTOGRAPHER LINDA JOHNSON

above left Like her Ukrainian grandmother Sharon enjoys baking delicious breads and other good foods for her family and community. KFN Archives. EMPC. Sharon Kabanak Family Images #4. PHOTOGRAPHER UNKNOWN

above right Sharon's paternal grandmother, Helen Kabanak, came to Canada from Ukraine and homesteaded with her husband and children in Saskatchewan and Alberta. KFN Archives. EMPC. Sharon Kabanak Family Images #3. PHOTOGRAPHER UNKNOWN

facing Sharon's father, Edward Kabanak (left) and Henry Besner circa 1945 in Vancouver. KFN Archives. EMPC. Sharon Kabanak Family Images #5. PHOTOGRAPHER UNKNOWN

childhood on the land with her parents and siblings. Father Morisset taught Mom and her sisters, my aunts and their cousins at his day school in the Catholic Church at Burwash. He baptized most of them and all of us kids when we were born. We were all baptized in the Catholic Church for several generations. We carry on our Southern Tutchone traditional teachings and spiritual beliefs taught by our parents and Elders and also respect our Christian connections, values, and beliefs to this day.

UKRAINIAN HERITAGE

On my dad's side I come from Edward Kabanak's family. His parents emigrated from Russia to Glasgow, Scotland, by boat while fleeing from the Russian Revolution. I found this listed on the book titled *The Wheat Fields of North Dakota*. There were seven families of Doukhobours, otherwise known as Christians who left the Russian Orthodox Church. They brought their wheat seeds from Russia and the Ukraine to North Dakota. The women also brought their memorized bread-making recipes with them. In those early days of homesteading in North Dakota, the women processed the wheat by hand with large flails and ground the flour for baking, then feeding all the families together.

In search of new land in Canada Grandpa Vladimir Kabanak travelled by horseback from North Dakota along the Etson Wagon Trail to British Columbia, Edmonton, and Grand Prairie and settled there for a rest. His name is listed as a farmer in the records of immigrants crossing the border into Canada. Grandma and her three children followed him by wagon train until they found him in Saskatchewan, and later they homesteaded in Eaglesham, Alberta. In a recording of her history Grandma Helen mentioned that she had a sack of flour and some salt to make pancakes for breakfast and some rabbit gravy stew for supper every day to feed the adults and their kids on that trip.

I did that as well when raising my two kids at a lone homestead on the shores of Kluane Lake. It is difficult to raise children on the land, but I did it too. When I lived and harvested my food like my grandmas, I was able to teach my children to do the same as they were growing up. In the fall time I hunted grouse, and we had plenty for dinner. In wintertime we had rabbits. All year around we had moose meat, and we considered ourselves well fed without having to go to town to find groceries to eat—except for the days when I craved European cheeses and other delicacies!

Grandma Helen had thirteen children altogether, and they all lived in one little house. She was famous for her pancakes, and she was a great gardener too! She made beautiful bread with seeds and fruit. Sometimes she changed the dough recipe and made perogies with potato inside—maybe 500 or more for a wedding. She loved to feed people and take care of them. Her love of baking for family and friends is part of my legacy to this day.

EARLY FAMILY MEMORIES

Mom met my dad around 1942, when he came through Burwash with the Alaska Highway builders. He was a CAT skinner and crane operator for the Proctor and MacIsaac bridge construction company. Dad and my uncle Henry Kabanak came North during World War II, while their brother my uncle Alexander went to the war over in Europe. Dad couldn't go overseas, because he had a bad right eye when he was tested.

There's a story about Dad and Uncle Henry in a book called *Cashing In*. One time it was 60 below in Teslin, and the highway crew was trying to get a CAT started. Nobody could get it going, and they had to stop construction on the highway. They had to find my dad and uncle Henry, who had gone into Whitehorse. They were at the Regina Hotel on their day off, but they got arrested in the bar and had to go back to work to start that CAT! Dad's best friend was another Henry, Henry Besner, who was a good machinist and mechanic too. They became mining partners and purchased land at Burwash Creek in the Kluane region.

Dad had staked a homestead at the entrance to Burwash Landing, across from the road that goes down to the lake, and built our log cabin home with Mom's two nephews. Later on there were five of us kids: Terry, me, Gerald, Hughie, and Harry. When I was young, I remember it was always windy at Burwash.

I only heard of Grandpa Jimmy because he had passed away before I was born. Grandma Emma was staying at Duke Meadow when I was young, so I knew her well and learned lots from her as a child. I did everything that the old people did. I learned to set gopher snares made with eagle feathers. Mom made little grayling nets from roots for me to use at the creek. Those kinds of things were lying around or hanging on the wall in the cabins everywhere then, but when you're a kid, horses were the favourite sport all the time. Riding was a tradition here. Every day somebody was gone on a horse somewhere. My willing godfather for baptism was Joe Jacquot, the outfitter, so he made sure I was always up on a horse from a young age. As stories were told to us by Grandma Jessie Joe,

above In her late teens Sharon travelled and worked in Europe, bringing home these AFRC (American Forces Recreation Center) badges from her adventures overseas. KFN Archives. EMPC. Sharon Kabanak Family Images #6, #7, and #8. PHOTOGRAPHER UNKNOWN

facing top Adventures in Kluane country included a 1990s trip to the Kaskawulsh Glacier in Kluane National Park, where Sharon stood at the edge of the ice field. KFN Archives. EMPC. Sharon Kabanak Family Images #9. PHOTOGRAPHER BOB JICKLING

"Your mom and your aunt Jenny [Johnson] were both the strongest horseback riders. They came home at sunrise, not sunset."

Our family travelled and lived in a trailer at Port Hardy and then at Fort St. John. When we came back to Whitehorse, we lived in Porter Creek. I went to Christ the King High and later F.H. Collins High School. I left because of cultural differences in the schools here at that time that made me uncomfortable.

ADVENTURES IN EUROPE

I went out to Vancouver Island to study at Camosun College, where several of my first cousins were also attending school. When I came back to the Yukon, I worked in housekeeping for a while at the Burwash hotel with my mom. I also worked as a cook's helper across the lake for Temple Outfitting. That was good preparation for the next phase of my life. I met people from foreign lands at the camp and was inspired to travel.

I went overseas, first to London with my boyfriend, who was a certified train engineer. He knew about a lot of places and natural resource jobs we could get. We travelled, made money, and lived in flats. We went first to Brighton in England. It's a very beautiful place, and I fell in love with the sea there. Then we travelled up to Cornwall. There were strawberry farms and sheep everywhere in the countryside. There was beautiful purple heather—flowers everywhere. I got to know the stinging nettles quickly and kept my distance. It was always misty in the mornings. We visited Stonehenge, a well-known tourist site.

Next we went to the Netherlands, and I worked at the Amsterdam Schiphol Airport for a year and a half. My partner, Michael, became a renovator for housing with the proprietors and worked on the place where we had to live. I worked in housekeeping at the hotel in the daytime, and at night I babysat for their family. We bought bicycles and rode around Holland. We saw the tulip fields, the windmills, and places like Apeldoorn. We rented a houseboat beside the food market. When we had enough money saved, we went to the south of France to pick grapes. We were given a cabin by the ocean by the proprietor of the grape field. This was at Meses Plage, in the south of France beside the Mediterranean. We travelled to the Pyrenees and through Spain on the train. It's really beautiful going by train to different countries, travelling high up in the mountains and through tunnels. We went down to Morocco and stayed there for a while.

Later on I worked at Reese Kasserne, in Augsburg, Germany, for the American Armed Forces as a Housekeeper/Kitchen Helper. I was transferred down to Chiemsee Armed Forces Recreation Centre, which was about 15 miles from Munich. I worked there for three months. It was a recreation centre organized by the Red Cross for retired or injured people who were healing and recuperating from service injuries. They could go relax, dine, and enjoy the view and services, sailing, go skiing in the Alps, bring their families, and stay in this beautiful place by Lake Chiemsee. There was lots of dancing too. After work we went dancing. It was a different life, and I had fun over there. Everyone treated each other with respect, and it was like a family life away from home.

BACK HOME TO KLUANE

I returned to Canada, but my mind was often far away thinking about those people I had met in Europe. I had my daughter, Elodie, whose father is Ted Yardley, in 1974. I turned my attention to compassionate work with people here. I took care of Elders with my mom at Burwash, and I looked after my baby. We helped Elders set their fishnets, get wood, and keep their fires going, and went out for walks with them. We would have tea and visit with them. I have renewed certificates and volunteered for forty years or so with the Red Cross First Aid and CPR, St. John's Ambulance, in the village work as a front-line Community Health Aide.

I moved to Burwash and married Robert White, who owned a fishing lodge, a lakeside campground, two cabin rentals, and a part-time furrier/taxidermy business. We raised my daughter and had one son together, Samuel. We ran our boating business called Kluane Lake Fishing Camp. Robert has passed away now. I have many good memories and photographs saved for my grandchildren.

Mom passed away in 1991. I thought a lot about how to balance my life within my two cultures. I had obtained my Indian Status in 1987 so I could live in the village, work, study, get a house, and provide for my two children when I became separated and we sold our fishing lodge. I realized there was no job except the highway gas station. Recreational jobs or activities were scarce, except for highway maintenance and the old museum; there was not much for entertainment or public services, except the Burwash café and bar by the lakeside.

So I found a niche for the alternative health work that would become my future field. My cousin Gloria and I became proactive in meeting with the Government of Yukon and expressing the needs for a health-oriented building at Burwash. Robert and I were separated but had been married for fourteen years and shared our children back and forth from Whitehorse until they became teens. His friend Archie encouraged the Chief and Council to get Yukon Government funding. The community held meetings to plan for a suitable building.

In pursuing training as a Community Health Aide (CHA), I developed a Standard of Care Protocol as a liaison between the village of Burwash Landing and the medical health clinic in Destruction Bay. This new building required proposal writing for a safe drinking water program, a sewage lagoon, personal support work, and health-related workshops with the Yukon Government. Health promotion and disease prevention programs became popular as gatherings by providing a lunch or dinner while the community attended workshops with government employees from Whitehorse. We worked alongside the federal First Nation Health Programs, and then 300 women across Canada started an organization that became very well known as the National Association of Community Health Workers. It spread across North America, New Zealand, and Hawaii, where conferences were held in educating Aboriginal health program workers. I applied for a trip to Honolulu and went there with another Community Health Representative (our title changes from Aide) named Barb, who is from my area in Kluane Country, and Tagish-based Elder and mentor Ida Calmegane, who was a CHR and a Traditional Healer.

above Sharon and her family are skilled hunters, enjoying healthy moose meat, fish, and other foods gathered from the land. KFN Archives EMPC Sharon Kabanak Family Images #10. PHOTOGRAPHER SAM WHITE

top Sharon's son (Sam White) and grandson Jared Dulac with large moose, circa 2018. KFN Archives. EMPC. Sharon Kabanak Family Images #11. PHOTOGRAPHER UNKNOWN

bottom Sharon has built on her first language, Dań K'è, learned from her mother as a child, by studying at the Yukon Native Language Centre in Whitehorse to earn her diploma in 2016, seen here celebrating with her daughter Elodie (back right) and grandchildren. KFN Archives. EMPC. Sharon Kabanak Family Images #12, credit YNLC. PHOTOGRAPHER ANDRÉ BOURCIER

facing top Working on tanning moosehide with Champagne and Aishihik First Nations Elder Marge Jackson from Haines Junction, circa 1990s. Pine cones and decayed wood are used to colour the hide. KFN Archives. EMPC. Sharon Kabanak Family Images #13. PHOTOGRAPHER UNKNOWN

facing bottom After tanning a moosehide Sharon creates beautiful and practical wearable art, such as these beaded mukluks. KFN Archives. EMPC. Sharon Kabanak Family Images #15. PHOTOGRAPHER UNKNOWN

As CHRs we met with the government on the Non-Insured Health Benefits process that linked in with the Alberta health protocols and adapted their health benefit into what is now the Home & Community Care Programs. With all that having been done I applied for funding to have five videos made for Traditional Healing Medicines in the Yukon Health Careers Programs. I was funded by the Council of Yukon First Nations through my work and had Elders and other support workers paid to teach land-based healing. A friend named Ruby worked side by side with CHRs and helped promote these videos with our Yukon First Nation Health Program Coordinator, Cheryl. Today Traditional Healing is a widespread component of alternative and natural healing education at the Whitehorse General Hospital and other centres.

Also, in my journey for educational pursuits in the 90s, I was notified by Linda from the Yukon First Nation Health Bursary Program that I was being awarded a bursary, which brought me to study the Wilderness Emergency Medical Technician-1. We were trained to do military-assisted life support (M.A.S.T.) with the pneumatic anti-shock garments. This fieldwork training was through the National Association of Search and Rescue. Some personnel from the army base assisted the plane or helicopter crash scenarios, while a cow moose watched from the distance. I think she knew we needed help as there were people lying about on the snowbanks waiting to be rescued. Our instructor was a graduate medic teacher from the army and held a degree in theology. She drove me back and forth to training in her Jeep, as I had no vehicle there. We all became a working family, study mentors, and friends.

I worked on the Kluane First Nation Self-Government and Land Claims Agreements with the KFN Land Claims Department staff to identify our areas of interest. We met with the Yukon Government over a ten-year period until the settlement process was agreed with their lawyers. A self-government book was made and distributed to all the members for future reference.

I studied Cultural Resource Management courses through the University of Victoria, B.C., by submitting a proposal to the Yukon Heritage Training Fund. I worked with the Yukon Historic Resources Board for several years as one of the Yukon First Nation representatives of the Council of Yukon First Nations. I also worked on their Special Projects Committee to encourage the development and funding of books by artists of Yukon ancestry.

FULL CIRCLE OF LIFE

After my mom was gone, I reached out to people in Alaska to regain my traditional balance. Mom had introduced me to her friend Ada Gallin at Northway, Alaska, who was a mentor in Native Arts. I had promised Mom that I would go to visit this woman and learn to sew on moosehide to make clothes for my family. Mom was happy that I was going to be able to look after myself and her grandchildren, Elodie and Samuel. Ada taught me to do birch-bark work. She was a birch basket artist along with Jenny Sandford, who was from Mentasta, Alaska. Jenny is related to me through my grandma's brother Bill Johns, who was from up in Northway a long time ago. They're always very kind and considerate and give me a place to stay. We're all distant cousins through Big Grandma's brother.

We went out in the bush together to get roots in different places. You have to pick the roots and get all the birchbark on the right days when it's good weather. That's not easy, because there are lots of mosquitos! You save up all the bark and roots for the wintertime. The Northway people travel all around: to Tok, Mentasta, and Chistochina in Alaska. I started my own small-business pilot project entitled Kluane Wild Berries. I bought cranberries, blueberries, and blackberries from Burwash and Northway Elders. Then one day I got a letter from a woman in Alaska who asked if I minded her borrowing my name for her business. I said I didn't mind at all. Now there's a business called Alaska Wild Berries at Homer.

I also design my own signature art-works with beads and other media. I do fine art beadwork on moosehide. I get my furs from my daughter, Elodie, and her husband, Marcel Dulac, who are trappers. My aunt Rita and uncle Thomas turned over their trapline across the lake to them. They have gone back to where my grandpa Jimmy Johnson and his sister Sophie Watt lived. They built their cabin beside the old cabins. I am very proud of my daughter and her husband, who are following the traditional ways of the Elders and respecting their desire to look after that parcel of land for our family. I am proud of my son, Sam, too, who also practices cultural conservation, participating in nature camps and travelling our heritage trails with the KFN Lands Department.

My first language teacher was my mom, who always spoke Dań K'è at home. Later I worked at Kluane Lake School and studied at the Yukon Native Language Centre to become a certified Native Language Teacher. Knowing our language ties into our responsibility to practice appropriate environmental behaviour. With our land claim agreements in place we are able to hunt in the Park now. We have to teach our kids to be respectful of the land and the animals. We tell them, "Always take the Elders with you to get the food they need and like." I think everybody should be able to find their gifts to work with their hands. Our kids and grandkids are fishing, hunting, trapping, and sewing their own clothes. So it's back to the old ways for my family. It's a cycle—a full circle of life.

We have to teach our kids to be respectful of the land and the animals.

GÙDÍA (SHARON KABANAK)

SALKAAYA
(BERTHA DORIS)

(b. 1954)

My Traditions Are Still in My Heart

I was born at Burwash Landing in 1954. The people that helped to raise me here were my grandma Tsal KàJana (Gopher Lady, Copper Lily) and my mom. My mom's name is Gushàka (Grace Margaret Johnson), and my dad's name was Frank, Frank Isaac, who was from the Aishihik area. I have three half-brothers, Freddy, Billy (William), and Henry. Freddy passed away in 1997.

facing Salkaaya (Going after Gophers, Bertha Doris), 2023. KFN Archives EMPC, Elders Portraits #34. PHOTOGRAPHER ROBERT POSTMA

LEARNING FROM OUR ELDERS

Growing up in Burwash was a wonderful experience, especially when we had our past Elders here. Joyce, Alyce, Gùdia Johnson, and I all grew up amongst these Elders. They taught us a lot about the land, how to survive, and about respect. They always took time to teach us new things, and we learned to be hard workers. Two things that we would do just to get a story from them was to pack water and wood for our Elders. It was fun to grow up around them. It was a very interesting life, learning new things every day. Life in Burwash has changed now to accommodate the western world lifestyles, but some of us still hold onto the traditional way of life. We try to continue the work and teachings of these Elders so that it can be passed on to the younger generations.

When I was 9 years old, I was taught to sew. I remember my mom cutting out patterns and encouraging me to try and bead it. I would sit with Mom for hours, watching how she would put items together that she was sewing and asking a lot of questions. Not only my mom taught me; Grandma Copper Lily and my great-aunt Jessie Joe also taught me. If my beading was not right and smooth, they would take it apart and I would try again. Sometimes it was frustrating to see what I had sewed taken apart. It had to be right. Today I am thankful for what they taught me as I continue to carry on this tradition of beading. I have sold products all over the world: in England, Ireland, South Africa, the United States, and across Canada.

Grandpa Moose Johnson taught us how to skin out a moose, quarter it, and process the meat, which we did as young children. It was a very good experience, and I have never forgotten this. I remember this very clearly. I can see now why they all worked so hard with us. People were living the traditional life back then. A lot of stories were told about how they had to travel for miles from camp to camp for food, on foot or with dog sleds. Now it is so easy; we drive a vehicle to the store and buy groceries.

Grandma Copper Lily was the most beautiful and inspirational person in my life. She was a very sophisticated, traditional Elder. She taught me so much. I did many things with her when I was young: picking berries at Silver City, chasing porcupine down the Cultus Road, hunting gophers at Duke Meadow. She would talk to me about being a good person, to be kind and gentle and most importantly to have patience. She would tell me, "Never quit sewing; you will always have money when you sew." I continue this hobby today.

She also talked about young girls turning to womanhood. This is an important part of a young girl's life. They are taught many lessons to carry on in their lives. Gùdia and I had to go through this. Gùdia still initiates this with her grandchildren (girls) who reaches puberty.

Grace Chambers was another Elder, and she was a wonderful grandma to all the children in the community. She would take us fishing and go on little outings. She always had a sled full of children and pulled us behind her Ski-Doo. Every Saturday we would head across the lake to go ice fishing. These were great memories for all of us children. Joyce and I used to call her the fairy godmother. She was a disciplinarian, caring, and loved every child in the community. She always had a gentle way of explaining things to us.

Moose Johnson taught us about dressing a moose and how to take care of it when it was brought back to the community. As food was sometimes scarce, it was important to share with everyone. This is how it was done a long time ago.

Here in Burwash I think my best memories are about Uncle Peter. He used to tease us so much, always joking and laughing. I'll never forget the time that he bundled up Joyce. She was just small, only about 2. We're only about a year apart, so I was about 3 years old. I remember him outside fixing the sled. He had this caribou hide, and he was patting it down. I said, "Where are you going, Uncle?" "Oh, I'm going to go across the lake," he says. I said, "Ok." Joyce went outside, and he hid her in the doghouse. He told her, "Just stand there."

Then he comes running in, and he says, "Look, there goes Joyce!" Grandma Copper Lily was just screaming, "Run after it! Get it! Bring her back!" Grandpa Moose and Uncle Thomas Joe and everybody were across the lake. So Uncle was sending supplies of food across to them, and he was just going to walk over behind the dogs. Grandma was panicking. I remember sitting at the table crying because Joyce was going across the lake alone in the sled. Then suddenly Uncle Peter comes in with her on his shoulders, and Grandma just about jumped up and down, she was so mad. I remember wanting to come home and see him all the time because he was always joking and teasing. That's one of my fondest memories.

Our Elders did a lot of hunting through there on the other side of the lake. It wasn't always playtime for us when we were here, because they were so busy trying to train us teenagers to learn about the land and to live off the land. When people travelled, we had to travel, too, and that's the way it went in summer and at Christmas holidays. We didn't have very many Christmases out here. When we did, we were always getting food. We didn't have presents or anything like that. We did go to church here.

Potlatches used to be held in the old school here, that round house. I remember Robin Johnson [now Bradasch] was so tiny, but she was just sitting and listening to what was going on. I've got pictures of her going to Chief and Council meetings too. I think she must have been about 6 in that picture.

OUR PARENTS DIDN'T UNDERSTAND ABOUT RESIDENTIAL SCHOOLS

I was sent to Lower Post Residential School in B.C. in 1960, when I was 5 years old. I was at the school for eight years,

facing Tsal KàJana (Copper Lily) tanning a moosehide at Burwash, circa 1970s. CYFN Archives. Photograph Collection #b82_f18_s5_8. PHOTOGRAPHER UNKNOWN

but I had the opportunity to come home at Christmas to Whitehorse, where my mom was living then, and I came back to Burwash in the summer months with my cousins. A lot of us received harm when we were at Lower Post. I find myself not wanting to go back to that time and to keep it in the past. Sometimes it's hard to erase, but I cannot hang onto it forever. It is the past, so leave it in the past.

Burwash was a very small community then. Off and on we'd come back here, but an Elder would be gone or somebody would be missing. The Elders here at that time were Big Jessie Joe, Copper Lily, Mary Jacquot, Moose Johnson, Nellie Johnson, Sam Johnson Sr., Jessie Johnson, Dick Dickson, and Joe Joe Johnson, but he would have been a younger man. It was hard on the Elders and our parents when we were taken away to residential school.

People were living a traditional life here then. That was the good thing about growing up in that era because we had the opportunity of learning everything on the land. The only thing was that we couldn't grasp our language, because we were forced to speak English when we went to residential school. Several of us were threatened not to use our language at school. When we went back home, we had to let our parents and grandparents know that. The school staff threatened us to the point we were scared to even speak it. Now we struggle to regain our language, and some of us work so hard as language champions to try our best to revitalize the language.

I was one of the fortunate ones. I had the opportunity to come home in summers. Some children couldn't come back, because their parents couldn't afford the bus fare for tickets. Maybe only four or five of us had that opportunity of coming back to Burwash or to wherever our parents were. My mom brought me home at Christmastime, summertime, and any lengthy holidays. I rode the bus from Lower Post to Burwash. My stepdad, Gilbert Nicholson, worked for Canada Bridge, so there were different destinations throughout B.C. where they were living during those years. Sometimes Mom and he were at Summit Lake, B.C. The bus would take me there.

To this day September still affects some of us psychologically. That's why as soon as September comes I'm out on the land hunting because in the back of my mind I keep visioning that September month is when they would come to take us away for school.

I have three brothers; one passed away in 1997. Freddy was the oldest, Billy is the second oldest, and Henry the baby in the family. The two younger ones were taken away in the 1970s to attend Yukon Hall for a very short time. Freddy had the opportunity to continue in school at Whitehorse Elementary and later at Christ the King High School.

By that time all the residential schools in Canada started shutting down. I thank Father Morisset for coming to Lower Post as the person in charge. As young children coming back into our community, we would tell him stories about how we were being treated at Lower Post. I am not sure if he was asked to come there or if he was concerned after hearing our stories about the school.

We felt comfortable with Father Morisset being there, and we trusted him. We had the opportunity to go and talk to him. He wanted to hear our stories, and he also witnessed some of the things that were happening. I believe he was the one that started the process of these residential schools to start shutting down and the truth coming out of how children were being treated in these schools.

Our parents didn't understand what was happening to their children. I feel bad for my mom and for my grandmother. They didn't understand what the Government of Canada was doing. I heard stories later that they were bribed by family allowance cheques. I am not sure if this is true.

I look at that experience as a lesson in life. I know there's a lot of people to this day that went through residential school, and they still hold onto that past. I had five close friends, but they are all gone now, passed on for different reasons. I still think of them a lot and often think about what they would be like today.

The residential school took away our dignity as First Nation people. A lot of cruel words were put into us; some I don't even want to mention. The word that sticks in my head is domesticate.

I was 13 years old when I left the residential school. My cousin Joyce and I did grade 8 at the Kluane Lake School before we moved to Whitehorse. Joyce went to Yukon Hall, and I stayed with my mom.

facing Women and children at Burwash, circa 1958. *Left to right:* Jessie Joe, Copper Lily Johnson, Joyce Johnson (in front of Copper Lily), Jenny Johnson (Daniel Tlen's mom), Helen Johnson, Mary Jacquot, and Margaret Johnson with daughter Bertha Johnson. KFN Archives. EMPC Robin Bradasch, Johnson Family Images #12. PHOTOGRAPHER UNKNOWN

above Bertha (in back) and her brothers, Henry Johnson, Frederick Johnson, and William (Billy) Johnson, in Whitehorse, circa 1965. KFN Archives. EMPC. Lena Johnson Family Images #9. PHOTOGRAPHER UNKNOWN

above left Bertha's sons in their teens left to right: Khià Tà (Aaron Christian Doris) and Nuzhią (Orion James Lee Doris). KFN Archives. EMPC. Bertha Doris Family Images #1. PHOTOGRAPHER UNKNOWN

above right Khià Tà (Aaron) in a beautiful beaded hide vest made by Bertha for his Native Grad ceremony in 2001. KFN Archives. EMPC. Bertha Doris Family Images #3. PHOTOGRAPHER UNKNOWN

facing Mother and daughter committed to preserving and reviving their language: Gushàka (Margaret Johnson) and Salkaaya (Bertha Doris) recording stories for the KFN Elders Memory Project at Jacquot Hall in Burwash, 2018. KFN Archives. EMPC. Elders Portraits #35. PHOTOGRAPHER ALISTAIR MAITLAND

WORKING LIFE

I came back to work at the lodge in Burwash. Joyce and I lived with Grandma Copper Lily. We were making something like $1.25 an hour, but to us that was big money. Betty Allinger was our boss. We both work in the kitchen.

After that summer I went to Whitehorse and applied for my first job at the Faro mine in 1976 or 1977. I married Herb Doris on March 10, 1977. We had two beautiful sons, Nuzhią (Orion) and Khià Tà (Aaron). I lived in Faro from 1976 to 1995 and later moved to Whitehorse. I started out in Faro as a supervisor in the Janitorial Department and later moved to the Finance Department, which I worked for nearly thirteen years. I moved on to becoming an equipment operator for the remainder of my stay in Faro.

Faro was a family-oriented community. Our children were never bored, as there would be numerous camping trips where a lot of family would participate in. Every event was geared to family. I moved my sons out of Faro in 1995. I worked several different jobs and continued my education in finance.

LANGUAGE IS OUR IDENTITY

In May of 2013 I was seconded from the Yukon Government by Kluane First Nation to come to Burwash to do a one-year pilot project through Council of Yukon First Nation. I enjoyed the language nest project, so when I was asked to continue a contract basis, I accepted. It was kind of strange that I would return to this community after twenty-seven years of absence from my people. Our success rate in the daycare is great. The first set of graduates from the daycare had achieved a grade 3 or 4 level in the language. They were tested by our KFN Elder linguist teacher, Daniel Tlen. We had our two oldest Elders working with the children, Lena Johnson and Grace Margaret Johnson, helping with this program and being the mentors for the language. We also had the late Peter Upton and Agnes Johnson, who helped with the language nest.

I continue to work with language and have started on the development of the KFN Language Department. Upon completion of this department I may consider retirement but would like to continue to do some work for Kluane First Nation that deals in the capacity of language. Language is our identity as people and I would like to preserve this for our younger generation as resources for them to use.

Language is our identity as people and I would like to preserve this for our younger generation as resources for them to use.
SALKAAYA (BERTHA DORIS)

KEITH JOHNSON

(b. 1954)

We Were Always Working

I was born in Burwash on January 14, 1954. I was born in what they used to call the Big House, which is a log cabin. I was delivered by Copper Lily Johnson, I believe. My mom is Lena Johnson. My father was Fred Chambers, now deceased.

facing Keith Johnson, 2017. KFN Archives. EMPC. Elders Portraits #36. PHOTOGRAPHER ALISTAIR MAITLAND

SCHOOL DAYS

I lived in Burwash until I was 6. Then I was sent to Lower Post Residential School, where I spent one school year. The next year I was sent to the convent in Whitehorse because I was a Non-Status Indian. I remember a few people from my school years, including William Atkinson and Harry Atkinson from Ross River. There was Robert Ward and the Goods from Squanga Lake: Helen Good, Wayne Good, Gordon Good. There were other kids, too, that were white children at the convent school: Anthony Boudreaux and a few others but I forget their names now.

In Burwash at that time there were many Elders. There was Sam and Jessie, Grandpa Moose, Grandma Nellie, Copper Lily, Big Grandma, who was Emma Johnson. I don't know how she got that name—she's so small everybody called her Big, I guess! Maybe she had a big personality. I'm not sure, but she always seemed quiet and she was always real nice. She used to get me to stay with her, pack wood and stuff, before I went to residential school.

There were lots of other kids around: Arnold Allinger and Sam Johnson Jr., who I played with. There were the regular kids, all Dorothy's kids, Sam Johnson's kids, my brothers and sisters (George Johnson and Gùdia Johnson). And then my mom took on foster kids Sheri and Bruce Atlin, whom she later adopted. They were from Carcross, but they lived here.

So I went to the convent for grade 2, 3, 4, and I think grade 5. Around 1964 Yukon Government allowed Native kids to go to public schools. I don't know exactly what happened, but they sent me to school out here anyway, at D-Bay. I felt a lot better then. Well, you're home, right? So you get to interact with your relatives, and it's just the family life. It's totally different than being in a convent or residential school.

Many of my memories are to do with work because I was the oldest of the family so I was always the one that helped Mom. She was a single parent, and so I had to basically raise up Gùdia and my brother, along with helping my mom. So I was always working even as a kid. I went to Kluane Lake School at D-Bay to the end of grade 8.

For grade 9 I went back to Whitehorse and into Coudert Residence. I was at Christ the King High until April, and then I got a call over the intercom saying, "Keith Johnson, report to the office." I walked in, and my mom was there. I said, "What's going on?" I thought somebody had passed away or something like that. She said, "Keith, I have to take you out of school because I can't make it by myself." So she took me out of school and brought me home to help her. I was 14, I think. Well, what could the school people say? Your parent says, "Take him out." There's no law saying that I have to be in school. There's a law of survival too.

VILLAGE LIFE

When we were going to school in D-Bay, we had work to do when we got home: go get wood, drag the wood in, cut it up. You had to go down to the lake and pack water, empty slop buckets. Village life. Bush life. You've got to go run the rabbit snare pretty well every day in the winter, gophers in the summer, get moose meat whenever somebody gave us moose meat because we couldn't really hunt ourselves. My uncle Joe Joe helped quite a bit. He helped us.

Our snares would be down towards The Point. We'd sometimes walk down to the mouth of the Kluane River or back up this way. There's an old wagon road that goes up towards Copper Joe subdivision that used to be called Half-Breed Creek, but now it's Copper Joe. So when I came back from Whitehorse as a teenager in the wintertime, my mom and I used to have traps down this way and in the wintertime we'd catch lynx, squirrels, and whatever we could catch and sell, which helped quite a bit.

There was a store at the lodge here at Burwash Landing, the resort it was called later, but of course it was never a resort. So we'd get some things here. Leland and Betty Allinger would get Mom charged up if we needed stuff, but mostly she shopped in Whitehorse. She had some kind of a deal with Taylor and Drury, which I think probably a lot of people all over the Yukon did. So she'd send a list in, and they'd package it and they'd send out boxes. I remember the freight truck used to stop right out in front of her house and then unload our food, and then Mom would just pay cash. COD, cash on delivery.

I would take whatever kind of work I could get those days. That summer and then in the fall of my 15th year, I went down to Victoria with Robert and Sandy Johnson. They wanted me to complete my education, so they took me down to Victoria and they enrolled me in the Institute of Adult Studies, I think it was called, in Victoria, but that was a total shock and I didn't last very long. I lasted until about April. Mary [Easterson] had a job teaching in Prince Rupert in one of the schools up there. They somehow got a hold of me in Victoria and told me they were moving up, and they said, "Come up." So I just basically quit school and hitchhiked up to Rupert and stayed there for that winter. Then there was nothing up there for me. No work or no school, so I hitchhiked back down to Vancouver, then I think I just ended up coming home, back to Yukon. I somehow got the fare together. Well, it was like $40 in those days, student standby. And then in those days hardly anybody travelled, so the plane was never, ever full from Whitehorse to Vancouver. CP Air it was then.

I came back to Burwash in 1970. I just started working for KFN, doing whatever odd jobs I could. I remember they had a store where I used to help unload groceries, and it wasn't much work, really. I'd go out hunting with Peter Johnson and Kenny Johnson whenever they went out if they needed some young muscle! Pack the quarter or whatever. We had a rowboat, so we'd always have a fishnet. We'd just row the boat out there to set and to check the nets. Fish always was in the lake, so easy to get and good fish too. Good food. I lived with Mom, and then we had looked after Bruce and Sheri too.

In those days I think the highest-paid person was the Band Manager at KFN, which always seems to be a white person. Somebody who can bullshit real good. The Chiefs in those days were Agnes Johnson, Charlie Eikland, Jimmy Enoch. I think Sam Johnson Sr. was Chief once for a while. There was just a community hall and band office in the 70s. Our Chief and Council chambers was our community hall then.

facing Keith as a teenager at high school in Whitehorse.
KFN Archives. EMPC. Lena Johnson Family Images #10. PHOTOGRAPHER UNKNOWN

And then right across the street was the band office, which was divided in half: one half was office and then the Band Manager's office was on the other side. In those days we had no running water; everybody had outhouses and water pails, yeah.

I remember the school we started at Burwash, Kêts'á dan' kų. Mary Easterson was teaching in that school and Sandy Johnson, but I don't think that lasted very long, about five years. I wasn't involved in that.

I was working odd jobs around Burwash then. If they built a house, Indian Affairs would always build one or two cabins every year, so I'd be involved in that. I don't think anybody from Burwash worked on the museum with Father Huijbers that I could recall. I know I didn't work on it. I think they just contracted the whole thing out to someone in Haines Junction, and they came up and built it. Contractor came up, threw it up, and took off.

From what I understand, they invited people to purchase memberships in that museum for $5 or so and for your $5 you got a share. So a lot of people did that, but they didn't understand the voting and how to structure it. So what slowly happened, they lost interest and said, "Here you can have your share. We don't want any part of it." So it was taken over by the white society from D-Bay and they still got it, but it's not like we have very much to do with it. We hardly have anything to do with it, but I'm going to say about the museum, it provided a means of support for the ladies where they could sell their sewing and some of the men, too, because the museum would sometimes ask people to go and, "Get a wolverine, a male and female wolverine." They paid good money for that; maybe it was $2,000 each or whatever. So, you know, that helped quite a bit for the local economy. I know Dorothy Johnson and Lena Johnson worked there for years. Later Agnes Johnson worked there too. I think Dorothy worked there until she retired because she, I think if I remember correctly, she got some kind of retirement package. I remember Mom saying something about that. Could have been Agnes worked there too.

FINDING WORK WAS TOUGH

I found the work wherever I could. I worked in Whitehorse for a bit, doing carpentry, labour and carpentry jobs, and whatever work I could, I did it. I staked claims, worked carpentry, and then I got into mining at Whitehorse Copper when I was just a young guy. I was 19 when I got on with Whitehorse Copper, working underground. Whitehorse Copper was good. I liked it because I was assigned to this one miner, and he got paid by his advance. He'd get a wage, but that wage would just pay his income tax, so he got paid by how much advance he did—he'd get paid by the foot. So that was his bonus, but his bonus was always bigger than his paycheque, so his paycheque went to pay his tax and his bonus was his regular pay. I wasn't into that, because I was just starting out, but I was assigned to this guy, so we'd drill and blast every day. Soon as he'd got in his one or two rounds, he'd say, "Well, I'm done." Some days he'd walk out at one o'clock in the afternoon. He was just young. I think he was a Ukrainian guy or something. He was a foreigner anyway. He had quite the accent. I'd be there after he left and then the foreman would find me something to do. I'd always be busy.

I knew that it was dangerous underground. There was potential there for being dangerous, but I thought about how many hundreds of people went through that mine before me and they're still walking around, so I figured, "Well, it's got to be safe, right? Not everybody's dead." There was blasting underground.

People operating heavy-duty equipment down there. There's rocks falling but not constantly. You'd always be safe. You'd put up a wire mesh, galvanized wire mesh, which is something like the fencing material that you use, and they'd drive them in with rock bolts, we'd call them, and that prevented anything from falling on you while you were working.

To an untrained eye the ore just looks like a big chunk of rock you'd find anywhere, but if you look carefully, you could see the copper, little veins of copper, and it didn't look like much, but apparently there was enough there to justify that mine. I believe there was gold, too, but I don't know. I wasn't involved in that process.

When I was 24, I spent the winter in CFB Borden in Ontario, where I took an aircraft maintenance course, but I should have done a little more research. I just kind of fell in love with the aircraft thing. I really wanted to be a helicopter pilot, but when I went for my test at the airport, they took me out on the runway and they were flashing these lights and I failed the colour test because I'm partially colour-blind. So I'm red, green, or something like that colour-blind. Anyway I had a hard time differentiating between white light and green light because they look so similar to me. So anyway after that I got the results. They called me up, so I went up to the airport and they said, "You're never going to be a pilot. You're colour-blind." After that I started thinking, "Well, maybe I'll get into aircraft maintenance." So I applied to Indian Affairs; I think that was putting it on. They just wanted people to train in different things, and they had this course on aircraft maintenance, so I applied for that and I got accepted. I went down to CFB Borden for September to May, and I took that aircraft maintenance course. And I come out on top of the class. That was '78 when I was 24.

above Keith Johnson working on the old community hall built in the 1970s and now being repurposed and upgraded as a Youth Centre for Burwash. KFN Archives. EMPC. Elders Portraits #37. PHOTOGRAPHER ALISTAIR MAITLAND

After I got back to the Yukon, I got a phone call from CP Air. I guess one of my instructors had called; he had a friend working for CP Air. Called me here in Burwash, and he said, "Hey, are you Keith Johnson?" I didn't know who I was talking to and I said, "Yeah," and he introduced himself and he said, "We'd like to fly you down to Vancouver at our expense. We'd like to show you around the maintenance hangars and stuff like that." So I went down, spent three days down there, and they showed me what they did and they asked me to go to work for them. At that time my son was just 4 years old, my daughter was just being born, and I didn't want to move to Vancouver.

So I took a job with Trans North helicopters in Whitehorse but really, really super low wages. I can't believe why I ever agreed to that. They're paying me $700 every two weeks. Al Kapty, he owned the outfit then. The wages they were paying—$710 every two weeks, but that was before taxes, and so like after my tax

was taken off, I was broke. I had a family to feed. So I lasted as long as I could in that, but I'd always go out in the hole. With a young family I just couldn't do it.

Then my uncle Joe Joe came to see me in Whitehorse, and he said, "You should come to work for me." And I said, "Work?" And he says, "Yeah, I got a contract to build two houses in Burwash," and he said, "I'll pay you good money." So we did those two houses in two months, and I made just as much in those two months as I would have done in the whole year for Trans North. And I was home all the time with my family. I built them a tent frame up at The Point because we used to live in there! After that I got into the carpentry side of things. That was '78, '79.

With my experience mining at Whitehorse Copper I got on up in Faro, which is an open pit versus underground, but because I had some experience in mining, I got hired. Once I got up there, I just didn't want to leave and go scratch around anywhere else, because I had a steady income. My family stayed in Whitehorse because I worked day shift and night shift, and we'd be working two weeks in, one week out. So I'd take my clothes up there and work my stint and change and head out and come back home. My kids went to school in Whitehorse.

I stayed up there for quite a few years. It got shut down in '84. There were a couple of strikes, too, in the 70s. We'd get shut down, and then I'd get called back. The thing I liked up there is they had the bunkhouse. So you could live in the bunkhouse and get your bed and your food. I stayed there for quite a few years.

I didn't have a problem with anybody. Maybe it was my attitude; I just didn't take no b.s., and I was willing to defend myself for anything. I was a good worker. You had to sign up for the union, Teamsters. So we signed up for unions, and the money was pretty good for those days and steady employment. I went back when it reopened again in '87. I was working for Curragh Resources. They called me back. I was surprised. They must have went through the old files and I must have gotten a good review, because they called me, so I went back and I stayed there until they shut down in the early 90s.

After that I moved to Atlin, and in the summer I fished on the Taku River for ten seasons. Salmon. And in the winter I just did whatever odd jobs I could. I built a house down there. I milled all the logs myself, all the planks, and all the lumber. We lived right on the Taku River. We fished from May to middle of September. We just moved right down there. Cold on the hands, but you know, it was lots of fun too. I mean, you wouldn't make it rich, but you had a good time. My wife at the time and two kids—we had our own boat.

In summers, before I fished, I worked in gold mines in Atlin, running equipment. I had a little bit of equipment experience. So, with that equipment experience, I got on with Golden Hill Ventures, building roads. We started in Beaver Creek, and my last stint was down at Iron Creek. We basically built that road right through to the other side of Silver City there; that last stretch was the last time I worked on the road. That was the government of U.S. trying to improve the Alaska Highway for their citizens travelling back and forth to Alaska. So I did that for a number of years. I think 2002 was my last year on the Shakwak Project. When I think about it, it only lasted so long. You'd be rich in the summer and broke in the winter—a pauper in the winter!

GOOD TO BE HOME AGAIN

I moved back to Burwash in '96. I was never into land claims. I was more a hands-on, practical guy. Over the course of time I always had employment with Kluane First Nation. I'd always be building something or repairing something or renovating something, but not for really long periods of time. If I got a more attractive offer, they understood that I'd be gone. If I got an offer to go to Faro or Fort Nelson or Watson Lake or whatever for a two-month job, I'd be gone. So basically I did that until I said, "Aw, I've had enough of this bouncing around." It's getting hard on the body, running CATs and bouncing on the hoe. It was really hard on the body. It's a young man's game, that, you know, where you can take the abuse and long hours. Bugs were not a problem when you're running equipment, but if you're a surveyor or a flagger, they are. When you're running a piece of equipment, they won't bother you.

After I left Golden Hill, I moved back to Burwash and I got a house. I moved in there, and I did work for the First Nation. I'd do contracting to renovate a whole house or whatever, and that's kept me going for quite a few years. And then they asked me if I wanted to go on permanent, and I thought, "Well, I may as well, you know; it's a paycheque." So I got on permanent as a carpenter, and then the public works position came up for Director, so I applied for it. I didn't get it the first time. They hired somebody from Outside, but he was only here for three months and then he left. The position came open again and so I applied for it, and at the interview they said, "Well, we're tired of hiring people that quit all the time, so we'll give you a try."

So I'm still here. So that's going on four years now. It's a good job because it's non-stop go. You're constantly running from here to there, and there's always some kind of a crisis you've got to fix, which I like. So it could be water mains, frozen lines, broken pumps. We build roads. We just put in another subdivision with twenty-six new lots. We've cleared two lots. We're going to be building two more houses next summer. So we're renovating a house right now.

Burwash has come from being a sleepy, little, backwoods town to a First Nation that has self-governing powers and the funding to back itself, and it's still growing. We want to build infrastructure where we keep our Youth here rather than them going out looking for employment. Hopefully Wellgreen will kick in in the future, and we'll grow our town into something that'll contribute not only to the Yukon's economy but to the well-being of our people and our members and the First Nation as a whole.

It feels good to be home. No worries. When you're not home, even Vancouver or whatever, doesn't matter, if you're not at home, you're always wishing you were at home. One thing I notice is that anywhere you go, anything that you want to do, you have to pay money for, but here you can just go for a walk or run over to someone's place and drink tea or snowmobile. There's no cost to live here, really. Whereas in Vancouver if you want to go seven or eight blocks, it's going to cost you $2.75 or $3.75 now to park your car.

We always hunt every year, and I'm just waiting for the ice to freeze a little more and then set a net and fish. We got two moose this year as a family to share. I don't hunt sheep; that's a young man's job. When you're 18, 19—but my brother, George,

facing Burwash seen from the bay in fall 2022. KFN Archives. EMPC. Landscape Images #26. PHOTOGRAPHER ALISTAIR MAITLAND

facing Keith Johnson recording stories for the KFN Elders Memory Project, 2017. KFN Archives. EMPC. Elders Portraits #38. PHOTOGRAPHER ALISTAIR MAITLAND

he's in such good shape even though he's 60 now, he still goes. He still climbs the mountains, and he smokes like heck too. I don't know how he does it. We set traps sometimes. My mom still loves going out on the land and setting traps. We've got cabins: one called the Gopher Cabin and then I built another cabin up where we hunt moose. We call that Moose Cabin. So we've still got our seasonal cabins but more comfort. We go by truck, snowmobile, ATV, and we're living in a stick frame–built cabin instead of a tent.

I was on Council as Elder Councillor for two terms, starting in 2015 and finishing in 2021. It is a very difficult and demanding job. Citizens expect a lot from their Council, and sometimes they can be unpleasant. If we could train human beings to be good to one another, there would be no wars and no famine and hardships. I also sat on the Wildlife Resources Board and also the KFN Development Corporation. Then I retired!

I travelled a lot before COVID: to the Philippines, Thailand, Vietnam, Singapore, Malaysia. They are very poor countries, so sometimes the conditions are pretty tough, with rickety hotels and accommodations, but it's interesting seeing how other people live. I've come full circle because I couldn't wait to get out of here when I was young and now I don't want to leave. So it's quite the roundabout way of finding out that actually home is where your heart is.

IT'S OUR FUTURE!

These days KFN is supplying employment for this whole area: D-Bay, Burwash. KFN is the economic driver. Without KFN there'd be just the highway crew here, probably wouldn't even be a nursing station. Actually they'd probably shut it down and run it out of Junction and Beaver Creek. Hopefully it will grow quite a bit with the new mine coming in. Who knows though? We've been at that since the 1950s, and every year they've been promising that mine to their investors. We have a lot of platinum in this area, and the price of platinum today is $300 below the highest point it's been. So all the investment advisors are saying, "Buy platinum. Now is a good time to buy platinum," because they figure it being such a limited resource and high demand that it's got to go up.

KFN has to get really involved in building this mine if it does come up. We have to get the economic benefits. We have to get the main contracts to drive that mine. We should be getting the catering, the road maintenance, the equipment supply. We should be in charge of labour, and that'll move us forward quite a bit. The techniques that they've used to mitigate environmental concerns have evolved so much in the last twenty years that it could be safely said that they could mine that without any future environmental impacts that could damage our ecosystem. So I'm sure that whatever they decide, KFN will have a big say in it because it'll have to come through the YESAB (Yukon Environmental and Socio-Economic Assessment Board) and we can intervene at any time that we feel it's unsafe to move forward. We can get into the environmental aspects of it, too, because everybody wants clean and green and you get a clean and green company, you're going to be wanted.

Education is crucial for our future. Our young people need to go to university. We need scientists, doctors, nurses, engineers, wildlife experts, financial planners, everything. We can support them to get their education; they just have to go and then work for their Nation. We need to protect and grow our financial assets, our wildlife resources, and our land. We have to make plans for all of this and act as needed. It's our future as a First Nation—for all our coming generations!

Education is crucial for our future. Our young people need to go to university. We need scientists, doctors, nurses, engineers, wildlife experts, financial planners, everything.

KEITH JOHNSON

GÙDIA
MARY JANE JOHNSON

(b. 1955)

It Needs to Be Done, You Do It

You introduce yourself from your mother's side. Á yį̨zhì Gùdia ùye Dań k'e (in the Peoples' way my name is Gùdia). Ama Tùlhàsèn ùye ch'e (my mother is Tùlhàsèn). Ama Ku'chan k'e Lena Johnson ùye ch'e (my mother is Lena Johnson in English). Asų̨ą Gùdia ùye ch'e na (my grandmother, who has passed, is Gùdia). Asų̨ą Ku'chan k'e Mary Johnson ùye ch'e na (in the English way my grandmother, who has passed, is Mary Johnson). Asų̨ą shäw Èna ùye ch'e na (my great-grandmother, who has passed, is Èna). Asų̨ą shäw Ku'chan k'e Emma Johnson ùye ch'e na (in the English way my great-grandmother, who has passed, is Emma Johnson).

facing Gùdia Mary Jane Johnson, 2018. KFN Archives. EMPC. Elders Portraits #39. PHOTOGRAPHER ALISTAIR MAITLAND

Atà Fred ùye ch'e na (my father, who has passed, is Fred). Atà Ku'chan k'e Fred Chambers ùye ch'e na (in the English way my father, who has passed, is Fred Chambers). Asìa Gă lhêla ùye ch'e na (my grandfather, who has passed, is Gă lhêla). Asìa Ku'chan k'e Moose Johnson ùye ch'e na (in the English way my grandfather, who has passed, is Moose Johnson). Asìa shäw Sida Tà ùye ch'e na (my great-grandfather, who has passed, is Sida Tà). Asìa shäw Ku'chan k'e Jimmy Johnson ùye ch'e na (in the English way my great-grandfather, who has passed, is Jimmy Johnson).

Khàjèt ích'e (I am of the Crow Clan). Lhù'ààn keyí ts'än ích'e (I am from the Kluane Lake country). Dzenu, Lhù'ààn Mân yū niìnje (today I live at Burwash Landing). I was born right here in Burwash, in the fall time at our old house, which was where the administration building is now. It was a big log building. Grandma Jessie Joe was there and Grandma Pete Jacquot.

EARLY MEMORIES OF BURWASH

I got tuberculosis when I was about 18 months old and was brought to the hospital in Whitehorse, then sent to Charles Camsell Hospital in Edmonton. After about eight months I was so homesick that I kept going downhill. My brother Keith also had TB, so the priest asked Mom to send Keith for treatment to be beside me. Mom agreed.

We came back here when I was 4. I couldn't go to the outhouse after being in the hospital with indoor plumbing, so Betty Allinger gave me a kid's potty. All we had was candlelight in our home.

I remember how loving all the grandmas and grandpas were—Big Grandma, Grandma Copper Lily, Grandpa Moose, Grandma Sophie Watt, Grandma Jessie Joe, Grandma Nellie, Grandma Mary Jacquot, Grandma Kitty Jamieson, Bill Jamieson, Grandpa Albert Isaac, Grandma Elsie Isaac, and especially Aunt Jenny Johnson and Aunt Helen—they were all alive. I remember going to a Potlatch at Champagne for Johnny Fraser, and all the Elders were dancing and singing. John Joe and his wife, Julia, were there from Marsh Lake. It was really strict for kids at a Potlatch then—no running behind the Elders when they were eating or playing around inside the room.

above Women of Burwash, circa 1960s. *Front row left to right:* Copper Lily Johnson, Ѐna Johnson, and Jessie Joe. *Back row left to right:* Mary Jacquot, Lena Johnson, and Jessie Kabanak. KFN Archives. EMPC Elders Portraits #40. PHOTOGRAPHER CATHARINE MCCLELLAN

Father Morisset was really helpful to people that had hardship. He took people in his little green pickup with the canopy. I don't know how he fit everybody in there. He'd drop us off at Pickhandle Lake in the springtime to hunt muskrats and at 1124 (Grandma Copper Lily's camp, where people would go to pick cranberries), 1120, Quill Creek, or Mile 1118 to pick berries. Sometimes he'd bring us to Beaver Creek and Northway to visit. He had a day school, where he taught young people reading and writing. Mom is one of the only people alive that didn't go to residential school. My grandmother Gùdia (Mary) passed away when Mom was 15, so she looked after Uncle Bernie, who was 8 months old; her sister, Eva; and brothers Joe and Harvey until Grandpa Moose married Grandma Nellie. When Lower Post Residential School was set up, the kids were sent there. My brother Keith went for one year. Father Morisset was here from 1943 until around 1965, when Father Huijbers came.

Mom contacted TB when I was 5. The ambulance took her away, and we ran behind it all the way up to the highway. We stayed with Grandpa Moose at first. Then Father Morisset came and said Keith and I had to go to school. Grandpa took George, who was just 3, across the lake while Mom was in the hospital. Our parents were separated, but Dad signed a statutory declaration saying we were his children, so we became Non-Status since he was enfranchised through his parents, Grandma Sue and George Chambers. Keith and I went to the Roman Catholic convent in Whitehorse from 1960 to '64. During those years we wrote to Mom because Keith knew how to write. It wasn't easy, but all of us at the convent became family: Rosemary Blair and siblings, Helen Good and her brothers, Vivian Jim and her brothers, the Chouinard kids, the Atkinsons from Ross River, and others.

People from Burwash came to visit us: Leland and Betty Allinger, Grandma Jessie Joe, George John, and Little Grace [Johnson]. When Grandpa Buck Dickson was in the hospital, Keith and I walked over to see him. They wouldn't let us in, so we visited at his window. When we went back to the convent, we were grounded for months. Leland Allinger picked us up at Christmastime and brought us out to Grandpa Moose. If he was across the lake, we stayed with Grandma Jessie Joe. She opened her door to many children in the community. That's how I remember my school holidays, always in the community with Grandpa, Grandma Jessie, or Big Grandma. She was one of the most wonderful grandmas, loving and kind, but when she just bring her voice up little bit, you know—oh, oh, trouble! Father Morisset drove us up to Pickhandle Lake, with the grandpas and grandmas, during Easter break to hunt muskrats and trap beavers. When we had to go back to the convent, Grandpa Moose would go out on the highway and flag down the Greyhound bus to take us to Burwash and Leland drove us to the convent.

When I was growing up, people would come from the Junction or Beaver Creek and camp here. Agnes Nieman and her kids came. She and her husband, Paul, were living in Whitehorse at that time, but she would camp here by Grandma Jessie Joe. Donjek and Dorothy Brown, with their son Gerald, Jack and Bessie Allen, Pardon and Lilly Kane—they would all come to camp in the summer. We always had lots of kids to play around here. Alex and Elsie Smith would come with their kids, Harry, Lena, Frank, and Mary Edna, in the summertime to fish, hunt gophers, and camp up at Duke

Leland and Betty Allinger had about fifty head of cattle, so lots of the younger guys had their first work experience planting and cutting hay for them. They had a hayfield at Burwash and a big hayfield up at Half-Breed Creek (now Copper Joe Creek). They had hay barns, so that was our play area. They had a big underground place up there for the cattle, but mostly they ranged free outside. There was an electric fence

above This first community hall in Burwash was built by Max McLeod, Edward Johnson, and Keith Johnson at the time of a Potlatch for Grandpa Moose Johnson, circa 1970s. *Left to right:* George John standing; seated are Jenny Moose, Grandma Nellie Johnson (second wife to Grandpa Moose Johnson), and Annie Nicholas; standing Mary Jacquot, Kitty Joe, Grandma Jessie Joe, Grandma Sophie Watt, Lena Johnson, Daisy Jackson, Solomon Charlie, and Jack Allen; unidentified man in doorway. KFN Archives. EMPC. Sandy Johnson Family Images #16. PHOTOGRAPHER UNKNOWN

around the hay area to keep away animals. When we were kids, we'd run as fast as we can to see who would grab the electric fence first and whoever got the tail end got the jolt!

Grandma Sophie Watt was like a boss in the village, with her sisters-in-law Big Grandma and Copper Lily. They were Khàjèt (Crow), and she was Agunda (Wolf). Grandma Sophie had traditional tattoos on her chest and her arms. She was a true sister to Grandpa Jimmy Johnson, and her half-sister was Elsie. Sophie was married to the "Old Doctor." When he died, she married Frederick Watt, who came from New Brunswick during the Gold Rush and was married to Suzie Pringle's sister at Lhu' Ghą (Dalton Post). When Suzie's sister died, Fred married Sophie and they had two children, Ada and Jim Watt. They lived at Cultus Bay until Fred died, then Grandma moved over to Burwash. Her house was where the Kluane Daycare is now. Grandma Sophie kept order in the community—she knew the Kwädāy Kwändür (long-ago stories) and saw that Potlatches were done right and babies were named properly.

Sophie raised up her kids here. Later Ada went to school in Vancouver. Grandma Sophie's son, Jim Watt, was racing dog teams with Walter David and Frank Joe on Kluane Lake on their way to sell fur at Frank Sketch's store by Kloo Lake. Frank was ahead, and when he turned his team around, he saw a black hole and knew they had both gone through the ice.

In 1966 Father Huijbers worked with Henry Besner, a gold miner at Burwash Creek, to get an old diesel-powered generator set up in the log garage at the Chouinards'. He got power poles and cable from Indian Affairs and ran one line down from the generator, then one line into every house. By fall everybody had one light bulb! Those years were still tough, with drinking and bad things happening in our isolated little community.

DESEGREGATING DESTRUCTION BAY SCHOOL

In 1964 Keith, Arnold, and I were allowed to go to the Destruction Bay school, and Mom came back. She had to wear a back brace, but I remember her walking to the Burwash airport to hunt gophers and in winter running squirrel and lynx snares. She wore that brace diligently for five years, and that's why she's still strong now.

Six of us from here went to the Destruction Bay school. We walked—cold, snow, or rain—up to the highway to pile in the station wagon driven by Charlotte McLean. Her husband, Doug, worked for Highways. Destruction Bay was a government camp for Canadian National Telecommunication (CNT) and DPW workers with their families. Kids from highway lodges and pipeline compressor stations also went to that school. Cindy Lambert,

Clinton and Kathy Boe, Kevin and Wendy McLaughlin, and Mark Wyatt—they got on the bus from the pipeline station south of D-Bay. There were others too: the Vanderveens, Gary and Karen, who lived in the army building by the lake; Terry Sakew; the Peirsons; the Jakestas; Buster and Judith Claire from CNT; from the other end of the lake at Silver Creek, there was Maureen Smith with her brother and sister; a few years later Mike and Jan Williams's kids came from 1128 by the Donjek and later Susie Radford and her sister from CNT; the Petersens, Woods, Tara-Lee and Kelly Backstrom, and the Thompsons from MOT (Ministry of Transport).

Keith, Arnold, and I were the first kids from Burwash to come back and go to public school. Grandma Helen was here, plus Big Grandma and Grandma Copper Lily. The aunties were the best, and they all looked after us. The community had to adjust to having kids at home and getting them to school every day. They couldn't go out on the trapline or to camp. For lunches we often had fried rabbit or bannock. Mom knew what she had to do, and she helped other families.

We still went out and trapped with Mom, Big Grandma, Grandma Copper Lily, Grandma Jessie Joe—everyone had to have money for school clothes. We trapped up to Copper Joe Creek (in those days it was called Half-Breed Creek); up Lewis Creek and along the highway through to the Duke; and Down Below. Sometimes they went across the lake but not much, because you needed a dog team. People didn't have snow machines then. Mom trapped and bought a gas-powered washing machine. Our last old log house was where the Jacquot Hall is now. In winter we packed water by the bucket from an ice hole on the lake, melted ice on the wood stove to wash laundry. There were no power saws, just a swede saw. We liked winter because we could hook up the dogs and pull lots of wood by sleigh.

facing Shukhwäya (Sophie Watt) was an Agunda matriarchal leader, seen here resting in front of her house at Burwash after chopping firewood, 1977. KFN Archives. EMPC. Elders Portraits #41. PHOTOGRAPHER NORMA MCBEAN

above Gùdia (front row, second on left) at Christ the King Elementary School, 1961. KFN Archives. EMPC. Gùdia Mary Jane Johnson Family Images #1. PHOTOGRAPHER UNKNOWN

NEW HOMES FOR BURWASH

Indian Affairs started to replace the old log homes in Burwash in the 1960s. Elijah Smith, Fred Jamieson, and Donnie Burns brought logs from the Watson Lake sawmill, and the kids peeled the rough-cut logs. One DIA-hired carpenter worked with a community crew, and by 1975 nearly all the old houses were taken down. There are only two original houses still standing: Grandpa Jimmy Joe's house that's beside the Jacquot Hall, and George John's and Little Grace's cabin.

The new houses were 20 by 20 feet, including one room with a counter and sink with bucket underneath to collect wash water for dumping outside, space for a small table and chairs, wood cook stove and wood heater, and two small bedrooms. I don't know how everybody fit in with six or seven people living in those houses. A gravel road was built from the highway to our new homes, and a school bus came in so we didn't have to walk up to the highway.

In 1968 Big Grandma got sick in the fall time. They took her into Whitehorse, and Mom said, "You guys gotta stay here and look after things. I'm going to go check in with Grandma." She passed away from leukemia. When we were at the church, Grandpa Moose said, "We're gonna say goodbye to your grandma now," so he brought me up there and said, "It's ok, grandchild, she's gone now. We gotta let her go." So then I understood what death was.

GROWING UP FAST

At that time you could only go to grade 8 at the Destruction Bay school. I finished grade 8 at D-Bay, then I had to go to Whitehorse to Yukon Hall, one of the Indian student residences. My brother Keith was over at the Catholic one, Coudert Hall. I said, "How come I can't be over there?" But they said no.

I was already working since I was 11 for Betty down at the lodge. You start working in the garden there, graduate to the laundry, then chambermaid and on to the kitchen starting with dishwashing, then prepping for the cooks. Finally you go to waitressing, where the tips were. I made it all the way up to be a waitress, but I took one order and just couldn't bring somebody's food to them. I did it at Potlatches, but at the lodge I couldn't do it.

So from working out here at the lodge, helping Mom, running the traps, raising money for myself, and contributing to the household income, I went to Yukon Hall and got grounded because I came back at 8:30 one evening. For my punishment I had to get up at six o'clock, sweep the stairs, and make toast for 180 kids. After this kind of treatment I told Mom when I came home at Christmastime, "I'm not going back there."

I packed up my stuff and went to Whitehorse to see a lady I knew named Linda from Montreal. We hitchhiked to Vancouver just after Christmas, and then we went to Montreal. I was 15 years old. I found a job looking after a family with six children, but after the summer I phoned Mom and told her I wanted to go to England to school. Mom said I should come home, so I hitchhiked back to the Yukon. I tried to go back to Yukon Hall and to school, but they wouldn't accept me.

I started working in Whitehorse, but I became pregnant, went to Vancouver to stay with my cousin Daniel Tlen's first wife, Jodi. I had to go to the Catholic Children's Services there, and after my baby was born, they tried to get me to give her up for adoption. I phoned Mom to say the baby needed a name right away. She got Grandpa Moose and Grandma Copper Lily to give Math'ieya her name.

My dad, Fred Chambers, lived in Haines, and up to then he'd never been in my life very much. I phoned to tell him the papoose was born, and he sent money for us to take the ferry to Haines. We stayed there with Dad for about two weeks, then went back to Burwash, and afterwards he made trips to visit us. Mom was going to the Yukon Vocational School in Whitehorse for upgrading, so I was on my own with my baby.

MORE CHANGES IN BURWASH

In the 1960s Indian Affairs officials came into the community and said there was no longer going to be a hereditary Chief but an elected Chief and Council. Grandpa Sam came from a long line of hereditary Chiefs. Big Grandma's dad was Tlinget Tlen, the Chief down in Fort Selkirk. Grandpa Jimmy Johnson's dad was Old Man Johnson, Chief at Aishihik. Grandpa Sam had been passed on that Chieftainship. The first person elected as Chief was Daniel Tlen in the mid-1970s. He was probably around 21 or 22. This election upset Grandpa Sam as well as other Elders.

Grandpa Sam's old house was converted, by where Dennis Dickson has his place now, to become the first band office for the Kluane Indian Band (KIB). I knew how to type, because that's what they taught you in high school, so I was the first secretary for the band at 16 years old! We set up an office and worked with Indian Affairs in Whitehorse to start several economic development projects and a small library through Yukon Government.

In 1973 we worked with Father Huijbers to dig a well and build a laundry with running water, three ringer washers, and two shower stalls. Everybody would pack their laundry down, wash their clothes, and hang them up outside at home. Later we built a bigger wash house on top of the hill. We converted one shower into a sauna because Betty Allinger, being Finnish, always had a sauna, and we had liked that as kids. Mary Easterson moved back to the community with her partner, Henry Michel, so we converted the old wash house into a home for them and their girls, Donalda, Juniper and Justina.

There were no more new houses being built, so younger people did not have a place to live. I lived in a tent for many summers with Math'ieya. I went everywhere, packing her on my back, and set up our tent by my mom's house, at the airport, or at Duke River. After I met my partner, John, I continued that lifestyle at Cultus Bay, Whitehorse, Champagne, and we lived in Grandma Pete's cabin across the lake seven winters.

When I was going to have another baby, there was no way I wanted to be in the hospital again after what I went through with Math'ieya. I went into Whitehorse and got checked up. I told my doctor I was going to have my baby in a tent. Grandma Margaret was living nearby, and when I told her, she said, "I'm gonna go get Agnes Nieman to help." I was helping Grandma Margaret work on her skins one morning and started to have contractions. Grandma Margaret and Agnes knew what to do. They got everything ready and my baby girl was ok. Grandma Margaret's husband Gilbert got scared and called the ambulance to take me to the hospital for a few days. Then I packed up our tent and came back to Burwash.

We moved down to Copper Joe Creek and started setting nets with Grandma Grace Chambers. Grandma Copper Lily made me a bibìa tth'al (birchbark baby basket) to pack Bibia on my back while I worked. We were getting eighty trout a day, which had to be cut and dried. Mom was at school in town and going to university in Alaska. She was in her 50s and had never gone to a regular school but now studying at university!

One day in July we came back to Burwash and were staying down at the old house. I could hear hollering, "Gùdi, Gùdi!" My baby was almost 3 months old. I looked out the window and saw Grandmas! So I grab Bibia, and I say, "Bibia, you gonna have a name."

facing Gùdia, in photo taken by her brother George Johnson, 1970. KFN Archives. EMPC. Lena Johnson Family Images #11. PHOTOGRAPHER GEORGE JOHNSON

above Gùdia's father, Fred Chambers (left), sheep hunting with Hank Jacquot near Burwash, circa 1950s. KFN Archives. EMPC. Lena Johnson Family Images #12. PHOTOGRAPHER UNKNOWN

Grandma Sophie Watt must have been older than 95 years that time. I gave her Bibia and she look at her and she said, "This one here is Diyet. Hello, Diyet. You—you got woman's name, Diyet. No baby name for you." She passed her over to Grandma Copper Lily, who said, "Hello, asheà (grandchild). Hello, Diyet, how are you, Bibia? No more baby name now, just Diyet, woman's name Diyet. Mmm, asheà." She pass her off to Grandma Mary Jacquot, who said, "Oh, this one, Diyet. Oh, you got big name. You name after your great-grandma sister, Alyce. That's the one this name, Diyet, mmm, Diyet." They pass her off to Little Grace, who call Diyet's name three times. Then she gave her to the youngest one, Grandma Jessie Joe, who sing her song. "Hello, Diyet. Gee whiz, Diyet, good to see you, Diyet." That's how all the grandmas talked. They all call her name three times. Grandma Sophie gave her back to me and said, "You say her name, Diyet, turn around, which way the sun go, hold her, call her name again. Diyet, this one here, Diyet." It was all right here on the road, where all of this big ceremony was going on.

Our names have to stay in order of Khàjèt and Agunda according to our mother's Clan. Grandma Sophie said, "Oh gee, my little sister gonna dance around with me," because it was her sister-in-law's sister's name she had given my bibia. The grandmas were all lined up on the fence from the two sides: Agunda, Grandma Sophie and Little Grace; Khàjèt, Grandmas Copper Lily, Mary Jacquot, and Jessie Joe. Diyet is a woman's name, meaning a skin house made on a willow frame—dyea. After that I was just so happy.

Grandma Amy Allen was alive around that time too. Johnny Allen had passed away, but she was still living and she came to visit Grandma Nellie all the time because Grandma was her oldest sister-in-law. Nellie's brothers were Johnny Allen and Jack Allen; her sister was Jessia, who was married to Sam Johnson. Lilly Birckel was the youngest one of the family from Monica Allen and Old Man Allen. Amy used to come around all the time, but she was starting to get forgetful at that time. When Math'ieya was small, Amy was delighted with her and made her little tanned gopher skin moccasins.

The museum was getting going in the late 1960s, and the Elders were working there. George John was making skin boats, with Jimmy Enoch and Joe Tom-Tom helping. Grandma Nellie, Grandma Jessie Joe, and Grandma Marge Jackson were all sewing for the museum. When Dorothy moved to the new log house Arnold Allinger built for her, the museum society made Dorothy's old house up on the hill a museum.

Later on Father Huijbers got the Yukon Vocational School to help design a church building, with Uncle Bernie and Lynn Lambert doing the drafting. It was bigger than the Catholic Church could support, so they turned it over to the Kluane Historical Society. Leland Allinger donated the land. They moved all the exhibits to that new Kluane Museum of Natural History. Father Huijbers got donations from miners like

Henry Besner. Every person in the community had some part in the building or the artifacts. The gopher and squirrel skin coat was made by the grandmas. Amy knew how to tan gopher skins. Grandma Nellie and Grandma Jessie Joe sewed the coat. Dorothy Johnson and my mom worked at that museum for many years.

I had Geordan at the old house when the ice was just going out at the end of May 1979. Mom was up the highway at a protest camp after the arrest of Grandpa Sam. Harry Allen and other First Nation leaders were there. Mom had forgotten the dog chains, and when she came to the house, she saw Grandma Jessie Joe and Little Grace boiling water. She said, "You're gonna have Bibia right now?" I said, "Right now." Geordan was the first baby born in this community in probably one and a half generations. Everybody went to Whitehorse to have their kids. George John always called me his Ämata (My Older Sister), so Grandma Jessie Joe said to pass on the name A'tanyata (Going Hunting along a Side Hill Trail) to my son from Fred Jamieson, George's younger brother. His nickname was T'àwa (Grayling) because she said that is what he sounded like when he cried.

Next day I was up! You can't go laying in bed if you have a baby—still things to do. I got two other kids to look after. Cook, pack water, load up the stove—still got all those things to do. Mom came back then, and I was very glad to see her.

DENIED OUR RIGHTS TO FOOD AND LANDS

The Game Warden had charged Grandpa Sam and Grandma Jessie for trapping muskrats down at Pickhandle Lake. Grandpa Sam had a rifle in the camp and traps. Ray Wootton was the Conservation Officer who came to their camp and tried to take their traps and the gun away from Grandpa Sam. He took the traps, but Grandpa Sam said, "You can't leave us without gun." They had a big argument. He was trapping in the Game Sanctuary, but the Game Warden didn't know that we had made an agreement to trap in that one area. They took his gun, and he had a stroke right after that and went to Whitehorse in an ambulance. He was never able to go out on the land again, although he and Grandma Jessie still camped at the Duke and at Burwash Creek. They had an apartment at Whitehorse, in the Marwell area, where he stayed to the end of his life.

Harry Allen was the head of CYI at that time. Daniel Tlen was working at the Indian Centre, too, along with Rosie Blair-Smith and Dorothy Wabisca. Community people rallied to come up here to protest: all the Chiefs, everyone from Yukon Native Brotherhood came. I think Oliver Jim and Willie Joe did some filming. They all camped up there at the campground where Ray Wootton took that gun away from Grandpa Sam. That wasn't the only time government officials did that. Game Wardens took Tom Smith's traps, and he got charged. Any fine was lots of money for our people at that time.

When we were growing up, we couldn't go across to the west side of the Alaska Highway, because it was the Game Sanctuary. We couldn't go over to set gopher traps by Grandma Grace's house or across the highway at Duke or at Copper Joe. When Grandpa Moose or another person shoot a moose over there, we would sneak across the highway and get the meat. I remember everyone sneaking across early in the morning to pack a moose out from Rashes Lake. The dogs were packed up too. When it's just getting daylight, we'd go. We'd cross one after another, some with a dog with its packs and just run fast across the road, then we'd just sit underneath a tree till everybody came. First thing we did was

facing top Mary Jacquot, Ruth (Pete) Jacquot-Donnelly, and Jessie Joe at Lhù'ààn Mân (Whitefish Place Lake, Kluane Lake), circa 1980. Gùdia remembers they were getting eighty trout per day, which had to be cut and dried. CYFN Archives. Photograph Collection #82_19_6. PHOTOGRAPHER UNKNOWN

facing bottom Granddaughter Aaliyah Zoe Burns-Symington in dunèn ra mäl (baby swing), 2020. KFN Archives. EMPC. Gùdia Mary Jane Johnson Family Images #2. PHOTOGRAPHER ERIN SYMINGTON

cut brush. If we hear a plane coming, then everybody would throw the brush on top of the meat and we'd all grab the dogs and hide underneath a tree till that plane would go over. Nobody moved. When the plane was gone, we'd come out, take all the brush off, pack up all the meat and the dogs as fast as we could. When we come back to the highway, we just wait. One run across, two run across, three run across, till the last one run across and we come back to the community with all the meat. We had to sneak to do that. That was a law that they made, and we had to break it to live.

TAKING CONTROL OF OUR CHILDREN'S EDUCATION

As our younger kids started to be old enough to go to school, I came to my auntie Sandy and my uncle Joe Joe and said, "Uncle, I don't want to let my kids go to that school down at Destruction Bay. If they can have our language, if they can tell our stories down there, then I will send my daughter down there." Sandy's daughter Robin was old enough to go to school. Their son Luke and my daughter Diyet were kindergarten age. Mary Easterson had her kids and was working here with her partner, Henry Michel. We talked to Harry Allen, and he put us in touch with Eleanor Millard to see if we can work something out for a school here. Eleanor was our champion, but she could not do much. The Minister of Education, Dan Lang, said, "If you want to teach your kids your language, your history, and your culture, you do that in your own home. You have every right to do that in your own home. We follow the B.C. curriculum."

So we started raising money. We did rummage sales, bake sales, everything. We asked Chief Billy Blair if we could use the money for two houses we got each year from Indian Affairs for a school. We would build two houses side-by-side with a walkway between for two washrooms, right beside the wash house, and hook up to the water system. Chief Billy said, "My kids are gonna go to school there too." So that's what we did. We lobbied the United Nations! We got money from Germany and other countries. We should have kept all their cheques. That's what allowed us to start Kêts'á dan' kų—the first school in our community—and to get supplies for it.

Mary Easterson had some teacher training, and Sandy Johnson was a teacher. We hired other teachers for the older kids: Peter Stewart, Bob Garrison, and Al Dion. I worked with the kindergarten kids. I had no idea what I was going to do in a school. So I thought, "Well, you gotta eat. There's no snacks and that around." So we learned how to make bread, do our numbers, and read by working in that little kitchen. In kindergarten and grade 1 that was their curriculum. The kids loved it. I had them making bread with me down at the old house. Once I was over across the lake bringing some stuff back before the ice broke up. When I came back, the kids had flour all over the house and they had put green dye in the bread. I had green bread for St. Patrick's Day. They were just happy as could be because they made green bread!

Students at the school included Edward Johnson and Jean Dick's son, Dwayne Edward Johnson; my children, Geordan, Diyet, and Math'ieya; Auntie Sandy's and Uncle Joe Joe's kids, Katie, Simon, Luke, and Robin. There was Billy and Mary Blair's son, Larry; Thomas and Rita Joe's children, Johnny, Darlene, and Helen; Mary Easterson's children, Donalda and Juniper and Justina; Gloria Johnson's sons Otis and Tcha-yah; Rosie Blair's children, Jolene and Curtis; Angel Peters's and Gordie Issac's children, Elena and Gordie; Pauline Sidney's child and Stan Peters's stepchild, Emmie; Kirk Johnson's son Shane; Agnes Johnson's children Janice and Gerald; and Dorothy Johnson's children Hughie and Richie. Richie was on a correspondence course because he was older but didn't want to go to school in Whitehorse. I think the most we had was eighteen kids. We taught kindergarten and grade 1 together. Grades 2 to 4 were more structured, with one teacher and all in one room. The other teacher had grades 5, 6, 7, and 8 and the ones doing correspondence for grades 9 and 10.

The Elders came in the afternoon and visited. Parents came and helped out during the school day; so it was really a community effort. We started developing stories from our language and writing down our language. We started developing curriculum based on Yukon history, not from the Gold Rush, but from as far back as we can remember: from the story of creation to where we are today. That is Yukon history, and that is what this Kêts'á dan' kų (Teaching People House, Burwash Community School) did. So without being acknowledged by anybody it made a difference to the whole education system in the Yukon.

Everybody was thrilled—it was a wonderful school. But the kids suddenly reached grade 9 and 10. People didn't want to send their kids to Whitehorse by themselves after what we went through as kids. Families started having to move because their kids had to go to high school. We're still dealing with that today. Families still move out of this community because of high school. They get established in Haines Junction or Whitehorse, then they come back in spring break or summertime, and it becomes a vacation spot just to visit your mom and dad here. I know that's our case right now, Ken and I.

During all of that time we were also working hard on the political situation in the Yukon. The people that wrote *Together Today for Our Children Tomorrow* were really instrumental in hearing what the Elders were saying and working with their words. Joe Jacquot was not a very public person, but he was strong. He was one of the building blocks of the land claims movement. He was involved with the Alaska land claims with his brothers Hank and Lawrence Jacquot. Joe came back to the Yukon and told Elijah, "There's been no land claim here. You need to get a land claim. This is what they did in Alaska, and this is what you need to do here in the Yukon." Elijah went to all the communities and met with all the Elders and told them what land claims means. It was here in this community, where Joe was raised up, that the modern land claims started. Joe Jacquot's mom, Ruth (Pete), donated all this land to the Indian people of Burwash Landing for $1. Because Native people couldn't own land, the Department of Indian Affairs got the land in trust for the Kluane people. In honour of that donation and the work that Joe did with land claims,

facing Gùdia (right) with baby Diyet in traditional baby carrier, visiting women friends around a campfire at the CYI Elders' Conference at Champagne, late 1970s. *Left to right:* Louise Joe, Rachael Thompson, Annie Charlie, Math'ieya Johnson, Elsie Isaac, and Gùdia holding Diyet. CYFN Archives. Photograph Collection #b49_f45_s5_91. PHOTOGRAPHER GEORGE ADAMSON

above Gùdia carrying her granddaughter Aaliyah Burns-Symington in a traditional bebia tth'al (birch bark baby carrier), 2020. KFN Archives. EMPC. Gùdia Mary Jane Johnson Family Images #3. PHOTOGRAPHER ERIN SYMINGTON

top Gùdia doing archaeology survey work in the icefields in the St. Elias Mountains. KFN Archives. EMPC. Gùdia Mary Jane Johnson Family Images #5. PHOTOGRAPHER LLOYD FREESE

bottom Gùdia at the Hoge Creek alpine camp measuring permafrost depths with Parks Canada staff in Kluane National Park & Reserve. KFN Archives. EMPC. Gùdia Mary Jane Johnson Family Images #6. PHOTOGRAPHER LLOYD FREESE

we named the community building after them—Jacquot Hall.

EDUCATION FOR A NEW CAREER

I separated from my partner John while the school was still going. I wanted to go and finish high school, then move on to some kind of academic training at university level. I packed up my kids, and Mom drove me to catch the ferry to Victoria. I stayed with Sandy's mom, Joan, at first, then I got a place and started looking for work. Dorothy Johnson asked me to look after her son Hughie, who had lost his leg in a motorcycle accident, and I said ok.

I was Non-Status, so there was no DIA education help for me. I had money saved up, but I still needed to work. I cleaned banks to make money. I'd get up in the morning and do my homework, get the kids to school, then I'd go to the college. I'd come home, get supper on, make sure everything was in order, and take the kids to swimming. I always had a whole list of things to do. Without me realizing it Math'ieya became a little mom, and she was second in charge of the household. I'd give the kids $40 and say, "These are all the items we need. You got your little calculator, and if there's some left over for a little treat for each of you, then you get your treat. If there's only enough for one treat, then you share it." I'd come home, and sometimes the dishes were done, sometimes not. I'd usually get home around 8:30, after I finished cleaning those banks, then get kids off to do homework, bathed, whatever had to be done, and do my homework. The next day it was the same thing again. I did that for three years in Victoria.

One of the first things I did at Camosun College was to take some computer courses. I finished my GED there and then took environmental courses at the University of Victoria. I came back here and started applying for jobs with Parks Canada. Most of my work experience was in this community. I had done some training and worked in community health in the 70s. Later I trained as a Community Education Liaison Coordinator with Frank Lacosse and Jeffrey Choy-Hee from Skookum Jim Friendship Society. So it was really hard to get on with Parks Canada. I applied three times and finally got an interview. It was difficult working with Parks Canada in Haines Junction, 45 miles away.

I went back to the University of Northern British Columbia in Prince George in the late 1990s. Ken moved down with our two youngest boys, Kenny and Curtis, while I went to university. I got a student loan while I applied for my Status under Bill C-32 because I still couldn't get DIA education support. When we came back, I returned to Parks Canada, then went out to the University of Alberta in Edmonton. Ken worked there and I worked part time, too, so we managed fine.

In 1995 I was planning to leave Parks Canada. Louise Gordon was working as the KFN Band Manager. I told her I didn't want to go back to work in Haines Junction, because it was not home for me and I was driving 150 miles a day to work. Louise said, "You're going to have to work until you're 60 or 65, so you might as well do a job that you like and that you're suited for. Who else can tell stories to visitors there? Nobody that they're hiring from Toronto, Edmonton, or Vancouver. They know how to run a park, but they don't know the stories of this country. Stick with it." When I retired from Parks Canada, I thought about what Louise had said. I worked there for twenty-four years, from March 1991 till October 2015. I worked in the old building at the base of Thechàl Dhàl (Rock-Scraper Mountain, Sheep Mountain) after they moved it out onto the flats there. Then I started doing

this page Gùdia making dry moose meat at the Congdon Creek Culture Camp in 2018. KFN Archives. EMPC. Elders Portraits #42 (top), #43 (above), #44 (bottom). PHOTOGRAPHER ALISTAIR MAITLAND

above left Gùdia and Diyet pulling fish nets out of the water at their ice fishing spot at Lhù'ààn Mân (Kluane Lake). KFN Archives. EMPC. Gùdia Mary Jane Johnson Family Images #7. PHOTOGRAPHER ROBERT VAN LIESHOUT

above right Gùdia and partner Ken Burns are devoted grandparents, enjoying time with all their grandkids from youngest to oldest, seen here with Samara Van Lieshout. KFN Archives. EMPC. Gùdia Mary Jane Johnson Family Images #4. PHOTOGRAPHER ROBERT VAN LIESHOUT

facing Gùdia with family and friends at the Congdon Creek Culture Camp she organized in 2018. *Front row left to right:* Jennifer Chambers, Gùdia, Robert van Lieshout, Diyet van Lieshout, Math'ieya Alatini, and Sheri Atlin. *Back row left to right:* Samara van Lieshout, Grace Dolson, Zander Moore, Malakai Alatini, and Skyler van Lieshout. KFN Archives. EMPC. Elders Portraits #45. PHOTOGRAPHER ALISTAIR MAITLAND

cultural resource management in Haines Junction, and in my last two years I was on secondment to Kluane First Nation.

GIVING THANKS

All through those years I travelled and did other things, but there's never been a year in my lifetime that I have not lived in my community. One thing that I know that sustains me is that I lift up this community. I practice my language every day that I live. Some way or another I consciously use my language. I consciously do something to lift up my community, and I do that with purpose. It's heartbreaking that there are many people who find that it's easier to tear down than to build. It takes effort, it takes strength, it takes commitment to build. And it takes love. And the only way that you're going to keep on that road is to do that consciously. No matter what you've done in your life to bring you to where you are, all through the stages of your life, on a daily basis, you have to make that commitment. All through that you don't think that, "Oh, it's something I can't do or it's impossible." It needs to be done. You do it.

We have to give thanks for all that we have. You don't learn how to remember orally unless you've been taught that way. I was blessed to have the grandmas and the grandpas to tell me stories. For them to teach me how to listen and to see what they see and to say, "How can you tell this story here if you're not paying attention?" So that's what I'm really, really worried about with this generation that's coming up.

I just talked to my granddaughter and held her and said, "I want you to say thank you to people. When Grandma does something for you, I stop what I'm doing in my life and I do something for you. I want you to look at Grandma and say thank you. I don't want you to go through your life without looking at people and saying thank you. I want you to be able to be a grandma and put your hand on your granddaughter, just like I'm doing now with you, and I want you to be able to say thank you. So when your granddaughter becomes a grandma, she can say the same thing too. The only way you're going to be able to say thank you is if you say thank you from your heart."

You don't learn how to remember orally unless you've been taught that way.

GÙDIA MARY JANE JOHNSON

ALYCE JOHNSON

(b. 1955)

Teachings from Our Trails

facing Alyce Johnson, 2018. KFN Archives. EMPC. Elders Portraits #46. PHOTOGRAPHER ALISTAIR MAITLAND

I am a member of the Southern Tutchone Khàjèt (Crow Clan) and a Kluane First Nation citizen. My ancestry also includes Upper Tanana through Ts'àgagia (Chickadee, Hutchi Old Allen) and Kändhäda (Singing to Herself, Monica Allen) from Alaska and with the heritage given to me by my late mother, Shada Zhan Mą (Humming As She Works, Jessie Johnson). My dad, Shùglità (Good Hunter, Sam Johnson Sr.), is of Northern Tutchone descent through the marriage of Sida Tà (Big Daddy, Jimmy Johnson) from Àshèyi (Aishihik) and Èna (Emma Jackson) from Hucha Hudan peoples, Fort Selkirk. I grew up on the trails of Lhù'àan Mân (Kluane Lake) region.

Our dad hauled three logs per day from Burwash Creek to build a two-room house for his family in Burwash Landing. We had approximately forty-five head of horses, and that is how he transported the logs. I was born in this log house to my parents, who loved the land, with its waterways, and they raised us on many of its trails.

As I look back on my life story, I reflect on where I have come from and where I am going. I thought at one point I was in control of my life and making my own choices. Then I came to realize all of my experiences had been directed by my Ancestors for one purpose, and that is to be part of the landscapes and waters—to be part of these mountains, the glaciers, the tectonic plates, and the rivers that transported them in many directions. My ancestral family directs my journey and the trails of my children and grandchildren forward.

ALWAYS LOOK BEHIND YOU

I have always been fascinated with trails. When we were very young, we walked on all the trails in the Kluane area. As young children we spent hours following different trails leading up into the mountains and exploring the lakes. We had no fear of our surroundings so walked everywhere to explore and experience those areas. My mother took me on some of those trails, and I became fascinated with them as she taught me to reflect on landscape markers. I became interested in maps and geography, then realized that it is our Ancestors that give us those experiences. They want us to experience that because they want us to transfer that knowledge on to our young people.

Those trails became very significant, and I see that even more now as my life story continues. My mother left me with teachings on those trails. One day she said, "Turn around and look. Just stop for a minute, turn around, and look behind you." Of course at the age of 10 you ask the "Why" question. She told me, "So that you know how to get back on the right trail." Now I know you need to be able to see from where you came; otherwise you would not find your way back. It becomes natural as you grow up on the land. When anyone travels on the land with me, I always ask them about the landmarks. What did you see? Did you see a mountain? Where was that mountain positioned? Which direction was the sun moving? Or from which direction did the moon come up? All of those things come into play, and it is not because I had to study that; it was because I grew up on those trails with my family and others in Burwash. As you look into who we are today and the way I grew up as a child, the whole community moved together. We made camps, and everyone feasted on the harvest of animals and medicines.

When I look at all the hills and mountains, I think about them in terms of mapping our knowledge. It is all embedded and layered upon all the other dimensions and through the generations on that map. They are filled with life stories, and every single one of us has stories that we can share. My late brother Naazhìa (Good Health and Well-Being, Kirk Johnson) and I travelled around together, and he told me stories about our grandfather Old Allen since I have no memories of them. Kirk shared stories of Old Allen trapping on the mountains, about the trails and mountain passes to get from Shézät Chù' (Swede Johnson Creek) to the Kala Dagür (Brooks Arm), where the horse trails are. Each generation has memories of those trails.

My memory of Chegär Män (Tincup Lake) is from age 4 travelling from the Shézät Chù' cabin. The trails are wide and well packed. I remember being bundled up in an eiderdown or a "90 x 90" bedroll in a sled. My mother would be in front and my dad at the back, with all the dogs pulling my brother and I. Our mother would be talking to the dogs and guiding them down the trail, crossing the river, going up into the mountain trail all the way to Thè K'u (Salmon Patch), where we would stop at the two cabins. I remembered that we stopped for tea and bannock before we kept travelling on to Chegär Män, which was another 10 miles or 16 kilometres further up the mountain.

I remember playing in the moonlight while sliding with my brother until the owls came out to hoot. Then we decided it was getting pretty late, so we had to go back to the tent. We were afraid of the owls, because we grew up with the stories of owls bringing "bad news," so we scrambled back up that hill to the tents. All of my sisters and brothers have stories about that area of Dad's trapline, and so do many others.

COMING HOME TO CHEGÄR MÄN

Our family went back there in the summer of 2018 and held a gathering to do some work and revitalize the area. We went up as a family with my grandson who was just 3 years old. It is a 4 kilometre hike up that trail, and the pathway remains wide and clear. My aunt Margaret Johnson named my grandson Khyen Thàät (Song Leader, Zander). Zander walked all the way up there and all the way back singing songs. We were on the tail end of the group that went ahead with four-wheelers to haul supplies. I could feel the power of that place when they yelled and said, "You're almost here." It was like coming home.

The power of the Ancestors' presence was welcoming all of us back. That is the sense I got when I came out of the trail and saw the cabins. We spent the weekend cleaning and preparing for future trips. It was very powerful. The children loved it. I am sure all the animals heard us from miles around! We walked up towards Chegär Män, maybe 2 kilometres, and took the children swimming in the creek. They had a wonderful time, and we were able to share our stories. I talked to them about being a 4-year-old child there. It had been that long since I came back to Salmon Patch. Our children need to grow up experiencing our childhood stories to create their own. It is so beautiful, and our children know a sense of place.

The next year after camping and being with my family at Chegär Män at the age

facing White fireweed is a rare form of the Yukon's official flower, which Alyce found on a trail. KFN Archives. EMPC. Alyce Johnson Family Images #1. PHOTOGRAPHER ALYCE JOHNSON

above Roses bloom in profusion throughout the southern Yukon in June, adding subtle hues of colour to the land and the aroma of summer on the wind. KFN Archives. EMPC. Alyce Johnson Family Images #2. PHOTOGRAPHER ALYCE JOHNSON

above Alyce netting fish in winter. She learned to hunt, fish, and gather food from the land and water as a child and continues those traditions to this day in her teaching career. KFN Archives. EMPC. Alyce Johnson Family Images #3. PHOTOGRAPHER UNKNOWN

facing Alyce graduating from UBC with her master's degree in education, joined by her niece Juniper Groves (née McLeod) and her sister Mary Easterson. KFN Archives. EMPC. Alyce Johnson Family Images #4. PHOTOGRAPHER UNKNOWN

of 5, I was taken to Lower Post Residential School. I remember waking up on the bus and screaming, and I would not stop screaming, because I didn't know where my sister was. They had the older sisters bring the little ones on the bus or the older brothers. You wake up in darkness, and all of a sudden there is no one around you. I realize in reflecting back that I learned a different kind of skill to survive, and that is knowledge. I spent three years at Lower Post Residential School. That is a long time not to see your parents or family. My older sister Gloria said that our parents came there; however, they were not allowed to see us.

One summer we got off the bus at Tl'äw K'à Chù (Burwash Creek) when I was 10 years old. Mom invited Elder Annie Ned to visit with us. She spent time training me as a young girl. She said, "This is how you sew with beads." I sat there for what seemed like a week sewing over and over, then undoing it. My mother said, "You have to redo it, because it does not look proper this way. This is how you do it." It's that kind of determination from training that makes you keep going. I later realized that Annie Ned also trained my sisters Mary and Gloria the same way.

I remember other things: listening to stories when we were out on the land and speaking our language. I thought English was my first language. Now I know that's not the case. I thought I had lost my language at residential school because my parents and older siblings spoke English to my younger brother and I. I recall early memories of writing stories in English. It was not until I went to UBC that a French professor asked me about my first language. I said, "It is English," and he said, "No, you have a first language. What is it?" I said, "I am Southern Tutchone, but I do not speak it. I know maybe twenty words." He said, "Your mind has been mapped in the language, because you heard it while growing up with speakers around you." I said, "Well, how would you know that?" He said, "Because of the way you learn French. Fifty percent of the students in this class will fail French, but you will not." I had high hopes. I kept studying and passed first- and second-year French in my third and fourth year of university. Even though they say we have lost our language, it is still embedded in our mind maps. After he said that, I thought eventually when the trail led me home that is when I would start to work in the language and to learn. While at Trent University in Peterborough, Ontario, I had a dream in a language; therefore I know it meant I would work in the Southern Tutchone language.

I developed curriculum for the Department of Education, for Kluane First Nation, White River First Nation, the Kaska Dene, and the Nlaka'pamux. I always included the languages, because that was very important to me. I sing the songs when my grandchildren are born, so they grow up singing and knowing those songs. I talked to them in the language, and the beauty of today is that my grandson will say, "I want to Facetime my grandma." We talk in Southern Tutchone, and he loves to sing. He sang all the way up that mountain, and I am sure all the animals heard us and were happy. The animals recognize you, and they know that you visit certain areas.

THE LAND PROVIDES FOR US

We moved around a lot with our mom and dad. Our dad worked in the summer for the Jacquot brothers' hunting parties. They hired our dad and his horses every summer. We camped with our mom down at Jedälį Tl'äw Käy (Duke Meadow). All the women would camp there and in other places while the men were out working. We had a campsite at Tl'äw K'à Chù, at Lhù'ààn Mân Jälí (Headwaters) near the Kluane River, and at 1120 (past 1118, Agnes Johnson's camp). We had all of these places where we grew up with our parents, and when we left Lower Post, we did not get off the bus in Whitehorse or Burwash. We went to the camps on the land, and Dákeyi (Our Country) sustained us.

Our people and our family hunted, trapped, fished, and gathered foods. The land provided for us wherever we were. We went to different places for different things. The gophers grew up on Duke Meadow, just like we did. They were growing up beside us knowing that they would one day become our food. We crossed the Duke River by linking arms with each other just to spend the whole day playing on the island there. When we returned before darkness set in, our parents were upset.

I remember being at Burwash Creek in the winter after we came back from Lower Post and we were allowed to attend public school at Kluane Lake School. We spent our Christmas breaks out on the land at Burwash Creek trapping squirrels and skinning them, while our dad trapped big game animals. Our mother's little dog would lead us to the grouse perched in the spruce trees, and she would get a few and we would have spruce hens for dinner. It was better than turkey!

Each generation shares different memories of being together at Duke Meadow. I have watched my children grow up on the Meadow. I brought my grandchildren back there to experience it and to understand, so that is three generations right there. When my grandson was 2 years old, he drew a map of trails leading from his house to my house. Keeping those stories and experiences through doing and practicing means that we pass knowledge on to each generation. There is no laughter at Duke

Meadow now. You do not hear the children playing the way it used to be, and it is silent. Imagine when residential schools took us away, how the places hear no sounds of children.

Duke Meadow was the central place for our peoples' camp. It was the main area where families gathered for seasonal rounds, because you walk the trails up the hillsides and listen to the stories that KFN has recorded with Elders. They talk about walking to Duke Meadow and arrived to find everyone gone to a Potlatch somewhere else. They left a message to let others know to where they had gone. They talked about going up Shar Nuh Chù' (Bear Colon Waters, Duke River) and crossing the Kaskawulsh (Tän shi, glacier). Our people used the glacier as a trail, and they crossed over to make their way across to Àshèyi (Aishihik) through Tsigra Chù (Jarvis Creek). Duke Meadow is central to who

above The Kluane First Nation General Assembly at Jedälį Tl'äw Käy (Duke Meadow) in 2017 was a very special occasion, when relatives travelled from Northway to share their songs, dances, and stories. KFN Archives. EMPC. Alyce Johnson Family Images #5. PHOTOGRAPHER ALYCE JOHNSON

we are and to who I am. I am like that grass that grows there. Every community member will be on Duke Meadow as the snow melts in April to look for the nàkhyela (crocus) and later on to pick the kwäntsì zhùr' (strawberries). I bring my grandchildren there to pick berries. We have stories wherever we lived and wherever we harvested. Our family was always camping on the land somewhere.

I married a Kāskā man and went back to Lower Post. My children grew up on the Nêt'ī̂ł Tūé' (Liard River), and they are rooted to the land too. I brought that with me, so my children were on the land experiencing the winter or the summer. The land is very important, and so my grandchildren also spend time on the land.

Äjukwänjìa (Curtis Carlick), my grandson, was 4 years old when his grandpa wounded a bull moose. He placed Curtis underneath a driftwood pile by the Liard River, and he stayed there while his grandpa hunted for the wounded moose. Being on that mountain and growing up on the land allows them freedom to move about without being afraid of anything and knowing we share this place with other animals. Being part of that landscape becomes part of who you are.

MAPPING MY FUTURE

The trail always brought me back to Burwash and to these places of memories. I did some of my education in Destruction Bay when they allowed us into the public education system. We were highly competitive students, always be trying to complete assignments first. When they had sports day, no one could outrun us. If they brought students from Haines Junction, they could not do it either. We worked very hard, and if we were on a team together, we made sure we came in first. We always took the top marks or first prizes in sports.

When I was in grade 6, I wrote about my future plans: I would finish school, go on to university, and get a teaching degree. I would get married, have two children, one boy, one girl, and I would live the experiences I planned. I knew that you need money to travel, have a home, and do all these things. So when I had my children, I had two girls before I had a boy.

When Mary [Easterson] was going to Simon Fraser University, she decided to take me, so I attended public school for six months in Vancouver. That was a huge step, moving from Duke Meadow and Kluane Lake School to Eric Hamber High

School in grade 8. I did well there and made the transition. I studied French, passed all my courses, and was in track and field. I was pretty independent, so I learned to map out the city, just like being on a trail. Mary was living there with her daughter, so I took care of my niece. I went to Victoria to visit family. I was about 14. Growing up on the land teaches you to be independent. I could move around in the city like I would move around in the bush. It did not matter where I was as long as I memorized the maps.

I started work in Burwash for Health Canada as a Community Health Worker. The nursing station was in Destruction Bay, so I volunteered my time to care for people in Burwash since the nurse was 10 miles away. I wrote a poem about it when I was 21 years old that was published in the *Yukon Indian News*, and Health Canada made it into a poster.

When I moved to Lower Post, the public health nurse and the doctor encouraged me to do community health work again. I worked for a couple of years, taking care of people, giving them medication, and was the liaison person with the Watson Lake medical team, even though I was new to the community.

I spent one summer working for Forestry, driving with my children, hauling groceries to firefighters at campsites. Sometimes I would receive a call. "You've got to turn around because the fire is crossing the highway!"

I was always interested in education, so I applied for a position as a Teacher's Aide. I worked very hard and enjoyed my time with the children. I volunteered on many committees and boards, wrote proposals for funding, and started a cultural program at the school. The students sewed their own outfits for a Rendezvous costume competition. We brought them to Lower Post to model their costumes for the community.

We raised money and took the children everywhere. When I was President of the Watson Lake Minor Hockey Association, the kids competed in Vancouver and won medals. My son was a hockey player. Around 1985 my daughter Shänch'ea (Poor Thing, Cute Little Person, Christabelle Carlick) was 9 years old and one of five students to go to Mexico, Disneyland, and Universal Studios. I wanted my children to have those experiences, so I worked hard to raise the monies.

NEW TRAILS TO FOLLOW

I was working many different volunteer positions and usually two part-time jobs, driving the school bus, working in various positions during the day, and volunteering at night. I had not graduated from high school, so I decided to take my Dogwood Certificate. I was up until two in the morning doing homework then at work again at six. I did seven courses over a year and a half to get my grade 12. I wanted decent marks to get into university. I went to Yukon College and moved my whole family. My husband at that time said, "Give me one good reason." I said, "Because I have given eighteen years of my life to this community and I am taking it back now, and I am moving with or without you." We moved to Whitehorse, bought a house in Crestview, and I started university courses. I volunteered for Whitehorse Minor Hockey Association, fundraising and getting my children to their activities. My son was active in hockey and soccer.

We lost our dad, and I almost quit my studies just before first-term exams. That was very challenging when we found out he had cancer in October and he was gone by the end of November. I had six exams to do in three days and two papers to deliver. It was seeing my dad and his determination—being on the land and how hard it was to get three logs every single day to build our house. That's determination, and a part of me just decided, "I am going to do those exams." I am sure the Ancestors and our dad were talking to me, saying, "You're not going to give up. You can do this. Your dad would never give up." It was just not something you do as a Southern Tutchone. You're brought up with that teaching that if you start something, you have to finish it.

I did my two years of study, then was accepted at UBC and I was happy! I did a bachelor's degree in English and a one-year teacher education program. It was very intense. In August 1994, on the night before my last exam, my granddaughter Savannah was born. I was trying to study for an exam in the morning, and my grandchild was being born that night before! I was hired in April to work for School District 87.

I packed up everything in a trailer and went to work in Lower Post for five years. The maintenance worker who was there when I was a Teacher's Aide was still there and said to me, "I have not seen the children like this before. They are really, really happy. I really see a difference because you are here." I said, "That's good!"

I applied to UBC for a master's program, spending six weeks in summers and doing some courses over the winters to complete my master's degree in 2000. We lost our mother when I was working on my master's degree. We lost our brother Edward while I was doing my PhD. I reflected on how I lost so many people in between doing all of those degrees and how our

lives intersected. Going back to Burwash has allowed me to do that, and it is like a lifeline that pulls you into a different spiritual realm. It is rooted to you to pull you back to the land. I see how I really was not in control. It is our Ancestors. My PhD focused on K'amà Dzêa (Ptarmigan Heart), where Aunt Jenny Johnson was born. I was at this site when she came to me, and I see how she has been part of my life. Her granddaughter Jenessa Tlen came back to our community, and I call her Auntie.

After five years I left Lower Post and purchased a house in Whitehorse. Then a friend who was the Principal in Lytton called me and said, "My kindergarten teacher just left, so can you come and help me? I cannot find anyone else." I moved in January 2000 to Lytton and did six months in a kindergarten classroom of thirteen students. I told the Principal, "This is the most important class here, so I need two EAs, one for the morning, one for the afternoon." He agreed. Lytton is a different type of community because some of the children lived way back in the hills and countryside. He said, "My kindergarten students are quitting school!" That was the story of the community, and so we worked very hard. I laid out a really good foundation for the EAs to help the students. One student quit kindergarten in October, and so I requested the Principal to take me to his home and introduce me. We walked in the dark amidst cougars! That boy started coming to check it out, and by February he was in school every day. When I left in June, the kindergarten class was reading and writing and the work paid off. The community wanted me to stay, but I could not live there with rattlesnakes, king snakes, black widow spiders, stinky bugs, and cougars!

I was hired by Kwanlin Dün that summer, but earlier in the spring I had applied to Trent University to start a doctorate program and I got in! It took me almost two months of self-talk to make that drive across Canada by myself. It was a huge experience when you have never done it before. I took my nephew with me. I did a doctorate in Indigenous Studies at Trent.

PROFESSOR OF THE LAND

UNBC called and offered me a job teaching, so I loaded everything into a trailer and drove across Canada again. I taught five courses at UNBC, and one year I also taught a course in the master's program at Yukon College. I flew to Vancouver and on to Yukon every Friday, taught all day Saturday, then flew back to Prince George for another week of teaching.

I had my granddaughter with me in Prince George. She did grade 11 and 12 there, graduating with honours. She didn't do well in English at Watson Lake, but I said, "You're in a new school. You can change that." I shared my experiences with her because when we went to register, they told her, "You may have been on the honour roll in the Yukon, but do not expect that here, because this is harder and you are coming from a little community." I said, "You do not have to live their story. You just live your own." I worked with her, and she came out with an A in grade 11 and 12 and made the Principal's List both years. She received an entrance scholarship to UNBC, and they were shocked. When I went to pick up her scholarship application, they said she would need really good marks.

facing Alyce's grandsons Curtis Carlick and Logan Moore after Logan's first moose kill in 2019. KFN Archives. EMPC. Alyce Johnson Family Images #6. PHOTOGRAPHER GORDON MOORE

above Chief Justice Robert Yazzie from the Navaho Nation and Grand Chief Ovide Mercredi of the Assembly of First Nations visited the students at Venetie School in Lower Post, British Columbia, in 1998 when Alyce was the principal there. KFN Archives. EMPC. Alyce Johnson Family Images #7. PHOTOGRAPHER UNKNOWN

I said, "I'm pretty certain she has." You have to have 85 percent or higher GPA. She finished her commerce degree in 2020!

I defended my PhD when I was at UNBC. I had never experienced a defence before. I travelled from Prince George to Ontario, then defended the next night. My external examiner was teaching at a university in Australia, and she Skyped in. Daniel Tlen was on my committee, so he was in Whitehorse, and Patrick Moore was at UBC in Vancouver. I was connected electronically to everyone. It was the first time Trent attempted that. I set it up so people could watch at the Yukon Department of Education and at Kluane Lake School for the students. I passed, and it was a great experience.

I taught Native Studies at UNBC from 2010 until 2013, then decided to come home. I worked at Whitehorse Elementary School, with Daniel as a Southern Tutchone language teacher, then I came home to Kluane. I was guided by our Ancestors; for whatever reason they saw fit for me to live those experiences. I wanted to go home. I wanted to go back to the cabin. I wanted to get back to the land.

I've always talked about being a professor of the land—that really is the highest achievement anyone can attain. Everyone thinks that getting a PhD is huge, which it is because it is a lot of work. On reflection I realized my Ancestors just moved me across a map and then brought me back to share those experiences. You meet people on your trails and on your pathway in life, and they influence you, guide you in a direction, or they support you.

GROUNDED IN PLACE

Anyone who is named after someone whose name is handed down in our family, I call them Auntie or Grandma. I treat them as though they are my grandma. This is the Southern Tutchone way. She is my auntie because she's named after my auntie, and I must treat her as though she's my aunt. She carries that name. She will pass that on to her children one day or her grandchildren. There are huge responsibilities. I treat her in a good way, so if she needs anything or wants help, I gift her. If I see something that I just think is so her, I pick it up and give it to her. She likes honey, so I'll bring her honey or some tea. The person who is named after our grandmother, I call Grandma and give her blessings. She's young, so I give her money because she's my grandma and that's the same way I would treat my grandma and how I would want someone to treat me as a grandmother.

It is important to pass on what I know from those life experiences and those life stories. There are many different layers to each story. I tell people, "If you want to learn something, I'm doing this at this time and you can learn." It's a responsibility to pass knowledge on to others. Our families work together to organize Potlatches. It's a great responsibility teaching the younger generation the importance and the value in all of that, to be rooted in it

facing top Alyce with her grandchildren at Dzäna Nanááje (Muskrat Camp) held at Edith Creek in 2018. KFN Archives. EMPC. Alyce Johnson Family Images #8. PHOTOGRAPHER UNKNOWN

facing bottom Alyce at Steele Glacier in the St. Elias Mountain Range. KFN Archives. EMPC. Alyce Johnson Family Images #12. PHOTOGRAPHER UNKNOWN

above Students and teachers from Kluane Lake Community School in Destruction Bay at Nanááje Muskrat Camp in spring 2020 with retired NHL Indigenous hockey players. KFN Archives. EMPC. Alyce Johnson Family Images #9. PHOTOGRAPHER UNKNOWN

so that we preserve that knowledge. I've named almost all of my grandchildren at our Potlatches. They know who they are.

I have been involved in political activities as well as cultural teachings. I attended the Alaska Highway pipeline hearings in Burwash in 1977. I remember the dialogue about paving the Alaska Highway, changing it from gravel to asphalt. I attended some of those meetings and made a presentation. We did protests against the governments, organized by my sister the late Mary Easterson, to get our rights back in Kluane National Park.

I was here when the Kêts'á dan' kų (Teaching People House, Burwash Community School) opened. I was eight months pregnant with my son. We did a lot of fundraising, travelling down to Teslin to sell bread and baking. I made three big bags full of bread! Uncle Joe Joe Johnson stopped in to see how I was doing and said, "What! They made you bake all this bread! You shouldn't be baking this much bread."

Mary was getting on a plane to go to Geneva to meet UNESCO officials about the Kluane Tribal Brotherhood's desire for a school to be located in Burwash Landing. She had raised the money, and she was going to tell the world: "We have the right to have our own school." The Yukon Government finally decided to support a school in Burwash. They did not want to do it; they wanted to keep busing Kluane children to Destruction Bay.

Our Burwash Community School was definitely a success. The statistics show that 65 percent of the students went on to get post-secondary education. My children were too young to go to it. In later years when I was in the Teacher Ed Program at Vancouver, someone said to me: "We know about this little village in the North, and they have a really high graduation rate, with lots of students going on to post-secondary." I said, "I am from that little village, and here I am! We're known for that."

The community really came together to support cultural activities at the school. Sandy Johnson and I wrote curriculum for a Muskrat Camp and developed some booklets. Learning and being grounded in place is very important. That's what I did when

top Grandma Alyce with her grandkids at Copper Joe Creek in 2017. KFN Archives. EMPC. Alyce Johnson Family Images #10. PHOTOGRAPHER JANESSA TLEN

bottom Alyce with great-grandson Nathaniel Magun at the 50th Anniversary Potlatch celebration of *Together Today for Our Children Tomorrow* in Whitehorse, February 2023. KFN Archives. EMPC. Alyce Johnson Family Images #11. PHOTOGRAPHER UNKNOWN

facing Alyce recording stories for the Elders Memory Project at Kluane Dana Shäw Corporation Offices, Whitehorse, 2018. KFN Archives. EMPC. Elders Portraits #47. PHOTOGRAPHER ALISTAIR MAITLAND

I came back to teach at D-Bay. When we were having our Muskrat Camp a few years ago, I asked, "How many generations have gone to Muskrat Camp here?" At least four! The first camp was held at Burwash Creek on our dad's trapline.

I want our children to know that place—learning and living those experiences, so then they become responsible for it. Going to Muskrat Camp is not just about going out to camp and setting some traps. It's knowing you're in a protected area. If you don't take care of that water, who's going to take care of it? Water falls out of the sky, but someone has to take care of the watershed. So they become responsible. I teach that to my grandchildren, and I also taught that to the children in the school.

MY TRAILS BROUGHT ME HOME

It's wonderful to be home! It's like my map just had its own trails and they brought me back. A new school is going to be built in Burwash, and money is in the Yukon Government budget. I am hopeful it will open in five years.

I have seen and participated in many educational developments, and I have been part of making change. I signed the 1973 *Together Today* document as a Youth representative from Kluane Tribal Brotherhood. I participated in the 1987 *Kwiya Report*, which recommended guaranteed First Nations' representation on School Councils. In the 2000 Education Act Review I volunteered to represent Yukon First Nations' interests. I recommended establishing a Yukon First Nations' Department of Education, a Deputy Minister for Aboriginal Education, cultural and language Protocols and initiatives. In 2007 I wrote rationales for education reform to establish Yukon First Nations' schools, including a high school.

I have a few adages to share, and one of them is, "Education is a trail that gathers no moss." Another one is, "My children are the future of my past." Those two are the most important ones to me. I am fascinated with maps because of the way I see how my Ancestors have influenced my life and who I am. We are all maps. We are maps of trails, of knowledge, of different layers of knowledge, peoples, places, and languages. In making memories we create that place and time in a dimension of generations as we share our stories. We are layers of knowledge, and each experience packs the trail down in multiple dimensions. Our Ancestors, our family members left us with a rich Oral History.

When Tsal KàJana (Gopher Lady, Grandma Copper Lily) said, "I guess she packed around her name," that to me was significant. Imagine packing that name on that trail that each of us are as a map through time! We are gifted that time for that period for a reason, and we don't always plan it. We think we do. A greater plan has been set and prepared unbeknownst to us.

We are all maps. We are maps of trails, of knowledge, of different layers of knowledge, peoples, places, and languages.

ALYCE JOHNSON

DA KWÄTHALA MĄ (JOYCE JOHNSON-ALBERT)

(b. 1956)

The Strength of Grandma Kept Us Going

facing Da Kwäthala mą (The Lady Floating in the Sky, Joyce Johnson-Albert), 2019. KFN Archives. EMPC. Elders Portraits #48. PHOTOGRAPHER ALISTAIR MAITLAND

My name is Joyce Johnson-Albert. My married name is Albert. My Dań K'è (Southern Tutchone) name is Da Kwäthala mą, meaning "The Lady Floating in the Sky." I'm named after my grandmother Copper Lily's sister Kitty Jamieson. My grandmother Tsal KàJana (Gopher Lady, Copper Lily) named me, and she's the one that raised me since I was a baby. She passed away in 1987, when she was 102.

I was born February 2nd, 1956. My mother was Rita Johnson, and my [step]father was Thomas Joe. Mom was sent away for seven years to Charles Camsell Hospital in Edmonton for TB treatment when I was a baby, so Grandma just took me over. In later years Mom showed us the scars on her back from her surgery. She said it wasn't like nowadays, when it just takes an hour for that operation; back then, she said, it was a very long surgery. My dad was a trapper. I remember pretty well all my aunties and lots of my grandmothers in Burwash when I was a child. I don't remember my grandfathers as much. It seemed like our grandfathers passed on before we knew them.

STRANGERS IN OUR FAMILIES

I was taken from Burwash when I was 5 years old and sent to Lower Post Residential School. So for seven years of my life I probably only saw my home for two months out of the year. We were mostly in northern British Columbia during that time. In just the little time I was with Grandma, I spoke Dań K'è fluently because Grandma didn't understand English. I didn't either until we went to Lower Post.

It was quite the thing to go there, not knowing where we were going. I don't think Grandma really understood what they were doing to us and why they sent us there. It was horrible. Really bad. My cousin Bertha was there, too, along with my other cousins: Alyce, Gloria, Louise, and some of our male cousins. There was a lot of us from Burwash, and we had relatives there from neighbouring communities, like from Beaver Creek and Haines Junction, too. I think the ones from Junction were older than us. We were separated into groups when we got there. Little ones stayed in one dorm and the next oldest in another dorm and the oldest in another one. So we really never got to see each other.

I cried a lot at first, and Bertha would always comfort me. She used to tell me, "Don't cry; otherwise they're gonna hit you, spank you." Bertha was only a couple of years older than me, but she watched over me all the time. We were so close together, her and I, along with a couple of my cousins from Beaver Creek, Angel and Christine, because that's who our family was. We looked after each other. We never really knew our parents, because we were taken away. We didn't know the comfort of our own family, and when we came back, it was like we were lost because we got separated at such a young age. We were just like strangers with our families, and a lot of our language was taken away.

We were ashamed to be Native, because we were brainwashed to think that "Natives were dirty." Then we would come home and try to relive our culture to try and understand. "Is that who we really are?" It was very hard. And then to try to tell Grandma, because Grandma couldn't understand. We were different people when we came back. Grandma wondered, "Who are you kids? You left here doing this, this, and that, and now you kids don't know nothing." How can you explain that to your grandmother when we had lost our language fluency and she didn't understand English very well? It was hard. I never did tell my mom anything until two years before she was gone, and that was just about four years ago.

My uncle Peter Johnson was taken away too. When Bertha and I were 11 years old, we told Grandma, "We're not going back." Grandma said, "No, you're going back." That was when Kluane Lake School at Destruction Bay was opening up for Status kids in the 60s. Uncle Peter said,

"No, they're not going back." We didn't know he had been at Lower Post School until maybe ten years ago or so, when people started speaking out. He told about the sexual abuse and other terrible things at Lower Post Residential School. We were just devastated. That's why he knew what we were talking about, but we never did tell Grandma. She wouldn't have understood.

When we were in Lower Post, the priests and nuns would say, "If you ever tell anybody what happened to you, you're gonna go to hell." So we were brainwashed to think if we said anything about what happened to us, we were gonna go down. Many years later as I had my own children, it started coming back to me. That's when I thought, "Why am I holding this inside of me? I need to tell somebody." I started talking to my husband about it, and he was appalled. When I did things, I was really unsure of myself. Everything had to be perfect. I didn't allow myself to make a mistake. If I did, I would be fearful. When I started bringing it out with Bertha and talking with my cousins from Beaver Creek, we cried and realized then it was ok to talk about it. It's ok, because all these years we were carrying that burden. It was supposed to be a secret, which it really wasn't. It was damaging us.

GRANDMA KEPT US GOING

You had to be strong to get through it. I think the strength I got was when we came back home briefly in summer. One thing I never, ever let go was my grandma. When I was in Lower Post, I always remembered the smell of my grandma because she raised both of us up, Bertha and I. That was the strength that kept us going. It was Grandma.

She was always so strong in our subsistence culture. When we came back home years later, even though she didn't understand what we went through, we still hung on to what she taught us. From then on we just continued learning, with her talking to us about turning into a woman and the responsibilities of that. We already knew a lot about that, I think, at a young age. My auntie Lena has said, "You and Bertha were so responsible when you were just 3–4 years old. You were making your own mitts, you were making your own gloves, just from Grandma." So we already had the technique of doing things on our own. We were already independent, just as little girls. Thanks to her we held onto it. I did not let that go. My grandma was my mentor. When we came back, even though we had all the hurts, we were back with Grandma. That's all I cared about—just to be with my grandma.

We came home in June each year, and then we would get taken away again in August. They sent us down there on the Coachways bus. We didn't have an escort, nothing. They just put all of us on the bus. They used to come right to the church, and

facing Burwash children on the steps of Lower Post Residential School, circa 1950s. KFN Archives. EMPC. Dorothy Johnson Family Images #11. PHOTOGRAPHER UNKNOWN

above Joyce's mother, Rita Johnson, circa 2002. KFN Archives. EMPC. Bertha Doris Family Images #2. PHOTOGRAPHER UNKNOWN

that's where they would take us. We would get on the bus at the church. I remember the second year they took us; I climbed out of the bus window because I already knew what they were doing. We caught on, but like I said, Grandma didn't understand. She thought she was doing good for us.

When I came back from Lower Post at the age of 11, I never really knew my mom. I didn't tell her lots of the stuff that happened to us, because there was no trust there. My trust was with my grandma, but I didn't want to hurt her by telling her what we went through. It would have been hard for her to understand. If I was fluent in my language like I was before I was taken away, I would have told her. Then in later years when Bertha and I finally told our mothers, they just broke down and cried. They said, "If we had ever known that, we would have never have let you go there."

We lived in Burwash when we were home. Grandma's house used to be right where the Jacquot Building is right now. Grandma had a big log cabin there. We used to look forward to the days just after Christmas, when Father Morisset would take Grandma and a whole bunch of other people to Koidern II. We would set up tents, and they would start muskrat trapping. In those days they had to dry everything because there were no freezers or anything. Bertha and I were always waiting for those muskrats to come in so we can cook the tails and go on the dogsled with Grandma.

In summer we would go to Koidern I, where Jim Cook's place is now. We used to camp back in there for moose. It was all seasonal travel. A bunch of people travelled together all the time. They would get a moose, then they would dry all the meat. We would stay there until fall time, then we would start picking berries. We'd start there, then we'll go down to 1124 for cranberries. There was not much blueberries around there but a lot of blackberries and cranberries.

From there we would go Duke Meadow to hunt gophers, dry them, and then go back to Burwash. In the fall time it's fish—fishing out across the lake. We're always moving all the time before Lower Post. That's a picture I will never forget, being with Grandma. Her and I did so much. To me Grandma was heaven. Just to do those things with Grandma and listen to her stories. We would sleep with her in the tent, and she would tell us stories of long time ago in Dań K'è.

Grandma never had any doubts about Bertha and I. She always knew if she told us to do something, we would do it and we would get it done. She didn't have to tell us again. I think she already saw the independence in Bertha and I. She never worried about us. She didn't have to tell us to clean the house. She didn't have to tell us to wash our clothes or pack water from the lake. We knew what had to be done. So she already knew we had that independence.

In the winter we'd have a little dog, and we would go down to the lake with buckets to bring water up. We used to go out with dog teams by ourselves. Uncle Peter would cut wood. We just hooked up our dogs and went behind Uncle Peter to haul the wood in. Everything we did was fun. We'd always be laughing, and we would find interesting things to do. That was not only us but Gùdia [Johnson], Alyce, and our whole group. Alyce hung around Grandma a lot, too, as we were growing up.

Daniel's mom, Auntie Jenny, used to babysit me and Bertha. I remember her because they lived right next door to Grandma's. Her mother was Emma Johnson. She used to put us in laundry baskets while she did house chores. She was a big part of our life, and Daniel was too. After Auntie Jenny was gone, Grandma took him over and he always called us his sisters because we all grew up together. We looked up to him a lot too. He was like a brotherly mentor to us. I think he's about ten years older than us.

TOUGH CHOICES

After Lower Post we went to school at Destruction Bay until 8th grade, and then I went into Whitehorse to finish my high school. One thing I wanted was for Grandma to see me graduate. At that time I was 17 and in grade 11, almost done, and happy that I had just one more year to go.

Then my grandma called me up. I didn't really know my mom and dad, but they got into alcohol really bad and the Yukon Government was threatening to take my younger siblings away. Grandma called me and said, "You have to come help me with these kids." I was not happy. "Why? I don't want to." I didn't know them, but Grandma said, "I need your help." I had to do it. I cried. I talked to my school counsellor, and she said, "Well, if you come back, you can't go back to high school because of your age. You probably will have to go to the Vocational School."

It was a tough choice, but I made it and I did go home. That was the fall of '72. They didn't like that black and orange Yukon Government car that came around all the time—with inspectors watching my parents. In the fall my mom sobered up. I didn't stay with her, but Grandma and I stayed close by and I would check on the little kids all the time, my two sisters and a brother. Then one day Mom called me, sat me down, and said, "I want you to forgive me for what I did to you." I kinda forgot all about it already. She said, "I pulled you out of school because of what I did, and I want you to go back to school." I said, "Well, Mom, I can't go back to school now. I have to go to Vocational School." She said, "Well, you do that, you go to Vocational School, and I'll promise you I'll never drink. I'll watch your brothers and sisters." From that day on she didn't drink.

NEW SKILLS FOR LIFE

I went to Vocational School in Whitehorse to do life skills training, but there was not really much there that I wanted to do. I went home again. Daniel Tlen and Mary Easterson were working at the Kluane Indian Band then. They started getting Youth involved in office work to see what our interests were. My interest was in the field of behavioural health and working with people. Now I'm a certified Behavioural Health Counsellor. I trained at the University of Alaska in Fairbanks.

It was around 1975 when I came home from Vocational School. I worked in the

facing Tsal KàJana (Copper Lily) with her great-grandson Timothy (Joyce's son) in Burwash, circa 1980. KFN Archives. EMPC. Bertha Doris Family Images #3. PHOTOGRAPHER UNKNOWN

above Joyce and her sister Darlene in Burwash, circa 2010. KFN Archives. EMPC. Bertha Doris Family Images #10. PHOTOGRAPHER UNKNOWN

back to where my father's from." My mom didn't like the idea, but I just told her that was where I wanted to be.

I married Terry Albert, Chief Walter Northway's grandson. We had four boys and a daughter. We lost our daughter when she was 3. She was born with a disability. I have four boys now and ten grandchildren: three granddaughters and seven grandsons. It's totally different from raising your own kids—they give you life again. That's how I look at it! They give you a whole new life, and you're watching for every little thing that they learn. I have a newborn grandson, who is 6 months old now. He's from my oldest son, Tim, who has five kids and lives in Fairbanks. Every day he'll send me pictures of the baby. I'm so involved with my grandkids. I just want to know everything that they do. My second-oldest son lives in Glenallen and has five kids. My two youngest boys don't have kids yet, but they are very busy as uncles. You can do anything you want with your uncle!

band office off and on. I took life skills classes here with Frank Lacosse, who was an awesome guy. He always came out to Burwash to check up on us and made sure we were doing well. Then Daniel got me into the First Nation office working in social programs. I think he was a Council member then. Daniel, Mary, and Sandy Johnson really worked with us Youth, organizing activities for us, just to keep us busy and helping us to stay out of trouble. They started our own school here. My sister Darlene Joe went to the Kêts'á dan' kų (Teaching People House, Burwash Community School) in Burwash, and my sister Helen Joe did too. That was the year I moved to Northway.

MOVING TO ALASKA

I had my first child when I was 24 and staying in Burwash. When my oldest son was 2 years old, I met my husband from Alaska, and he moved to Burwash with me for a couple of years. I fell in love with Alaska, because that's where my grandma's father came from. Copper Chief—he's from down Chistochina area. When I told Grandma that I wanted to go to Alaska, she was ok with it. She said, "Yeah, I was always hoping to hear some of my grandkids would go

LEARNING MY HISTORY

I am starting to learn more about the history of the Kluane area now. I remember a little bit of the stories Grandma told me about the time when the highway was going through. When the American Army was around here in the 1940s, Grandma had never seen Black people before.
I always remembered Grandma talking about the 40s when my mom and the other girls had to run away when soldiers were trying to bother them. At the time my mom was probably 17 or 18 years old. She told us about that. Father Morisset was here then and looked out for the people. Grandma and the others here were afraid, mostly for the little girls.

Later when we were probably around 10 or 11, some U.S. Army guys were going through to Alaska. It was summertime, and the old people used to tell us to run into the bush and hide. This one time these guys came into the village, and they were hollering, making a big ruckus, and banging on people's doors. I remember they banged on our window. Grandma pushed us onto the floor and went to see who it was. She opened the door, and it was a Black guy. I heard her say in her language, "Oh my God, what kind of man is that out there! I can't see his face, just two eyes looking at me." She freaked out and told us in her language, "You girls, you stay there. I'm gonna run next door." Auntie Jenny [Johnson] and the others were there. Those men were looking for women, so Grandma ran over there. Grandma's not scared, and she's just really strong. She went over there and made sure that everything was ok. I think they got Daniel to run up to Father Morisset's. Father came down and told those guys they had to leave. I remember every little piece of that.

I just heard a little bit about the establishment of the Park after the war, when we weren't allowed to go hunt muskrats no more. Our people did not understand why, and no one was telling us the background or anything about it. Regulations just started coming in, and our community was just really staring in the face of a new reality. People wondered, "What's going on?" These were all really big changes.

That's when a lot of alcohol started to come into our community. All the new regulations were stopping them from going to the places that had been their life: trapping, berry picking, fishing. They took it all away from them, so what were they supposed to do? Their kids were gone too—taken away to residential schools. They never really knew how to be parents, because they never had kids here in those years and the responsibility of being a parent. That's why I keep saying Grandma was our mentor when we came back. At a young age Grandma had taught us all that,

facing top Joyce and her baby daughter, Timara, circa 1980. KFN Archives. EMPC. Bertha Doris Family Images #4. PHOTOGRAPHER UNKNOWN

facing bottom Joyce's son Chad Albert with his brother George's baby Timara in Northway, Alaska, circa 2020. KFN Archives. EMPC. Bertha Doris Family Images #5. PHOTOGRAPHER UNKNOWN

left Joyce's son Roger Albert (far left) with his children in Glennallen, Alaska, circa 2020. Children left to right: Rajan, Ryan, Raylee, and Rene. KFN Archives. EMPC. Bertha Doris Family Images #6. PHOTOGRAPHER UNKNOWN

Bertha and I. When we became parents, I never had a hard time, because I always remembered Grandma's words, "When you become a parent, you have to be responsible for everything." Now I see a lot of young people having kids, but they're not ready for it and it's sad.

I could never let my mom and dad watch my kids, even though Mom would say, "You can leave Tim with me." I couldn't, because of the experiences I'd had being taken away from Grandma and her not knowing what I went through—the hits and everything else at residential school. I'm not saying that my mom was going to do that, but I had to see everything all the time with my kids. I had to see them, have them in my sight all the time. That's how my two boys are now too. If they're gonna go somewhere, their kids have to be home because that's just the way I was. Tim says, "You know, Mama, I see how you were raising me up, how you made sure we were well fed, had clean clothes, clean home, and I'm doing the same thing. We were safe, and I'm doing the same thing with my kids." That's all from Grandma. Just that little piece I hung on to; it's gonna carry on with my kids.

Another thing that Grandma used to tell us, "When you go out and you get your moose or you get your muskrat or rabbits, you just get what you need. You have to

top Joyce with her pup visiting Burwash. KFN Archives. EMPC. Bertha Doris Family Images #7. PHOTOGRAPHER UNKNOWN

bottom Joyce celebrating her birthday. KFN Archives. EMPC. Bertha Doris Family Images #8. PHOTOGRAPHER UNKNOWN

leave some for other people. Don't overdo it. There's other people that want to eat." She used to tell us about long time ago when they travelled with their dad from Copper Center all the way down to Burwash. She said, "Summer camps—we used to stop, and when we would get rabbits, or whatever, we dry it, put it up in a cache for the next group to come. That way they have food." She used to tell me, "You don't see that no more nowadays. People, they hide everything now. That's not good. I don't want you kids to be like that. You always share, even though it's the one rabbit; you always make something big out of it, like soup that everybody has a taste of it." I always remember that.

LAND CLAIMS BRING CHANGE

When all those land claims meetings were going on, I pretty much stayed home in Northway raising my kids. I never really went anywhere much until my kids were older, maybe 13–14. I would come home sometimes to visit Mom and bring the kids over, but not for long stays, just short visits. My kids were into a lot of activities, so it was hard to get them away.

I noticed a lot of the changes that came with the land claims. I am still learning about it now because I wasn't really involved in it. Uncle Joe Joe Johnson used to come over all the time and give me updates. Him and Sandy would come every year, spend time with my husband, my kids, and I. He would always let me know what was going on. My children don't really know anything about land claims in the Yukon and Canada, because they were born in Alaska. It is so totally different.

Grandma Jessie Joe signed the land claims papers. I was home for that, and two years after that she passed away. I don't think I was really too excited about it, because I really had never known much about all the negotiations over the thirty years. I was gone probably twenty-five years of that time, living in Alaska and just coming in and out once in a while.

KEEP YOUR TRADITIONS AND SHARE YOUR CULTURE!

In recent years I've been coming back more often, doing a lot of work with the language. We're bringing our Dań K'è language back. We just finished our first book, and now we're working on the tape recordings of songs that I recorded with all the Elders in Burwash when I was 17 or 18. I was the one that recorded them all: Aunt Margaret and all of them. My aunt Sandy got a grant for that work, and I went around and recorded everybody.

My great-great-grandfather Copper Chief [Copper George Joe's father] came from over in Alaska, so I don't feel like I'm in a different country living there, because we are from both sides of the border. Grandma said if that border wasn't in there, we would have a lot of family going back and forth. There's a lot of people over there that always ask me about their family here. My husband, Terry's, grandma Lily Northway is actually from over here, but when that border went through, they couldn't come back and forth. A lot of them have families in Dawson. So it's really not different. I understand their language over there, Upper Tanana. I always did because I used to go over there with Grandma when she would talk to Chief Walter Northway. I could hear it, and Grandma understood it because of her father.

People ask me if I would ever move back over here. I probably would if my mom was still here. My last older connections over here are my aunt Margaret and uncle Peter, and they are very elderly. I probably would not come here permanently, because my kids are more into the culture over there and they're raising their kids in Alaska. My sons all work up north on those oil rigs, so if they were to come over here, I don't think they would know what to do. Their thing is oil rigs, union work, outdoor labour. It would be culture shock for them if they came over here. They always say they would like to try, and I say, "Well, you would just need to prepare yourself; maybe two years ahead of time, maybe go over there and feel it out." It's all office work over here, and they're not office workers. Only one, the youngest one, he's an environmental worker. They don't really know many people here. The two older ones do but not the two younger ones. The only ones they really know are Aunt Bertha, Grandma Margaret, Uncle Peter, and my dad. Beyond that they are not really close with our relatives here. They do have their family tree, so I tell them, "If you guys ever go over there after I'm gone, you just take your family tree and it's all there."

In Northway my husband and I and his family teach kids on the land. We take them out hunting and fishing. We teach them how to survive off the land, to dry fish, dry meat, and hunt the traditional way. They don't bring out four-wheelers. They have to go out on the land, get their moose, pack it in—that's just showing respect. How their grandfathers did it. We do a lot of berry picking with them and cultural activities: singing, dancing, making regalia, and using the language. Our Potlatches in Northway are very strong.

My oldest son always talks about Grandma Nelnah, Bessie John from Beaver Creek. She was a strong, strong lady. Oh, she had words for everything! She just had the wisdom. I remember after Grandma was gone, I used to stop by Bessie's place in Beaver Creek. She would just hug me and cry with me because she came to Burwash to see Grandma Lily all the time. I think she was the matriarch for Beaver Creek. It takes a lot of wisdom and knowledge and respect to get to where she was. She was just so well respected. When she spoke, she spoke with a lot of love and care. You understood where she was coming from. She didn't beat around the bush; she was just right to the point. And she had a lot of love behind it, a lot of love.

Our family still has some really tight bonds here. We are all really close to my uncle Peter, who is being cared for at Thomson Centre now in Whitehorse. My dad, Thomas, is at Copper Ridge Centre. They all have that wonderful smile. There have been a lot of changes, I know that, since I've been living in the Yukon. I'm just new at this cultural work, and I really enjoy the learning. Just knowing the changes that have happened, the history of land claims and seeing what it's going to do for our younger generations. Hopefully they'll step into our shoes and keep it going, keep it strong.

My best advice for future generations is to get along, share your culture, your wisdom, and your knowledge. Care for each other because that's the most important thing. Share what's out there; don't keep it to yourself. It's very important that the next generation learns what we learned and they pass it on. That's how you're going to keep your culture and your traditions alive.

above Joyce and husband, Terry, fishing at Lhù'ààn Mân (Whitefish Place Lake, Kluane Lake), circa 2015. KFN Archives. EMPC. Bertha Doris Family Images #9. PHOTOGRAPHER UNKNOWN

> **My best advice for future generations is to get along, share your culture...**
>
> DA KWÄTHALA MĄ (JOYCE JOHNSON-ALBERT)

ERNEST MARTIN

(b. 1958)

Lessons from Grandma Grace

My name is Ernest Carl Martin. I was born in Chilliwack, B.C., in 1958. My parents were Kluane and Bill Martin. Her parents were Grace and Carl Chambers. My dad was a Cree Indian from Manitoba. My mom was training as a lab tech in a Vancouver hospital at that time. Then after I was born, we came back up here to Burwash when I was about a year old. My mom worked in Whitehorse General for forty-two years as a lab tech.

facing Ernest Martin, 2017. KFN Archives. EMPC. Elders Portraits #49. PHOTOGRAPHER ALISTAIR MAITLAND

BUSY GRANDMA

I stayed with my grandmother Grace Chambers here in Burwash often when I was young. Then I stayed in Whitehorse when I started school. I came out here for a few summers and for some winters when I was in school at Destruction Bay. It depended on where my mom was. If she was in Vancouver taking training, which she did for years on her job, I'd come out here with my grandmother until my mom got back. I went to Whitehorse Elementary School for grade 1 and up to grade 9. After that I went to Christ the King for grades 9 and 10 and then I went to F.H. Collins and did my grade 11. I was just getting into grade 12 and could have graduated in five months, but I came back out here to give my grandmother a hand. I didn't graduate. I had things to do out here.

By that time she was getting old. Her husband, Darrell Duensing, was mining, so I came out here to help her when he was away.

We fished all the time in the summer, and we'd sell fish to the Burwash Lodge, sometimes three or four big tubs of whitefish. In the winter she'd get fish for the dogs, whitefish, and she'd bring it up to all the dogs. She'd start at Jessie Joe's, and I'd go and give Jessie Joe two fish. I'd take it out to her dogs, and then we'd go to the next house and feed all the dogs in Burwash. And give the person of the house a fish, too, a whitefish. She was a consistent food supplier for people here.

Gùdia, John, and Math'ieya, and all the kids lived across the lake, and in the spring when it broke up it would take a while. As soon we could take a boat over there, we'd take a bunch of groceries over to Gùdia and John. Then he didn't have a job, and Gùdia wasn't working, either, so I took them trapping up the Big Arm. We were catching lynx and all the other animals.

Then we went, me and John, down to Little Arm. That's my grandmother's trapline, and we trapped there. We trapped a big lynx on my trapline.

When I was young, I trapped with my grandmother all the time. We sent all kinds of animals that we live trapped to Al Oeming in Edmonton. Al Oeming had a game farm there. We sent anything that would walk except the moose and wolves. No wolves. It would be anything from wolverine right down to a weasel. We'd catch them, and then we'd have them until the plane came in to Whitehorse. Al Oeming knew Grandma from when they were young. He came up here in the 1940s after the highway was built. He heard of this woman of the Great White North, so he had to meet her. He asked around Burwash and went out to the house and met her. I was about 10 years old and sitting right there. He said, "Gracie, now I need for my game ranch wolverine, lynx, coyote, foxes, anything, like even weasels, squirrels, stuff like that." So she agreed. She said, "Ok." So we started trapping live animals.

We made live traps designed by my stepgrandfather, Darrell, using 45-gallon fuel drums. I've got them up at the house. A 45-gallon barrel with a slide door on it, and you put bolts in it so the wood part will stay and then the slide door. There would be tin on the inside of it so they can't scratch through, and you can lift that up and down. Then there would be a little wire from the front of the barrel that sticks into the door, so that holds the door up. Then inside from that wire a stick would go through and it would be tilted on a nail, so that's where you put your bait. So when the animal goes in there, he pulls on that bait with that string hooked to the nail to hook that door. Pull on it and the door will go down, and then he's locked in. He can't get out.

We'd take them and put them on our Ski-Doo and drive them back here. To start with, when you first get them in the barrel, they're growling and raising hell, like in the bush. Then within about two days they kind of calmed down, but they would be growling away, like you know, deep growls from a wolverine or a "Wahhh," like that, from a lynx. All these little noises going on in the garage, right? They're all together in barrels in one garage.

You have to feed them, give them water. There's the open little thing on the top of the barrel. And you'd chop up the ice and make it about 2 inches round and as long as you want, then stick it through that barrel hole. Then you'd get fish and chop it up and stick that through the barrel hole, and whatever else you wanted to feed them, you'd stick it through that hole. So their water was actually ice. You'd stick a chunk of ice in there, and you'd hear them chomping, chewing it up. Then you'd stick some fish in there; you'd hear them eating that.

facing Grandma Grace smiles at little Ernie. KFN Archives EMPC. Ernie Martin Family Images #1. PHOTOGRAPHER UNKNOWN

above Old live traps built by Darrell Duensing in the 1950s for capturing wildlife to ship to Al Oeming's game farm in Alberta. KFN Archives. EMPC. Ernie Martin Family Images #2. PHOTOGRAPHER LINDA JOHNSON

We'd have to change the barrel traps, prepare a clean one and all that. We'd maybe have three or four wolverine in the garage and maybe two lynx in the barrel traps. At one time we'd have seven or eight barrel traps in there and all the animals in them. We'd have to keep them for maybe four or five days. We'd come back here with the animal, and we'd phone Al Oeming and tell him, "Well, we've got two wolverine, a lynx, and a fox." He would get everything together down there, and a small plane would come into Whitehorse, just for these animals.

Al sent big heavy boxes out here from Edmonton. We would grab our 45-gallon barrel in the garage, lift it up, and flip it on top of the box, open the door of our barrel, and the animal's sitting up trying to hang on so he won't fall through into the box. So you'd take a stick poke at them a bit, and pretty soon he'd fall in the crate. We'd put lots of fish in there, through that hole, and lots of ice and then off you'd go. We went by truck to Whitehorse. My grandma was the first to have a Ski-Doo in Burwash and one of the first to have a truck. Everybody else had dog teams. First of all she had a 1951 one-ton Chevy. A 4 x 4 open in the back. After a while it didn't even bother me, because you get used to it.

above Sisters Grace Chambers and Babe Southwick pulling fish net with a big catch on Kluane Lake, circa 1940s. KFN Archives. EMPC. Ernie Martin Family Images #3. PHOTOGRAPHER UNKNOWN

facing Grace working at a mine site, late 1940s. KFN Archives. EMPC. Ernie Martin Family Images #4. PHOTOGRAPHER UNKNOWN

After they got to Al, he let them out of his crate and they'd take off in the wild again at his farm. He had 300 miles of fenced land with all these animals: moose, caribou, elk, grizzly bear, black bear, squirrels, weasels, and lynx. Grandma went down there to see it in the early days, when she was younger, and I went one time too.

GRANDMA'S DICKSON FAMILY

Dickson was her maiden name. Tom Dickson and Louise were her parents. There were a lot of kids. Grandma told me there was fourteen, but two passed away. So it ended up there were twelve kids in the family. They grew up down below here, to the north of Burwash. They had a cabin down by the river, about 2½ miles down the Kluane River. They've got a homestead there. They had a cabin on the lake, too, up the Little Arm. So they'd go up there trapping in the winter and hunting and all that in the summer.

She said there's people that come up from Northway, come up here running dogs, and they would get to Kluane Lake here and they'd start fishing. She said they'd freeze fish together on a dog sled. They have a dog sled, and they'd freeze it together so all these fish were frozen in this dog sled. They would be going to Haines, Alaska. So they'd come up from Northway, through here, get a haul of fish to keep going, eating it themselves and to feed their dogs. They'd go down to trade at Haines. I don't know what they were trading in the 30s. Probably furs.

Tom Dickson come up through North Dakota in '98, I think. He was here real early. And later on there was this guy poaching horses in the Yukon. He'd come from the border, the Alaska border. He'd come over to the Yukon, and he'd steal horses from people around here; that's in about the 20s, something like that. So Tom, Tom Dickson, was always on the prowl looking for him, and then my grandma said he would shoot to kill, eh? Because this guy was stealing horses for years, so he shot him. He shot him in the leg and that was it, but he got away because he had all these horses. So he jumped from one horse to the other to the other, and he'd have a fresh horse all the time. So Tom couldn't catch him, because he wouldn't pack with three, four horses behind him to switch off. So he could never really get close to him, but he got close enough to shoot him in the leg with his pistol. Yeah, and the guy got away. My grandma said he didn't come back after that. End of the horse thieving. I guess so, because they never seen him after that. Maybe he didn't survive, might have been injured and bled to death. Nobody knew who he was, really.

Then Tom did go after that mad trapper too. Yeah, he was one of the corporals who were outside the house shooting at the building. Al Johnson wouldn't come out, wouldn't come out, so they started throwing dynamite at that house, that shack there. And then he got out the back door, back window, and took off again and that's about as far as I know that story, but they finally got him. Albert Johnson. Yeah, he did go after him, too, with all these other corporals because Johnson was a marksman and Tom Dickson was a marksman.

My grandma said he could pull a pistol out and shoot a spool of thread. I mean, a spool of thread at 50 feet, just pull it out like that, and bang! And he'd hit it, yeah. She said he can do it three times in a row, you know, no sweat. But she said he was always shooting, all the time. Must've had good eyesight too. And then later on in his years he's walking along with a horse and he flicked a branch, my grandma said. He'd flick a branch off and peel it down and use it as a toothpick. Well, he flicked a branch off one time and a piece of that branch went in his eye, and it blinded him in one eye. So that's when he got blind.

She told me a story about how he always packed his tobacco in his pocket, and one day he was filling his pipe up and somehow a .22 shell got in there and he didn't know it. He was puffing away and puffing away, and then he put his pipe down there and he went to get something and his pipe blew right up. Because the shell got hot in there. And then it took off, yeah. It's a good thing he didn't have it in his mouth. Yeah, he was just puffing on it and then he put it down and walked maybe six, seven steps and there it blew up. She told me about lots of things.

Everybody knows my grandma and Sue Van Bibber and all the Dicksons, all her siblings. Most of them were born right down at the homestead here. They didn't have no doctor or anything. And to go to Whitehorse my grandma said it would take them three days on horseback just to

ride into Whitehorse one way. On the old Jaçquot Trail, yeah. Then when they got wagons, well, that was even worse because it would take them four or five days to get to town because they'd be getting stuck all the time. So then after that they didn't take the wagon into town at a certain time, like spring. So they'd go to town, pick up stuff, and bring it out here. And then pretty soon the store at Silver City started up, so then they would just go get their stuff from there. They travelled a lot in the winter on the lake by dog team.

ADVENTURES WITH GRANDMA

As a child living here, everywhere she went, I went. When she went across the lake, I went. When she went up Big Arm with Belle Desrosiers, I'd go. Belle Desrosiers used to own my trapline, and before Belle Babe Southwick owned that trapline. I don't know who owned it before that, but I think Babe was the first one that got the trapline over there when they started coming out with registered traplines. So Babe sold it to Belle Desrosiers; that's her sister. And then I bought it off of Belle in the mid-70s, about '76. I bought that trapline for $500, but I don't know what it's worth now.

One time we went up to Little Arm, me and my grandma, and we put out a net. Then the next day we got a smaller boat, just a little small wooden boat there. It was only maybe 10 feet long, yeah. Mostly people built their own boats. So we went up the next day. I guess we were maybe 300 or 400 yards out in the middle of the lake. We were running this fishnet, and I was stomping on these fish, killing them. I stomped on one and it ricocheted, and I put a hole right through that boat with my heel. So I pulled it back out, and there was water coming out—coming up through there about maybe 6 to 8 inches high. So I stuck my foot back in there, and Grandma rowed to shore while I was holding my boot there. We just got to shore! There were at least, oh, I'd say 8 inches of water in the boat, and I was trying to bail it out. She'd be about 45, 40, something like that then. Yeah, she was rowing! She just said, "Now put your heel back in that hole! And bail!" And then she rowed. Yeah, it was no big deal. We got there! She wasn't mad or anything. She said, "Oh, well, things like that happen."

Oh, lots of adventures with her, yeah! When I was younger, she'd go down to the mine and sit around and maybe go panning while Kim and Ron Holway were filling their box with gold. We'd be up on the bank there, panning gold. And what we got out of there, we'd keep for ourselves.

WARTIME ROMANCE

Grandma's first husband was Carl Chambers, and my middle name is for him. They had three children, Kluane, Louise, and Ron. Her sister Sue married Carl's brother George. So the two sisters married two brothers.

Grace and Darrell met during World War II down at the Jacquot Lodge in Burwash. She was working there for a dollar a day in the kitchen and laundry downstairs and waitressing. All the jobs that were there—she'd do whatever. From 14 or 15 years old.

Darrell was in the American Army. I think he was a sergeant, something like that. He was coming through here with the construction of the highway. They had a big camp here at one point, the American Army, at Destruction Bay, and they had a camp here in Burwash, and then the next camp was Donjek. So every 40 miles or 30 miles they'd have a camp, with these Jeeps and tents. Lots of army people.

She didn't talk too much about the army. Darrell didn't tell me too much about the army, either, because he was overseas and I guess he just wanted to forget all about that. Him and his three brothers, they all went to war at the same time. They were on three different boats, but they all survived, came home.

Afterwards he came here when they were building the highway. They took 4,000 men, and some worked from Tok, Alaska, coming this way and others coming the other way and they all met up. Nine months. Hundreds and hundreds of U.S. troops all along this road.

So they met during the building of the highway. She already had the kids. My grandfather [Carl Chambers] was a drinker. She said he'd come home after drinking up in the village here and all over, and two days after that he'd start making moonshine in the house. Then, a couple of days later, he was gone again. He'd take that whole barrel of booze with him, yeah. And go drink it, sell it, have a party. So she kind of got rid of him. She was raising three kids by herself after that.

After Darrell left here, he went down to some island in Fiji for a couple of months. Then when the war ended, he came back up and stayed here. Every six months he'd go back to the United States or he'd drive up to Tok and stay the night because he didn't have Canadian citizenship, so he couldn't stay here year-round. Every six months until he finally got his Canadian papers. So it's a real World War II Alaska Highway romance!

MINING FOR GOLD

Darrell was a miner. His dad was, too, and they had a gold mine down in Chico, California. His Ancestors were German, and he was born about 1925. His dad went from Germany to California in the 20s, even earlier, maybe 1915 or after the First World War. Darrell was telling me his dad was digging up gold when he was 10 years old at Paradise. It's south of L.A. and inland. They owned a couple of miles of land back in that time.

When Darrell came back up here, he and Grandma would drive out to California in the early days, like in the 50s. They'd go to Chico; from Chico they'd go to Reno and they'd gamble a bit, and then they'd come back to Chico and stay there for maybe a month or so. Come back here in the start of the winter and then they'd go again during the winter. We'd all take off from here and go down to California at Christmastime once in a while. Sometimes we'd go down in the spring or the fall. She'd go down maybe once every two, three years with

facing Grace with dog in the 1940s. Dogs were constant companions for bush families like the Dicksons, essential workers for transportation, security against prowling bears or other predators, and friendly beings to help pass the time during long, cold winters. KFN Archives. EMPC, Ernie Martin Family Images #5. PHOTOGRAPHER UNKNOWN

facing top Grace Chambers's cabin in 2022 on the west side of the Alaska Highway across from Burwash. The cabin was built by Ed Kabanak for his family in the 1940s and later purchased by Darrell Duensing as a home for Grace and himself. KFN Archives. EMPC. Ernie Martin Family Images #6. PHOTOGRAPHER LINDA JOHNSON

facing bottom Receipt for goods purchased and fish delivered on credit by Grace at the store in Burwash, 1955. KFN Archives. EMPC. Ernie Martin Family Images #7. SCANNED BY LINDA JOHNSON

him, or she'd stay here and he would go down for a month or so.

Darrell lived a long life and died in 2014. Grandma died in 2007. They stayed together all that time; the only time they would be apart is if Darrell would go down to California for a month during the winter and do whatever he has to do. He'd go down and see the dentist, doctor, little things like this, and then he'd get his papers, whatever had to be done, and then he'd come back. Darrell mined across the lake in Gladstone. He was up there with Park Southwick, Babe's husband. He was in Reed Creek just up by the Donjek in the late 40s, early 50s. He mined in these creeks around here looking for gold and all across the lake. He got some big nuggets. One was the size of your hand. That came from Reed Creek, that nugget. It was about the size of the palm of your hand, and it was about maybe an inch to half an inch thick.

We cleaned the sluice boxes there at the mine site, put in all the gravel and the gold that came out of there. We'd take it and put it in the truck and then drive it back home and put it in the garage. So there was bags of gold in the garage that has to be sluiced through a little box. We'd just stack those bags up in the corner. Me and Darrell would be in the garage sluicing during the winter, all winter, yeah. And then sometimes in the fall. He was mining here, and Ron Holway was mining Dublin Gulch, in the Mayo district. That was around the 60s and 70s. They would take the gold and meet in Whitehorse at his place and then go through all the gold and separate the gold from the sand.

That was worth lots of money—could have been half a million in those bags at one time, because we would take just about a whole truckload by the time we shovelled it and put it in all these big bags and put them on the truck. It would be a couple of hundred pounds of dirt in these bags, then we'd put them in the garage and just leave them there, go back mining and then come back again. We'd do that all summer and then there'd be three truckloads in there, just bags of gold. Or more sometimes, because it depends on how often we'd clean up. You'd have to clean your sluice box out every two, three weeks. So there'd be lots of gold in there.

OLD-TIME BURWASH PEOPLE

There were lots of people, Elders, here when I was growing up. Moose Johnson. Albert Isaac. A lot of old timers, yeah. The old timers would play cards for .22 shells and bullets. At Albert Isaac's place. Albert Isaac from Aishihik. He was a really old man by the 60s. In 1980 I think he was mid-80s. Albert was probably 87 years old, and he took a boat from here, a rowboat, a little, tiny boat, and he rowed across the lake by himself. Then he went back up into that lake back there by the Little Arm, and he killed a moose. Then he hauled it—from there he hauled it out to the lakeshore, and he started cutting it up, hanging it, and smoking it, and then nobody knew where he was. They go, "Well, where's Albert?" Well, he's not in Burwash anywhere, and nobody took him anywhere. So now they're starting to fly around. Like John Ostashek just got here by that time; he had a plane. So he was flying around. Me and my grandma were looking around all over the lakeshores for him. Then we finally found him, and here he was, 80-some years old, killed a moose, happy as can be. Yeah, just sitting there. He didn't want to come back here! We told him, "Come on, we've got to take you back to Burwash." "I don't want to go to Burwash; that's why I came over here," he said. So we finally conned him into it. We brought his moose over and him too.

Grandma always had money—a little bit of money anyways—all the time, working at the lodge, trapping, fishing, selling

furs, this and that, all the time when she was growing up. She was a real entrepreneur. Yeah, and then she worked with the outfitters. The surveyors that come up here in the 30s and were surveying all this land back behind here in the Park and all over the place. So my grandmother worked there for, oh, fifteen or so years.

We'd say you'd always know where Grace was because a helicopter would go by and there'd be a stove hanging underneath the helicopter, so you'd know that's her helicopter; that's the one she rides in all the time. She'd be cooking for forty people way up in the mountains. Middle of the sticks, yeah. Just in tents. That was the 50s, 60s. There was platinum exploration just after the war. They were up here for years. My grandmother worked for them, so that's what she was doing. They would be here in the summer, and then they'd leave in the winter and she'd go trapping and fishing and this and that, so she always had money. She wasn't broke like some of the people that only have $10 every couple of months or whatever. She was saving money, stuff like that.

In the 50s she's regularly selling fish at the lodge. In Burwash and Destruction Bay. We have the receipts that show what she was selling and buying. Kleenex, three sardines, four pounds margarine, bread. That was '55. June 5th, 1955. Five dollars and 54 cents for something. And Klim, that's milk. Powdered milk. Two dollars and 54 cents for a big container of it, 10 pounds or something. Four dozen eggs, $2.80. Bacon, $1.50. Fish credit, July 3rd, 1955, at maybe 30 cents for something like 44 pounds, fish credit $13.20. Forty-four pounds of the best fish. She must have liked sardines because they're on quite a few of the receipts. And 5 pounds of spuds, 2¼ pounds of spare ribs. Not moose spare ribs, she was getting some beef spare ribs or pork spare ribs. This was likely an account with the lodge here because back in that day they had a building down there.

My grandfather Darrell would sell fur, and he had a little store there. You could buy groceries down at the lodge at this little store he had. Leland owned the lodge, then he'd [Darrell would] run the store and the trading so people could get

DATE, July 8 1955

M

		ACCT.	FWD.
		25	26
1			
2	Credit	10	00
3		15	26
4	July 11-55		
5	½ doz apple		40
6	July 12-55		
7	1 Ham		45
8	5# Spuds		65
9	2¼# Spare ribs	1	24
10	1# Butter		85
11	5# Sugar		78
12	1 Can Sardines		14
13			
14			
15	46		

MOORE BUSINESS FORMS WESTERN LTD.

above Grace Chambers's greenhouse had an elaborate wood heating system designed by Darrell Duensing, consisting of a barrel stove and pipes that were dug into the ground beneath it. Many families maintained greenhouses heated by wood to produce fresh vegetables in summer because of the long distance and high costs involved in buying food from stores in Whitehorse. KFN Archives EMPC Ernie Martin Family Images #9 PHOTOGRAPHER LINDA JOHNSON

their supplies for trapping. You could buy jeans and everything there. Whatever you wanted, you'd tell Darrell and he would write it down and send out for it, then it'd come to the store and then you would buy it from him.

As kids we lived across the highway, not in the village here, so my grandma would say, "Always stay away from the highway. Don't go out to the road. You go out the road, then you stay away from the highway, just stick around the house." You had to stay close anyways, because there was a bear in the yard every week, every two weeks, because there's a road right from the house where I live right back to the pipeline; it goes straight back there. So bears would go up and down the pipeline, and moose, all these animals—they'd turn into that road sometimes and come right into the yard. Grizzlies, yeah. Oh yeah, because there was always fish. Oh yeah, we'd have to shoot them sometimes. Especially in the fall time. We'd have a moose hanging, and there'd be bears all the time.

Darrell and Leland had cows around here. Cattle. Leland Allinger. Every fall him and Darrell would go and kill a nice bull and hang it up just down by the lodge there, and just across the highway from us there was a big barn. So we'd hang that meat up there, and they'd phone each other at a certain time to go up and check the meat. Even at twelve o'clock, three o'clock in the morning. It was like every so many hours they'd go up there and check on it.

The Jacquots' boat was the *Josephine*. Yeah, the Jacquot brothers took that to Silver City and back. So anybody coming out of the bush or mining or with horses, they'd just park it here and then they'd go over with that boat, pick up their grocery order. Or they'd come out of the bush and drop off their grocery order at the lodge, and then they'd leave again, go back up there, and when the groceries came in a week or so later, two weeks, they'd come back to Burwash, pick up their stuff, and go back up in the gold fields. The *Josephine* had a one-cylinder motor in it. Inboard. My grandma said you'd ride in it and you'd hear the noise of that motor going along; Grandma had an outboard motor. Most people here would just have had a small rowboat. You wanted a boat, you go build it.

When I was about 12 years old, my uncle and my grandma's sister Ruth McFarlane [née Dickson, then Jacquot] and I went down to Vancouver. We went on a tour around the U.S., and we hit every state in the United States except Hawaii. My uncle bought a brand new Cadillac, so away we went to all the states and all the places everywhere. So later on I went to Hawaii just to hit every one of them.

GOING AWAY TO WORK

I worked up in the village here building houses in the 80s. Before that I worked at Junction, at Parks Canada. I was a mechanic's helper for all the Parks trucks. So that's what I was doing in 1976.

I moved to Dutch Harbour, Alaska, around that time. I was about 18, 19 when I moved there. I went there for three or four years, fishing. On the big boats. There was a Russian boat came over from Saint Petersburg into United States waters, just off the edges of it. Then we went out to meet it and we invited the boat to come into U.S. waters, and it followed us just out of Dutch Harbour, somewhere there, a few miles out of Dutch Harbour, and anchored down. We would drag net fish. They were looking for salmon, so we'd drag net for salmon. When the net was full, then we'd give the lines to the Russians and they would haul that net up onto their boat, and they would have regulators there that would make sure only salmon comes out of that net and goes in the hull; everything else goes overboard. So we did that to fill that boat up. I think it was five, six days we were just there constantly. Oh, one of those big fishing boats is huge. It'd be a couple of million dollars for that thing. You see them on TV now on that show.

So I went over there and stayed in my girlfriend's bunkhouse. It was just a series of trailers put together. There was about 180 women living there. Then I got working on the boats, and most of the women would be working at the factory right in Dutch Harbour. So we'd go out, we'd catch fish to send down south, and then we all would cut it all up. And then once in a while a boat from somewhere else would come; like there was some of them coming around from Sweden to get salmon, and we'd fill them up too. And other boats would be filling up at the same time. One big boat like that one was about two football fields long. So there'd be three, four fishing boats drag netting for them to fill their boat.

KLUANE IS STILL HOME

After that I moved back here full time and been here ever since. The most places I would go is maybe Whitehorse and back again, just around the Yukon. I was born and basically have stayed here. Back home I was trapping my grandma's line. And Joe Joe Johnson had an overlapping area. Grandma just said to him, "Ok, you can have that part of the trapline because I don't go up in those mountains anyways." And I don't think he did, either, but he took that part of the trapline. Well, it's just over between Big Arm and Little Arm, and right in the middle there's overlap.

One time I was jumped by a wolverine. That was across at the Big Arm. I took off from the cabin and I was going down the lakeshore and a wolverine was running along so I thought, "Ok, I'll go out there, and I'll shoot him." So I went out to get closer to him, and I shot at him about three times. He was on the run. He had my snare around his neck. He chewed the rest of the toggle down to about maybe a foot long. He was running along. I run out of shells, so I chased him back into shore a little ways. I got a big club and went back out there, and he jumped me. He jumped on me, and he finally fell off of my back, after he

above Ernie loves to travel on the lake by four-wheeler or snowmobile in winter, regardless of the cold and wind! KFN Archives. EMPC. Elders Portraits #50. PHOTOGRAPHER ALISTAIR MAITLAND

top Darrell Duensing's gold mining operation at Reed Creek up the Donjek Valley in the Kluane Mining District, circa 1970s. KFN Archives. EMPC. Ernie Martin Family Images #11. PHOTOGRAPHER UNKNOWN

bottom Darrell Duensing (right) and Fred Holway at Darrell's gold mining operations at Dublin Gulch in the Mayo Mining District, circa 1970s. KFN Archives. EMPC. Ernie Martin Family Images #10. PHOTOGRAPHER UNKNOWN

facing Ernie Martin recording stories at Jacquot Hall for the Elders Memory Project in 2017. KFN Archives. EMPC. Elders Portraits #51. PHOTOGRAPHER ALISTAIR MAITLAND

overleaf Since the late 1940s newcomers to Kluane First Nation have arrived by driving north on the Alaska Highway, with the first sighting of Lhù'ààn Mân (Whitefish Place Lake, Kluane Lake) and Tṣ̀echàl Dhàl (Rock-Scraper Mountain, Sheep Mountain) signalling the dramatic landscapes and vibrant lifestyle lying ahead. KFN Archives. EMPC. Landscape Images #27. PHOTOGRAPHER ALANNA DICKSON

tore up my coat and Ski-Doo seat. They're ferocious. Well, that was a mistake, yeah.

My grandmother and Joe Jacquot started all this land claims, and they got the government to notice that there's Indians up here and First Nations all over the place and you've got to do something about this. So Joe Jacquot and my grandma and Dick Dickson and them just started on the government: "Now we're a First Nation, we need this, and we've got to have that." Then they started all this meeting. It started with my grandmother and Joe Jacquot. They went into town and started talking about how there's no housing in the 1950s, 60s. They started it, and it took a long time for the government to realize that there is a First Nation out here and they do need some help.

I don't know about the future here. I don't know what's going to come up around here next. The big new mine would do something around here, but I don't think there's that much gold up there. They're looking for other things, platinum and stuff. So I don't know how that would go, because it was mined in the 40s, 50s, 60s, and 70s. Now they've got to figure out what's there and if it's feasible to go down deeper.

It's like Burwash Creek: everybody's been kicking rocks there for a hundred years and more. My grandfather said the best place to dig up Burwash Creek would be the tailing piles, because they didn't care about fine gold if it was just big as mosquitos. The gold they wanted was something as big as your fingernail, little nuggets. So everything else, just throw them away, so there'd be some in the tailing piles.

When I look back on it, I had an amazing childhood! Days full of adventure with my grandma and her husband. My wife (Wendy) and I still love to travel, and we've been to many interesting places too. California, New Orleans before the big hurricane, and other places. But Kluane is still home!

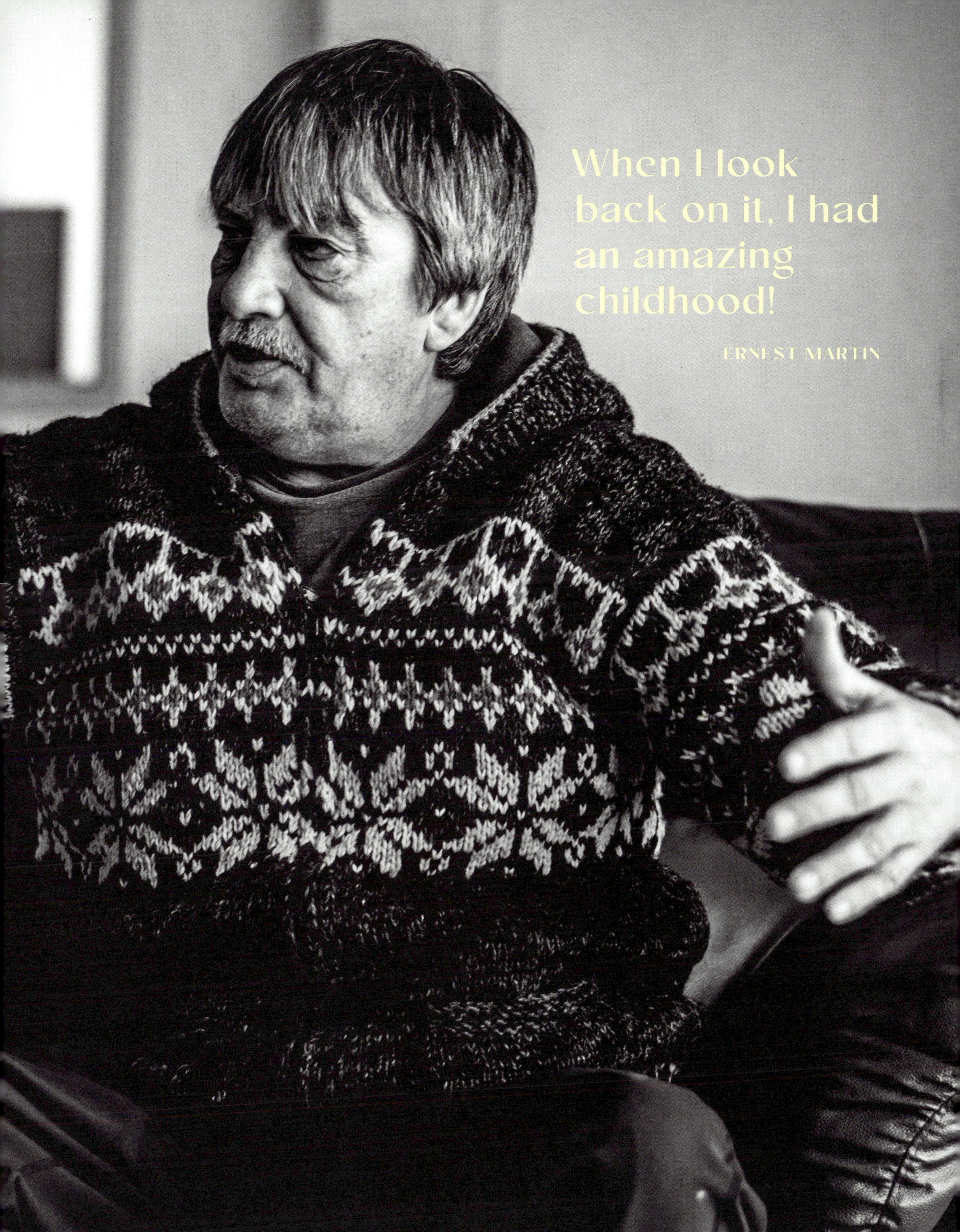

When I look back on it, I had an amazing childhood!

ERNEST MARTIN

Many people from distant places have joined our families through the years and contributed much to the growth of our community. We appreciate them all for their hard work. Three of those people—Joe Bruneau, Sandy Johnson, and David Dubois—told their stories for this book.

ANTERA (JOE BRUNEAU)

(b. 1947)

You're Never Too Old to Learn

My name is Joseph Serge Bruneau; that's my full name. I was born in 1947 in Sentinelle, Quebec. It's about 400 miles north of Montreal, 50 miles away from Val-d'Or. People in Burwash call me Little Joe because I am shorter than Joe Joe Johnson, who was the Chief for many years. In Southern Tutchone they call me Antera (Little Person).

facing Antera (Little Person, Joe Bruneau), 2018. KFN Archives. EMPC Elders Portraits #52. PHOTOGRAPHER ALISTAIR MAITLAND

WE MOVED AROUND A LOT

My parents were Joe and Simone Bruneau. We stayed there in Sentinelle for a few years. My dad was a mechanic. So we moved around a lot in our young age; we didn't really stay in one place too long. When we left there, we moved to Madison, Ontario, which is just across the line from Quebec, and from there we hit Timmons, Sault Ste. Marie, and Red Lake, Ontario. He built a house there, so we thought our travelling days were over, but no; because of the work he was doing, it would run out in certain places. Instead of being away from the family a lot, he wanted to keep with Mom. She'd always go ahead with him, and he'd rent a house. Then they'd come back and get us.

My family all spoke French in Quebec, but when we moved to Ontario and I started school there, of course it was an English school. But once we got home, we had to speak French. That's my mom's way. If I brought a friend with me, an English friend, that's ok; I can speak to him in English. But if it was just the family that was home, we spoke French and that was her rule. You know, we still speak it today, but if it wasn't for her, maybe not. Because my dad, he didn't really care if we spoke English or French. What do I tell people today? Well, if you want your kids to learn, you've got to be able to speak it yourself. To me it's very important. Our mom ensured we spoke French, all of us kids. We still can go back to Quebec. It doesn't take me long; I get all the words back. Boom, boom, and then I'm just talking as fast as they do!

We kept coming this way, west. I went to school when we stayed in Elgin, Manitoba. Finally we moved to Yellowknife, Northwest Territories. That would probably be when I was 7 years old, so around '54. Well, Yellowknife was just small. Giant Mines—the big gold mines were going there. I was about 7 or 8 when we moved there, and from there we went to Hay River and stayed there for a while. I was getting up in age now, so I stayed with my oldest brother when my parents went back to Quebec to visit their families. I stayed with Guy and finished school.

Then I started in the work world. I stayed in Hay River for quite a while, five or six years, doing carpentry, a little jack of all trades, master of none—that sort of thing.

My other brother had a company called Leon Fortin and Company. He built houses. We travelled a little to work. We'd go to High Level, Alberta, and wherever there was need, we'd go. Then I got a job at Hub City Machine Services in Hay River driving truck for them, CATs, and all that.

THE SPELL OF THE YUKON

By then my parents had moved up here to Destruction Bay. Dad had met Clyde Wann, and he told him, "Come on up here," because Clyde owned a lot of lodges up here. So Dad said, "Ok." He told Mom, "Let's go up to the Yukon and try it now the kids are gone." He ran the garage here for two or three years in Destruction Bay. It's not there no more.

I thought, "I'm going to go up and see them." Dad was still working as a mechanic at the Destruction Bay Lodge. I come up to visit. I just fell in love with this place, the whole Yukon—like holy man, the mountains all over! I was here for a while. I liked it and I thought, "To heck with this. I'm going back to Hay River, pack up, and I'm out of there." And that's what I did. I come back up here. I've been here ever since 1973.

I've been out for a couple of months here and there, but the Yukon, the spell of the Yukon, keeps bringing me back. I don't know why, but it does. Nobody's in a big rush up in this country. The rat race ain't here yet. Not that I don't like going out; I like Vancouver Island.

When the Destruction Bay lodge was sold, my parents went back east for a while. What happened there was that it didn't work out with whoever bought the lodge, so the former owners came back. Then my dad came back here, too, and that's when my mom died. She was 73. After that Dad just left and went back to Quebec. He couldn't handle it here without her.

My brothers had come up, too, but they were in the Faro area. Gilles was driving truck, and my brother Guy had a business in Faro working on the highway trucks for White Pass. He just contracted out to fix their trucks. Later he moved down to Princeton, and that's where he stayed until he passed away.

EVERYONE HELPED EACH OTHER

I stayed here in Burwash. I worked at the lodge, and that's when I got to know some of the people here. I used to go to the lodge, and they had a little grocery store. I got to know all of the KFN Elders, their kids, and everything. When I first came here, Jimmy Joe, Bill Jamieson, Sam Johnson, Little Grace, George John, Ruth Johnson, Aunt Nellie, and old Sophie Watt were all alive then. I think Sophie was the oldest one in Burwash at that time.

Jessie Joe—she used to tell me stories all the time. We used to go up to Burwash Uplands, hunting, her and Jessie Johnson. She told me when they were kids, they'd go up there and they'd get on a hill and then they'd start playing. They'd forget all about time. They were supposed to go up there, see their dad for something, but by the time they got there, it was pretty late. They were kind of scared they were going to get heck and all that, but they were kids, you know? They wanted to play. I think they were going up there to get meat or something.

I trapped with Thomas Joe, who was another Elder. Thomas and Rita. They needed help, so I went along and I learned how to trap, just watching them, see what they do.

I remember they used to have a little hexagon hut here. They had land claims meetings in there. That place was just packed! If there was a meeting about it, everybody went. It was just the way it was. At the beginning they were all excited,

facing Moose crossing Alaska Highway near Burwash. KFN Archives. EMPC. Wildlife Images #13. PHOTOGRAPHER ALANNA DICKSON

above Pair of Cedar Waxwing birds in winter. KFN Archives. EMPC. Wildlife Images #14. PHOTOGRAPHER JOHN MEIKLE

but over the years, after the process got started and people started to learn a little more about it, then it started to break apart. I saw it cause a big divide in the community. I really did. Why I loved it here—the people, when I first met them, they helped each other. It was amazing. I never seen anything like that in the white society. Here if somebody wanted help, boom! They were there to help.

We used to go and hunt moose across the lake. Whatever you could pack, you kept. That's how they shared. See, we had the kids there too. They'd pack little pieces, but they shared it along, and when we got over to this side, you kept what you had in your pack. Three miles sometimes we had to pack meat to the lake to get to the boat. So there was a lot of sharing then. Lots. Everybody shared. People didn't hide the moose and then run home and put it in the deep freeze. Even today I don't hunt, but it's the same thing. I get more moose meat than the person who goes out hunting because I help this guy, help this guy, help this guy—everybody's giving me meat. What the heck? Why should I hunt?

My partner is Agnes Johnson since 1984. I used to drink like a fish then. I quit in '89. I went to treatment in Whitehorse. I had a friend there, Joe Jacquot. I hardly knew him, but he took me in. He took me to his place, and I got to stay there for a month. And one day I told him, "Joe, look, I've got to go back to Burwash. If I'm going to deal with this, I have to go back there." But I'll tell you the support I got from the people here was overpowering. It saved my life. Oh, it did, it did. Because if they hadn't supported me, I could have started drinking again. I'm 71 and I'm still going now.

The Elders called me in at that time, when I came back. Charlie Eikland was the Chief. I was nervous, wondering what they were going to say. Maybe they were going to ask me to leave, because they had sent other people away. He said, "The Elders want to make you an honorary member of the community." Boy, was I surprised! Just stunned. I was worried they were going to chase me out, but instead they gave me a KFN hat and a T-shirt and some other things. That was in 1989.

I STAYED HERE IN BURWASH

Agnes went to Whitehorse for about three years because she was taking up social work. So she was in town for a few years. That's before we started going around. When she came back here, the kids went to school here. They played hockey here. After that they went to Christ the King High School in Whitehorse. They're all back here again now, except for Lillian. She got married Outside.

Agnes and I looked after her seven kids for years. If you are going to live with somebody and you care for them, you love them and all that, you've got to care for everything about them. You can't just care about her and not her kids. I couldn't do that. There were hectic days in them days.

I remember when we used to go to meetings here and people would say, "What the

facing Joe was friends with everyone in Burwash, learning to hunt and fish with Elders, enjoying time with families in the community. Friends left to right: Peter Johnson, Kathleen Johnson, Gerald Dickson, and Russell Dickson, early 1970s. KFN Archives. EMPC. Agnes Johnson Family Images #7. PHOTOGRAPHER UNKNOWN

left Joe walked everywhere in the bush, carrying a walking stick like his Elder friends and his binoculars to be on the lookout for moose and other wildlife. KFN Archives. EMPC. Agnes Johnson Family Images #8. PHOTOGRAPHER UNKNOWN

heck is the matter with the children?" You know, I can't see nothing wrong with them. One day I got so angry about that and I got up and I says, "Why do you guys keep saying what's the matter with the children? You should be happy. We taught them that. They watched us; that's all we did."

There were two buildings put together for the community school here in the 70s. One of them was a storeroom, and the other one was a classroom. I was a tutor at the school, believe it or not. I just helped the kids with their math and all that. I was also putting the water in the school. We used to pump it from the wash house with a garden hose, fill up the tank every two or three days. I'd do that. Keep the septic from freezing in the winter. I made a barrel, put a torch underneath it, heat up the water to steam, and I'd steam it out. You had to have it for the school. Not too many people had running water here then; just the school was about the only one.

YOU CAN DO IT!

I was not against land claims, but because of how fast it came, nobody was prepared for it. I said to the people at that time that it's going to be harder than going to residential school because that is going to stick with you for the rest of your life. And that's what's happening now. There's big divides in this community, and you've got to have good leadership here to stop and say, "Ok, what's wrong with this community?" Yes, we can't fix it, but we just try; that's all we can do is try. Oh, it's a tough job, but you've got to start somewhere. Whatever you want to be, you can do it. That's what the whole land claims is about: to govern themselves.

I worked for KFN in a lot of different departments. Jack of all trades and master of none! I became an NNADAP worker in 1983. That's when I set up a little unit here with the old video games because I see a need for the children. They've got to have something to do. I'm telling you, that little machine could make money like you wouldn't believe. It was a guy in Whitehorse that had video games, and he set them up here. What you did, you got half the profit for running it for him. We had Batman and one of those football games. It was always going. It was 25 cents to play. But it gave the kids a place to go at night. It used to be in the old school.

above left Joe in his backyard at Burwash cutting lake trout caught in Kluane Lake, September 2003. Fish of this size are becoming rarer at Kluane Lake, one of the many signs of environmental change of concern to Joe and everyone in Kluane First Nation. KFN Archives. EMPC. Paul Nadasdy Images #1. PHOTOGRAPHER PAUL NADASDY

above right Joe putting his boat in at Mile 1118 and heading for Dawson City with his dog Lucky in 2005. KFN Archives. EMPC. Paul Nadasdy Images #2. PHOTOGRAPHER PAUL NADASDY

I was an NNADAP worker for about four or five years. I think it started in '83; that's when they started handing some of the programs to the First Nations. I worked in the Health Department; I was Acting Director for a while. This Elders Room used to be our offices. After that I was Acting Director of Housing. Then I retired five years ago at 65. I couldn't wait—I'm outta here!

I like this country. I like walking around. I like seeing things. Usually I'm out in the bush. In the winter I'm out cutting wood. I'd sell a few cords here and there; I just don't go at it big. And then in summertime we go to the cabin down below at Salmon Patch, you know, cruise around down there. When you've got Agnes as a wife, there's always something to do! She still sews.

There was alcoholism in the community in the past, but the thing is, people still cared for each other. They shared everything; it was amazing to see. Burwash—it's got everything today for a good life. It's got a lake with fish in it, all kinds of game; it's got rabbits, grouse. Agnes says, "Oh, we've got to cook a turkey!" For what? Just go shoot two grouse. That's good enough! Why always turkey? Let's change it to grouse. You can eat that anytime!

The biggest problem I have here now is the darkness. The winter. That is my biggest problem. You're at home and you want to go Ski-Dooing, but you've got to be back in time. Three hours, four hours and it's dark.

NEVER TOO OLD TO LEARN!

When you look at the land, you've got to help protect it. You've got to help protect the animals. Take only what you need. Because if you're going to overharvest, then they're going to suffer. Well, that thing has been with me since I've been here. Now I'm not saying I've never shot a moose; don't get me wrong there. See, I went with people hunting, but I remember Joe Joe sends me up there and he says,

"Just shoot it, Joe. A bad shot and he'll come down right to us." Ok. So I'm walking up there, I see the moose, he gets up, he's taking off, holy man, bang! Moose drops, little Joe Joe's down there with Kenny Johnson and that Joe Joe—well, he wasn't laughing because then they had to come up to get it!

I remember another time we were coming back—Peter Johnson and I, Joe Joe and Kenny—we were pulling a moose on the hide. Man! It just wouldn't slide, so all of a sudden, here comes Kenny and Joe Joe; they had put rails, poles, underneath their skin. So Peter and I, we put rails on ours, and that made all the difference in the world, like a little sleigh. Yeah, but we're laughing. We're going to get to the lake first, and we're going to have to wait for these guys, you know, but here they come! Just kept going. So that's something I learned!

You're never too old to learn. I learned lots from the young kids here. There was one here one time saying, "Why do we always build a whole bunch of buildings here for everything? Why can't we just make one place that does for all?" To me that made the best sense I've heard. You can have volleyball, basketball, and other activities; you don't have to play in 80 or 90 miles an hour wind, because you're indoors. Now they've got the covered skating rink.

I've been all over this country, and it's beautiful. You've got to go out and look at it. Not too far from Ptarmigan Heart I was coming through there with a horse one time, and I came to this little creek. It's just like somebody planted the grass and everything with little flowers growing there, and it went right to the water's edge. I thought I went to heaven. It was beautiful—people couldn't have even done it that good. This was nature. And that's what I like about nature. Nature does good things. But you've got to protect it.

I used to go on hunts, and it was always a together thing. We used to go up to the lake with Joe Joe; Katie was there, too, when she was small. We'd set a tent and stay in the tent: Katie, Peter, and I. Then from there we'd go out on the lake and hunt and do whatever we wanted to do. So it was a good life. I'm heading for 75. After that I'll see—do it yearly!

above Joe enjoying winter splendour on a snowmobile trail at Sleepy Cabin near the mouth of Kluane River, March 2004. KFN Archives. EMPC. Paul Nadasdy Images #3. PHOTOGRAPHER PAUL NADASDY

> **Nature does good things. But you've got to protect it.**
>
> ANTERA (JOE BRUNEAU)

SANDY JOHNSON

(b. 1947)

There's a Lot Going On Here

My name was Sandra Bastin before I married. I was born and grew up in Victoria, B.C., in the late 1940s. My mother, Joan Honor Varley, was a war bride, and she came out to Canada from England after World War II. She was an interesting lady because she was totally deaf and she read lips. She didn't use sign language. None of us kids ever learned how to sign. She lost her hearing when she was 2 years old from scarlet fever. Her family had owned a hotel in London that was completely destroyed during a German bombing raid. They had to move to the country for the rest of the war.

facing Sandy Johnson, 2022. KFN Archives. EMPC Elders Portraits #53. PHOTOGRAPHER ALISTAIR MAITLAND

My dad, Aubrey Archibald Bastin, was born in England, too, but raised in B.C. His father was English, and his mother was from New Brunswick. Dad joined the Armored Division of the Canadian Army and went to England in 1939. He met my mother during the war, when he was stationed there waiting to go over to the continent to fight. They were married in 1943 before he left England. His unit was on a ship headed to Italy when it was sunk by German torpedoes. All the men were rescued, and he was taken back to England. By that time the war was mostly over, so he did not see action. He never really talked much about the war.

A RELIGIOUS CHILDHOOD

When the war ended, my father was sent back to Canada right away. My mother had to wait a couple of years before she came. She was a pretty fearless lady to do that. They settled in the interior of B.C. for quite a while because my dad worked as a surveyor. He surveyed electrical lines that were built throughout B.C. after the war. Once we were old enough to go to school, we moved back to Victoria and lived with my grandmother for a while before we found our own house.

We were three girls. I'm the oldest, and I have a sister Sydney, who is two years younger than me, and a baby sister, eight years younger, called Susan. Sometimes we lived with my father's mother, and other times she lived with us. She was a really old-fashioned Victorian lady. Her father, Ernest Purdy Fluelling, was an Anglican missionary who travelled to many different places including Hawaii and Puerto Rico. He wife died young, so he left his daughters, my grandma and my great-aunts, at All Hallows Anglican Boarding School in Yale, British Columbia. My grandma married an Anglican minister, Reverend John Bastin, who travelled to various parishes all over the Chilcotin region on horseback. Grannie B. was really well educated, but she was hard to get along with. I was a strong-willed teenager, and she was really strict. I wish that I had liked her better because she had lived in such interesting times. Now I wish I had been able to learn more from her.

My father was not at all interested in the Anglican Church. When I was in grade 3, I had a teacher who invited all of her students to come to Vacation Bible School. I was interested in it and went for several weeks one summer. When my parents came to our final celebration, my father was converted to this group.

It was a Canadian evangelical group called the Brethren, and my parents went into this new religious group wholeheartedly. That religion really shaped a lot of our childhood. I got out of it once I went to university. I remember having lots of arguments about that group and its beliefs with my father. Not with my mother, because she really wasn't able to talk well enough to debate issues like that back and forth.

In Victoria I went to Monterey and to Willows elementary schools first. Then we got a house near present-day Mayfair Mall, and I attended Quadra Elementary School. I went to Oak Bay High School. My sisters were sent to a Christian, one-room school, which was very strict and religious. To this day my sisters are not interested at all in religion, because almost every night of the week they had to attend some type of religious service. My dad and mom were really busy in that church, sometimes doing good community work such as visiting elderly people in nursing homes. They often took us along, and I can remember making corsages for Mother's Day and that sort of thing.

left Sandy Johnson's parents were married in England in 1943. KFN Archives. EMPC. Sandy Johnson Family Images #1. PHOTOGRAPHER UNKNOWN

facing top The whole community turned out for the wedding of Sandy and Uzi Tà (Robbie Johnson) at Burwash in 1969. KFN Archives. EMPC. Sandy Johnson Family Images #2. PHOTOGRAPHER UNKNOWN

facing bottom Robbie's grandmother Tsal KàJana (Copper Lily) and Sandy's Grannie Adela Bastin at Robbie and Sandy's wedding in Burwash. KFN Archives. EMPC. Sandy Johnson Family Images #3. PHOTOGRAPHER UNKNOWN

ADVENTURESOME TEEN

I went to UVic after graduating from high school. I had really wanted to become a doctor, but I gave that up pretty early on. I spent two years at UVic and then decided I wanted to travel. I worked for a year at Royal Jubilee Hospital as a Nurse's Aide. I must have been interested still in becoming a doctor at that point because the head nurse went out of her way to involve me in what was going on at the hospital. They let me sit in on their meetings, so it was pretty interesting. When I had enough money, I took off to Europe with a friend. We travelled for a while, and when we ran out of money, we settled down in Bilbao, Spain, to teach English for about ten months.

That was in 1967, the same year as the [Six-]Day War in the Middle East. My girlfriend met a guy then, and we had a falling out. I decided to keep travelling because I wanted to go to Italy and Greece. On the boat to Greece I lost my money and my passport. So I found a job cooking for an English man who had his boat moored in the harbour at Corfu. He arranged a ride for me on another boat, so I could get back to Italy and pick up a new passport in Rome.

I was very adventurous! I was travelling by myself for most of the year, leaving in September 1966 and returning home the following August. My friend and I reunited in Europe and came back to Canada together. Expo 67 was happening in Montreal, but I just wanted to get home. I have an aunt and uncle in Montreal, where we stayed overnight. The next day we got on the train and kept on going to Victoria.

I went back to UVic for another year. I needed a job for the summer of 1968 and went to a job fair at the university. Somebody gave me a copy of the *Mile Post*, and I sent resumés to all the places along the Alaska Highway. Burwash was the farthest away, and the lodge owners responded that I could work there. So I came here to work. I washed dishes, cleaned rooms, made beds, and did the laundry. I liked the Yukon right away, that's for sure.

TRAGEDY AND NEW BEGINNINGS

I met my first husband, Uzi Tà (Caribou Daddy, Robbie Johnson), that first summer in Burwash. He was a Kluane First Nation member. When we married, I got Status from him because in those days a white woman marrying a Native man would legally become a Status Indian. I didn't go back to school in Victoria that year. We stayed in the Yukon and moved to Whitehorse. I got a job as a housekeeper at the hospital. Robbie was going to the

above Robbie and Sandy Johnson's daughter, Chùsi (Robin), circa 1973. KFN Archives. EMPC. Sandy Johnson Family Images #4. PHOTOGRAPHER UNKNOWN

Vocational School, finishing his grade 12. We lived in the three-storey Log Skyscraper. I think we were on the middle floor, and we could feel the building shake when people walked up the stairs! We had many visitors from Burwash—non-stop!

We stayed in Whitehorse for a year, then we went to Victoria because I needed to finish my last two years of university. Robbie was starting classes at Camosun College. By that time I had decided I didn't want to be a doctor. I was doing a BA with a double major in English literature and biology, which really wouldn't be great for getting a job, but I liked them both so I continued.

Tragically Robbie drowned in a canoeing accident near Victoria in February 1971. We had a memorial down there for him, then we had to get his coffin on the plane to bring him home to the Yukon. I discovered about two weeks after he died that I was pregnant. I went back to Victoria and received my BA from UVic that spring. Robin was born in October 1971 in Victoria. I thought, "She's got to know her grandparents in the Yukon." I think if I hadn't been pregnant, I would have stayed in the south and who knows where I would've wound up. But I had this little girl, named Chùsi by Little Grace. I really wanted her to know her grandma Grace ghra (Little Grace) and her husband, Ts'adasha (Grandpa George John). So we came back to Burwash every summer.

I did a fifth year at UVic to get a teaching certificate. I did that as a single mom, which was tough. I wasn't able to get a teaching job up here right away. My first job was in the community called Owikeno [Wuikinuxv] on Rivers Inlet, B.C. It's a fly-in community, and they were crazy to hire me! The year before, the school went from being a two-teacher school to just one teacher because their enrollment went down by one kid. I had twenty-six K to 8 students in my first year of teaching. I didn't have a clue what I was doing! Those poor kids! I only stayed there for one year, and then I worked in Gold River on Vancouver Island for a couple of years.

I was bound and determined that I was going to come back here and live in Burwash. There was a school in Destruction Bay, and I applied for jobs there but was not accepted. I remember somebody from the Department of Education saying to me, "I suppose you're going to try and use your Indian Status to get a job with us." I moved back to the Yukon anyway in 1974.

I decided I was going to build a log cabin in Burwash. I had taken a log building course in Gold River, B.C. I had bought a piece of property beside the lot where my current house is located. This was prior to land claims, when you could actually buy a parcel of property, which I did for about $300. I had to get it surveyed, which didn't cost much. I thought, "We're going to try to build a house." I didn't know what I was doing, and so Robbie's cousin Mats'an Nats' ats'ulia (You Expect Something from Him, Joe Joe Johnson) helped me out with the construction.

Joe Joe and I got together later that year, in 1975. I had three more children with him: Gă lhêla (Luke) and our twins, Lasänmą (Katie) and Kayenà (Simon). We lived in that little log house with electricity but no running water or plumbing—just an outhouse.

It was a lot of work. I had a wringer washer, and we hauled water or ice from the lake to wash all those baby clothes!

Joe had gone to the Baptist Mission School in Whitehorse in the late 1940s. He left school early, after grade 8, and went to work right way. He came back to Burwash and worked for the Dicksons as a wrangler and a guide. Later he worked in B.C. as a logger, along with several of his cousins. He came home in the early 1970s to spend time with his father, Moose Johnson. [Joe] was a hunting guide and trapper and later became Chief of Kluane Tribal Council. Land claims had started in 1973, and he was involved right from the beginning.

BUCKING THE SYSTEM

I finally did get a job at the school in D-Bay but only worked for one year there. Then we decided to start our own school here in Burwash. In those days we could not get Native language or any other cultural programs taught in the school at D-Bay. Kluane First Nation parents staged a protest and took all their kids out of the school. I really believe that because they did that and said, "We're going to do this ourselves," it scared Yukon Government enough to start looking at First Nations programming.

The idea for the Kêts'á dan' kų, our community school, came from several parents in Burwash. Gùdia Johnson and her kids were living across the lake. She had been homeschooling them, so it gave the rest of the community the idea that we could educate our kids too. Mary Easterson was involved as a driving force from the very start. I think Daniel Tlen was here at the time too. It was very difficult because it required so many people. We didn't really have enough people to do all the work, because land claims were happening and those negotiations were very demanding as well for our small community.

We went ahead and did it without any YTG help at first. It certainly caused alarm in the Education Department! We raised our own money. We had a walkathon to Whitehorse, bake sales, hockey pools, and many other fundraisers. I can remember Joe and I going to Yukon Indian Days down at Brooks Brook with one hundred boiled gophers wrapped in tinfoil to sell to people! We did so many things; that's how we made money. Everybody got involved.

For the first year our school was in a log building that had been built as a community hall. After that we moved further down the road to some housing units that were converted for the school.

top Mats'an Nats' ats'ulia (You Expect Something from Him, Joe Joe Johnson) taking daughter Robin Johnson out on the lake with dog team, circa 1975. KFN Archives. EMPC. Sandy Johnson Family Images #5. PHOTOGRAPHER SANDY JOHNSON

bottom Chùsi (Robin), twins Kayenà (Simon's name given by his aunt Tùlhàsèn—Lena Johnson) and Lasänmą (Katie), and Gä lhêla (Moose Johnson's namesake, Luke) Johnson camping out on the land in a wall tent north of Burwash Creek, circa 1980. KFN Archives. EMPC. Sandy Johnson Family Images #6. PHOTOGRAPHER SANDY JOHNSON

We had to plan our own curriculum: myself, Gùdia, and Mary. Some of the other parents were involved too. I was hired as a teacher and Mary Easterson, who also had her teaching degree. It was scary! We had enough students for two classes, so I think we probably had about fifteen kids because we also had some children from White River First Nation. That was before the split between KFN and White River. We didn't run for very long, just four or five years. When the school closed, everybody here was really sad. I felt really bad, but it was just so hard to keep it going.

Getting the building fixed up so that it was meeting the building code was not really possible, but there was always water and washrooms. You can't have a school with kids going to an outhouse. You've got to have running water, and that was sometimes a problem because it would freeze up in the cold winters. It was hard to find enough people for maintenance and to clean at night. Just to keep everything going was hard. It was also really hard work to keep everybody happy.

Mary and I taught together. We only ever had two teachers at a time. We did hire some people from Outside. I didn't work the year when I had my twins. We had Peter Stewart and Mary Easterson that year. We only had two rooms for K to 8. Many of our students have done really well. Donalda is a lawyer. Juniper works in finance. Robin, my daughter, has worked in government and now at the university. Math'ieya and Diyet both have had great successes. Luke and Geordan went to university.

The big thing was that we were home in Burwash and it was so nice to be there. For gym lots of community people would come out, and we'd play soccer or baseball on the field next to the school. Elders came into the school every day, and we finally had our Native language classes!

YTG came on board pretty quickly with some funding and other logistical supports. I really believe they thought, "We don't want this to get too far out of hand." We never knew when somebody from the department was going to show up, and we had to toe the line as long as they were funding some things. We had to make sure we covered all the basics, then we could do the cultural programs we wanted to do. It was somewhat limiting because the Yukon used the B.C. curriculum and YTG supplied our textbooks. When the Clinton Creek mine and townsite closed down, we got boxes and boxes of supplies and equipment from there.

I had four kids and I was teaching full time! I can remember getting up really early in the morning when everybody was still asleep, coming here to work, getting everything ready for class, then going home and getting my kids out of bed. It was pretty crazy. Joe was not always the most reliable in those days, because he was away a lot. He was the Chief then and often in Ottawa or Whitehorse for meetings.

Well, we all did that then. We looked after kids and worked full time with minimal services in our small log homes.

When the YTG superintendents came through, the D-Bay teachers would phone and say, "They're on their way!" It was our early warning system. Half the time we weren't ready anyway when they came. We always felt we were really under scrutiny. When we finally shut down the school, I felt it was my fault. I had sent Robin out to school for a year with my sister for grade 9. It did not go well, so I knew I had to bring her home and move to the Junction for her to go to high school. I put in for a transfer, and so me and all four of my kids left. Then the government said, "There aren't enough kids left for the Burwash school."

KFN still want a school in Burwash. It's something that comes up at every General Assembly. We're still trying to get a school built here, even though we have a small number of children. Actually there's no children in Burwash anymore. All of the children now live in Destruction Bay or at Copper Joe subdivision. It was hard then, and it still is the same problem: Once you've got a child who is in grade 8 or 9, you have to move. Sometimes I wonder how on Earth we ever did all those things! KFN are persistent. These days we have built a windmill to generate electrical power and many other things. We are pretty progressive here and determined!

THE LAND CLAIMS YEARS WERE VERY BUSY

Joe was Chief of KFN for many, many years, right through the land claims process. The kids and I moved to Haines Junction around '84 or '85, but we came home every weekend. I thought that he was going to move down there, but he never did, so we just went back and forth all the time. He was not always Chief, but he was always working in some way on land claims as a negotiator. He was gone a lot: to Ottawa, Vancouver, Whitehorse. Sometimes they had meetings here in Burwash too. I was home looking after the kids. It was a very, very busy time.

I remember when Kluane First Nation signed their agreements, the leaders made sure that they recognized all of the people that had worked on this claim from YTG, Canada, and the First Nation. Everybody came to this big party. I said, "Holy smokes! Look at all those YG and federal people compared to the tiny KFN group." There was only a handful of people from here, and they had to do everything. They had one lawyer, Dave Joe, but the other side was formidable. I don't know how they did it to keep going back every day and trying to argue over this or that, bargain over one or both sides of a creek and so many other details.

Robin definitely remembers that time. I don't. I don't know where I was half the time, because I was so busy. Robin remembers clearly Elijah Smith coming to our house and Dave Joe; they'd be talking about land claims. I think Joe felt that it was worth giving up something to get something, because First Nations people had nothing before. Something was better than nothing. I don't know if he would be disappointed with the situation today or not. I think he felt they were getting a lot more control and power than they have in actual fact. There's some power but in terms of land and what can be done with it, whether or not we can stop a mine or other issues. I don't know. I think he would still say something is better than nothing because that's what he felt they had before—nothing.

People's attitudes were so racist back in the 70s and 80s, and some people are still like that even today. When my first husband, Robbie, and I would walk down the street in Whitehorse, people would yell at us, "What are you doing with that?" Joe and I would sometimes try to rent a

facing Big sister Robin with twins Simon and Katie on toboggan and Luke behind at Burwash, circa 1982. KFN Archives. EMPC. Sandy Johnson Family Images #7. PHOTOGRAPHER SANDY JOHNSON

above Joe Joe and Sandy Johnson in Venice, circa 2008. KFN Archives. EMPC. Sandy Johnson Family Images #8. PHOTOGRAPHER UNKNOWN

facing top left Joe Joe Johnson leading a guided wilderness cultural camping trip with his horses near Cultus Bay, circa 2007. KFN Archives. EMPC. Sandy Johnson Family Images #9. PHOTOGRAPHER UNKNOWN

facing top right Sandy and Joe Joe out for a walk in the fall near Cultus Bay, circa 2008. KFN Archives. EMPC. Sandy Johnson Family Images #10. PHOTOGRAPHER UNKNOWN

hotel room in Whitehorse. If he went in, the clerk would often say, "No, there's no room," but I could go in right afterwards and have no problem getting a room. That happened often. I think that's partly why people started going to the Yukon Inn because it was the first place that welcomed Native people. They didn't have a colour bar. It was really, really terrible and annoying. Joe used to get very impatient in a restaurant. He was not willing to wait for very long, because often they would just ignore him at restaurants, hoping that he would give up and go. He could get quite miffed by that. It's still happening, but it's just gone underground. Today Native people have money to spend, and that's making a huge difference. I look at something like the Yukon Native Hockey Tournament, which is a big economic boost to Whitehorse. It's only in the last few years that it's been given real recognition for its contributions.

After the passing of the 1993 UFA we began to see a difference. It took a long time for non–First Nation people in the territory to really get on board with land claims and how to live with it. Maybe it didn't feel so much like things were changing in Burwash or in the Junction. When I first went to work in the Junction, Champagne and Aishihik First Nations had already signed their agreements. I lived on Rainbow Street, and there was very little interaction between the people in CAFN (Champagne and Aishihik First Nations) and the rest of the Junction. White kids did not go and play over there. I remember trying to take my class to the CAFN office on a field trip, and it was a big deal for some non–First Nations people. They weren't sure if their kids were going to be safe going there.

GRATEFUL FOR GOOD TIMES

I retired from teaching in Haines Junction in 2007. Simon had graduated from high school, and I thought, "This is ridiculous, kicking around here by myself." Joe was still in Burwash, so I came back here. He was often gone a lot working on various boards and committees, especially those established under the UFA like the Fish and Wildlife Management Board and the Yukon Historic Resources Board. He liked meeting with people and found that work interesting.

We were able to spend a lot of time together on the land during those years, trapping and travelling, looking after our horses, staying at our cabins at Big Arm and Cultus Bay. We ran culture horse camps for Skookum Jim Friendship Centre at Cultus Bay. We had a small guiding company called Donjek Wilderness Tours that took visitors out on horseback to Burwash Uplands. We travelled in Europe, to Mexico, the United States, went camping in Hawaii and on several cruises. Joe loved meeting new people, and people enjoyed hearing his stories about his life in the Yukon. I am grateful we had those good times before Joe became ill in 2009.

I have served on the Rec Board here, and we've done many fun projects. We organized crib tournaments, a moose stew cook-off once a year, and other events in the community. I worked at the Library too. There are not very many boards for me to join, because you have to be a KFN citizen to be on most of them. Kluane First Nation asked me to sit on the Dän Keyi Renewable Resources Council. I don't know very much about it, but it's interesting, that's for sure.

I organized a community greenhouse program for Burwash, and we've got two greenhouses out here now. One belongs to the daycare and the day camp in the summer, so I work with kids on that. I haven't found anybody who will take it over when I move to town. People get to eat the food, but there's not a lot of participation. The kids go out to work in it. We have one of Bob Sharp's super green construction greenhouses out here now, and the KFN Archivist, Adam Hicks, looks after that in the summer. The kids from daycare always take some veggies home with them, and they go to the KFN offices or to Elders' homes and give the food to them. We have lettuce, kale, zucchinis, cucumbers, tomatoes, and green onions in there. We've grown pumpkins too. Adam grew turnips this year. Somebody said, "You know, I don't eat that kind of green stuff. I eat potatoes, carrots, and turnips." I really wish we had that kind of root garden and there is a place where we could do it; maybe next year.

We're pretty busy with crafts too. Wednesday night started off as a women's sewing group. We made quilts and other projects. Then the Heritage Department took it over, and for the last two years they've done moccasins, slippers, high-top moccasins, packsacks, drum covers, mitts, gauntlet mitts, vests, and all kinds of things like that. There's only about 80 people in Burwash now, probably it's half KFN and half non-First Nations people. The Heritage Department has always been really inclusive, and if there's somebody that works in KFN who wants to come out and learn how to make moccasins, great!

We have a ball diamond, a skating rink, and a beautiful gym beside it. We always have the problem of not having enough capacity to keep things like that going. There are just not enough people to do everything. A lot of people here are over 65 now.

above Sandy volunteers as a gardener to grow fresh greens in summer with Burwash kids in greenhouses built by Kluane First Nation behind Jacquot Hall. Old Copper Joe's cabin is in the foreground, one of the few remaining original log buildings in the community. KFN Archives. EMPC. Sandy Johnson Family Images #13 PHOTOGRAPHER LINDA JOHNSON

DEALING WITH LOSS AND CHANGE

Joe died in 2010. At that time he was very worried that Burwash was going to turn into a community of old people. He really wanted KFN to turn its attention to economic development and felt that was pretty important. I don't think he felt that he could do the work, but it needed to be done. KFN needs to create economic opportunities so people have work options besides the ones at KFN. Gradually that is happening. I think he'd be quite happy with the two KFN development corporations: Kluane Dana Shäw Corporation, which manages KFN's investment capital; and the Kluane Community Development Limited Partnership, which is responsible for creating jobs through operating KFN-owned businesses like the store and the gas bar, mine services, and other related activities.

The Big Nickel or Wellgreen mine could bring some more promising developments in future. Some people worry about mine development, but it's provided many KFN people with employment. It will bring KFN young people back here in time, mostly in the summer at first. We had a really nice summer in 2017 when four young adults, none of whom grew up here, came back and worked on mine-related projects. It was really nice. Nice for them and nice for older people in Burwash. When you think about it, there are a lot of high achievers from Burwash—they are just somewhere else right now!

It's hard to bring young people back to live in a small community. Families have pushed hard for a school in Burwash to keep their kids here all the way through high school. In the end it's still hard to keep them here. When kids get to be 14 years old, they want to go to Whitehorse or to Junction, where there's more young people. They want to be anywhere but here, so it's hard.

I'm busy here in the summers, but I live in Whitehorse now in the winters. Luke is here and working on language projects. My girls are in Whitehorse. Simon is the only one that's a long ways away, down on Vancouver Island. Services for seniors are limited in Burwash. There's a nursing station in Destruction Bay. We have KFN health and social workers here, which is a great service. I have somebody who helps me clean and others to help with wood and heavy chores I can't do anymore. So that's good, but if somebody gets sick here, that becomes problematic. It's really hard. When Joe was ill, I was able to keep him here at home with help from the nurse from Destruction Bay. He didn't require very much help until pretty close to the end. He just wanted to be here at home in Burwash.

I have seen a lot of change over the five decades I have lived here. What keeps me here has something to do with the physical environment—the mountains and the lake. We still have our cabin at Cultus Bay, but I find that very hard to go there since Joe passed away. I don't have anybody to go out in the winter with me anymore. We always did lots together. We were out all the time on the land. I really enjoyed that,

but I never got good enough at doing those things to feel confident to go by myself. I go to the cabin in the summer by myself, but it's not as much fun, that's for sure. Sometimes I think, "Why do you stay?"

When I first came to Burwash, I think the attraction was in finding a community where everybody looked after everybody else's kids. Men played with the kids. Everybody played with the babies. I hadn't come from that in my family at all. So that was part of the attraction, but also the scenery and being out in the bush. I liked being able to produce our own food too. Joe did the hunting, and I did the growing. I'm not much of a fish person, but he loved fishing and we ate fish often. The community was a little bit bigger then, probably about 120 people, and the lodge was still operating.

I had to learn to be less social and to entertain myself here in such a small community. Land claims was all consuming for many people for so many years. I heard somebody say that the striving for that or trying to catch it was way more fun than when you finally got it. Now it's a different kind of work for implementation, much less exciting.

When Joe was growing up, the kids here were more carefree and they could go anywhere. They would go down to the Duke Meadow by themselves and all over. Even my kids—they didn't go that far on their own, but they certainly were free to go wherever they wanted around here, whereas now people don't let their kids out the door alone. It's different now, for sure.

We built a playground here many years ago, and when we expanded the Jacquot Building, we had to take it down. We had to move it, but we couldn't move it without a professional playground technician. So we had to raise money to get a new playground, and we decided to put it up at Copper Joe subdivision because that's where the kids are living these days. We still need one here, too, when we have Potlatches and for staff who have kids at the daycare, so we have a small one here beside the Jacquot Building. Our daycare is small, but in the summer it gets bigger when more people come home. We've got great daycare workers.

It's wonderful that we've got our store going now in Burwash, with takeout food, basic groceries, and the self-serve gas station—all part of the KFN development corporation's economic development projects. We're all reaping the benefits. Yes, there's a lot going on here, it's true!

facing Sandy and Joe Joe with first-born grandson Nàdaya (named after Old Man Johnson), son of Luke Johnson, circa 2004. KFN Archives. EMPC. Sandy Johnson Family Images #11. PHOTOGRAPHER UNKNOWN

above Sandy Johnson with her children, their partners, grandchildren, nieces, and nephews, circa 2016. KFN Archives. EMPC. Sandy Johnson Family Images #12. PHOTOGRAPHER UNKNOWN

I liked being able to produce our own food too.

SANDY JOHNSON

DAVID DUBOIS

(1949–2021)

Kluane—Beautiful Land, Beautiful People

I was born in Ottawa on June 5, 1949, in the Grace Hospital. We moved to a farm in Low, Quebec, in 1956. Low is a little Irish community. My grandson's name is Liam, and my mom's an O'Neil. My dad's a Frenchman. Dubois. I lived there from the age of 9 to about 15. I left home young and moved to the city, to Ottawa. From then on I pretty much travelled back and forth across Canada and the States until I came up here. This is the longest I've ever been anywhere for one period of time—twenty-seven years in one place. Here.

facing David Dubois, 2017. KFN Archives. EMPC Elders Portraits #54. PHOTOGRAPHER ALISTAIR MAITLAND

RESTLESS YOUTH

We lived on a farm. I worked like a dog as a kid, so at 15 I had enough of it. I wish I had've stayed. I loved that place. It's as beautiful as here. Our farm is right on the Gatineau River and Manitou Lake, God's Lake, is right behind us. It was beautiful country. I didn't mind working; I really didn't mind farming. It was just a small farm, and we produced cream. We used to have thirty-five cows. We only milked fifteen of them. My dad milked eight, I milked seven, all by hand of course—morning and night. It was a good life, just a lot of hard work. I saw a counsellor up here for a while, and he said, "That was slave labour." No payment for me but I took care of them well. My daughter, before she had the baby, said, "Dad, what if I go into labour on the way to town?" I said, "Don't worry. I've birthed a lot of calves." We had to know how to do it. Now I am a grandfather to Liam David Joseph Dubois. Joseph is after Grandpa Joe Bruneau, who is his great-grandfather on his mom's side.

After I left home, I spent a couple of years in Ottawa and then I took a train out west. Isn't that what everybody does? Head west, young man? I headed west and made it to Chateau Lake Louise in Alberta. I worked there for a summer making metal ornamentals for houses. Then I worked building highways. Must've wanted to be a highway builder, you know. I always played with trucks and bulldozers on the farm and made little roads all over the place. That was my thing.

At Hotel Lake Louise I spent a summer working as a plumber even though I didn't know anything about plumbing. I very quickly gassed myself with chlorine, and they took me off that job. I ended up working in the laundry, and that was pretty much it for the summer. There were a lot of college students there for the summer, so it was a party place and we had a lot of fun.

Then I headed back east and joined the army in '68. I spent several months there, and then I asked them to let me go. I did basic training in Shilo, Manitoba. My group of engineers was sent to Chilliwack, B.C. I liked playing with dynamite so I did learn that, but it wasn't for me. I was an excellent soldier. In Shilo I did very well. I got a lot of congratulations. Only problem was, when we graduated, the Captain proposed a toast to me at our dinner and said, "I hope I never see you again." Simply because I had a good ability with people and so the troop listened more to me than the authority figures!

I was the Pied Piper, and that followed me all the way through. When I wanted to get out, they kept saying, "Well, you have great leadership qualities." Yes, I do, but that was not my thing. I just did it because I was bored. I got out of there in July '68.

I went to work for a company in Ottawa called The Treble Clef, and I worked in every one of their music stores. After the first year I became a manager. I worked the Rideau Street store first. Then at Carlingwood Shopping Centre, then the one way out on Bank Street. At that same time I got into a lot of not good stuff.

Up in Low some friends and I started a little rock band, and we called ourselves The Prowlers. I was the lead singer, front man. Terrified but I was still the front man. That only lasted for about a year, because then I hit the road again. I was living out on Vancouver Island, along the coast in a little cabin. The Treble Clef main store on Sparks Street Mall was going down the drain. So they sent one of the supervisors, who was a good friend of mine, out to find me and bring me back. I lasted for about a year and got it straightened out, but I burnt out. That was the last time I ever worked for them.

I played guitar and sang. I sing all the time around here. People here say, "If Doobie's around the bank and the post office and he's not singing, then be careful: he's gonna be yelling." I have a very wonderful greeting.

After that period I went to Calgary. I'd manage a store, but I always had this ability to burn out. I just worked too hard. I wasn't able to delegate authority very well. That was my problem. I worked off and on for Treble Clef, and I used to go back and forth across Canada. I'd wear out my welcome, and I'd go out to the West Coast. Usually Vancouver Island. And then go back East.

I became a mess, a really bad mess, which lasted for twelve years. I worked, because I was one of those who was capable of working still. Seeing as I managed the place, I had to be there on time and I had to close it up. I always managed to work until I'd burn out, and then I wouldn't; I'd just party on. Then I couldn't go on any longer. I just couldn't keep going. I was 33 and I was finished. I wasn't capable of anything anymore. I ended up in Calgary in a treatment facility. I was so afraid to leave it, I stayed for nine months. I was so afraid of the world because I just didn't know it anymore.

I left there after nine months and started a brand new world of my own making. That is pretty much what happened. There's so many things from my very young age that are just too much to talk about. How do you tell a life story in minutes? You don't; it just goes on and on. And that's the whole thing about it. I was writing the book, and as I kept writing, of course time was passing. I realized, "This'll never end. This is an ongoing book. That's what it is: it's an ongoing story, an ongoing book."

A YUKON FANTASY

The Yukon was somewhere I always wanted to go. It was a fantasy in my mind: "The Yukon." But in those days I thought it was so empty. In my mind it was just completely empty of people, and I needed lots of people to live the life I was living. I got injured on a job in construction, and I got put on Workers' Compensation. I wanted to go into childcare work because I was working towards a degree in psychiatry. Of course any nutcase coming out of that type of a life wants to help. So I wanted to help. But, for some reason, the Workers Comp people said, "No, we're gonna put you in accounting." The Advisor at Algonquin College said, "What're they doing? That's not where you belong." They had done tests with me. I said, "I know, but they wanna give me $2,000 a month. And so I'll take it." The profs in the business school kept saying, "What are you doing here?" I said, "I have no idea, but they keep giving me money, so I'll come." Just recently I was going through some of my old papers, and I found my final exam marks. I ended up with a B-plus overall. So that was pretty good for a guy who had no interest. I finished school and I needed a holiday,

facing David as a young schoolboy in Low, Quebec, circa 1957. KFN Archives. EMPC. David Dubois Family Images #1. PHOTOGRAPHER UNKNOWN

above Flowers are everywhere in summer in Asi Keyi (Grandfather's Country). KFN Archives. EMPC Landscape Images #28. PHOTOGRAPHER ROBERT POSTMA

so it was the Yukon. And I fell in love, probably starting around Dawson Creek.

I drove. I had a little mattress in the back of my pickup, and I slept in there. Had a little cooking stove. I took my time. I don't even think I knew where I was going. I just wanted to make it to the Yukon. I wasn't coming to stay, that's for sure. Like that old story I wasn't coming to stay here; I just wanted to see it. I didn't bring anything. Some clothes and that was it, pretty much. I think I wanted to go to Dawson actually because I thought there was something about Dawson. But I got to Whitehorse, and I met a few people. I met one fellow who I became really good friends with, and he says, "There's an old guy up the highway. You gotta meet him." So we headed up the highway to meet this old guy named Scully. Used to make burl bowls up here.

Well, he's the granddad of burl bowl making in this neck of the woods. I met him. And when I walked in his shop, I had the most amazing thing happen. I walked in his shop, and it was dim in there, very dull, but all of a sudden it was like a million-watt light bulb going off! The first thought I had, "Oh God, I wish I had known about this at the age of 23." I immediately saw a whole different life than I had lived. Scully was a pretty interesting character. He was definitely a character.

I headed back to Whitehorse, and I was gonna go work for that woman just outside of Whitehorse, at Fish Lake, who had a riding business. I went up to see her because she wanted a bookkeeper. That was too freaky for me so I left. I thought, "I want to do this bowl thing." So I went up to 1118, and I said to Scully, "Could I be your apprentice?" He said, "Dude, just do it." So I watched him, and I started to just do it.

That was it. That was the beginning, in 1990. That was up there on the old highway where it used to go right down by the river and by Kluane Lake. Anytime I'd come into town, I'd drive down that way. As soon as you leave 1118, when you go down by the river, I'd burst into tears. It was so beautiful. I just fell in love again, just like when my daughter was born. I fell in love. Can't leave her, can't leave here.

I was very naive and ignorant of what was going on here. I didn't have a clue about First Nations people. My dad's great-grandmother was Ojibway, but he never talked about it. He kept that hidden from us all, for whatever his reasons were. He was a bad drunk. Might have had something to do with it. I said, "I'll never be like him," and then I became way worse than he ever did.

I was in awe here. The first two people that I met were Elders. I remember them coming to Scully's, because Scully knew everybody around here. I saw these two Indian ladies, Jessie Joe and Jessie Johnson. I'm a pretty talkative person, and once I get going, it's pretty hard to shut me up. When they came in, I pretty much just looked at them because this was something totally different. They giggled. They giggled a lot. I fell in love with Jessie Johnson. I married her granddaughter. I still don't understand it through all this time. When I first came here, I thought I knew some stuff. Over the years I learned I knew nothing about First Nations ways, their traditions, their knowledge. I accept it now. And I'm allowed to be here. I'm allowed to be in the community; people accept me. Even when they don't, they still accept me. I get along. I get along with everybody.

I stayed there at Scully's for four years, and then I moved down here to Burwash where the garage was, just above the museum. My friend who brought me up to Scully's moved into that place and invited me to come start a burl shop. We called it Burlbilly Hill. I spent four years up there on the hill with Obie, and then we had a falling out. I moved down to D-Bay. At Destruction Bay Lodge I had a little shop there, making bowls all the time. Oh, it was wonderful. I just loved doing it. I made a pretty good living at it, but at the end of the season I never had any money. I had to go from October to the next April because my business was selling to tourists.

In those days the bowls were cheap, so cheap. We'd sell a little bowl for $15 or $20 that are now selling for $80 to $100. The bigger bowls that now sell for a couple of hundred dollars, we were selling them for $50 or $60. There's a young fella I met a few years ago. The second year he was here he came to me and said, "Would you show me how to make bowls?" I could see some enthusiasm in him, and I said sure. So I showed him how I do it, which is pretty much what Scully showed me. Within a year he was a great bowl maker. I sold my tools to him because I just needed a change from the bowl making thing.

facing Dubie (David Dubois), as he was nicknamed and known by all in Burwash, took up burl bowl making and carving when he first landed in Burwash, coached by Scully, the famous burl master himself. KFN Archives. EMPC. David Dubois Family Images #2 PHOTOGRAPHER UNKNOWN

above David at his burl-manufacturing site, Burlbilly Hill, at Burwash. KFN Archives. EMPC. David Dubois Family Images #5 PHOTOGRAPHER UNKNOWN

* "B.O.A.L.S."

BUMP ON A LOG SHAPES

BY DUBIE

BLACK SPRUCE BURL BOWLS

Black Spruce are predominantly from Central British Columbia, northwestern Alberta, northwest Yukon and Alaska.

A burl in the dictionary is defined as a knot i.e., a burl in a rope, in hair.

University of British Columbia defines a Spruce burl as starting out from any irritation to the tree such as fungi-bactéria-a bump, a scratch, bugs, etc. (in humans, our body sends healing to say a scratch and when healed quits sending) the tree sends extra sap (healant) to the irritation, but for nature's own reasons doesn't quit after the wound is healed. So with this over abundance of healant creates a growth or burl. Because I find trees with burls mostly in small patches I tend to think they are hereditary maybe a sub species of Black Spruce.

We quite often walk miles thru the forest and never spot a burl and when we see one there is always more.

Many types of trees do produce burls but none that I know of in the same manner of Black Spruce trees such as Birch and Maple may grow from 1-5 on a tree. Black Spruce may grow as many as 100 from the size of your finger nail to 3 feet all on the same tree.

We choose trees that have been dead for up to 50 years because the wood is dried naturally and the finished bowl should not crack. Green to semi-green woods are prone to crack when made into a thin sided bowl.

I use an electric chain saw to carve out most of wood when making a bowl.

I boil the partly finished bowl to remove the bark from the outside and retain bug marks the Spruce bug larvae has created. Then a rotary rasp is used in a drill press to bring the bowl to a proper thickness, followed by a rotary sander to smooth it. A coat of new clear Epoxy is then applied, let to dry for 48 hours. Any cracks or blemishes are patched with a mixture of sawdust and Epoxy. The bowl is sanded one more time and dipped in Epoxy once more (hope no bugs or dust get on it) and finale.

"The joy is in the journey"

Dubie

BEING A DAD

My daughter, Pascale, was born in 1999. Her mother is Janice Dickson. I met Janice when I first came to the Yukon. She was a young girl then. I was 42 or 43 and she was 21. There was a bar up at 1118. I didn't drink, but I used to go there every night, hang around, and talk. This pretty young girl came in. Little did I know that so many years later, I would marry her, we would have a child and now a grandchild. You know, I'm only 70 years old, so who knows—maybe a great-grandchild someday.

I worked for KFN in construction for a few years and then as the janitor. In 2005 I had a little shack down in D-Bay, and Pascale moved in with me to go to school there. Then we moved into the old daycare for a year. Next we moved into Jessie Joe's old house out in Copper Joe subdivision. That's where Pascale and I ended up.

I can't hunt anymore. I can hardly walk. My hips are shot. I used to go out, but I didn't hunt. I had an experience when I was a kid on the farm and I used to go hunting with my dad. I went out early one evening by myself. I hid and waited for the deer to come out. This deer came out. It was a doe and she come out of the bush and I just raised my rifle and was lining up. Then this little thing all wobbly came out, and that was it. I couldn't do it anymore. I couldn't shoot. I never had a desire to shoot again.

I used to love fishing. I can't cast. I'm afraid of water, so I didn't have a boat. Oh, I'm even afraid when there's 5 feet of ice. Crazy! I used to go out on the land back many years ago. I used to go into the back country a lot. I loved it on the other side of those mountains there—it's just beautiful back in there. I did a lot of running around in the bush. With the burl business initially I got my own. Then as time went on, it got pretty busy, so I didn't. The best part was going out and getting it, but I had to make that money because now I had a wife and a kid so I had to find cash. So I just started to make things, and I bought burls from different people.

Scully initially—any trees you'd see with the burls sliced off, that was Scully. That was back in the 80s when he first came out here. They still are prevalent around here, even though they've been harvested for over thirty years or more.

The lodge was operating then. The old band office was really small. The place they use for Chief and Council now was the store and post office. And it's still there. I'm glad they kept it.

STRAIGHT-TALKING MAN

In the early years of land claims I'd come down here to quite a few activities, and Janice was part of the signing of the agreement. People didn't talk about it a lot. It was as though people weren't really sure that they wanted it, because there was something not right about it. That's what I felt too. It's kinda bizarre that the government is giving back the land to the people that rightly belongs to them. It still upsets me immensely. I think *O Canada* should go, "Our home and Natives' land," not the way they sing it, because it's Natives' land. So that part was kinda strange to me. It just seemed wrong, still seems wrong.

I don't know if it's a benefit. I don't know if taking on the ways of the federal government is good for the people. I think there's something wrong with it too. I work for the bank now and the post office, and the bank tells me that I can't cash KFN's cheques unless people have an account with our bank. I said, "Wait a minute. You take government cheques. I have to cash those. Doesn't matter if they have an account with us or not. KFN is self-governing, so they're a government and you're telling me I can't cash their cheques. Are you discriminating? You're making a difference in their governments? I cash Yukon Government's, I cash federal government's, but I can't cash KFN's?" So I do. They stopped fighting with me, so I just do it.

It's all capitalism. They want to get their monies, so they're telling me. I said, "All the Elders have bank accounts. It may not be with your bank, but I'm not going to tell them that I'm not going to cash their cheque unless they open an account with us so we can take their $10 a month. I'm not going to do that." So a couple of times they gave me a hard time about it. I kept doing it, and today they don't even talk to me about it anymore. I tried to explain to them that this is Kluane First Nation. It's a little village, and there may be sixty people here during the winter. I said, "If we have any problems here, with anything, I know where everybody lives." I said, "Let me handle it." They said, "David, it's not how Toronto wants it." I said, "I don't care." The manager said, "Well, what if an auditor from the main branch back in Ontario comes out there?" I said, "And says what?" "Well, lets you know that you're not doing things the way they want it done." I said, "I tell him to go to . . .!"

Burwash has totally changed since I arrived. There were a lot of little old cabins here when I first came around. Then they started building new homes, like Jessie Joe's house. They started building along here, and they removed the old cabins. This Jacquot Building has totally changed too. It was so much smaller. The biggest change I've noticed is we're running out of Elders. We really are running out of Elders.

facing Dubie's business card and promotional information for his burl business. KFN Archives. EMPC. David Dubois Family Images #4 and #5. PHOTOGRAPHER UNKNOWN

above Dubie in characteristic ball cap, circa 2020. KFN Archives. EMPC. David Dubois Family Images #6. PHOTOGRAPHER UNKNOWN

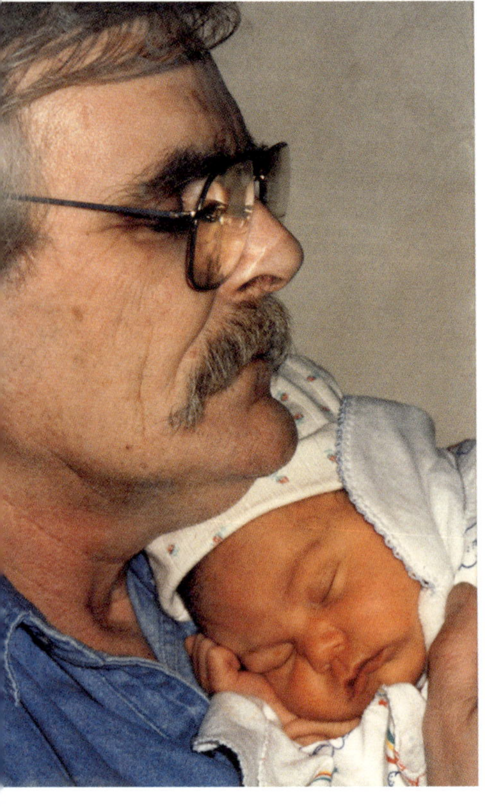

There's only a few left here. I wasn't that old when I first came here, and the young people who were kids then were beautiful. Now I see they're all grown up, with families of their own. A lot of the younger guys are becoming Elders now. But the elder Elders, not many are left: just Agnes Johnson, Peter Johnson, Lena, and a few more.

I hope this area doesn't develop. I like it the way it is. The only opportunities that anybody ever really talks about is the Wellgreen mine, which would be the ruination of this community. It may be a benefit financially in some way. I'm anti-capitalism, so I don't like the idea of things like that taking over, because it changes everybody's mind. Not for the better, I think.

I always think of the term self-supporting through our own contributions. I used to go to AA, and that was their thing. We are self-supporting through our own contributions. Nobody's going to have control over us by contributing to us. I see how right that is. It's like that influence of the money-lenders controls the people. I think if we're self-governing here, then let us govern. Our way. To hell with their way. We do what we have to do to get what we have to get in the game, the capitalism game. But otherwise take care of our people.

I despise what the feds have done to the First Nations people forever. I really do think it's wrong. And I think people have to take a stand like Gerald Dickson did. I remember one time he wanted to block the highway. He said, "This is our land," and he's right. It's KFN's land. You wanna pass our land, you get our permission. You don't just bulldoze your way through. And that's what went on. That was part of that self-governing thing that I didn't like. I just felt there was something not right. People made a choice, and that's for the KFN people to decide. That's their thing, not mine. So I stand outside and I run all this through my head, and when I get an opportunity, I talk with people about how I see things. Don't get very many answers.

The house where my daughter lives now was built by Bobby Dickson, who is the Chief now. I did the drywall in that place in '96. I didn't want to do construction anymore, but I just did it for Bobby. I had first met Bobby and a couple of his friends stuck up there at 1118. It was 37 below and Bobby said, "We need a drive back to Burwash." This is January sometime. I said, "Oh man, it's 37 below. I don't know because my truck's not plugged in." Anyway somehow it started. The four of us packed into the cab and went down the highway, and it was all humour all the way! These guys were laughing about me, the crazy white man, coming out at 37 below. Anyway we made it back, and that was another connection with the community.

Bobby is my brother-in-law also, so he's always been there for me. I've gone to him on occasion with issues I've had in the community and things that I didn't like that were going on. So in that way I have a voice here. I have a very loud voice, and I'm not afraid to share my ideas, no matter what the consequences. I think I've put myself in some bad situations sometimes, but I think it's important to state it as I see it. I think people know that about me. I'm going to be straight with them. I'm not going to try to mess them around. Hopefully they come back at me straight; that's all I ask.

TIME FOR MYSELF

I'll die here unless they run me out of town. I am semi-retired and I enjoy what I do. I'm a very introverted person. I like being at home. I read a lot. I fight with the TV, because I watch the news all the time. I read, and I write a bit. So when I come out to the post office and the bank, I get to interact a lot. It's just three days a week. It's plenty. There are jobs I've been offered here, but they're full time and I don't want to do the full-time thing anymore. I need time for myself.

I think the Kluane world is fantastic the way it is. The thing is, more is going to happen. I think partially because it has to happen. Which is kinda sad. You always hear about the dream of going back to the land, but nobody's gonna go back to the land. It's been too long. It's the same thing with Ancestral Knowledge. Nobody ever talks to me about Ancestral Knowledge. I've always been curious about the spirituality of Southern Tutchone people. It's secretive. Nobody will talk to me about it.

I don't know what spirituality means, really, to anybody. I think it's an individual thing, and it's so important to have that in our lives, not in the traditional religions. I'm anti-traditional. When my life turned around, I had three questions in my mind that I had to ask of myself. First one: What does it mean to be a man? Second one: What are the traditions I've been living by? And third: What are the rituals? Looking into that I realized that none of those traditions were mine; they were passed on through my parents, and they came from wherever they came from. I knew that wasn't the world I wanted anymore. I had to come to what it meant to me to be a man, not whatever society I was living in said it was. I had to come right down to the fine points of those things. What does it mean for me to be a man, for myself? And I didn't want any more traditions in my life, because they weren't mine. I'd create my own if there were going to be traditions. And the same with the rituals that I live by. They weren't mine either, and if I was going to have rituals, I became God, I guess.

Takes a long time to explain that. So I think when I look at things, and I look at people, and I hear people and where they're coming from and what they want, and what they believe and all those things that people live by, I think I heard very clearly what people were saying to me. I also feel I hear clearly that most people don't know what they're saying, because they haven't reached that point where they have to take a look at themselves. What does it mean to me, as an individual, to be human? What does it mean? I think it's even some kind of trauma in life that causes a person to get there.

SO MUCH TIME HAS PASSED

I wouldn't want to be anywhere else. Scully's 90 now and he lives in Edmonton. He's still making canes. He figure's that's lucrative because there are a lot of old people! He's living with his daughter, Laurie. They built him a little cabin because he couldn't live with anybody. He's still functioning. Helen died, his wife, when he was in his 80s, about ten years ago, and he left here. He brought his brother-in-law up and they started working together and he pretty much finished his time working with his brother-in-law. He's from northern Saskatchewan. His real name is Gordon Scollon.

Scully fell in love with my daughter. I brought Pascale up to him just after she was born. I got a bunch of pictures of him and her. He made up these little sayings to go with the pictures, as though he and Pascale were talking, but she couldn't talk in those days! So he made it up. He's a character—one of the most amazing guys I've ever met. He built the Dempster Highway, so he had been up around this neck of the woods a long time. He met Helen, his wife, in Dawson. He was 36 or something and she was 17. He lived out in Burnaby for a time, where they had a home. He used to build furniture there, and he never really got into the bowl making until he came up into this area. So he'd be here for the summer, and then they'd go Outside every winter.

I think he had something to do when they were putting the pipeline in, and he got hired on to do the clearing for it. That's how he knew everybody here because he hired

facing David with baby daughter, Pascale, circa 2000. KFN Archives - EMPC. David Dubois Family Images #7. PHOTOGRAPHER UNKNOWN

above David hamming it up with his daughter, Pascale, at his burl shop, circa 2000. KFN Archives. EMPC. David Dubois Family Images #8. PHOTOGRAPHER UNKNOWN

facing David Dubois recording stories for the Elders Memory Project at Jacquot Hall in 2017. KFN Archives. EMPC. Elders Portraits #55. PHOTOGRAPHER ALISTAIR MAITLAND

all the guys to come work with him. He had a way with people. Scully had been a drinker, so he understood. He'd say, "Well, boys, you've got to do it. You've got to do it." He'd get the guys and they'd all do their work and party on the weekends and then Scully would come and drag them all out. I remember when they were going to put the pipeline through again. They wanted to put it under the lake. That freaked me out.

So much time has passed—twenty-seven years! I ran into Marissa [Mills] yesterday. I didn't even recognize her. I was wondering, "Who is this beautiful young woman saying, 'Hi, Doobie'?" Then she hugs me and I say, "I really don't know you. Who are you?"

MY CONNECTING PLACE IS HERE

I freak out when I go to Whitehorse. When Pascale had her baby, I kept saying to her, "When you get home, you'll feel so safe. So safe, honey. I remember bringing you home and the feeling of walking through the door and going, 'Phew.'" That was so important to me, and I think that when she got home last night, she realized what I was saying. It's so important to be home.

Without her foundation with KFN, her grandmother, the other people in the community, my daughter may have ended up like I did because I had no foundation. My dad was a Frenchman, and he was embarrassed by that. My mom was from England and she had very few connections, and I never really got an identity. My family has no idea why I stay here in the Yukon. They cannot grasp it, and they have no desire to come here. I've gone back three times since I've been here and twice to bring my daughter back to see my family. My connecting place is here now. I've had other kids in my life, but never parented until I had Pascale. I parented her. I made that commitment when she was born.

My daughter has an identity. It's the people here, and it's so darn important. To her it's everything. Belonging. That saying, "It takes a community to raise a child." That is her foundation. Her grandma Agnes Johnson used to take her out as a little kid to go gopher hunting and catch six of them. Then they would sit there, build a fire, and eat them. Her grandma did a lot of grounding things with her—because my world is not my daughter's world. I'm a white man from the white man's world, and she's Indian.

I think what's happened for me is I've learned to respect another culture as not my own. It's not something I can ever be, because I wasn't raised in this culture. I don't have the language of this culture, and without the language it's pretty hard to have the culture, but it's still there. I accept that. It's simply an acceptance of my role. My part in this community is simply to be who I am. I'll never be an Indian. I'll just be this guy, and that takes a whole bunch of worry off me in one sense that when I'm gone, she'll still have the community. She'll still have that foundation, and that's so important.

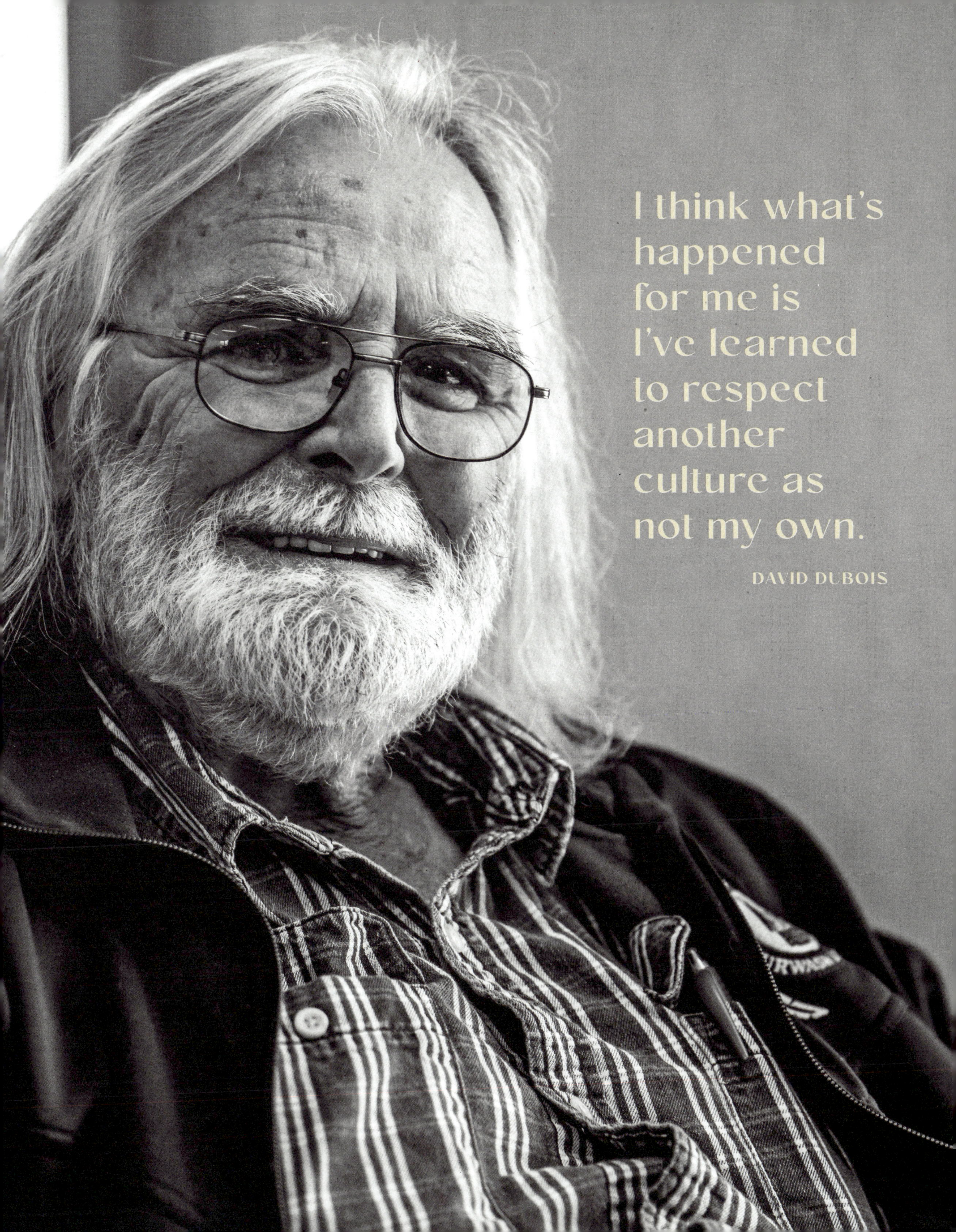
I think what's happened for me is I've learned to respect another culture as not my own.
DAVID DUBOIS

PART THREE

LHÙ’ÀÀN MÂN KEYÍ DAŃ KWÁNJE NÀÀTSAT

(Kluane Lake Country People Speak Strong)

overleaf Fireweed and delphinium bloom in June and July throughout Asì Keyí (Grandfather's Country).
KFN Archives. EMPC. Landscape Images #29.
PHOTOGRAPHER ALANNA DICKSON

above Sign marking the site of Category B Settlement Land at Thechàl Dhàl (Rock-Scraper Mountain, Sheep Mountain), for which Kluane First Nation owns the land surface but not the resources below the surface.
KFN Archives. EMPC. Landscape Images #40.
PHOTOGRAPHER ALISTAIR MAITLAND

Since 2003 Kluane First Nation has worked diligently to build a self-determining governance organization needed by our citizens and to pursue diversified economic development for the betterment of present and future generations.[1]

Kluane First Nation is governed by a Constitution, developed in accordance with the Self-Government Agreement, which established five branches: the General Assembly, the Council, the Elders Council, the Youth Council, and the Kluane First Nation Court. Every eligible citizen has the right to vote in elections for a Chief and Councillors, including an Elder Councillor and a Youth Councillor. The Council acts as our Executive, overseeing our organizational structure, budget, laws, and strategic planning.[2]

Our Final Agreement provides ownership and/or management rights over key lands and sites of long-standing importance to our Nation. Some provisions of our agreements have been affected by the status of the White River First Nation, which to date has not finalized agreements for land claims and self-government and remains an Indian band under provisions of the Indian Act. The traditional territories claimed for our two First Nations currently overlap on 100 percent coverage of lands in our region, an outstanding issue to be resolved in future negotiations. KFN has identified certain core areas of exclusive use. Our Traditional Territory is currently overlapping with White River First Nation's asserted territory because WRFN chose not to complete their own agreement. The overlap is due to the previous historical amalgamation of the two nations by the Department of Indian Affairs. The overlapping territories extend from the southeastern end of Kluane Lake northwest to the Alaska border and from the St. Elias Mountains north to the Donjek River–White River confluence.[3]

Kluane First Nation owns the following Settlement Land:

- 647.5 km2 of Category A Land for which the First Nation owns both the surface of the land as well as what is below it (such as minerals, oil, and gas)
- 259 km2 of Category B Land for which the First Nation owns the surface of the land but not what is below the surface
- 6.81 km2 of Category C Land allocated per section 4.3.4 of the Final Agreement, i.e. lands within Burwash Landing.

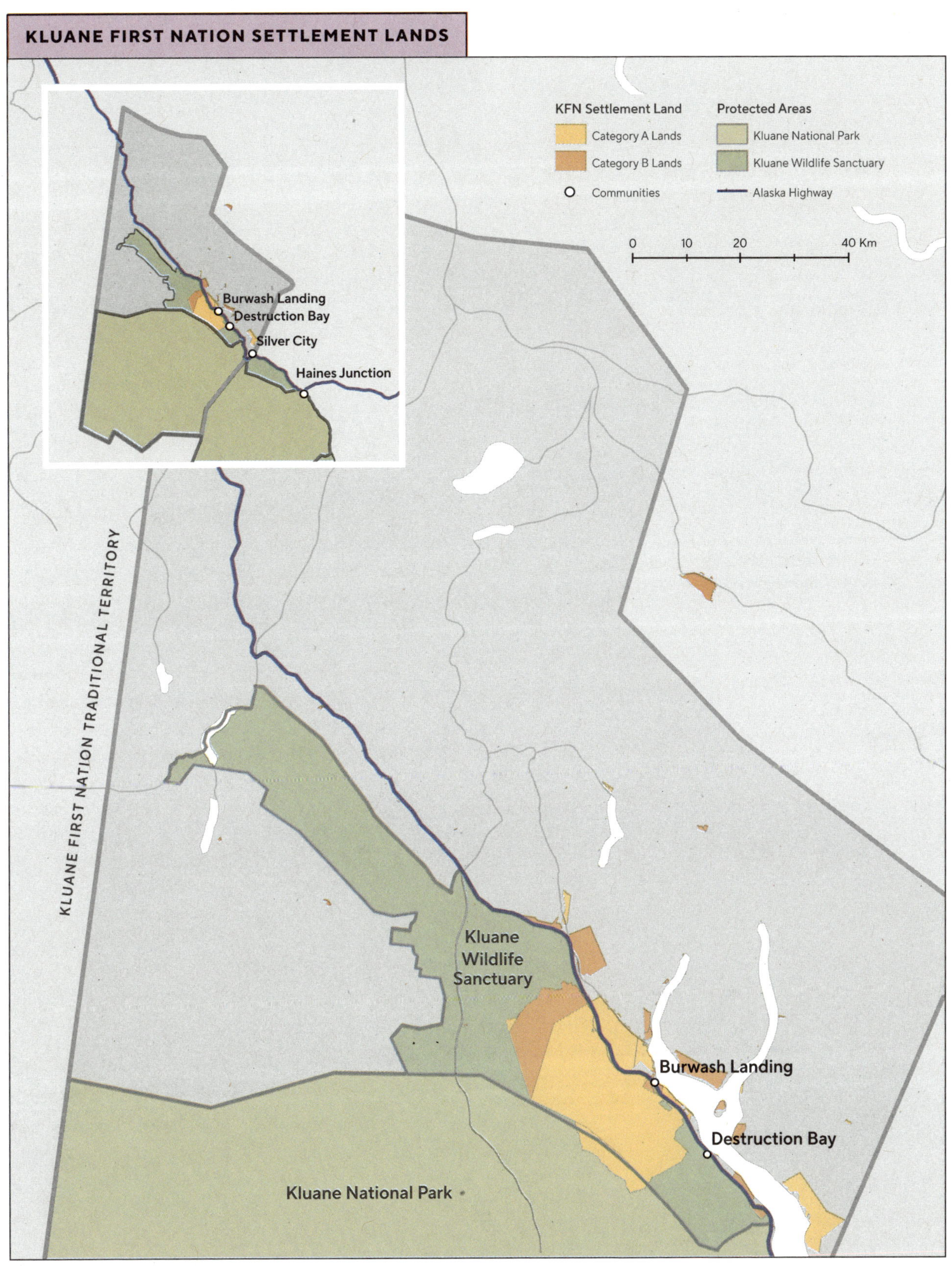

Map prepared by Frank Anderson,
KFN Lands Resources and Heritage

top (both) Kluane Dana Shäw Corporation opened a store and fuel station in Burwash as an economic development project, which is a welcome addition to services for the community and highway travellers. KFN Archives. EMPC. Landscape Images #30 and #31. PHOTOGRAPHER ALISTAIR MAITLAND

bottom Kluane First Nation operates Lhù'ààn Chù' Shàw-kwa-than Kù' (Kluane Good Water House) to ensure safe drinking water for the community. Jason Tapp, Water Operator, testing the water before delivery in the KFN water truck. KFN Archives. EMPC. Landscape Images #32. PHOTOGRAPHER ALISTAIR MAITLAND

facing, top left Magreya (Isabella Stickle) drumming at Lake Creek Culture Camp, 2017. KFN Archives. EMPC. Landscape Images #33. PHOTOGRAPHER ALISTAIR MAITLAND

facing, top right Amber Berard-Althouse and Sam White at the Big Horn Culture Camp in 2018 preparing sheep horn for use in making sheep horn spoons. KFN Archives. EMPC. Landscape Images #34. PHOTOGRAPHER ALISTAIR MAITLAND

facing, middle Kluane Lake School students learning to set traps from Marcel Dulac during Muskrat Camp at Pickhandle Lakes, 2015. KFN Archives. EMPC. Landscape Images #35. PHOTOGRAPHER UNKNOWN

facing, bottom Joe Joe Johnson and granddaughter Shakina Johnson at the Healing Broken Connections project in Kluane National Park, circa 2008. KFN Archives. EMPC. Landscape Images #36. PHOTOGRAPHER UNKNOWN

We created two new Special Management Areas: Pickhandle Lakes Habitat Protection Area and Asì Keyí Natural Environment Park. The former was designated under Yukon's Wildlife Act, while the latter was designated under Yukon's Parks and Land Certainty Act. Special management area provisions regarding the Kluane National Park and Reserve are also included in the Agreement. Our representatives participate as designated members for the management and planning of those unique areas that have long been important for our people (Kluane Park and the two new Special Management Areas). As well we identified sixteen heritage routes under provisions of our Final Agreement.

Kluane First Nation received financial compensation of $10,016,557 (measured in 1989 dollars), in fifteen annual payments starting on October 18, 2003. As a self-governing Yukon First Nation our government has the authority for taxation for local purposes on Settlement Land. KFN can enter into arrangements with Canada and the Yukon to share tax-generated revenue. KFN passed the Kluane First Nation Income Tax Act in 2004. Under Chapter 21 of our Final Agreement KFN pays property taxes for some, but not all, Settlement Land; property taxes are not paid on unimproved rural Settlement Land.

The KFN Final Agreement also provides for measures to create opportunities for our people to participate in the Yukon economy and benefit from the Agreement. In recent years our people have worked as Kluane National Park and Reserve employees, as well as serving on advisory committees and planning projects. Our traditional names appear on interpretive signs today, our stories are told to visitors, and we have access once again to our special places and spaces, including opportunities for some limited hunting and gathering.

We work cooperatively with the Yukon Department of Education to plan and deliver cultural programming for our children at the Kluane Lake School in Destruction Bay. One of the most exciting developments in recent years was the announcement of funding for a new school to be built at Burwash! After more than a century our children will have a government-funded school in their home community, fully supported by the Yukon Government, with programs incorporating our language, history, and culture. We have named the school Kêts'á dan' kų, after our first community school and honouring our Elders, teachers, and students of the 1970s who worked so hard to establish the dream of a school for and in our community.[4]

Other KFN programs addressing the needs of children and Youth include our language nest for preschool children at our daycare, our culture camps on the land, and our language program, which produces high-quality teaching resources for home and school. We built a beautiful community meeting centre—Jacquot Hall—with a gym, Elders Meeting Room, kitchen, and community library; nearby is our arena for outdoor sports.[5]

KFN invests in numerous health and wellness supports for citizens, including counselling, treatment services, and assistance to Elders and those needing extra care. The Nation owns and maintains sixty-two houses in Burwash, a fourplex unit, and fifteen homes in the Copper Joe subdivision for citizens and government employees. Our public works staff operate water delivery and sanitation services, as well as maintenance services for the community.[6]

Our government works with citizens to build our investments for the future. We have two corporations to manage our investment funds: Kluane Community Development Limited Partnership (KCDLP), which develops economic opportunities, building projects, and infrastructure; and Kluane Dana Shäw Corporation (KDSC), which has a mandate to generate long-term wealth for KFN through for-profit business investments. Currently KDSC has interests in energy, construction, aviation, transportation, and mineral exploration. One very exciting future project is the Kluane Ńts'i (Wind) Energy Project, to be built on the lakeshore south of Burwash, which will generate green energy for our communities, replacing current reliance on diesel power generation.[7]

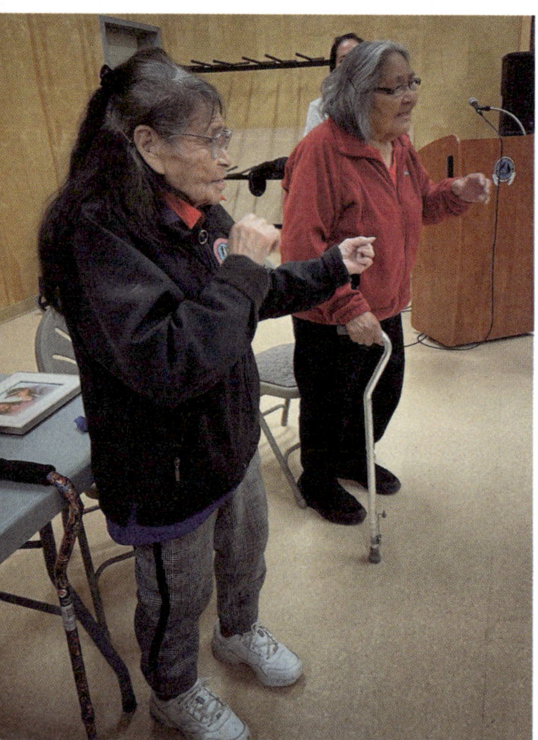

top left Champagne and Aishihik First Nations Elder Chuck Hume, Joe Bruneau, and KFN Elder Michael Johnson sharing stories at a culture camp, circa 2015. KFN Archives. EMPC. Elders Portraits #56. PHOTOGRAPHER UNKNOWN

top right Margaret, Agnes, Lena, Dorothy, and Peter Johnson at Elders Story Camp in Kluane National Park, circa 2006. KFN Archives. EMPC. Elders Portraits #57. PHOTOGRAPHER SUSAN HOWLETT

bottom Gushàka (Margaret Johnson) and Tùlhàsèn (Lena Johnson) singing at a Potlatch in Burwash, circa 2020. KFN Archives. EMPC. Elders Portraits #58. PHOTOGRAPHER KATIE JOHNSON

KFN citizens contribute to national, international, and Yukon initiatives for Reconciliation to support long-needed reforms to overcome historical wrongs arising from racism and colonialism. Our citizens were strong leaders in the fight to identify and bring to justice the many people who abused our children in residential schools, joining the Yukon Trail Blazers group, which brought the first lawsuits against former staff connected to Lower Post, Choutla, and other schools.[8] We also support the women and organizations that uncover crimes against Missing and Murdered Indigenous Women and Girls. We work to ensure that families and individuals receive help to recover from trauma inflicted by colonial policies and practices.

Kluane First Nation is participating in numerous scientific studies related to climate change, a key concern for our future as a people, our lake, and our homeland. In recent years studies have documented falling water levels in Kluane Lake owing to glacial melt in the mountains and reduced water flow in the Slims River. This is a real threat to the very existence of our beautiful lake in future decades if present conditions persist or grow more extreme. Lower water levels will expand shorelines, changing critical habitat for wildlife and reducing water depths in the lake, which affects the fish and other aquatic species. We could lose our lake and all its resources and cultural and spiritual connections. Lhù'ààn Mân (Kluane Lake) is our namesake as a Nation, and we must do everything possible to slow down and mitigate these negative impacts.[9]

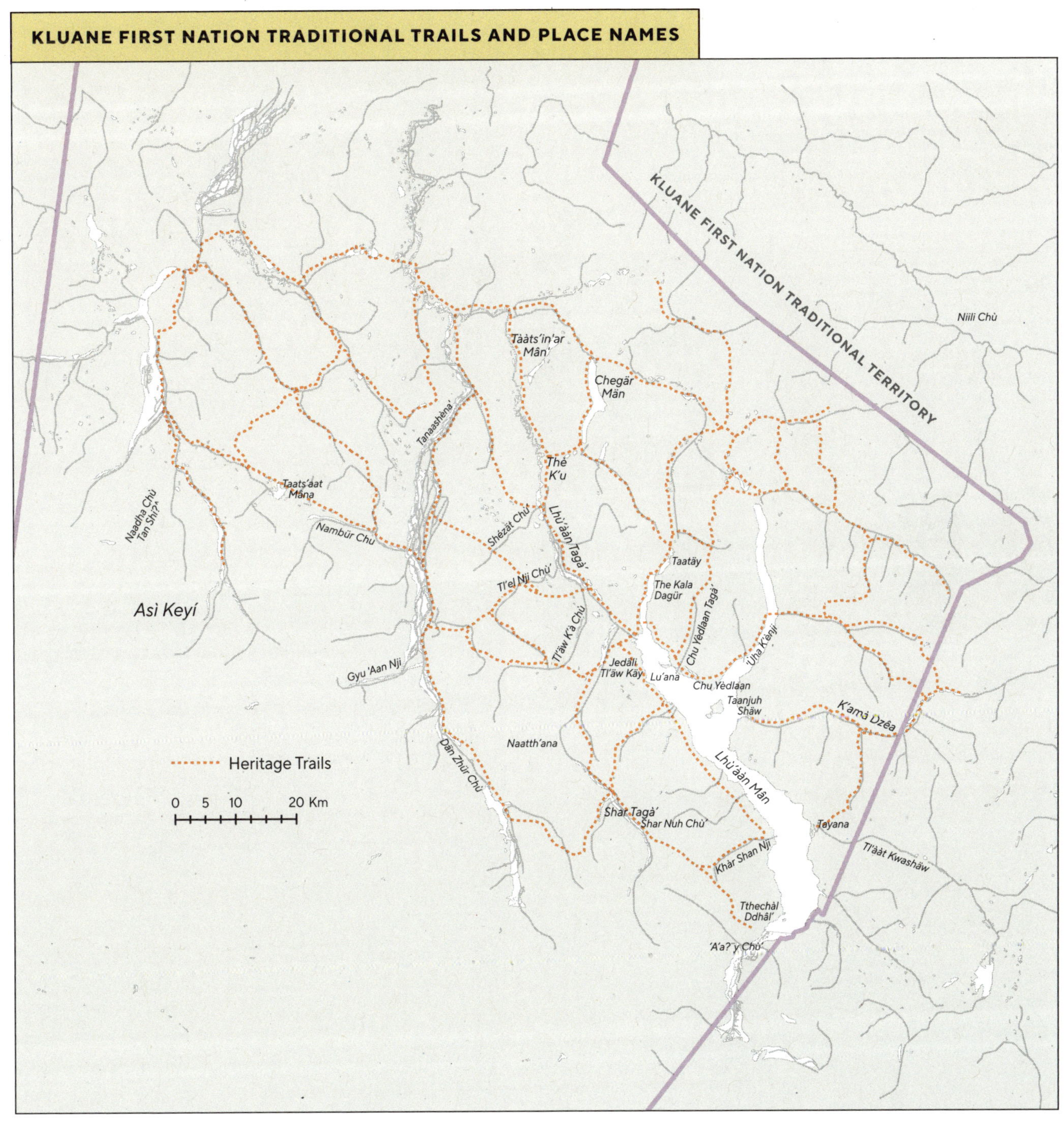

Map prepared by Frank Anderson,
KFN Lands Resources and Heritage

The Kluane Museum of Natural History in Burwash has an outstanding collection of artworks made by Kluane First Nation and other Yukon First Nations Elders in years gone by using traditional bead, hide, fur, and bone resources.
All photographs courtesy of the Museum.

1. Beaded mukluks by Margaret Johnson.
2. Beaded mukluks by Mary Jacquot.
3. Ceremonial cape by Kluane First Nation women.
4. Man's gopher skin jacket by Nellie Johnson.

5 Beaded hide ceremonial shirt by Burwash women.
6 Hunting bag by Copper Lily Johnson.
7 Baby carrier by Bessie Allen.
8 Hunting bag by Mary Jacquot.
9 Netted bag with lynx head by Sarah Tom Tom.
10 Beaded necklace by Lena Enoch.

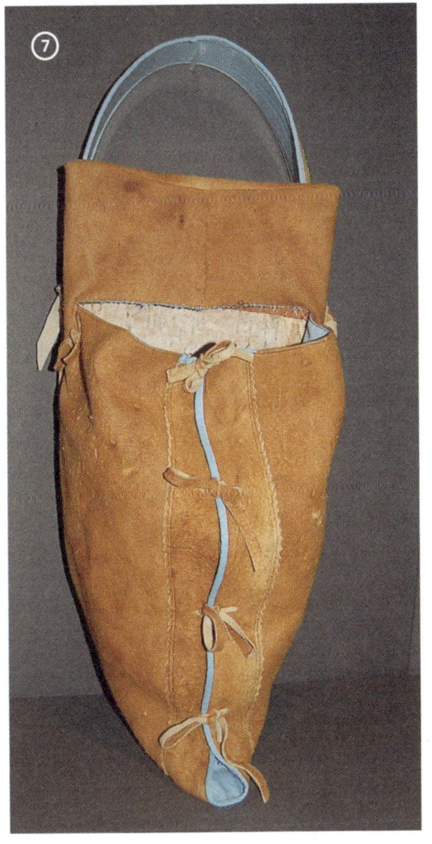

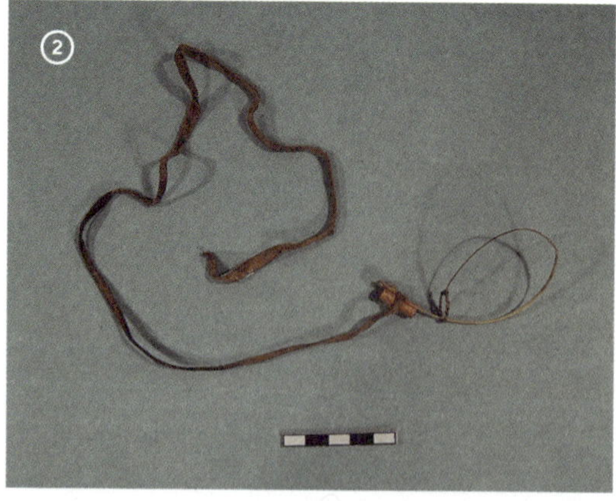

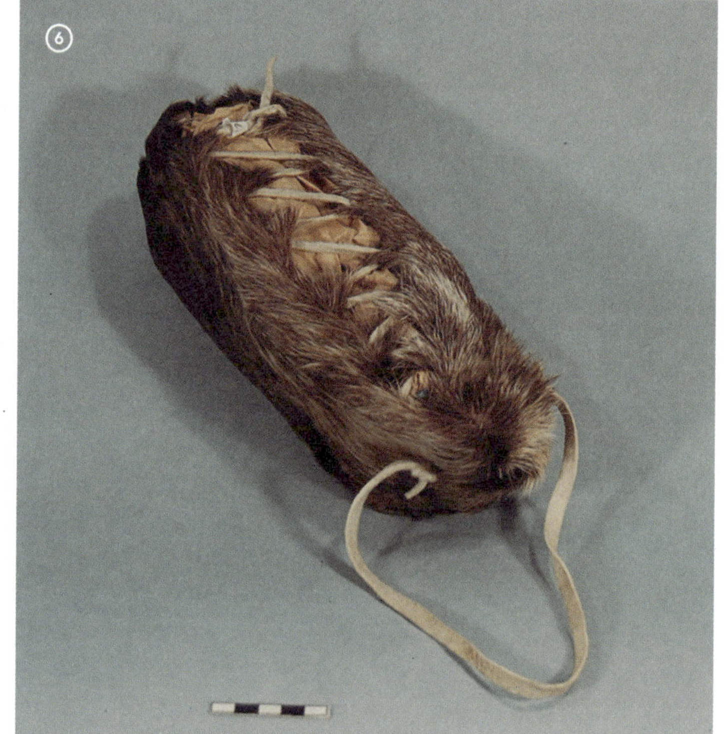

1. Wooden frame for moose skin boat by Joe Tom Tom.
2. Eagle feather gopher snare by unknown artist.
3. Fish spear with barbed antler point by unknown artist.
4. Child's moose skin toy yo-yo by Jessie Joe.
5. Potlatch spoon made of sheep horn by unknown artist.
6. Caribou skin toboggan by Copper Lily Johnson.
7. Collection of works by various artists.

above Burwash seen from the air, circa 2020. KFN Archives. EMPC. Landscape Images #37. PHOTOGRAPHER FRITZ MUELLER

facing Kluane First Nation Elders gathered with Champagne and Aishihik First Nations Elders in Jacquot Hall in 2011 to celebrate their language, culture, and family connections. KFN Archives. EMPC. Elders Portraits #59. PHOTOGRAPHER UNKNOWN

overleaf Chief Robert Dickson showing Youth a musket he made from a kit at a firearms safety workshop at Duke Meadow in 2020. KFN Archives. EMPC. Landscape Images #38. PHOTOGRAPHER UNKNOWN

Today as Lhù'ààn Mân Ku Dań (the Kluane Lake People) we continue to rise up and stand tall together—teaching, speaking, and preserving our languages; planning and evolving new pathways to success for all ages; reclaiming time for multi-generational activities on our lands; incorporating traditional and contemporary ideas for health and spiritual well-being; and recapturing and celebrating the strength of our Ancestors, past and present Elders, and leaders over many decades. We know we must take care to preserve our lands and waters, culture, languages, heritage, and pride so that we can continue to live well in our beautiful Lhù'ààn Mân Keyí (Kluane Lake Country). We're still here! It's up to us to make a good path for the next generations![10]

EXIT

We're still here! It's up to us
to make a good path
for the next generations!

ACKNOWLEDGEMENTS

KFN is grateful to the many people and organizations who contributed to the creation of *Lhù'ààn Mân Keyí Dań Kwánje Nààtsat, Kluane Lake Country People Speak Strong.* The book was envisioned and guided by KFN Elders from its beginnings to the final printing of the stories and images. Their life histories form the content of this book, and it would not exist without their hard work and dedication over more than six years, including difficult times during the COVID-19 pandemic.

The project had three phases:

Phase 1: Oral History Project and Archival Research, 2017–2019

Phase 2: Manuscript Development, 2020–2021

Phase 3: Publication, 2022–2023

KFN Lands, Resources and Heritage Department staff led all phases of the work, with Director Geraldine Pope providing oversight and direction. Heritage Manager Gùdia Mary Jane Johnson initiated the project, guiding the oral history phase and development of the historical overview. Subsequent Heritage Managers Rachael Thom and Alyssa White provided support with funders and resources. KFN Finance and administrative staff managed ongoing financial requirements.

The KFN Elders Council reviewed proposals for recording Oral Histories and archival research, contributing significant details to guide the work. Katie Johnson (Bella Elite Events Planning & Consulting) and Linda Johnson (Linda Johnson Research & Consulting) organized and conducted the oral history recording sessions with twenty-two Elders in Burwash and Whitehorse from 2017 to 2019, then worked with Elders and family members to finalize content and scan images from family photo collections for each Elder's chapter. Robin Bradasch and Sandy Johnson assisted with genealogies and photo identifications for the book.

Hiedi and Josh Cuppage (Transcriptions North) and Michele Taylor transcribed all of the Elders' interviews.

Diana Jimmy transcribed two Southern Tutchone stories from the Yukon Native Language Centre for the traditional stories segment. Diyet van Lieshout and Daniel Tlen contributed research and transcriptions of traditional songs from the Tutchone Heritage Society *Dáh Shäw Yên* song project. KFN language consultants Margaret Johnson, Bertha Doris, Joyce Johnson-Albert, and Diyet van Lieshout translated place names, personal names, and other technical terms.

Alistair Maitland produced digital portraits of Elders and images of community events and special places. Alanna Dickson provided images

above Yat'äy Dàk'àn (Northern Lights) dance above Lhù'ààn Mân (Whitefish Place Lake, Kluane Lake). KFN Archives. EMPC. Landscape Images #39. PHOTOGRAPHER ALANNA DICKSON

of landscapes, flora, and fauna. Parks Canada contributed images from various events held at Kluane National Park and Reserve. KFN Archivist Adam Hicks and Yukon Archives staff identified and copied historical images. Donna Darbyshire located and identified images in the Council of Yukon First Nations (CYFN) Archives. The Kluane Museum of Natural History and Yukon Government Cultural Services staff contributed images for artworks held in the museum. David Dickson provided images and information from Dickson Outfitters collections. Other photographers are acknowledged in individual photo credits. David Ashley contributed design motifs.

Figure 1 Publishing in Vancouver provided professional editing and creative design expertise to take the manuscript to final publication as a beautiful book. The KFN Elders Council, Chief Bob Dickson and Council, KFN Youth Council, and individual Elders reviewed design options for the cover and interior pages. Frank Anderson, KFN Lands Manager, worked with Figure 1 designers to produce maps for the book. Elder Tùlhàsèn (Lena Johnson) composed the name for the book.

The Yukon Government Community Development Fund and KFN funded Phase 1 of the project. The Government of Canada Indigenous Languages and Cultures Program and KFN funded Phases 2 and 3. Yukon University partnered with KFN to obtain a grant from the Yukon Foundation to support publication of the book. KFN greatly appreciates all of the assistance from funders and their staff, which was essential to the success of this project.

Many more people and organizations have supported the production of this magnificent book. We thank everyone for their help in bringing our Elders' life stories forward to inspire all present and future generations.

NOTES

History of Lhù'ààn Mân Keyí (Kluane Lake Country)

1. Kluane First Nation, *KFN 101* (Burwash: Kluane First Nation, n.d.), p. 4.
2. Margaret Workman, compiler and translator, *Kwädąy Kwändür* (Whitehorse: Yukon Native Language Centre, 2010), pp. 80–83 and pp. 36–47, respectively. Text for The Crow Made the World was transcribed from Daanji's recording of Copper Lily (YNLC Tape #853, side A, story no. 1). Text for The Wolf Story was transcribed from his recording of Jessie Joe (YNLC Tape #856, side B, story no. 3). Stories have been reproduced exactly as they appear in *Kwädąy Kwändür*, including spelling, grammar, and transcriptions.
3. Tutchone Heritage Society and Kluane First Nation, *Dáh Shäw Yên, Songs of Our Elders, Lhù'àan Mân Kwanje Kluane Dialect* (Burwash: Tutchone Heritage Society and Kluane First Nation, 2022), pp. 4–5.
4. Ibid., pp. 10–11.
5. Ibid., pp. 26–29.
6. Ibid., pp. 30–31.
7. Ibid., pp. 34–35.
8. Ibid., pp. 48–49.
9. Ibid., pp. 50–51.
10. Angela Sidney in Catharine McClellan, comp. and trans., *My Old People Say* (Ottawa: National Museums of Canada, 1975), p. 75.
11. Mary Jacquot in Catharine McClellan, comp. and trans., *My Old People's Stories: A Legacy for Yukon First Nations*, Part 1: *Southern Tutchone Narrators*, Hudē Hudän Series, Occasional Papers in Yukon History, no. 5 (1) (Whitehorse: Cultural Services Branch, Government of the Yukon, 2007), pp. 177–78.
12. Mary Jacquot in Margaret Workman, comp. and trans., *Kwädąy Kwändür* (Whitehorse: Yukon Native Language Centre, 2010), pp. 12–15.
13. Ida Calmegane in Kwanlin Dün, *Dă Kwăndur Ghày Ghàkwadîndur, Our Story in Our Words* (Whitehorse: Kwanlin Dün First Nation, 2010), p. 100.
14. Ibid., pp. 73, 93.
15. Catharine McClellan, *Part of the Land, Part of the Water: A History of the Yukon Indians* (Vancouver: Douglas & McIntyre, 1987), pp. 106–7.
16. Mary Copper Jacquot and Josephine Jacquot Sias, "The Copper Family," Kluane First Nation Archives, Manuscript Collection, n.d., pp. 1–13.
17. Elmer Harp Jr., *North to the Yukon Territory via the Alcan Highway in 1948: Field Notes of the Andover-Harvard Expedition*, Hudē Hudän Series, Occasional Papers in Archaeology, no. 14 (Whitehorse: Archaeology Programme, Government of the Yukon, 2005).
18. Kluane First Nation, Kluane First Nation Elders Memory Project (Burwash Landing: Kluane First Nation, 2020), Transcripts 2018–2020.
19. Ibid.
20. Jimmy Joe and Jessie Joe, "Jimmy Joe's Stories" and "Life of an Indian," in Margaret Workman, comp. and trans., *Kwädąy Kwändür* (Whitehorse: Yukon Native Language Centre, 2010), pp. 56–68.
21. Catharine McClellan, comp. and trans., *My Old People's Stories: A Legacy for Yukon First Nations*, Part 1: *Southern Tutchone Narrators*, Hudē Hudän Series, Occasional Papers in Yukon History, no. 5 (1) (Whitehorse: Cultural Services Branch, Government of the Yukon, 2007), pp. 3–4; ibid., Lily Birckel, "Crow Gets the Sun, Moon and Daylight," pp. 159–62.
22. Lena Johnson, in Kluane First Nation, Kluane First Nation Elders Memory Project (Burwash Landing: Kluane First Nation, 2020), Transcripts 2018, p. 3.
23. Richard J. Hebda, Sheila Greer, and Alexander P. Mackie, *Kwäday Dän Ts'inchi, Teachings from Long Ago Person Found* (Victoria: Royal B.C. Museum and Champagne and Aishihik First Nations, 2017), pp. 151–83.
24. Julie Cruikshank, *Through the Eyes of Strangers* (Whitehorse: Yukon Archives, Yukon Government, 1974), pp. v–2.
25. Linda Johnson, *The Kandik Map* (Fairbanks: University of Alaska Press, 2009), pp. 10–12.
26. Ibid., pp. 127–54.
27. Paul Nadasdy, *Hunters and Bureaucrats: Power, Knowledge and Aboriginal-State Relations in the Southwest Yukon* (Vancouver: UBC Press, 2003), pp. 27–32.
28. Paul Nadasdy, notes to Linda Johnson, September 9, 2022.

29. K'akhyuama is listed as the wife of Copper George Joe in Margaret Workman, comp. and trans., *Kwaday Kwadan* (Whitehorse: Yukon Native Language Centre, 2000), p. 11.

30. Unnamed author, "Notes on Burwash Landing, the Jimmy Johnson Family, the Allen Family, the Copper Family and the Dickson Family," Kluane First Nation Archives, Manuscript Collection, n.d., pp. 1–4.

31. Ibid.

32. Mary Copper Jacquot and Josephine Jacquot Sias, "The Copper Family," Kluane First Nation Archives, Manuscript Collection, n.d., pp. 1–13. Mary Jacquot's traditional name is spelled as Nach'ädn̈ch'ea, in Margaret Workman, comp. and trans., *Kwaday Kwadan* (Whitehorse: Yukon Native Language Centre, 2000), p. 168. Two different spellings for Mary Jacquot's father's Indigenous name appear in various sources. Dháldatà is from the biography of Mary Jacquot in *Kwaday Kwadan*, p. 11. Thul-da-ta is from "The Copper Family" cited above.

33. Unnamed author, "Notes on Burwash Landing, the Jimmy Johnson Family, the Allen Family, the Copper Family and the Dickson Family," Kluane First Nation Archives, Manuscript Collection, n.d., pp. 1–4.

34. Edward J. Glave, *Travels to the Alseck* (Whitehorse: Yukon Native Language Centre, 2013), p. 320.

35. Frederick Schwatka, *Schwatka's Last Search* (Fairbanks: University of Alaska Press, 1996), pp. 1–3.

36. Al Wright, *Prelude to Bonanza* (Sidney: Gray's Publishing, 1976).

37. Kluane First Nation, *KFN 101* (Burwash: Kluane First Nation, n.d.), p. 8.

38. Ibid.

39. Library & Archives Canada. Canada Census 1921, 1931 online. KFN Archives, "Descendants of Thomas Alexander Dickson" manuscript.

40. John F. Reisenauer Jr., *Brothers in the Yukon*, 2nd ed. (Kennewick: self-published, 2007), p. 26.

41. Ibid.

42. Paul Nadasdy, *Hunters and Bureaucrats: Power, Knowledge and Aboriginal-State Relations in the Southwest Yukon* (Vancouver: UBC Press, 2003), pp. 27–32.

43. Marjorie E. Almstrom, *A Century of Schooling: Education in the Yukon, 1861–1961* (Whitehorse: self-published, 1990), p. 137.

44. Ibid., p. 138.

45. Julie Cruikshank, *Dän Dhá Ts'edenintth'é, Reading Voices, Oral and Written Interpretations of the Yukon's Past* (Vancouver: Douglas & McIntyre, 1991), p. 93.

46. Elmer Harp Jr., *North to the Yukon Territory via the Alcan Highway in 1948: Field Notes of the Andover-Harvard Expedition*, Hudē Hudän Series, Occasional Papers in Archaeology, no. 14 (Whitehorse: Archaeology Programme, Government of the Yukon, 2005). https://emrlibrary.gov.yk.ca/Tourism/occasional%20papers%20in%20yukon%20archaeology/north-to-yukon-territory-via-alcan-highway-andover-harvard.pdf

47. Ibid., pp. 19–20. All excerpts reprinted with permission.

48. Ibid., pp. 26–27.

49. Ibid., pp. 27–29.

50. Ibid., pp. 35–36.

51. Ibid., pp. 38–40.

52. The names in this diary entry are Harp's renditions and only vaguely correspond to actual terms. Terms in square brackets are modern and more accurate.

53. Ibid., p. 44.

54. Ibid., pp. 47–48.

55. Ibid., pp. 48–50.

56. Ibid., p. 52.

57. Ibid., pp. 54–55.

58. Ibid., p. 57.

59. Ibid., pp. 59–63.

60. Ibid., pp. 71–73.

61. Ibid., pp. 74–75.

62. Ibid., pp. 55–56.

63. Ibid., pp. 91–93.

64. Ibid., pp. 93–96.

65. Ibid., pp. 99–100.

66. Ibid., pp. 101–2.

67. Ibid., pp. 103–5.

68. Ibid., p. 108.

69. Catharine McClellan, *Part of the Land, Part of the Water: A History of the Yukon Indians* (Vancouver: Douglas & McIntyre, 1987), pp. 85, 91–94, 98–99, 174.

70. Paul Nadasdy, *Hunters and Bureaucrats: Power, Knowledge and Aboriginal-State Relations in the Southwest Yukon* (Vancouver: UBC Press, 2003), pp. 32–34.

71. Catharine McClellan, *Part of the Land, Part of the Water: A History of the Yukon Indians* (Vancouver: Douglas & McIntyre, 1987), pp. 85–86.

72. Paul Nadasdy, *Hunters and Bureaucrats: Power, Knowledge and Aboriginal-State Relations in the Southwest Yukon* (Vancouver: UBC Press, 2003), pp. 38–41.

73. Ibid., pp. 41–42.

74. Linda Johnson, *With the People Who Live Here: A History of the Yukon Legislative Assembly, 1909–1961* (Whitehorse: Yukon Legislative Assembly, 2009).

75. Paul Nadasdy, *Hunters and Bureaucrats: Power, Knowledge and Aboriginal-State Relations in the Southwest Yukon* (Vancouver: UBC Press, 2003), pp. 42–43.

76. Marjorie E. Almstrom, *A Century of Schooling: Education in the Yukon, 1861–1961* (Whitehorse: self-published, 1990), pp. 216–20.

77. Helène Dobrowolsky and Linda Johnson, *Whitehorse: An Illustrated History* (Vancouver: Figure 1 Publishing, 2013).

78. Kluane First Nation, Kluane First Nation Elders Memory Project (Burwash Landing: Kluane First Nation, 2020), Transcripts 2018–2020.

79. Ibid.

80. Paul Nadasdy, *Hunters and Bureaucrats: Power, Knowledge and Aboriginal-State Relations in the Southwest Yukon* (Vancouver: UBC Press, 2003), p. 33.

81. Ibid., pp. 34–51.

82. Ibid., pp. 34–38.

83. Ibid., pp. 48–49; Catharine McClellan, *Part of the Land, Part of the Water: A History of the Yukon Indians* (Vancouver: Douglas & McIntyre, 1987), p. 94.

84. Katie Johnson, *Łù'àn Män Ye Shäw, Burwash Landing Elders* (Burwash Landing: Kluane First Nation, 1995), pp. 1–33.

85. Lily Gontard and Mark Kelly, *Beyond Mile Zero: The Vanishing Alaska Highway Lodge Community* (Whitehorse: Lost Moose, 2017), pp. 157–62.

86. John F. Reisenauer Jr., *Brothers in the Yukon*, 2nd ed. (Kennewick: self-published, 2007), p. 68.

87. Paul Nadasdy, *Hunters and Bureaucrats: Power, Knowledge and Aboriginal-State Relations in the Southwest Yukon* (Vancouver: UBC Press, 2003), p. 46.

88. Kwanlin Dün, *Dǎ Kwǎndur Ghày Ghàkwadîndur, Our Story in Our Words* (Whitehorse: Kwanlin Dün First Nation, 2010), pp. 181–84.

89. Dennis Dickson to Linda Johnson, personal communication, September 2022.

90. Yukon Native Brotherhood, *Together Today for Our Children Tomorrow* (Whitehorse: YNB, 1973).

91. Gùdia Johnson to Linda Johnson, personal communication, September 2022.

92. Kwanlin Dün, *Dǎ Kwǎndur Ghày Ghàkwadîndur, Our Story in Our Words* (Whitehorse: Kwanlin Dün First Nation, 2010), pp. 184–85, 194–96.

93. Paul Nadasdy, *Hunters and Bureaucrats: Power, Knowledge and Aboriginal-State Relations in the Southwest Yukon* (Vancouver: UBC Press, 2003), p. 49; Kluane First Nation, Kluane First Nation Elders Memory Project (Burwash Landing: Kluane First Nation, 2020), Transcripts 2018–2020.

94. Kwanlin Dün, *Dǎ Kwǎndur Ghày Ghàkwadîndur, Our Story in Our Words* (Whitehorse: Kwanlin Dün First Nation, 2010), pp. 194–201.

95. Kenneth M. Lysyk, Edith E. Bohmer, and Willard L. Phelps, *Alaska Highway Pipeline Inquiry* (Ottawa: Supply and Services Canada, 1977), p. 157; Kwanlin Dün, *Dǎ Kwǎndur Ghày Ghàkwadîndur, Our Story in Our Words* (Whitehorse: Kwanlin Dün First Nation, 2010), pp. 22–23, 81–121.

96. Kwanlin Dün, *Dǎ Kwǎndur Ghày Ghàkwadîndur, Our Story in Our Words* (Whitehorse: Kwanlin Dün First Nation, 2010), p. 196–97.

97. Kluane First Nation, Kluane First Nation Elders Memory Project (Burwash Landing: Kluane First Nation, 2020), Transcripts 2018–2020.

98. Paul Nadasdy, *Hunters and Bureaucrats: Power, Knowledge and Aboriginal-State Relations in the Southwest Yukon* (Vancouver: UBC Press, 2003), pp. 56–59.

99. Kluane First Nation, Kluane First Nation Elders Memory Project (Burwash Landing: Kluane First Nation, 2020), Transcripts 2018–2020.

100. Linda Johnson, *At the Heart of Gold: The Yukon Commissioner's Office, 1898–2010* (Whitehorse: Yukon Legislative Assembly, 2012).

101. Paul Nadasdy, *Hunters and Bureaucrats: Power, Knowledge and Aboriginal-State Relations in the Southwest Yukon* (Vancouver: UBC Press, 2003), pp. 56–59.

102. Kwanlin Dün, *Dă Kwăndur Ghày Ghàkwadîndur, Our Story in Our Words* (Whitehorse: Kwanlin Dün First Nation, 2010), pp. 198, 211–14.

103. Linda Johnson, *At the Heart of Gold: The Yukon Commissioner's Office, 1898–2010* (Whitehorse: Yukon Legislative Assembly, 2012).

Lhù'ààn Mân Keyí Dań Kwánje Nààtsat (Kluane Lake Country People Speak Strong)

1. Kluane First Nation website: KFN.ca

2. Kluane First Nation Constitution in *Kluane First Nation Annual General Assembly Package* (Burwash: Kluane First Nation, October 29, 2021), pp. 5–33.

3. Kluane First Nation, *KFN 101* (Burwash: Kluane First Nation, n.d.), p. 15.

4. KFN.ca, Kets'ádan Kù Project.

5. KFN.ca, Lands, Resources and Heritage; Wellness and Education.

6. KFN.ca, Housing and Public Works.

7. Kluane Dana Shäw Limited Partnership website Kluanecorp.ca; Kluane Community Development Limited Partnership (KCDLP), on YFNCC (Yukon First Nations Chamber of Commerce) website and KCDLP Facebook site.

8. Gùdia Johnson to Linda Johnson, personal communication, September 2022.

9. *Community Adaptation Project. Burwash Landing and Destruction Bay Landscape Hazards Geological Mapping for Climate Change Adaptation Planning, 2013*. Whitehorse: Yukon College, Yukon Research Centre, Northern Climate Exchange; Melissa Mills and Laurie Bouvier, *Wildlife Observations and Community Interviews, 2022*. Destruction Bay: Dän Keyi Renewable Resources Council.

10. Kluane First Nation. *Nän/Land Use Plan Summary, 2015*. (Burwash: Kluane First Nation), p. 29.

SELECTED BIBLIOGRAPHY

Almstrom, Marjorie E. *A Century of Schooling: Education in the Yukon, 1861–1961*. Whitehorse: self-published, 1990.

Cohen, Stan. *The Trail of '42: A Pictorial History of the Alaska Highway*. Missoula: Pictorial Histories, 1990.

Coutts, Robert. *Yukon Places & Names*. Sidney: Gray's Publishing, 1980.

Cruikshank, Julie. *Through the Eyes of Strangers*. Whitehorse: Yukon Archives, Yukon Government, 1974.

Dobrowolsky, Helène, and Linda Johnson. *Whitehorse: An Illustrated History*. Vancouver: Figure 1 Publishing, 2013.

Glave, Edward J. *Travels to the Alseck*. Whitehorse: Yukon Native Language Centre, 2013.

Gontard, Lily, and Mark Kelly. *Beyond Mile Zero: The Vanishing Alaska Highway Lodge Community*. Whitehorse: Lost Moose, 2017.

Green, Lewis. *The Boundary Hunters*. Vancouver: University of British Columbia Press, 1982.

Harp, Elmer Jr. *North to the Yukon Territory via the Alcan Highway in 1948: Field Notes of the Andover-Harvard Expedition*. Hudē Hudän Series, Occasional Papers in Archaeology, no. 14. Whitehorse: Archaeology Programme, Government of the Yukon, 2005.

Hebda, Richard J., Sheila Greer, and Alexander P. Mackie. *Kwäday Dän Ts'inchi, Teachings from Long Ago Person Found*. Victoria: Royal BC Museum and Champagne and Aishihik First Nations, 2017.

Johnson, Katie. *Łù'àn Män Ye Shäw, Burwash Landing Elders*. Burwash Landing: Kluane First Nation, 1995.

Johnson, Linda. *At the Heart of Gold: The Yukon Commissioner's Office, 1898–2010*. Whitehorse: Yukon Legislative Assembly, 2012.

———. *The Kandik Map*. Fairbanks: University of Alaska Press, 2009.

———. *With the People Who Live Here: A History of the Yukon Legislative Assembly, 1909–1961*. Whitehorse: Yukon Legislative Assembly, 2009.

Kluane First Nation. Elders Memory Project. Transcripts. Burwash Landing: Kluane First Nation, 2020.

———. *KFN 101*. Draft prepared for new staff and families moving to the community. Burwash Landing: Kluane First Nation, 2022.

Kwanlin Dün First Nation. *Kwanlin Dün: Dă Kwăndur Ghày Ghàkwadîndur, Our Story in Our Words*. Vancouver: Figure 1 Publishing, 2020.

Lysyk, Kenneth M., Edith E. Bohmer, and Willard L. Phelps. *Alaska Highway Pipeline Inquiry*. Ottawa: Supply and Services Canada, 1977.

McClellan, Catharine, comp. and trans. *My Old People's Stories: A Legacy for Yukon First Nations*. Part 1: *Southern Tutchone Narrators*. Whitehorse: Government of the Yukon, 2007.

———. *Part of the Land, Part of the Water: A History of the Yukon Indians*. Vancouver: Douglas & McIntyre, 1987.

Nadasdy, Paul. *Hunters and Bureaucrats: Power, Knowledge and Aboriginal-State Relations in the Southwest Yukon*. Vancouver: UBC Press, 2003.

Reisenauer, John. *Brothers in the Yukon*. 2nd ed. Kennewick: self-published, 2007.

Robb, Jim, and Julie Cruickshank. *Their Own Yukon*. Whitehorse: Council for Yukon First Nations, reprinted 2016.

Schwatka, Frederick. *Schwatka's Last Search*. Fairbanks: University of Alaska Press, 1996.

Tlen, Daniel. *Lhù' Ààn Mân Kwánje*. Burwash Landing: Kluane First Nation, 2018.

Tutchone Heritage Society and Kluane First Nation. *Dáh Shäw Yên, Songs of Our Elders, Lhù'àan Mân Kwanje Kluane Dialect*. Burwash: Tutchone Heritage Society and Kluane First Nation, 2022.

Whitehorse Aboriginal Women's Circle. *Finding Our Faces*. 2nd ed. Whitehorse: Whitehorse Aboriginal Women's Circle Publication, 2018.

Workman, Margaret, comp. and trans. *Kwädāy Kwändür*. Whitehorse: Yukon Native Language Centre, 2010.

Wright, Al. *Prelude to Bonanza*. Sidney: Gray's Publishing, 1976.

Yukon Native Brotherhood. *Together Today for Our Children Tomorrow*. Whitehorse: Yukon Native Brotherhood, 1973. Reprinted by Council for Yukon Indians. Brampton: Charters Publishing, 1977. www.cyfn.ca/agreements/together-today-for-our-children-tomorrow/

INDEX

Photographs and maps indicated by page numbers in italics

C

H

I

J

K

W

Y

LHÙ’ÀÀN MÂN

KEYÍ DAŃ

KWÁNJE NÀÀTSAT